SAP R/3 Administration

Related titles published by Addison-Wesley:

ABAP/4 Programming the SAP R/3 System Bernd Matzke

SAP R/3 System: A Client/Server Technology Rüdiger Buck-Emden and Jürgen Galimow

SAP R/3 Administration

Liane Will
Christiane Hienger
Frank Straßenburg
Rocco Himmer

Translated by Jason Miskuly

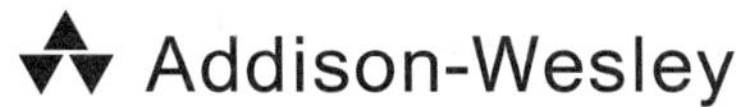

Harlow, England • Reading, Massachusetts • Menlo Park, California
New York • Don Mills, Ontario • Amsterdam • Bonn • Sydney • Singapore
Tokyo • Madrid • San Juan • Milan • Mexico City • Seoul • Taipei

First published by Addison Wesley Longman Verlag GmbH 1997
as *Administration des SAP-Systems R/3*

Addison Wesley Longman Limited
Edinburgh Gate
Harlow
Essex CM20 2JE
England

and Associated Companies throughout the World.

Cover designed by OdB Design & Communication
Illustrations by Pantek Arts, Maidstone
Typeset by 43
Typeset in 9.5/12pt Palatino
Printed and bound in the United States of America

First printed 1997

ISBN 0-201-92469-2

British Library Cataloguing-in-Publication Data
A catalogue record for this book is available from the British Library

Preface to the first edition

'The Walldorf-based SAP AG is expanding throughout the global market with incredible speed. No end to the climb is in sight and the signs point to a favorable market position...'

(*Handelsblatt* 24 October 1994)

'Success in the USA, the motherland of the computer, is one chapter in the success story of SAP. Now SAP sells its products in all corners of the world in a dozen languages...'

(*Tango* 22 October 1994)

'Software from SAP has become the industry standard: 90% of the top 500 companies in Europe work with it.'

(*Börsenzeitung* 24 September 1994)

'The R/3 development system offers everything that is being discussed today as state-of-the-art in software engineering: Client/Server support, information models for data, visual depiction of functions and processes, graphical user interfaces and a host of tools and libraries.'

(*Informatik-Magazin* 6/1993)

'Or are the users like lemmings, believing everything SAP says and following it into destruction?'

(*Wirtschaftswoche* No. 12, 16 March 1995)

Critics of SAP's software product express similar opinions. In many respects, R/3 is unique. The development costs and labor reflected in R/3 have created a software product unique in the history of data processing.

We wish to show what R/3 can do, to demythologize R/3 as the 'Great Unknown'. We base this book on our own experience and support during implementation of R/3 with ADABAS D database software. We have sought to examine more closely the administration, run-time optimization, repository, correction and transport system and the programming language ABAP/4.

This book hopes to serve as an aid for those who must keep an R/3 system running and for others interested in its subject. Business concerns play almost no role. The complexity of R/3 simply overwhelms the capacity of a single book. Nonetheless, we wish to share our experience and spare readers from making mistakes similar to our own. Perhaps we can also save you from many sleepless nights spent trying to solve problems with the system. We have spent enough sleepless nights for both of us. Even if the book cost us many evening and night hours, the effort was worth it.

We wish to thank all those who made allowances for the hours we spent on this project and managed without us. We also thank the many, many contact persons at SAP in Walldorf for their tireless efforts in converting difficult material into clearly understandable form. They contributed greatly to the success of this book.

We thank SQL Datenbanksysteme GmbH and, especially, Dr Rudolf Munz for technical support. We especially thank our colleague, Anna Witkowski, who proofread this edition.

Not the least, we thank the editors, Dr Gerhard Paulin and Dr Ludwig Claßen for helpful discussions and suggestions. We thank Uta-Dorothé Hart at Verlag Technik for the pleasant time spent in preparing the book.

For the additional care expended at Addison-Wesley Publishing, we thank Claudia Lucht and Fernando Pereira.

Liane Will
Christiane Hienger
Frank Straßenburg
Rocco Himmer
Berlin, January 1996

Preface to the second edition

A year ago the press celebrated the SAP R/3 system with jubilation. Today one hears more critical voices. Many have raised doubts about the future of the system and its efficiency for business needs.

Yet SAP closed its previous fiscal year with record volume and profit.

'Market leaders often stand in the media's line of fire,' observed SAP Chair Dietmar Hopp in an interview with *Computerzeitung* (No. 21). His judgment certainly looks in the right direction.

In any event, with R/3 release 3, SAP has brought a new, very much improved generation of its product to the market. The very success of this release was enough reason to revise this book and update it to the current release level (3.x).

Liane Will
Christiane Hienger
Frank Straßenburg
Rocco Himmer
Berlin, October 1996

Contents

Trademark notice
AIX, AS/400, DB2 for AIX, DB2/400, Presentation Manager, 4232-302 printer, LU6.2, **IBM**. Netview6000, **IBM Digital**. HP-UX, HP256x, HP9000/715, Laserjet II, IIIP, III, IIID, IIISi, Open View, **Hewlett-Packard**. Micro Focus, **Application Builders Inc**. MultiCash, **Intel Corporation**. Oracle, **Oracle Corporation UK Ltd**. OSF/1, OSF/Motif, **Open Software Foundation**. QMS-PS 410, **QMS Inc**. Quantum, trademark of **Quantum**. R/2, R/3, **SAP AG**. SAPGUI, Macintosh, **Apple Computer Inc**. SINIX, **Siemens AG**. SNI 4009 lineprinter, SNI 9014-12 lineprinter, 9021, 9026 printers, **Siemens Nixdorf Information Systems Ltd**. UPIC, **Siemens Corporation**. Solaris, **Sun Microsystems Inc**. Symmetrix, trademark of **Symmetrix**. ULTRIX, LN07, DEClaser 1000, DEClaser 22, **Digital Equipment Corporation**. UNIX, licensed through **X/Open Company Ltd**. Windows 3.1, Windows NT, Access, Mail, Office, Resource Kit, SQL Server, Visual C++, Windows, Windows for Workgroups, **Microsoft Corporation**. NetVault, **AT & T**. Q47 Robots, **Breece Hill Technologies, Inc**. Insight Manager, ProLiant, **Compaq**. Informix, Informix Online, **Informix Software Inc**. CI-1000, CI-500, **Itoh**. F-1200, F1200S, P-2000, **Kyocera**. MT600, **Mannesman Tally**. ML3410 lineprinter, **OKI**. 4440XT lineprinter, **SEL Alcatel**. ADABAS C, ADABAS D, DDB/4, Entire SQL-DB, Reflex, **Software AG**. Sybase Server, **Sybase Inc**.

Introduction

For some time now, the SAP R/3 system has set the norm in the area of standard business software. R/3 offers standard solutions for the entire information processing needs of a company.

The system consists of integrated functions for the following areas:

Production Planning (PP)

Sales and Distribution (SD)

Office and Communications (OC)

Controlling (CO)

Material Management (MM)

Human Resources (HR)

Quality Assurance (QA)

Asset Management (AM)

Plant Maintenance (PM)

Project System (PS)

Industry Solutions (IS)

Financial Accounting (FI)

The database contains several gigabytes of data even before customers enter their own data.

In addition to these standard solutions, the SAP development environment and information system provide customers with powerful tools for development and adaptation of the system to individual requirements (customizing). The development environment of the R/3 system even offers the user its own fourth generation programming language (ABAP/4), created especially for business needs.

The powerful range of services provided by the system, however, is only one cause of the success enjoyed by R/3. SAP supports the concept of the open system and builds interfaces, GUIs, services, etc., upon current standards.

In the broadest sense, this book concentrates on the administrative, technical and informational side of R/3. The system's business aspects and their operation do not constitute the center of our purview.

Chapter 1 describes the system architecture and its various possible features. It also discusses how the system resides in and works with other components: the network, the operating system and the RDBMS. Section 1.1 presents the theoretical basis of client/server architecture and the various configurations it makes possible; Section 1.2

introduces SAP system services. The interfaces made possible by the flexible architecture of the R/3 system find an extensive treatment in Section 1.3. Read Section 1.4 to become more familiar with process flows and concepts. To close this series of topics, Section 1.5 treats technical aspects related directly to computers.

Chapter 2 explains the basic service elements of R/3. It treats setting the profile as well as the creation of clients and users as the first steps required after installation of the R/3 system. This chapter also presents the equally important creation of connections to SAP support systems.

A functioning R/3 system is one thing; an efficient system is another. Chapter 3 discusses the tools available to the database administrator (DBA). It describes the most important tools used to evaluate system performance and how the tools are used. The organization and execution of data backups form an important part of this section. R/3 provides special administration of these tools.

Within the R/3 system, the ABAP/4 workbench provides an area to create, process and administer every kind of object. Chapter 4 focuses on a presentation of the workbench tools and their use.

Chapter 5 introduces the R/3 repository as the central source of information with the system. It explains the individual Basis objects and object classes. Using practical examples, it shows how objects are created and administered in the repository. In the process, the chapter treats both the information system and version administration.

A description of ABAP/4, the programming language, forms the basis of Chapter 6. Here the reader learns the basic elements necessary for the development of individual programs.

Any developer expects a user-friendly, multi-user development environment to provide, among other things, tools to monitor object modifications and an ability to transfer those modifications into other systems. R/3 meets these expectations with its comprehensive correction and transport system, described in Chapter 7.

1 R/3 architecture

This chapter provides the basic general understanding necessary for the administration of the R/3 system. It describes the host system: the system environment (both hardware and software) on which the R/3 system is installed. However, a general overview of only the host system would furnish inadequate information. A sketch of the architecture of the R/3 system offers greater assistance to the administrator. System administration does not begin with the analysis and resolution of bottlenecks or errors in an up-and-running system. Design defaults and decisions made as early as the installation phase determine the level of effort required to administer the entire R/3 system.

Nonetheless, the chapter makes no attempt to present a detailed description of the R/3 system; please see Buck-Emden and Galimow (1996) for more particulars.

1.1 Client/server architectures

1.1.1 General introduction

A total of three components make up client/server architecture: the client component, the server component, and a communications connection between the first two components which functions as the third component.

The client component (hereafter 'client') requests the performance of a particular task from the server component (hereafter 'server'). In other words, the client fulfills the role of an employer who issues contracts for specific services or tasks. The server then functions as an employee or contractor, who accepts and performs the services required by the contract.

Some examples will furnish the best understanding of this model:

- The hardware-oriented viewpoint and
- the software-oriented viewpoint.

The **hardware-oriented viewpoint** primarily takes the participating components into account: computers, printers, plotters, scanners, etc. Each part of this configuration fulfills a very specific task (a printer server, for example). This methodology results in a hard and fast division of tasks. It views each program as a closed unit that can run on only one computer. Connections between personal computers (PCs) as work stations and background processors serve as a good example of the hardware-oriented model. The background processors offer services such as file systems, database systems, or simulation calculations. However, not only powerful mainframe computers can function

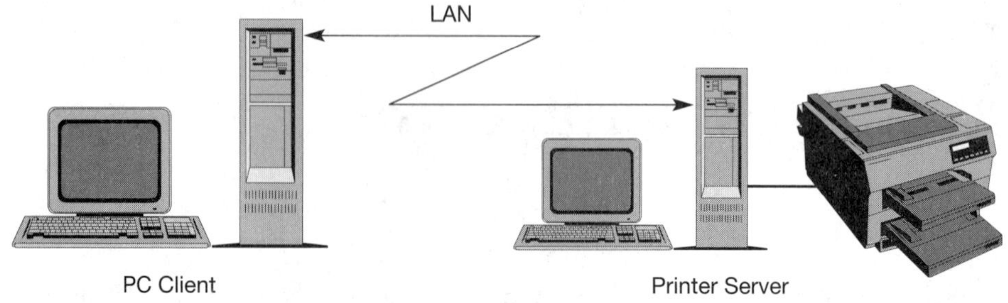

Figure 1.1 PC client with printer server

as background processors. Printer servers or plotter servers function in exactly the same manner. The required communication takes place over local area networks (LANs). Figure 1.1 shows an example.

Several examples describe the **software-oriented viewpoint**. Structured programming languages allow the categorization of services into sub-programs made available to the main program (considered a client). Communication between the two components takes place over mechanisms (e.g., parameter lists or global variables) established by each language. Taken one step further, this model can also offer extended, prepackaged services (libraries). Most programming languages offer math libraries, for example.

The execution of and communication between various independent programs builds the next level of the client/server model. Creation of data in a database provides a good example. On the one hand, the database management system functions as a distinct service. On the other hand, when the data-creation program runs it requires the use of a special portion of the database management system that allows it to store data in the database. Communication between both programs takes place in a shared memory (SHM) area. See Figure 1.2.

Following this line of thinking to its logical conclusion, it becomes clear that different programs can run on different computers. The program issuing the calls is the client; the program calls up functions as the server. Communication takes place over already-present connections, either LAN or WAN (wide area network). Figure 1.3 shows a configuration with these features.

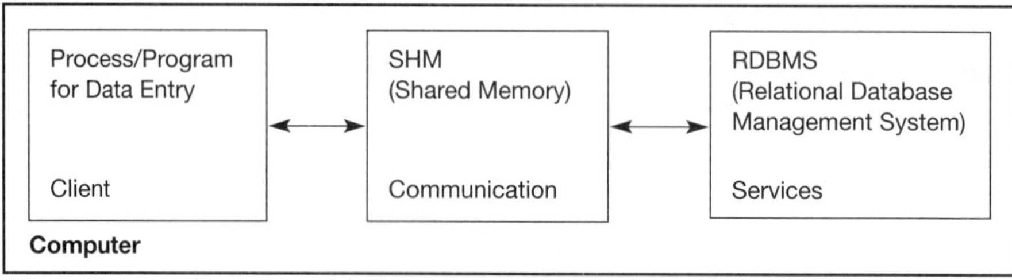

Figure 1.2 The client/server model at the program level

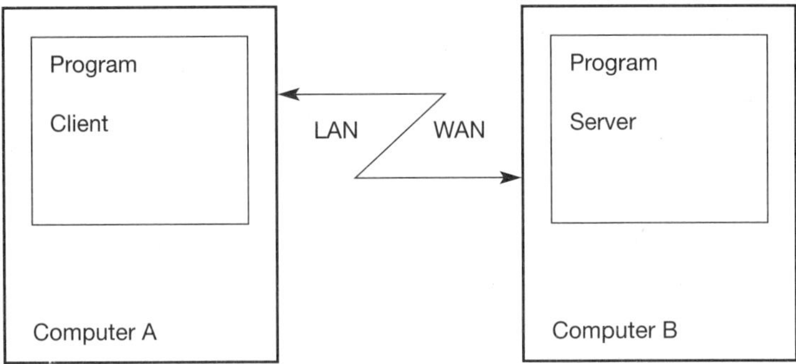

Figure 1.3 General, two-level client/server model on different computers

A more exact observation of these systems will reveal a certain level of parallelism between the hardware-oriented and software-oriented viewpoints. The software-oriented system, however, allows far more flexible and expandable systems and features. The software determines when and how the hardware functions rather than a system requiring the opposite. For the software to function in this manner, however, the design of the software system must have been designed accordingly and must allow for it.

The advantages of the division of labor provided by this model, however, need not remain limited to two computers. Systems display more and more of a tendency toward client/server architecture of three and more levels. Figure 1.4 shows one example of the possible configurations.

Two distinct methodologies exist to process requests between the client and the server: synchronous and asynchronous.

When operating **synchronously**, the client must wait until the server has executed the task the client has submitted to it. Only after the server returns the results of the task can the client continue with its own activity.

When operating **asynchronously**, the server acknowledges receipt of the task. As a result, both components can continue processing in parallel. According to this scenario, the client can even, if necessary, request the results of the task at a later time. The client

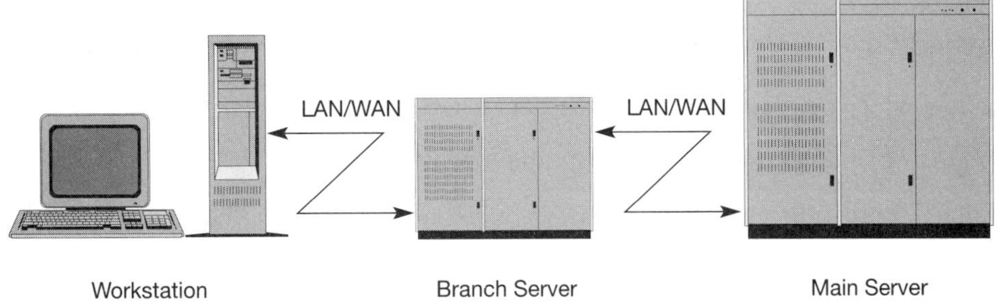

Figure 1.4 General, three-level client/server model

might also retrieve the results in file form, thus working independently of the server. A print request provides a good example. The client need not wait until the printer has completed all 99 pages of a document. The client requires only the relevant knowledge whether the server could complete the entire task, up to the very last page.

1.1.2 The client/server architecture of the R/3 system

The hardware-oriented viewpoint allows us to distinguish between three levels of information systems. The tasks executed by each component create the criteria for categorization into the following three levels:

- Presentation,
- Application and
- Data storage.

The same levels form the R/3 system. Defining interfaces (see Section 1.3.2) that regulate the exchange of data between the various levels quite exactly makes it possible to choose between the varied properties of the architecture. Accordingly, the R/3 system can be individually adapted to the most demanding customer needs.

Before we present the possible properties of client/server architecture more exactly, we need to examine some terminology. SAP terminology defines a 'service' as any task provided by a software component. According, a service may comprise anything from a specific program (e.g., the message handler process) to a combination of programs (e.g., the application server). The program(s) thus form the server for the given task. In the process, the server programs can run on different computers.

The following components make up the presentation level:

- SAPGUI (SAP's proprietary Graphical User Interface),
- Window Management.

The application level contains the following components:

- Dynpro Interpreter,
- ABAP/4 Dialog Processing,
- Dispatcher,
- Work processes.

The following component describes the data level:

- ABAP/4 Updates in connection with the RDBMS

Section 1.3 provides more detail about each component; Figure 1.5 illustrates the three levels.

By definition, all programs and software components assigned to a database make up the SAP system. In the following, we will examine the basic configuration possibilities of the SAP R/3 system.

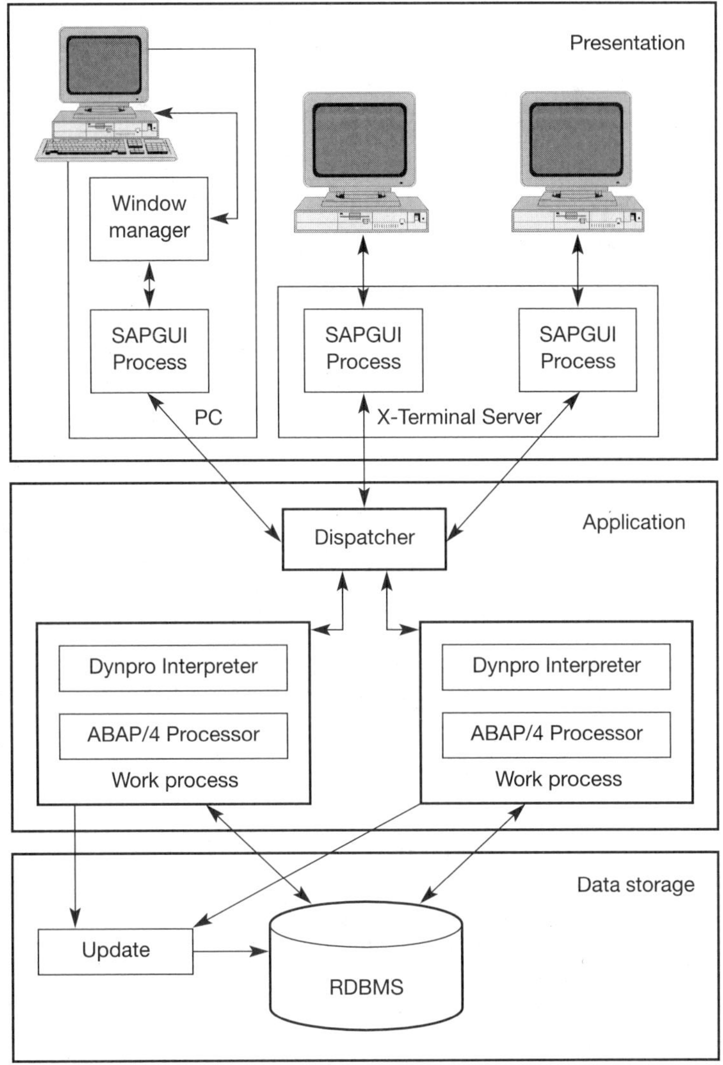

Figure 1.5 The three-level structure of R/3

In a **centralized system**, all three levels exist on one computer. Such a system resembles a classic configuration on a mainframe. X-terminals with graphics capability simply replace the earlier, character-based terminals. Figure 1.6 illustrates this situation.

In **two-level architecture**, the computer running the RDBMS and the applications does not administer the terminals; a separate computer, the presentation server, takes over these functions. The second computer runs the presentation software that controls the input and output functions of the R/3 system. A PC or X-terminal server often performs these tasks. An X-terminal server would then have a larger number of X-terminals connected to it. Figure 1.7 displays an example of two-level architecture.

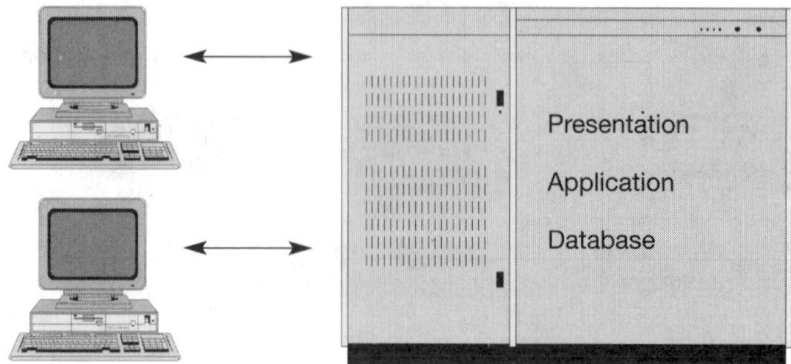

Figure 1.6 Centralized system

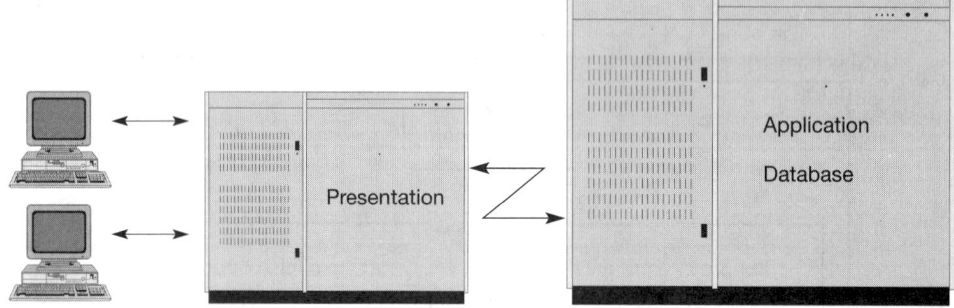

Figure 1.7 Two-level architecture (first model)

Decoupling the database creates a variation on two-level architecture. In this case the presentation programs and the application programs run on one computer while the database runs on another (see Figure 1.8).

In three-level client/server architecture (Figure 1.9 shows its most simple form), each level exists on its own hardware platform. This arrangement allows the optimal choice of platform for each application area. According to this scenario, each software application determines the type and performance of the hardware. The system can therefore use

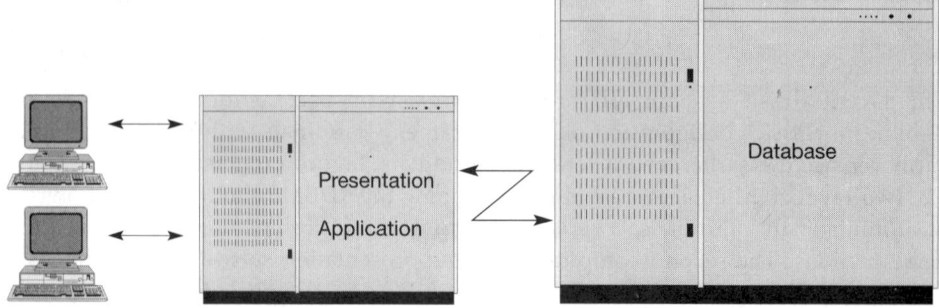

Figure 1.8 Two-level architecture (second model)

Presentation
Application
Database

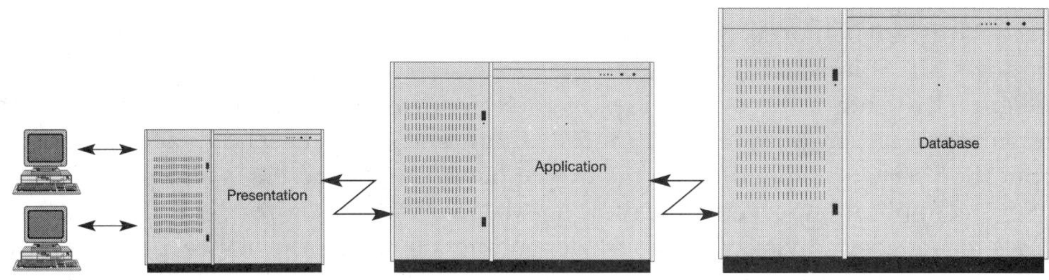

Figure 1.9 Three-level architecture

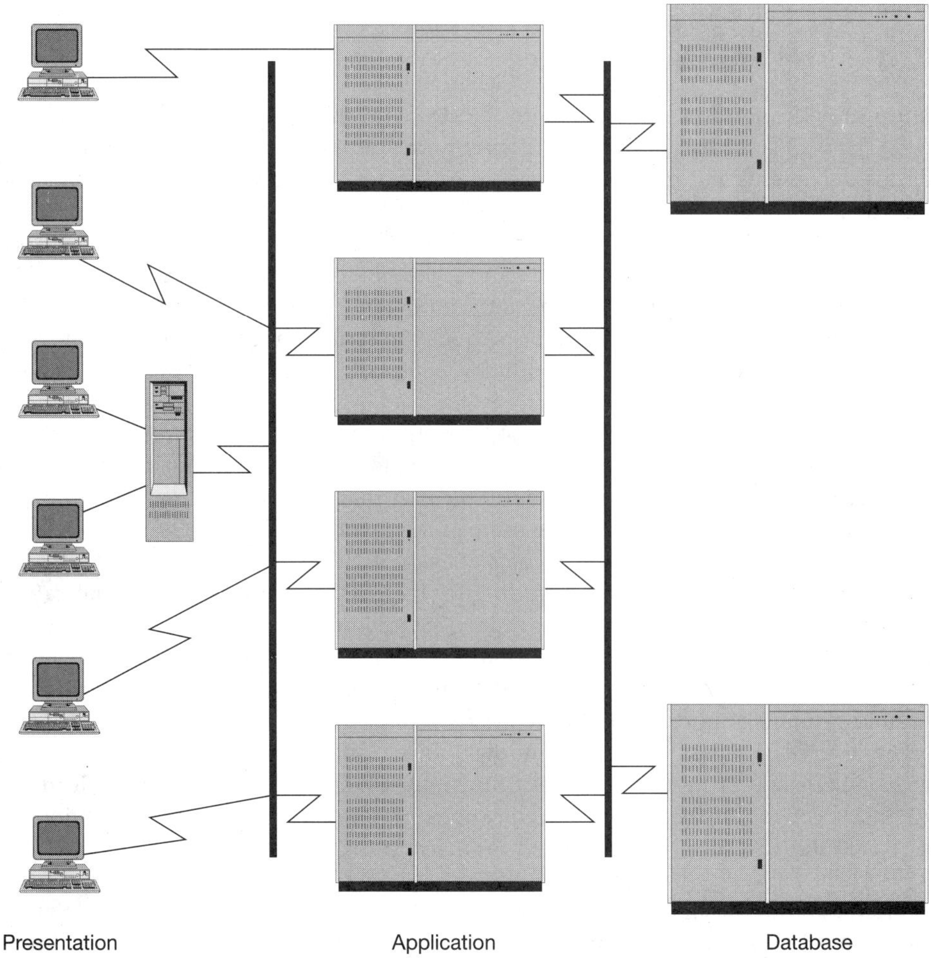

Presentation
Application
Database

Figure 1.10 Example of three-level client/server architecture

mixed hardware platforms (HP, IBM, SUN, etc.) with different operating systems (UNIX, Windows NT, Solaris, AIX, etc.).

Figure 1.10 shows the possibilities of three (and more) level architecture. With the presentation server (also called an **R/3 front end**), the user can access different application servers, depending on the task at hand. Parallel access is also possible.

Several application servers can access one database server, or **back end**. This provision allows for a good division of labor; depending on the performance profile of each application server, the system chooses it for a specific task. Direct or network connections provide communication between the individual servers. The design of the R/3 system allows it to accommodate all variations of client/server architecture.

1.2 R/3 services

1.2.1 Presentation service

Figure 1.5 indicates that the user communicates with the R/3 system at the presentation level. The R/3 services offered at this level regulate the input and output functions for various documents and graphics on each presentation server as well as communications with the application service.

The **SAPGUI** (SAP Graphical User Interface), a proprietary SAP terminal process, exploits the possibilities of the available presentation software. It realizes the graphical images of the R/3 system, including data input and output, on individual hardware components. SAP offers the GUI for various presentation environments, allowing a choice between the most familiar products, such as OSF/Motif or Microsoft Windows. See Section 1.3.2 for a complete list.

The system always offers the same GUI functions on each platform. A few exceptions depend on the possibilities of the installed presentation software. This flexibility makes the operation of the R/3 system significantly easier than one might otherwise expect. The user must learn the system only once but can then work on the most varied platforms – without ever having to learn the specifics of each platform.

To achieve an optimal fit or embedding of the SAPGUI into the conceptualization of each environment, the system takes the services offered there into consideration. Accordingly, some systems may offer individual functions that do not appear in other systems. The differences, however, depend on the details of specific installations; they do not hold primary importance for system operation.

The SAPGUI relies on the 'Windows Style Guide' (among other sources) for ergonomic design of input and output functions. The results of research performed by SAP itself constitute the design specifications of the user interface. In addition, SAP has based the design on standardized tests according to the norms of EC 90/270 and ISO 9241.

Stipulating the design of the user interface achieves a notable consistency. Symbols, icons and other graphic elements always appear to the user in identical form and the same location within the same function regardless of the application in use. This consistency allows the user to learn new applications and to take full advantage of

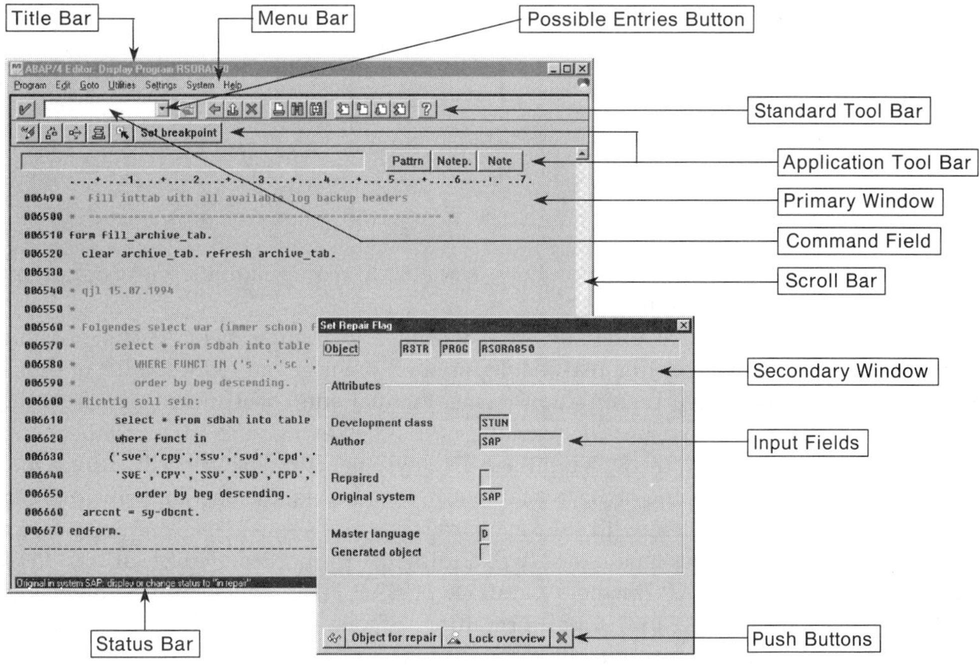

Figure 1.11 Screen interface

the possibilities of known applications rapidly and easily. Default settings support adherence to the standards even for individual development (see Chapter 4). See Figure 1.11 and the following for an illustration of some properties of the graphical interface design.

On-line help provides the user with one of the most important properties of the interface. It offers the user assistance in unknown or insecure areas. At any time, the user can access context-sensitive help by using the **help menu** or pressing **F1**. The system delivers documentation on the operation of the R/3 system to the user. Hypertext links allow the user to navigate through various units of information. Access to on-line help can take place from any application. Alternatively, the user can start from the glossary.

Service elements make up the next group of properties: **input and output fields**, **check boxes**, **list boxes**, **push buttons** and **radio buttons**. **Scroll bars** allow for movement, or scrolling, through the contents of the screen when the information does not fit into one window.

Menus enable navigation through the applications. Built hierarchically, the menus also allow lateral movement. In most cases, users must move directly from one level to another. Because the system provides a unified tree structure, menus are always used in the same way. The main menu leads to the application areas. From there, the user moves to the working level, at which concrete tasks can be performed. From this level onward, the individual operations of the task determine the contents of the menu bars. In addition, the user can also define individual menus for a specific activity field.

Standard tool bars aid the user in navigating between the various levels. A list of the most common functions follows:

- Back,
- End,
- Cancel,
- Help.

A **push button bar** makes function keys available to manipulate the most important functions of a given application.

Several **input values** are often possible within a particular field. If the possible alternatives limit themselves to a reasonable number, the user can request a list of them.

In addition to the visual presentation forms, manual entry instruments, such as the **mouse** and **keyboard**, also exist. The user still needs the keyboard to enter numbers and text (data entry). However, the R/3 interface displays such a mouse-friendly design that the user can often avoid using other instruments. Nonetheless, the user, in principle, can also operate the entire system with the keyboard.

The presentation server possesses two additional properties. First, various local graphics tools, such as SAP Business Graphics or SAP Hierarchy Graphics, allow the display of data for editing and visual formatting. Second, the SAPGUI can operate in several languages: it administers all text portions of input forms and output lists separately. The system merges texts into the screen display only during output of the screen layout. When logging onto the R/3 system, the user can determine which of the available languages to use. Because it uses a double byte character set, the R/3 system can display not only Latin characters, but also others (e.g., Japanese).

Finally, the SAPGUI also supports the abilities of client/server architecture. The communications possibilities of the presentation service enable storage of the SAPGUI on a separate platform without any difficulties. In addition, the system allows for connections between computers via not only LANs but also WANs. These platform-independent connections have a great advantage. The user need not fear any difficulties posed by performance losses: the system does not send completely formatted images to the presentation computer. Representations of that sort would demand the transmission of an incredibly large amount of information. Instead, the system transmits generic, platform-independent descriptions of the images between the presentation and application servers.

The capabilities of the presentation software currently running create the graphical image of the interface on and for that computer only. These circumstances limit the flow of data required for each change of screen required to one or two KB.

1.2.2 Application service

The **application level** serves as the switching center of the R/3 system. The **ABAP/4 programs**, which mirror the business logic of the R/3 system, run here. In addition, the logic of the image flow control takes a preeminent place next to the business logic. The image flow control contains the dialog step control, the **dynpro**. For further details

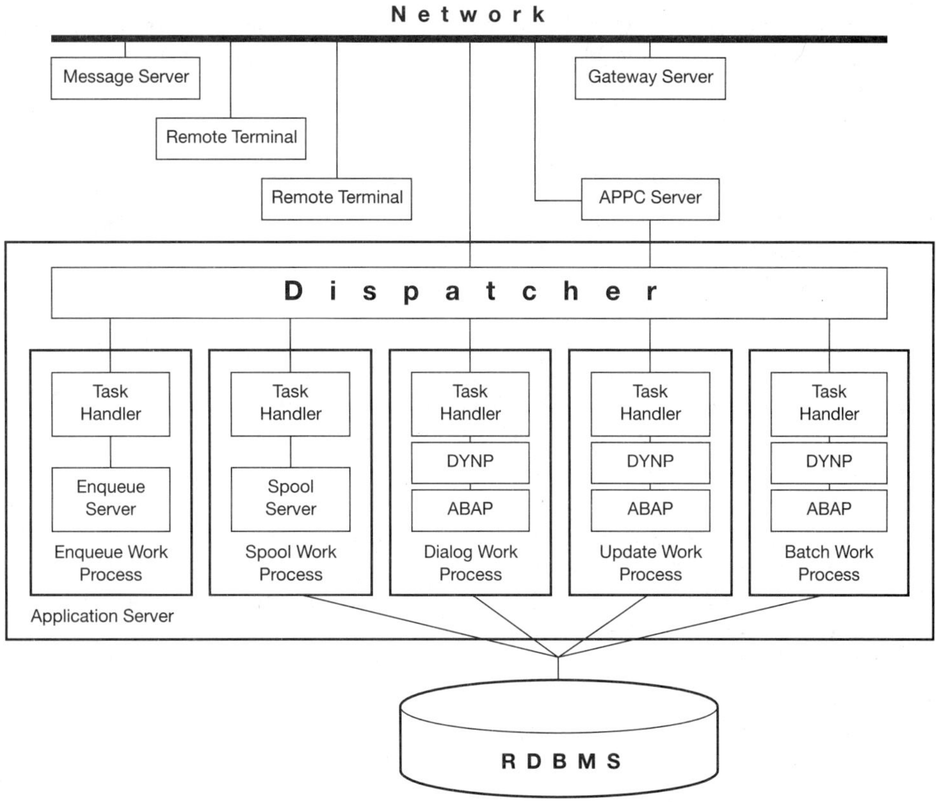

Figure 1.12 Application server

about and relationships between ABAP/4 programs and dynpros, see Chapter 4. Transfers between ABAP/4 programs and dynpros take place via the **R/3 runtime system** that contains the necessary processors: the ABAP/4 processor and the dynpro processor. Processing of both logics (languages) takes place interpretatively.

Along with both processors, the various software components form the application server. Figure 1.12 provides an overview.

Figure 1.12 clearly shows that in any **application server** only one dispatcher exists. The server, however, also contains a large number of work processes (WP). The user can establish the number of work processes (see Appendix B). Each **work process** can complete one specific task. Processes exist for dialog processing, updating data and document changes, batch processing, print spooling and for blocking management (enqueue/dequeue). The dispatcher determines the task that a particular work process must complete. Each work process can process each function.

The **dispatcher** functions as the control unit among the R/3 processes. It assigns the waiting processing requests among the various work processes. In other words, it accepts user entries from the presentation level. Other application servers (see Section 1.4) also send requests for service to the dispatcher. It is also responsible for setting priorities among update processes. The dispatcher sends the results provided by various work processes to the proper recipient.

Besides these duties, the dispatcher performs a host of other functions because it works very closely with the various operating systems. The dispatcher manages all the data traffic of a work process, unless the RDBMS handles it. The **APPC server** (Advanced Program to Program Communication) forms a constitutive element of the dispatcher. The APPC server can redirect all tasks to a software gateway that serves as the interface to the transport logs.

The **task handler** enjoys responsibility for the coordination of activities within a given work process. As needed, it actives either the ABAP/4 processor or the dynpro processor. It must also start activities for work processes that run without user interaction (e.g., the work process for batch (background) processing).

Dialog work processes handle the demands of the current user session. However, no hard and fast connection between a given user and a given dialog work process must exist. In a less than ideal situation, the system allocates a different dialog work process to the user. As a logical consequence, there may be many more users than dialog work processes at any particular time. Any work process can serve the needs of any user. This concept, however, makes queues unavoidable. The user will rarely notice such a situation in normal cases, especially if the configuration of the entire system has taken it into account. In the best of systems the number of dialog work process and the number of users (and user requests) balance each other well: usually five to eight users per dialog work process.

R/3 Release 3.0 contains a new feature: the ability to bind a dialog work process exclusively to the processing of a complete SAP transaction (see Section 1.4.3 for a definition of this term). This feature minimizes changing the allocation of dialog work processes from user to user, improving the performance of the entire R/3 system.

When a dialog work process accepts a task, it processes exactly one dialog step. After completing its task, it is free to process another task request made by the same or another user. The SAP system defines a **dialog step** as the processing of data. The processing begins with the initial screen and ends with the return of a reaction data packet and the screen layout that results from it (see Section 1.4.4).

During the processing of a dialog step, the system will inevitably have to address the RDBMS. Assume, for example, that the system must prepare data for the output fields of a screen layout. At the same time, it must transfer entries made by the user to the RDBMS. Such movement takes place via the **database interface**, implemented as a constitutive part of the work process.

Background processing forms another type of work process: a **batch work process**. Batch work processes execute ABAP/4 reports and programs at a particular time or in response to a particular event. The **batch scheduler** triggers batch work processes at given, adjustable intervals. The scheduler is a program interpreted and processed by a dialog work process.

Execution of batch programs cannot be interrupted. These programs must follow the same rules as on-line dialogs. Batch programs generally have a lower priority than on-line dialog work processes. This arrangement avoids any blockage of user sessions.

The batch work process also exchanges data with the RDBMS. Obviously, this exchange occurs when the process starts to run. Yet a scheduler dialog work process must be able to read data from the RDBMS to trigger the batch process. At least the starting time has significance.

The **spool work process** administers workflows for the buffered transfer of data to output devices such as printers or fax machines. This work process can administer and move data in both a LAN and a WAN environment. It almost always works in conjunction with the appropriate host spool system on the computer. The spool work process reads the data to be processed from the RDBMS. The system uses the following procedure to process tasks properly:

- Transfer of the output data to a **TEMSE file** (TEMporary SEquential file),
- Use of a separate print request that specifies the use of TEMSE file contents more closely: e.g., print on printer XYZ.

The **enqueue work process** plays a very special role within the internal lock management component of the R/3 system. For data structures, the locking behavior must orient itself, above all, to the realities of business. The definition of data objects (e.g., matchcodes or R/3 views) across several relational tables takes place easily. To exclude the possibility of bottlenecks and other difficulties in the locking behavior of the RDBMS, the system features built-in lock management. This component solves the following problems and meets the following requirements:

- Simultaneous locking of various tables in the RDBMS,
- Maintaining locks during a change of process (when, for example, various dialog work processes deal with a given transaction or when the data is updated apart from the dialog),
- Maintaining locks until a predetermined endpoint (for example, until the application program explicitly returns data or until the end of the SAP transaction),
- Use in client/server configurations (all application servers in such a configuration must recognize the locks because they apply to all applications),
- Use on multi-processor systems,
- System-wide validity of the locks.

To ensure the correct performance of the locking tasks, the enqueue work process works only on the lock table stored in main memory. Access to the RDBMS is not required. This implementation provides better performance.

Each dialog transaction generally consists of several dialog steps. In some cases, the dialog steps attempt to change tables in the RDBMS. Executing each of these relatively small actions would require an enormous level of communication between the work process and the RDBMS and would simultaneously lead to a significant loss in performance. To avoid such problems, the desired manipulations are written to a log record. The record contains all the information necessary for the change. Once the dialog portion of the transaction has ended, the update (i.e., the execution of the log record) can follow; the **update work process** performs this task. Should a rollback be issued before the beginning of the update, the log record no longer applies: access to the RDBMS was not required. Section 1.4.5 provides a more detailed presentation of how updates function.

Several update work processes can exist in one R/3 system: each of them must have access to the RDBMS.

The following sections refer to instance names according to the naming conventions valid in the R/3 environment (see Section 1.4.6). The German word for update begins with a 'V.' Therefore, when a particular instance offers update service, a 'V' forms part of the instance name.

1.2.3 Summary of services and servers

Now that we have examined the general structure of the application server, we can turn our attention to a sketch of the possible variants or types of servers. Consider the following possible variations:

- Dialog server,
- Enqueue server,
- Update server,
- Batch server,
- Spool server.

In addition to the other processes, at least one dialog work process must also exist – independently of the type of server. Communication between the application and a special server requires this dialog work process. It can also, as in the case of the batch work process, perform the tasks of the scheduler (Section 1.2.2).

The following presents the various types of servers, beginning with the **dialog server** (see Figure 1.13).

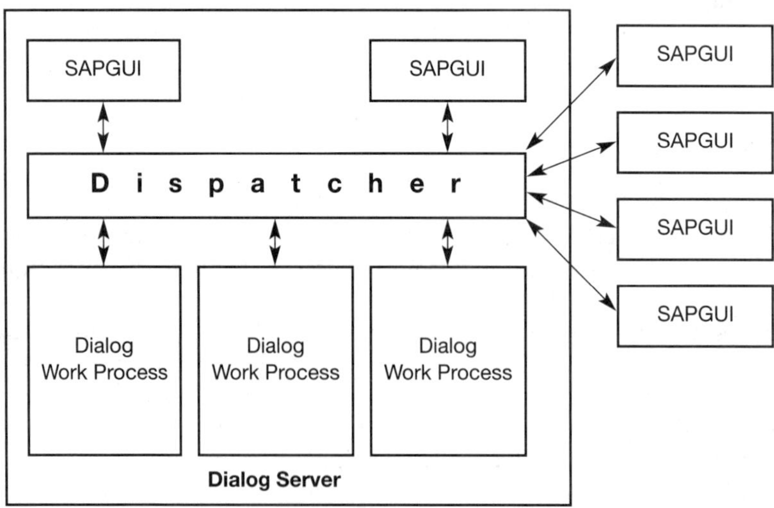

Figure 1.13 Dialog server

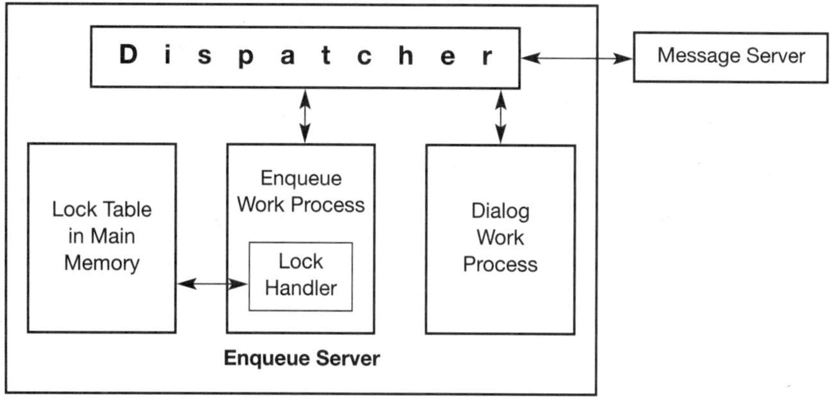

Figure 1.14 Enqueue server

The dialog server enjoys is own distinct characteristic: it consists of only one specific type of work process. Processes are limited to 'dialog' tasks.

In any given R/3 system only one (!) **enqueue server** (see Figure 1.14) may exist. In normal cases, only one enqueue work process can perform all the queued tasks: the special tasks of the enqueue work process have already been discussed.

All other work processes must either communicate with the enqueue server via a special work process (the message server, described in Section 1.2.4), or form an integrated part of it. These work processes can execute 'enqueue' (lock) and 'dequeue' (unlock) functions on their own. This procedure avoids any unnecessary communication between the enqueue work processes and other work processes running on the same computer and thereby avoids performance losses.

To the same end, an **update server** can be installed (see Figure 1.15). This server generally runs on the same computer as the database software, thus providing shorter communications routes.

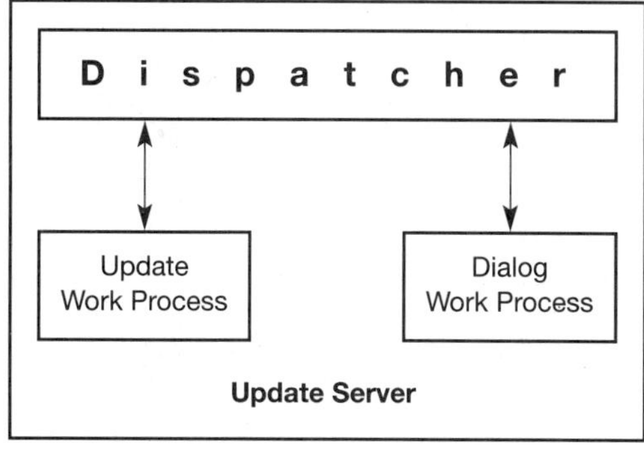

Figure 1.15 Update server

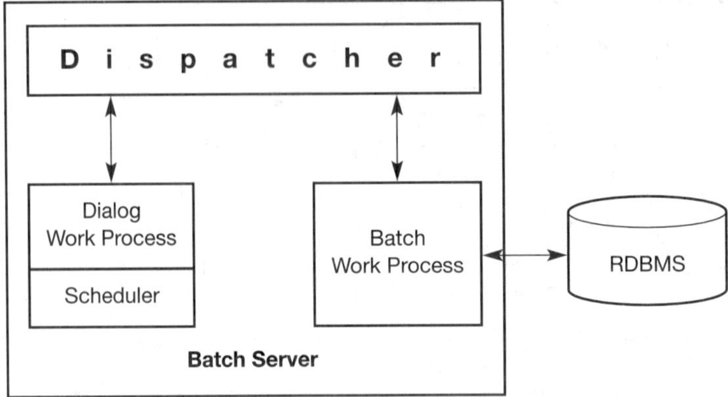

Figure 1.16 Batch server

Figure 1.16 illustrates the background server (**batch server**). See Section 1.2.2 for a description of the function of this server.

Starting a batch work process always requires a dialog work process.

The **spool server** is presented in Figure 1.17.

Section 1.4 discusses process flows and concepts in detail.

1.2.4 Additional R/3 services

In addition to the previously described services at the application level, other services exist. These additional services become significant when, for example, the R/3 system works in a distributed environment. The services described in the following regulate communication within a distributed R/3 system and with other R/2 and R/3 systems. Provisions must exist for the ability to exchange data between the R/3 system and other external systems.

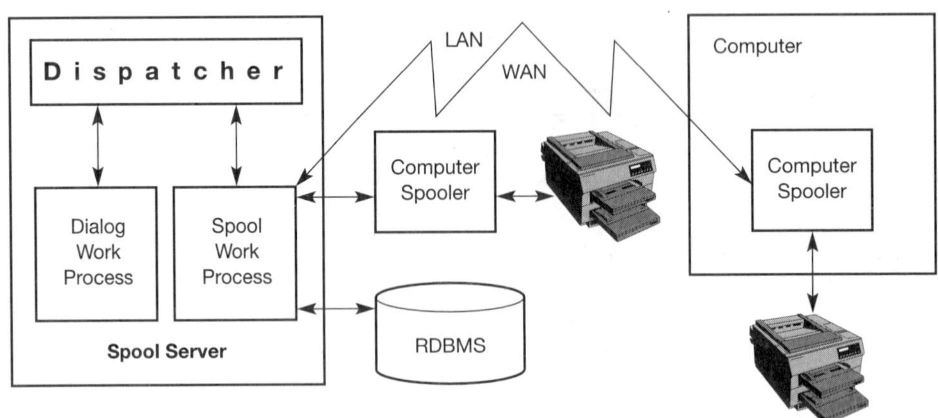

Figure 1.17 Spool server

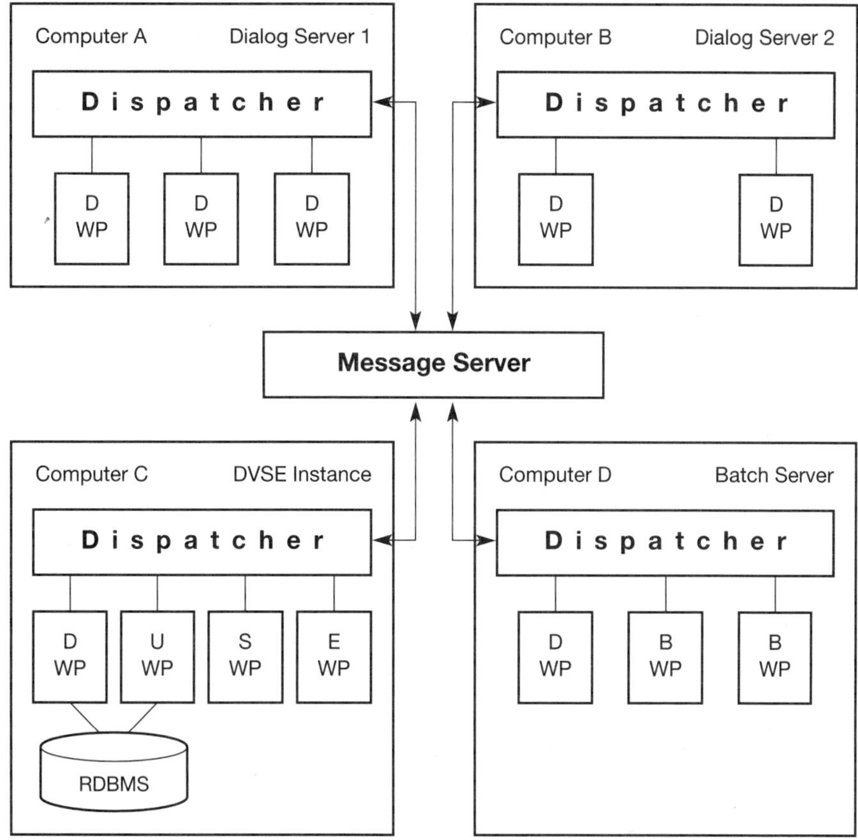

Figure 1.18 Message server

The **message server** holds responsibility for communication within a distributed R/3 system, one, for example, that includes several dialog servers and a batch system. Only one can exist within a given R/3 system and it belongs to the small group of processes that have no access to the RDBMS. By way of example, Figure 1.18 shows the use of a message server.

The short messages that exchanged between the application servers are normally of the following types:

- Update trigger,
- Batch job trigger,
- Enqueue/Dequeue,
- Exchange of tasks.

To identify sender and receiver uniquely, application servers address the message server with a unique name. As seen in Section 1.5.3, each application server knows the names of the update, enqueue, batch and spool servers. The unique 'target addresses'

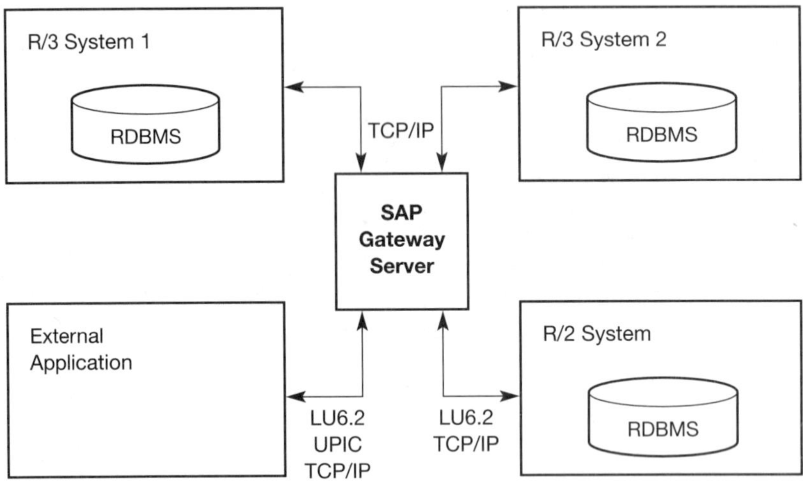

Figure 1.19 CPIC server

that the application servers provide for the message server enable the work of the corresponding service to become active.

Leaving the confines of an R/3 system requires the use of the **gateway server** (often called the **CPIC server**). Figure 1.19 shows an example.

To communicate with other systems, the server uses the CPI-C protocol. The volume of data treated here is generally much greater than that transferred by the message server. The transport of application data between various systems (R/2, R/3, external) causes the increased level of data.

As Figure 1.19 indicates, the processes of the SAP gateway server communicate with their clients via the TCP/IP transport protocol whenever UNIX systems are involved. On mainframes the server uses protocols such as LU6.2 from IBM or UPIC from Siemens. Of course, the computer running the SAP gateway server provides the hardware and software components necessary for communications.

Another available service is **SAPcomm**; Figure 1.20 illustrates how this service fits into R/3 architecture.

This service generally runs as its own process on its own computer or an application or database server. This service regulates the use of communications products offered by third parties. The products themselves handle communications with the external standard communication services. SAPcomm provides support for products that permit the exchange of documents. For example:

- EDI documents (Electronic business Data Interchange),
- Mail documents (X.400, among others),
- Telecommunicataions documents (telefax, teletex, telex).

SAP offers an interface, **SAPcomm API** (Application Program Interface), to connect to hardware and software products offered by third parties. Within SAPcomm a

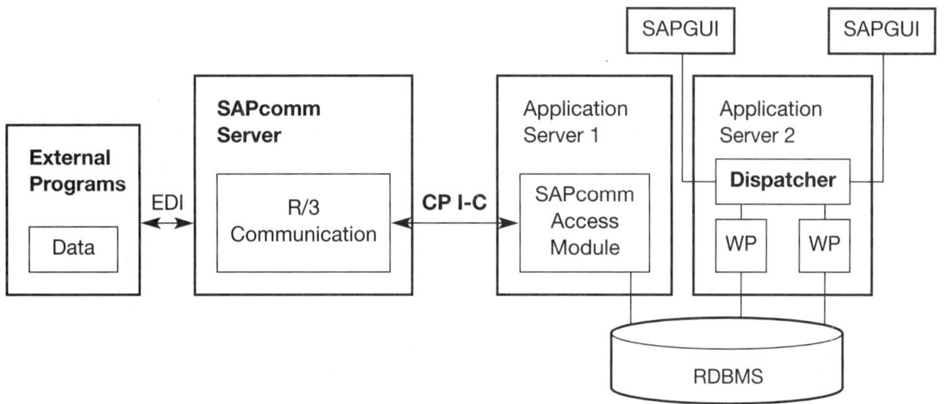

Figure 1.20 SAPcomm server

product-specific communications component must exist to allow the system to undertake control of the external communications portions of a given task. One of these internal components can also create a connection to another R/3 system. The number of connected R/3 systems plays no relevant role. SAPcomm, unlike third party products, treats all connected systems in the same manner. In an extreme case, one could even imagine an operation that has no connections to an SAP system.

To control remote spoolers and printers, the R/3 system offers an output processor, **saplpd** (also written as SAPLPD). This program accepts print requests (for example) from the spool work process. Such a procedure becomes necessary whenever remote communication at the operating system level between the client computer (where the print request is issued), and the printer server (where the print request should be executed), does not function properly or should not be used at all. This situation can arise when the R/3 system does not support particular print command interfaces.

Generally, print requests are issued over a LAN or WAN; Figure 1.21 illustrates these functions.

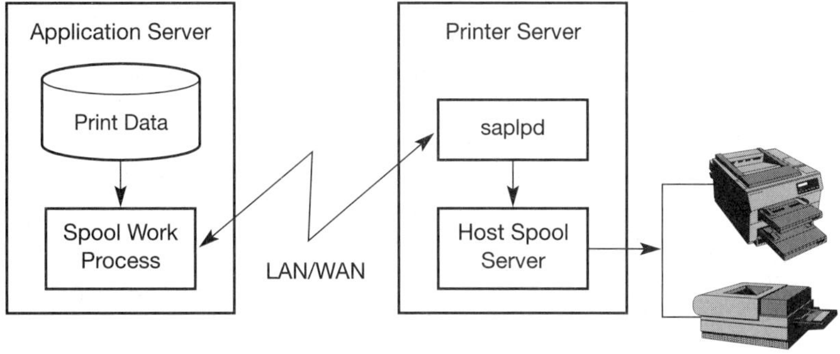

Figure 1.21 saplpd

1.2.5 Database service

The R/3 system is an open system, based on standards. The same is true of the database interfaces and the database service. Only SQL commands are used for the definition and manipulation of data. To deal with all the differing linguistic issues (syntax and semantics) raised by various database systems with as few problems as possible, the system stores the necessary information in a few isolated modules. The R/3 system can therefore use all relevant RDBMS currently on the market. The use of a particular RDBMS depends only on its efficiency and capacity.

To allow for even more independence from the SQL functions of a given RDBMS, the R/3 system makes two SQL levels available in the ABAP/4 Development Workbench (see Section 5):

- ABAP/4 Open SQL,
- ABAP/4 Native SQL.

ABAP/4 Open SQL corresponds to the entry level according to the SQL2 Standard (Technical Committee ISO/IEC, 1992). This linguistic expansion of ABAP/4 guarantees complete independence from the RDBMS in use. Accordingly, any RDBMS used by the R/3 system can run applications that use only this language.

Implementation of the extended level takes place by means of ABAP/4 Native SQL. This level enables access to all the RDBMS functions currently used by the application. Even the extensions specific to the manufacturer can be called upon. To minimize the porting requirements in such a database-dependent environment, the system combines all instances of this language into a few modules and identifies them as database dependent. If the R/3 system is ported to another RDBMS, only these modules need adaptation. Figure 1.22 illustrates this process.

The R/3 system stores application data in transparent tables. This procedure thus contributes to the required open nature of the R/3 system. Besides the tools provided by the database manufacturer, tools used by standardized access interfaces, such as ODBC (Open Data Base Connectivity), must have access to the data. Figure 1.23 displays these circumstances.

The R/3 system uses a variety of methods to minimize the communication necessary in client/server environments. On the one hand, R/3 applications take advantage of allowing the RDBMS to execute quantity operations (e.g., array fetch). On the other hand, the system uses buffers to limit the number of accesses to the database. Database services, a constitutive part of the R/3 runtime environment, supply these buffers, which are available on every application server. Because of their implementation on the client side, they are called a 'client cache.' They serve as an intermediate storage point for data required frequently by the application. This procedure not only lessens the traffic on the network, but also significantly lightens the load on the database server. The following list indicates information types particularly well suited to client caching because they change very little.

- ABAP/4 programs,
- Dynpros,

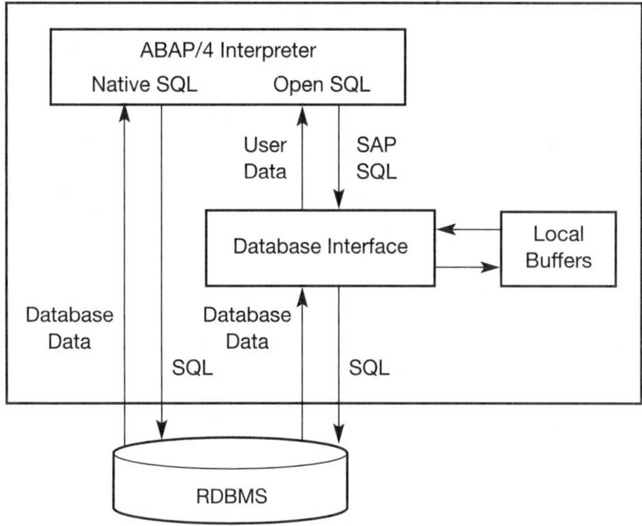

Figure 1.22 ABAP/4 SQL

- ABAP/4 repository information,
- Business parameters.

The application knows nothing about these optimizing activities. It usually uses buffers in read-only mode and normally passes queued changes to the RDBMS immediately. The message service ensures that the contents of the affected buffer are also changed on the other application servers. A user need not worry about the synchronization of buffer contents should one application server or a network fail. Because they are stored in the computer's main memory, they are automatically deleted upon rebooting. The runtime behavior of the application rebuilds the contents dynamically.

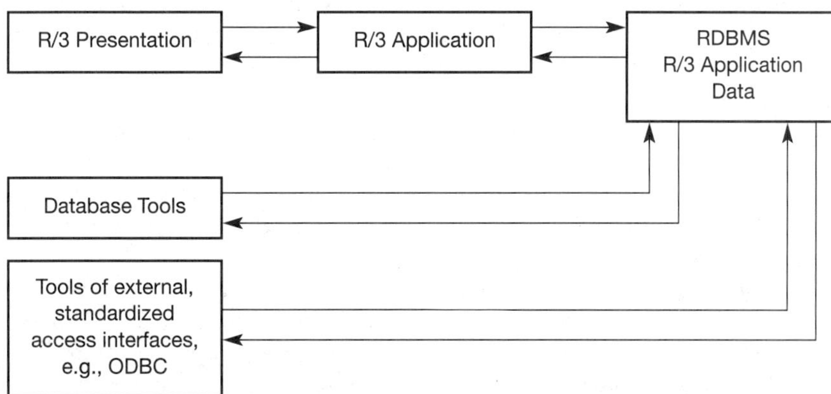

Figure 1.23 Access to the RDBMS

When an application starts, its programs are dynamically loaded from the RDBMS into the application server's buffer. The programs are thus available to all users of the server. Accordingly, when the server is installed, no thought need be given to the applications or functions that will run on it. This procedure offers a high level of flexibility during the configuration and installation of client/server networks. It allows for the implementation of a dynamic distribution of applications on application servers.

1.3 R/3 interfaces

1.3.1 Interface architecture

Figure 1.24 illustrates the basic interface architecture of the R/3 system. This design, based on the model of levels with generally independent interfaces, allows the system to achieve various goals:

- Support of client/server configurations,
- Scalability of available computer services (which components of the R/3 system can run on which computers, thus allowing for the highest possible level of performance for the entire system),
- Portability (the ability to use the most varied hardware and software platforms),
- Use of ergonomic user interfaces,
- Linkage to third party software (openness and interoperability),
- Expansion possibilities for the entire system.

The **system interfaces** ensure independence from the services of various hardware platforms (and their operating systems) as well as from many database systems. These interfaces are written in the C programming language to achieve a high level of portability.

The **application level**, responsible for the business functions and processes in the R/3 system, is written in ABAP/4, an R/3-specific, fourth-generation programming language. Section 5 treats the features of this programming language in detail.

Flow control takes responsibility for coordinating the actions necessary for the user session and the efficient use of R/3 system functions. Among other things, it must regulate memory management for the R/3 processes and/or decide which action to process next (dispatching). Many of these functions could have been left to the operating system without further ado. However, to ensure the desired portability of the system, the R/3 system itself manages these functions.

The design of the R/3 system combines the interfaces for the system environment (operating system, database system and other software standards, such as TCP/IP for communication) at one unique level. The design ensures, among other things, a high portability of the entire system. To gain a foothold in a new environment, only that level requires new development. The rest of the R/3 system is completely independent of any given hardware or software environment.

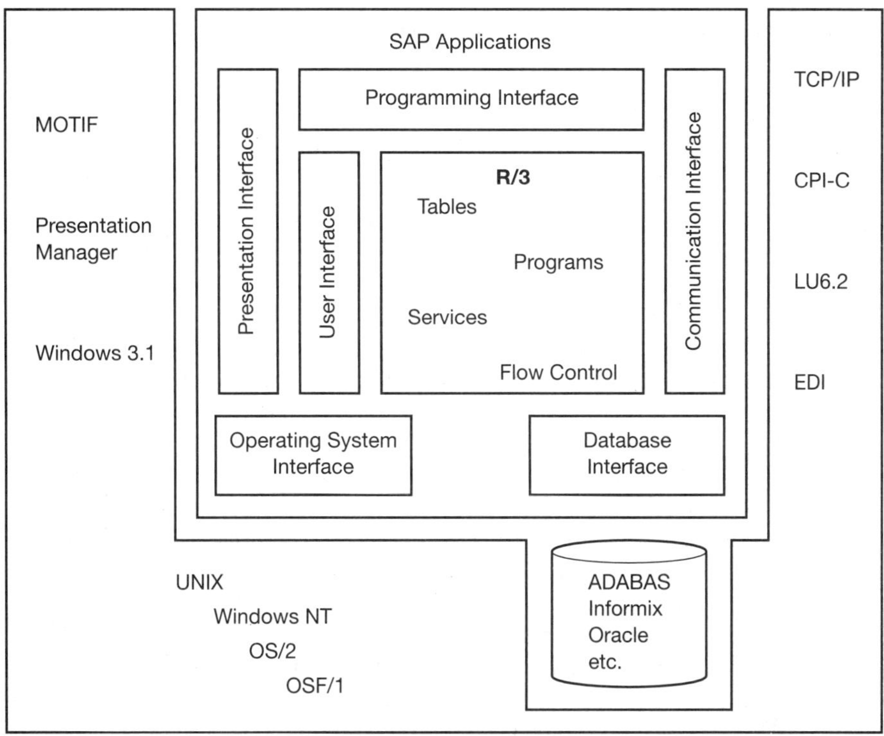

Figure 1.24 R/3 interfaces

1.3.2 System interfaces

Presentation interface

The presentation interface creates the optical, interactive connection to the user. Using presentation computers requires systems with graphics capabilities; only these computers are supported. Such computers offer the quality required for the display of the SAP user interface. Accordingly, the system must employ PCs or smaller workstations and X-terminals. The presentation interface ensures that no functional difference in the dialogs appears at the various front ends.

The presentation interface works closely with the software of the presentation hardware platform to achieve this goal. In doing so, various graphical operating elements of the dialogs are realized within the interface itself. System-independent portions, however, are defined in the user interface (see Section 1.3.3).

Although the color graphical display can be adjusted for monochrome monitors, color terminals work better. The standard, default settings used in the installation process assume the presence of color monitors.

The R/3 system currently supports the following presentation software:

- OSF/Motif,
- Presentation Manager,
- Windows 3.1,
- Apple Macintosh.

Database interface

The definition of the database interface enables it to connect relational databases from various manufacturers to the R/3 system. The interface contains settings or adjustments that compensate for the differences in SQL syntax and semantics between the individual RDBMS.

Section 1.2.5 already indicated the tasks of the database interface. Here we will provide more detailed information.

The R/3 system contains many extensive data structures. These are ultimately converted into SQL and, thus, into simple, relational tables. Relational tables likewise contain the information (in compressed form) necessary for the conversion. This information is integrated in the database interface.

The database interface also implements functions that improve performance. Consider **cursor caching**, for example: it allows repeated use of a previously created access path to the database. The interface also manages the full exploitation of internal buffers for data processing. The reuse of optimized SQL commands also falls within the purview of this environment. As is true of the execution of SQL commands, both syntax analysis and access optimization demand a great deal of time and resources from the RDBMS. If a particular SQL command produces a very small 'hit rate,' the preparation (syntax analysis, etc.) of the command may have used more resources than the subsequent reading of the data. It is therefore crucial to the runtime characteristics of a RDBMS that once SQL commands have gone through the optimization process, they do not get 'lost' too quickly. Every RDBMS offers its own means to recreate optimized SQL commands. Some examples include:

- Storage in fixed access-plans and
- Dynamic buffering.

Since these functions depend upon the RDBMS in use, they are stored in the database interface, thus ensuring application independence.

The demand for openness in the R/3 system also applies to the interface for data management. Specifically, this means:

- All R/3 application data must be stored in transparent tables of the RDBMS.
- Access to data must be possible both with the SQL tools of the RDBMS in use and by means of standard access interfaces, as is true of ODBC (Open Data Base Connectivity).

- An external user must have the ability to find data in tables and table columns, so that she can gain the information she requires. Access authorization, of course, is the primary precondition for access to the data.
- The enterprise model serves as an orienting point for business applications.
- In R/3 applications, no limitation requires addressing only one special RDBMS in a given R/3 system. Quite the contrary: the user can access additional RDBMS in the R/3 system by using and taking full advantage of the transparent distribution concepts of the database manufacturers.

Currently, the user can choose between the following RDBMS:

- ADABAS D (formerly Entire SQL-DB),
- DB2 for AIX,
- DB2/400,
- Informix Online,
- Microsoft SQL Server,
- Oracle.

Operating system interface

Access to operating system resources takes place primarily through the dispatcher and its environment. It must manage tasks such as signal handling and the use of the queue. It cannot avoid working closely with the operating system.

Likewise, the R/3 system must turn to the operating system for communications and file/memory management. The R/3 system can be used with the following operating systems:

- OSF/1, ULTRIX,
- HP-UX,
- AIX,
- SINIX,
- Solaris,
- AS/400,
- Windows NT.

1.3.3 User interface

The user interface defines the interaction with the user. The R/3 system can use this interface to present itself to the user identically and in a functionally equivalent manner, regardless of the type of front end in use. A user who has learned the R/3 system on one platform can easily use it on another.

To make learning and operating the R/3 system as easy as possible, the system must provide the user with as ergonomic a user interface as possible. The user interface should also exhibit a structure similar to that offered by other manufacturers, so that the user can work with the interface more familiarly and rapidly. The requirements of the standard **CUA** (Common User Access) and the Windows Style Manager serve as a basis here. The interface contains additional rules, beyond the requirements of these standards. The field assignments establish defaults for the following points:

Texts	terms, abbreviations, function keys, help texts,...
Flows	compilation of menus, scroll functions,...
Optics	colors, grouping of fields, fonts,...
Controls	title bar, menu bar, application area, dialog windows, command lines, function key lines, scroll bar,...

1.3.4 Communications interface

The communications interface determines the procedure for the electronic exchange of information. As examples, consider the communications among R/3 systems or the communications between an R/3 system and another application system.

As is typical in an open system, this interface orients itself toward current standards. Data exchange therefore takes place in heterogeneous environments by means of CPI-C (Common Programming Interface-Communication) or RFC (Remote Function Call) standards. The interface also used the standard network protocol TCP/IP (Transmission Control Protocol/Internet Protocol). Table 1.1 provides a list of the standards and protocols used by the R/3 system.

Table 1.1 Network protocols and standards

Application services	EDI	Electronic Data Interchange Exchange of business messages
	X.400, X.500	Electronic mail interface
	LU6.2/APPC	Logical Unit IBM Network Protocol Advanced program to program communication
	CPI-C	Common Programming Interface-Communication
	RFC/RPC	Remote Function Calls/Remote Procedure Calls High level programming interface
	OLE	Object Linking and Embedding Microsoft technology for the integration of PC applications
	DDE	Dynamic Data Exchange
	ODBC	Open Data Base Connectivity Standard procedure from Microsoft for table-oriented data access
	ALE	Application Link Embedding Message-oriented distribution of business objects
	API/Q-API	Application Program Interface/Queue Application Program Interface Communication between application programs (also asynchronous)

Transport services	Sockets	
	TCP/IP	Transmission Control Protocol/Internet Protocol Open standard network protocol
	IEEE 802	Protocol and hardware interface for Ethernet
	X.25	Communications protocol, WAN Corresponds to the German DATEX-P
	X.21	Hardware interface
	ISDN	Integrated Services Digital Network, WAN
	Ethernet	Network hardware in LAN area
	Token ring	Network hardware in LAN area
	FDDI	Fiber Distributed Data Interchange High-speed network, LAN, two bi-directional network strands

1.3.5 Programming interface

This interface comprises concepts developed by SAP Software Technology that go far beyond the features of normal APAB/4 language elements and, to a great degree, determine the structure of SAP applications.

The units found here allow for and implement remote calls of dialogs and functions. These units provide the basis for distributed applications at the application level.

A function library allows for the centralized storage and reuse of recyclable modules that can be applied throughout the system.

Besides using SAP SQL, the system also allows direct access to the RDBMS. The 'EXEC SQL' command available for this specific purpose is, logically, stored in the programming interface.

Direct access to the RDBMS can lead to the danger of dependence on a particular system.

1.3.6 Additional interfaces

Most of the remaining interfaces deal with communications with external entities. The **office communications interface** allows for the transmission of texts to any user of the same or another R/3 system or to any other office communications system. Information for the users of telecommunications services (telex, telefax or teletex or X.400 subscribers) also flow through this interface. The interface can also direct information to a printer.

MAPI (Messaging Application Programming Interface) is yet another interface. A constitutive element of Microsoft Windows Open Service Architecture, MAPI is used by SAPmail, the integrated electronic mail component of the R/3 systems.

The CCMS (Computing Center Management System) contains various **open interfaces** that allow for the integration of Open View (HP) and Netview6000 (IBM, Digital). The

CCMS also contains an interface for the collection of performance-related data from the operating system, the database system and the network. Another interface allows CCMS to use services (data backups, for example) provided by external tools. Yet another interface enables the processing of R/3 management data by external management tools; like some of the CCMS interfaces, it is based on SNMP (Simple Network Management Protocol).

1.3.7 Data interfaces

Data interfaces are actually special procedures, based on the standard methods in use, to allow for data transport.

The **delta manager** controls the flow of copies of tables (data flow) between the calling programs and the calling function modules. Figure 1.25 illustrates this flow.

To minimize the data flow, internal tables are copies 'by reference' (1). Later manipulations to the common table take place only via a log table (2). Handling is based (partially) on the RFC (Remote Function Call) standard.

Based on the CPI-C standard, the data is transferred directly, i.e., **synchronously**, by an ABAP/4 program. During the process, however, interruptions can occur. Among them, the user may encounter any of the following possibilities:

- The partner system is unavailable.
- The receiving side is stalled.
- The connection between the system has been interrupted.

In most cases, the user can expect difficulties on the sender's side in addition to the interruptions noted above. In a best-case scenario, this means a delay in the runtime behavior of the user session. In a worst-case scenario, the user may face a loss of data, leading to later recreation of the lost information.

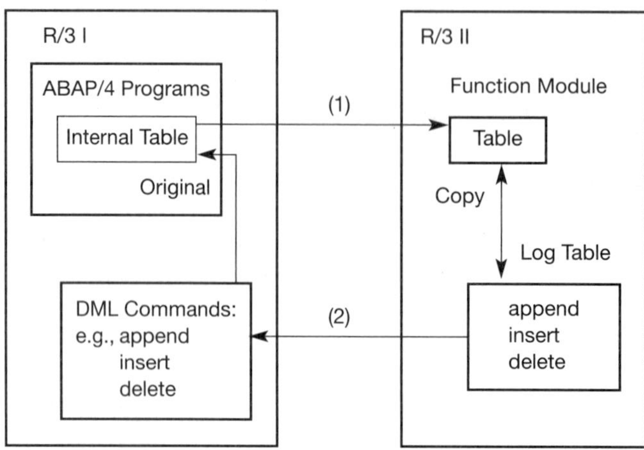

Figure 1.25 Delta manager

Besides the **synchronous data transfer** the system can employ **asynchronous data transfer**. The system temporally decouples the sending and receiving in this case. Accordingly, it must place the data in intermediate storage. A driver program then transfers the data at a particular time. The action ends only after successful transfer of the data.

The R/3 system implements a **wait queue** for the transfer of **buffered data** from one system to another.

One method of transferring large amounts of data is **batch input**. This automated procedure is often called BDC (Batch Data Communication). As in the case of on-line data input, data consistency must be guaranteed. To do so, the system applies the same buffer mechanisms to the transfer data as it does on-line. When a user enters data via a screen field, it is subject to the same consistency checks that would apply had he entered it on-line. The actions of a batch input must also meet the requirements of the SAP user authorization concept (see Section 2.2.1).

Data intended for transfer is temporarily stored in a **batch input session**, a queue file. A batch input session mirrors a collection of business events. Execution of a batch input can be seen as a simulated user dialog.

Sequential datasets, stored in an external file, can be read with the READ DATASET function, or written with the TRANSFER DATASET function.

Because of its exceptional importance within the R/3 system, the **correction and transport system** (CTS) is described, in detail, as a data interface in Chapter 7. Here, however, we briefly note the goals of the CTS:

- Verification of developments in and changes to objects in the R/3 development environment.
- Tracking objects in the R/3 development environment from one SAP system to another.

1.4 Process flows and concepts

1.4.1 Architecture concepts

The architecture of the R/3 kernel

Figure 1.26 illustrates one possible use of the design of R/3 architecture. A separate process is started for each user and for each parallel user session. According to the depiction, the process consists of the following parts: interface control, dynpro processor, ABAP/4 processor and database interface. Some of the more significant disadvantages of this configuration include:

- Loss of operating system resources:
  - Each process lays claim to the same amount of main memory. This situation leads to unfavorable paging behavior while the process is running: in main memory, the processes that can run displace those currently not in use.

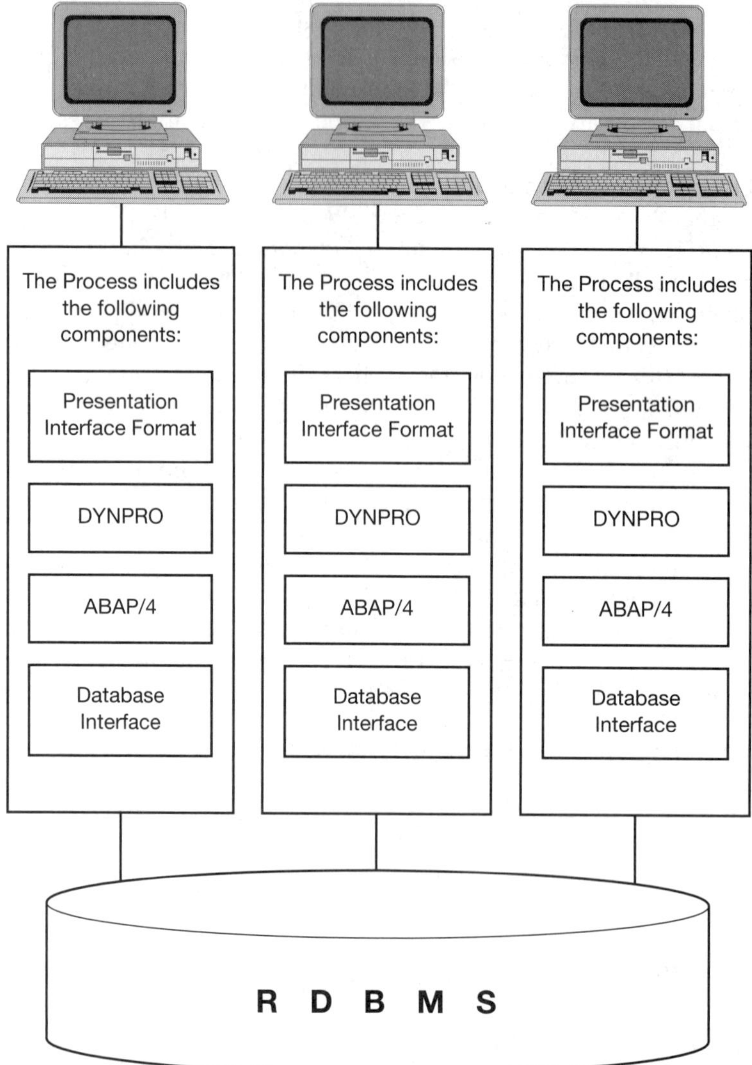

Figure 1.26 The use of R/3 architecture at the process level

- Each process executes, on its own, the formatting of the screen interface. Such individual execution requires a great deal of processing and places extraordinary demands on the computer's CPU (Central Processing Unit).

- The configuration does not apply the principles behind client/server architecture to all parts of the system: it uses them only to access the RDBMS. A distribution of tasks and load among the R/3 components cannot be implemented.

Accordingly, SAP has decided to employ the distribution illustrated in Figure 1.27.

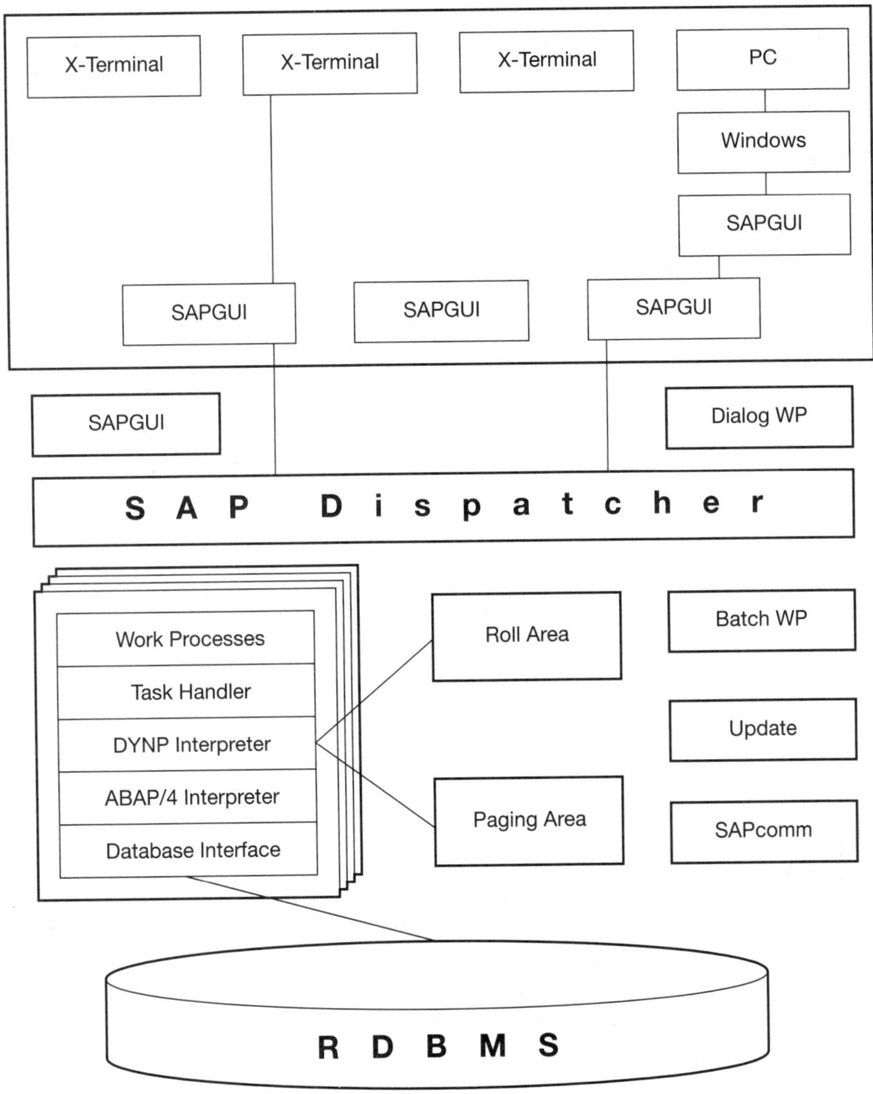

Figure 1.27 R/3 architecture

The user's entire context (ABAP data, screen data, etc.: see Section 1.4.4) are temporarily stored in roll and paging areas. This distribution allows every work process the ability to execute the tasks of each user.

Figure 1.28 provides an example of the process links in the R/3 system environment. The figure presents an overview of how all the components mentioned above collaborate at the process level.

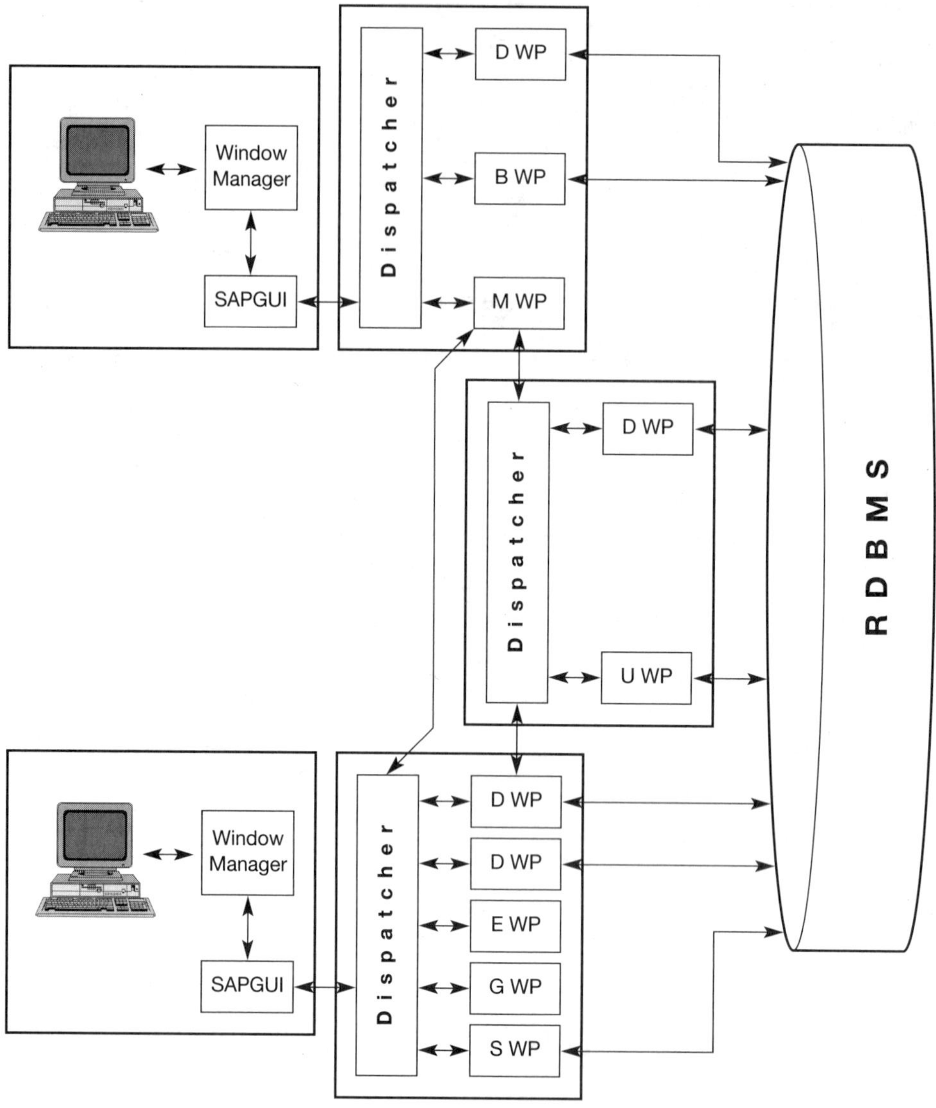

Figure 1.28 Process links

Architecture of the work process and its immediate environment

Figure 1.29 gives an overview of the architecture of a work process. The following comments mention components not directly related to the actual work process only for the sake of context and better understanding.

The **task handler** coordinates all the activities that can occur in a work process. These activities include:

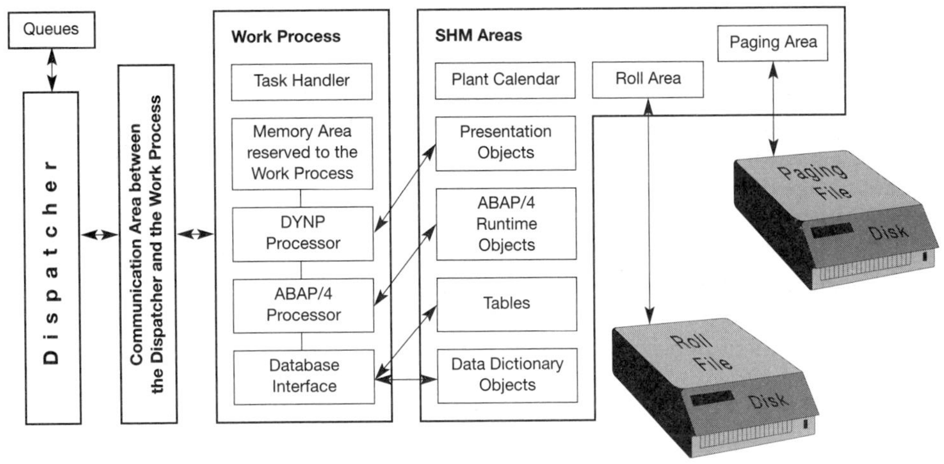

Figure 1.29 Architecture of the work process

- Communication with the dispatcher,
- Calling the dialog interpreter (screen processor),
- Calling the ABAP/4 processor,
- Control of the writing of input and output of the user context to and from roll and paging areas at the beginning and end of a dialog step.

The architecture of a work process includes memory areas for the temporary storage of data for various lengths of time and for storing data beyond the immediate scope of the work process itself. Depending on the configuration of the application server, either main memory or the hard drive (removal from storage) contain the **roll** and **paging areas**. Other memory areas that must be retained beyond one dialog step (such as those used to input data) are always stored in **shared memory areas**. Various work processes use these areas.

The **paging area** serves as the storage location for data from application programs: internal tables and report lists, for example. The **roll area** stores user-specific data. This class of data includes input data from previous dialog steps, management information for ABAP/4 and the dynpro processor and data characterizing the user (access authorizations, for example).

Local buffers exist in addition to those used beyond the immediate boundary of the work process. Every work process, for example, has a private roll area. These private areas contain a copy of the global roll area for the latest user. Before any exchange of data between the two areas, the system checks to see whether, coincidentally, the same work process has been allocated to the previously logged in user. In this case no need to copy the required data exists: it is already located in the proper place. This configuration accelerates the working speed of the R/3 system and provides the user with better performance.

The roll area can be addressed directly. The system allocates it to the work process only when the dialog step changes and removes it afterward. However, the system grants the work process access to the paging area only when needed.

Since the database interface also comprises part of the work process, we must treat it here again. The interface does not use any of its own network components. Rather, it takes advantage of the features available in the RDBMS: it must respect any procedures specific to the manufacturer.

Assume that the ABAP/4 processor issues a query (Open SQL/Native SQL) to the database interface. The system must first analyze (parse) the query. The functions of the interface perform this task. In the process, helpful information from the repository (e.g., table type, client dependencies, etc.: see Chapter 5) comes to the fore. The query is thus translated into a form that the system can send to the RDBMS. This procedure would take place if the examination of the local R/3 buffer did not find the required information. Accordingly, the system can avoid accessing the RDBMS if the information still exists in the buffer. SAP buffer management determines whether the system needs to communicate with the RDBMS at all.

1.4.2 The new 'main memory management'

The advancing maturation of the R/3 system has steadily increased the scope and amount of data. The APAB/4 area supplies ever more complicated data types. Previous experience with the behavior of versions 2.1 and 2.2 of the SAP system indicated that users could expect increasing problems with performance and processing speed. For this reason, release 3.0 of the R/3 system included the installation of a new main memory management system.

In light of the ever increasing cost/benefit improvements in the main memory market, SAP has forced the expansion of main memory resources on the host system. The following rule applies:

Main memory and swap have no better replacement than more main memory and swap!!!

Each user works with a user context typical for her activities. The context describes the processing status of the current transaction (see Section 1.4.3). Before release 3.0, the roll and paging areas contained this information. It could also be copied into the memory area of the currently active work process. The data would be copied back to the roll and paging areas at the end of the dialog step.

As of release 3.0, the system stores the largest portion of the user context in generally accessible shared memory (SHM) areas. If necessary, this area can be enlarged to a limited degree by requesting additional SHM areas. Only a small portion of data, mostly administrative, remains in the roll area.

Transfer of data into the working area of the operating work process occurs via a representation of the user context area in the address space of the work process (mapping). Since the mapping function replaces the time-intensive copying of data, access to all required internal tables, lists and data has become much more efficient.

However, sufficient main memory and swap space must exist. To save the time and effort of copying, complete internal tables and lists must now be held in the user context.

We have already noted the expansion possibilities of the general SHM area for the user context. Additionally, however, the SHM can also be expanded at the local work process level. The need to do so might arise when the adjustable setting (ztta/roll_extension) of the largest SHM area has been exceeded or the 'shared' expanded memory has been exhausted. The ability to increase the size of SHM at the local work process level must also exist for batch or update processing. Because the context does not change during such processing, an expansion of the process-independent SHM area is impossible.

When the work process expands local memory, it changes to PRIV(ate) mode. One effect of the PRIV mode is that the work process becomes linked to the processing of a given user context until it is released at the end of the transaction. Afterward, the demands of the operating system require a restart of the work processes so that it can leave PRIV mode and release the main memory it used.

A short description of some of the adjustable parameters in this environment follows:

abap/use_paging	0 : New memory management active 1 : Old memory management active
abap/heaplimit	Memory size in bytes: if exceeded, the corresponding work processes are restarted.
abap/heap_area_dia	Heap memory is the local process memory. This parameter indicates the highest allowable storage request for the dialog work process in bytes.
abap/heap_area_non-dia	This parameter indicates the highest allowable storage request for spool, batch and update work processes in bytes.
abap/heap_area_total	Total highest allowable storage request of an application server in bytes.
ztta/roll_extension	Size, in bytes, of the memory available for growth of the user context in expanded memory.
ztta/roll_area	Size in bytes (at least 1MB) for the user context. If the size is exceeded, additional storage space in expanded memory (configured SHM areas (em/initial_size_MB)) must be requested.
rdisp/ROLL_SHM	Cache size for the roll buffer in 8KB blocks.
rdisp/ROLL_MAXFS	Size of the roll buffer in 8KB blocks.
rdisp/PG_SHM	Size of the paging buffer in 8KB blocks. This parameter has no meaning for the new memory management.
rdisp/PG_MAXFS	Size of the SAP paging file at the host system level in 8KB blocks.
em/initial_size_MB	This parameter provides the size of the expanded memory in MB. This pool is taken from the shared memory are of the host system.
em/blocksize_KB	Size of the expanded memory segments in 1KB blocks.
em/stat_log_size_MB	This parameter helps create statistical values in the new memory management. Only SAP may change it.
em/stat_log_timeout	See em/stat_log_size_MB.

1.4.3 Transactions

A transaction is generally defined as a process that changes a given condition. The transaction brings the system under consideration from a defined beginning condition to another consistent condition (end condition) without interruption. The end condition forms the starting point for the next transaction. To perform this function, two preconditions must be met:

1. If anything causes interruption of a transaction, the system must be returned to the condition it enjoyed before the start of the transaction.
2. During the transaction, some procedure must guarantee that all condition variables do, in fact, lie within the competency of the person starting the transaction. No one else may change them.

This comprehensive definition of transaction corresponds to the term '**logical unit of work**,' abbreviated as '**LUW**.'

The general term, transaction, applies both to the database level and to the R/3 system. Nevertheless, differences between the objects of the definition exist. At the database level, a transaction means the following:

- A **database transaction** is a sequence of one or more processing steps. It operates on database objects such as tables, views, joins, etc. It must maintain the ACID conditions: atomic (indivisible), consistent, isolation, durable (Hagen and Will, 1993).

In the R/3 system however, logical business structures take first place. Therefore, we define an SAP transaction as follows:

- An **SAP transaction** is described as a sequence of consistently business-related, functional and logically related dialog steps. Since the objects addressed are subordinate to the business management viewpoint, they can encompass several database objects or portions thereof.

This definition arises from an **application-oriented perspective**. One can also consider the **system-oriented**, expanded definition:

- An **SAP LUW** (SAP Logical Unit of Work) encompasses the totality of all the dialog steps of a transaction, including the corresponding changes in the RDBMS.

Figure 1.30 shows the difference between the definitions of an SAP transaction and an SAP LUW. We assume that the time axis moves from left to right. Updates normally execute changes in the RDBMS.

Figure 1.30 shows that with the start of an SAP transaction, an SAP LUW begins. An SAP transaction can – independently of the actions to be executed – comprise several SAP LUWs. When the following speaks of transactions or LUWs, it refers to SAP transactions and SAP.

The characteristics and interplay of transactions, LUWs and their environment can be described as follows:

- Every dialog step (see Section 1.2.2) means a database transaction.

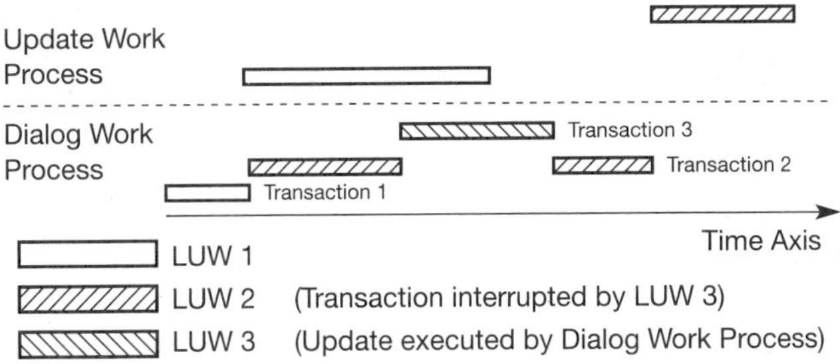

Figure 1.30 SAP LUWs and transactions

- Updates in the RDBMS always take place within a database transaction.
- LUWs consist of one or more dialog steps.
- LUWs are always executed either completely or not at all (ACID maxim).
- LUWs end with a 'COMMIT WORK' or with the end of an update belonging to an LUW.
- A transaction consists of at least one LUW.
- The use of ABAP/4 language elements allows for the nesting of transactions and LUWs.
- Various work processes (see Section 1.2.2) can process transactions and LUWs. As of R/3 release 3.0, a work process can be linked to the processing of an entire SAP transaction.
- An update belonging to an LUW can be executed asynchronously or synchronously.
- Work processes that operate on an LUW with asynchronous updating can run on different computers. The dialog portion can run on computer A and the update portion on computer B.
- The SAP system guarantees the logical interrelation of the dialog steps belonging to a given transaction:
  - It can ask an application program to lock access to a specific business object, allocating it exclusively to one user session, for the duration of the LUW.
  - Within a given LUW, that may be running in various screen windows, it must allow a rollback of all RDBMS changes until the LUW has completed its task successfully.

  In practice, users should adhere to the following rule of thumb:

A transaction should not involve more than 5–10 dialog steps.

1.4.4 User session

A user session begins when a user logs onto the R/3 system. The user then executes the steps (R/3 transactions) necessary for her work. When she has completed her work, she logs out of the system.

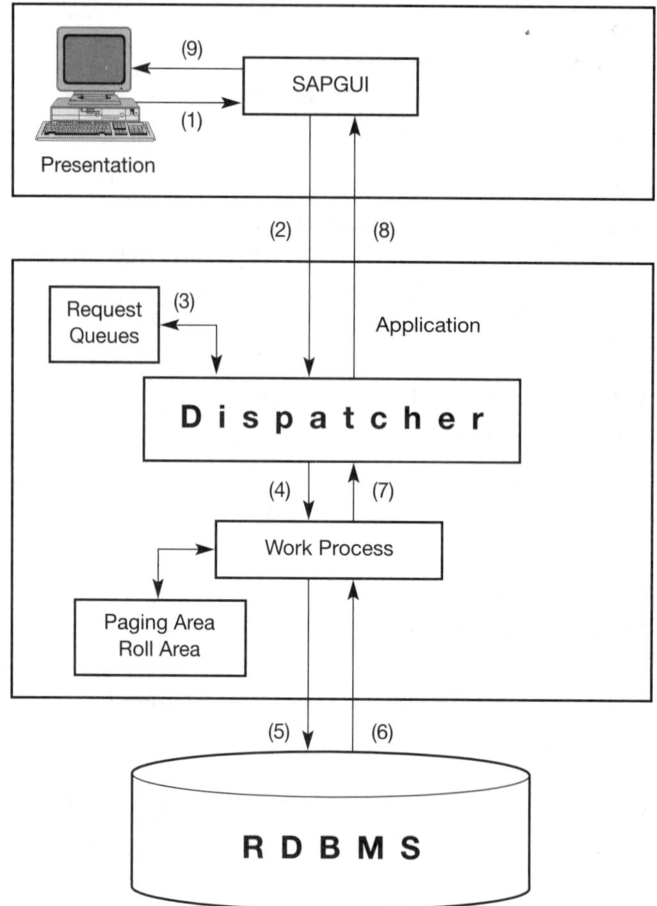

Figure 1.31 Data flow during a dialog step

During a session, the R/3 system allows the user to execute several parallel activities. Doing so requires the user to open a corresponding number of windows: the system designates these windows as **modes**. These windows or modes allow parallel processing of various transactions in any order, as long as the transactions do not depend upon each other directly. Since the R/3 user can begin a transaction in one window (mode) or continue another transaction in a different mode, she experiences little, if any, down time while processing her work.

The data flow begins with the input of data or the choice of a menu option and ends with the corresponding reaction from the system. How does this data flow work in practice? Figure 1.31 provides an initial impression.

The user executes a given action on the screen. She chooses an option from a menu or fills in an entry field to begin an RDBMS query. In each case, the SAPGUI accepts the

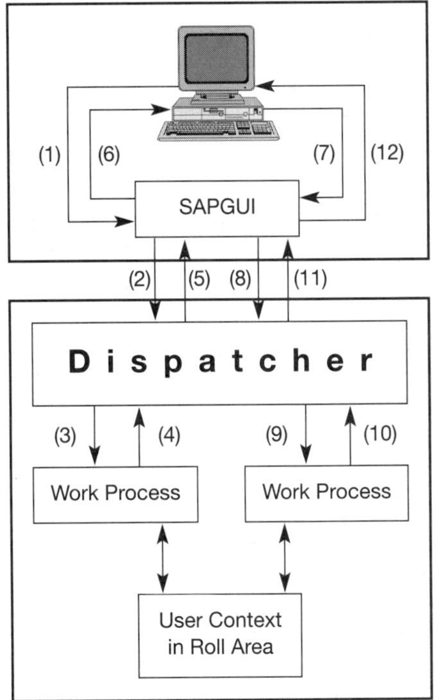

Figure 1.32 User session

user's entries. The system then converts the entries into an SAP-specific format and sends them to the dispatcher of the application server.

The dispatcher first enters the processing request into a request queue file. As the broker for the exchange of information between the SAPGUI and the work processes (in this case dialog work processes), the dispatcher must distribute a large number of processing requests among a relatively small number of work processes. It must continuously take processing requests from the request queue and dispatch them to free work processes.

The work processes handle the actual processing of the tasks. Depending on the actions to be performed, ABAP/4 and the dynpro processor are addressed. In general, the database interface carries out the movement of data to and from the RDBMS.

The work process passes the results to the dispatcher, which, in turn, sends them to the SAPGUI. The SAPGUI then interprets the data it has received and creates the new screen layout for the user.

Figure 1.32 displays two cycles of a data flow, indicating that the same work process need not process every input/output. On the contrary: users can expect a different work process to process each dialog step. A dialog step comprises exactly one input/output.

1.4.5 Service concepts

Update

Section 1.2.2 has already presented the concept of an update. Here we will expand that description.

Two parts comprise a user transaction (see Section 1.4.2): a dialog portion and an update portion. The latter contains all the information necessary to change and update the data in the RDBMS. The parlance of the R/3 system calls the tables containing these log records the **VBLOG**.

Manipulations of the RDBMS always take place after the dialog portion ends. Changes to the data can follow either immediately or a few minutes later, depending on the communications load on the R/3 system and the RDBMS. How does the system choose a synchronous or asynchronous update procedure? Generally, the system leaves the decision to the application program.

Synchronous updating makes the most sense when the application demands a high level of immediate data throughput. This approach has an obvious disadvantage: the application must wait for the completion of the update.

Decoupling 'dialog' from 'update,' i.e., asynchronous updating, makes the most sense when the data in the RDBMS does not require an immediate update. Using an asynchronous procedure provides better performance: neither the dialog work process nor the user must wait for the completion of the update. The system detaches communication between the update work processes and the RDBMS from communication between the user and the dialog work process.

The R/3 system subdivides the asynchronous updating of a log record into several parts, each one called an **update component**. Differences in time and importance distinguish two types of update components: primary (especially critical) and secondary (less critical). The former are known as **V1 components**, the latter as **V2 components** (see Figure 1.33).

This division allows the dispatcher to act according to the prioritization noted above, wrap up the corresponding tasks and distribute them.

The R/3 system always makes sure that it completes processing all V1 components before it begins treating V2 components. As Figure 1.34 illustrates, processing of V2

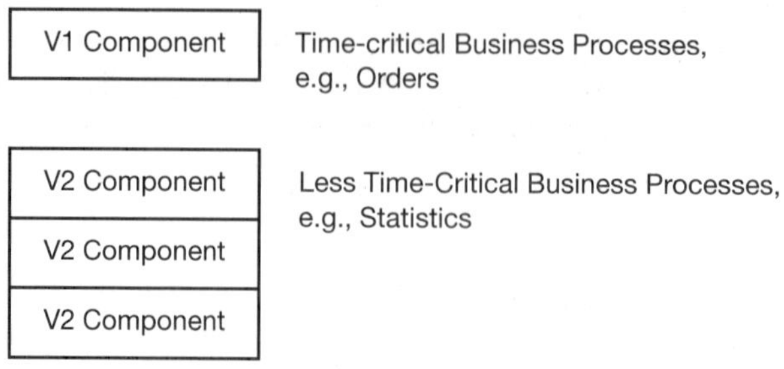

Figure 1.33 Update components of a log record

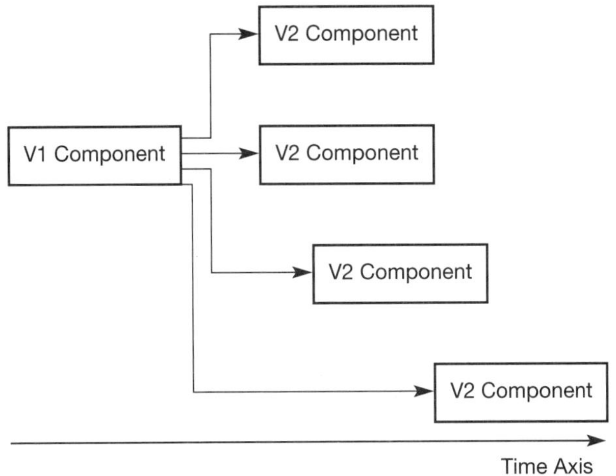

Figure 1.34 Processing the update components

components can proceed in any order desired. If the system finds enough free update work processes, it can process V2 components in parallel.

Several different update work processes can handle V1 components, provided, of course, that they belong to different update records.

During asynchronous updating, only technical errors can occur, such as overflows in a file or a database buffer. The system administrator must solve such problems. The system notes all logical error situations, such as illegal entries by the user, during the dialog phase and returns them to the user for correction. If the system discovers a technical error it proceeds as follows after the execution of a V1 or a V2 component:

1. When the error appears in a V1 component:
   - All changes to the RDBMS are canceled (rollback).
   - All changes to the RDBMS initiated by other V1 components of the same log record are also canceled (rollback).
   - V2 updates are not executed.
   - The log record is marked, but not removed from the VBLOG table.
2. When the termination appears in a V2 component:
   - All changes to the RDBMS already initiated by this V2 component are canceled (rollback).
   - Already closed RDBMS transactions initiated by the V1 component or other V2 components remain in effect.
   - The corresponding log record is marked, but not removed from the VBLOG table.
   - Remaining V2 components are updated.

In both cases, the R/3 system informs the user of the problem with an express mail message. The user can then evaluate and deal with the interrupted update. The transaction concept of the R/3 system always ensures the consistency of the data in the RDBMS.

The update programs that initiate the updating of the target tables in the RDBMS are written in SAP's own programming language, ABAP/4. The same applies to the dialog program. The update work processes described above execute the programs.

The system stores log record data in the RDBMS. The dialog work process that issued the request, with help from the message service, sends a short message to the update work process. The update work process can then begin processing the update.

Background processing

The R/3 system enables users to process programs without dialogs, offering batch work processes to this end. The system management of R/3 provides a good example: it must collect an extremely wide variety of information (see Chapter 4). With a corresponding number of batch work processes, almost any number of parallel background programs and on-line dialogs can operate at the same time.

Spool processing

The SAP system transfers data to output devices (fax machines, printers, etc.) in buffered form. The processes (spool work process, saplpd) designed for this task do not themselves 'drive' any devices. The computer's own spool system must perform this function: the R/3 processes collaborate with the operating system's spooler. The spool system has to perform two essential functions:

- It must manage spool requests. This function includes the display and release of current print requests, deletion of a request, changes to print attributes and the supervision of print requests.
- It must make the output devices connected to the computer available to the SAP system. The spooler system must know the names and types of the available devices: the user enters the required information in the R/3 system profile (see Section 2.4).

In addition to addressing printers connected to the same computer as the spool work process, the spool mechanism of the R/3 system can also administer and send print requests to other computers. Communications between the computers can occur via LANs or WANs. The R/3 system also allows for the configuration of several spool work processes. However, only one process can exist for a given instance (server). Section 2.4 treats printer installation and this point in detail.

Lock management

While discussing the enqueue work process, Section 1.2.2 noted the necessity for lock management. How does the system respond to these needs? Some sort of system-wide administrative instrument must exist that records locked business objects. The enqueue work process uses a lock table as just such an instrument. For several reasons, including fail-safe measures, independence from communication paths, performance, etc., the system stores the table in the main memory of the computer running the enqueue server.

The system never sets locks (enqueues) implicitly. The application program must explicitly request all the locks it requires. Such requests must include information on the tables involved, the lock arguments, the lock mode (shared or exclusive) and the lock fields. This data is stored in the SAP repository. The application program, or the update program itself, can delete the locks. If the update program deletes them, however, it can do so only after successful completion of the update (business transaction).

The enqueue server reacts to lock requests according to the information found in its lock table. If the object is already locked, the enqueue server reports this condition to the user program, which then issues a message to the user. To avoid a collision as early as possible, the following procedure applies:

- Most changes in the RDBMS result from previously read data. Even before reading the data, therefore, the system requests the enqueues it will need later. The system is thus prepared in advance to react to denied lock requests.

1.4.6 Instances

Sections 1.2.2 and 1.2.3 introduced the services of the R/3 system and discussed the creation of certain types of application servers. Here we present how individual parts combine to build a centralized or distributed R/3 system. Consider the term **instance**:

- An instance is an administrative unit. The components of the R/3 system (application services) are allocated to an instance.
- The components belonging to an instance are started and stopped simultaneously. They read a common profile (see Section 2.1).
- The name allocated to an instance arises from an identification code indicating the services offered by the instance. A unique number for each computer follows these codes, resulting in the **instance number**:

  D : Dialog
  V : Update (see the end of Section 1.2.2)
  E : Enqueue
  B : Batch
  M : Message
  G : Gateway
  S : Spool

Examples: DVEBMGS00, DVM01, DB27, etc.

One must distinguish between a **central instance** and a **system with distributed instances**. A central instance comprises all the services offered by an R/3 system (DVEBMGS). A centralized system can easily become a distributed system by the addition of further instances.

Instances are normally installed on separate computers. It is however possible to configure several instances belonging to the same R/3 system on one computer. Figures 1.35 to 1.37 illustrate a central instance and various possible distributed systems.

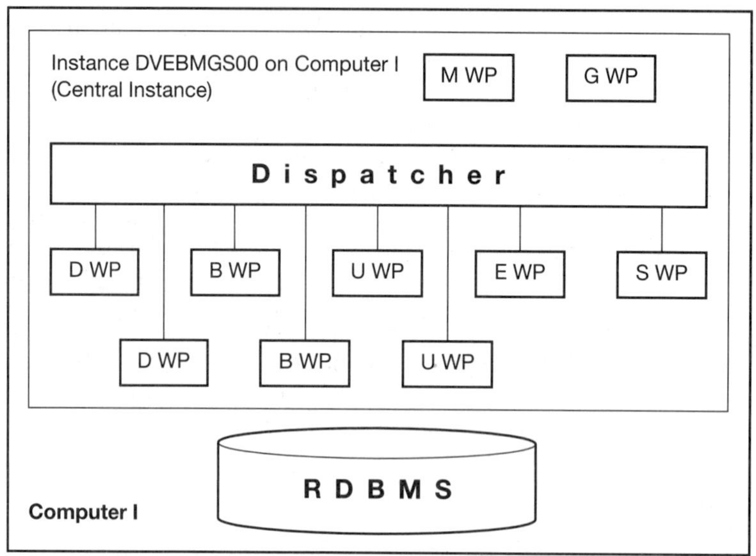

Figure 1.35 Central instance

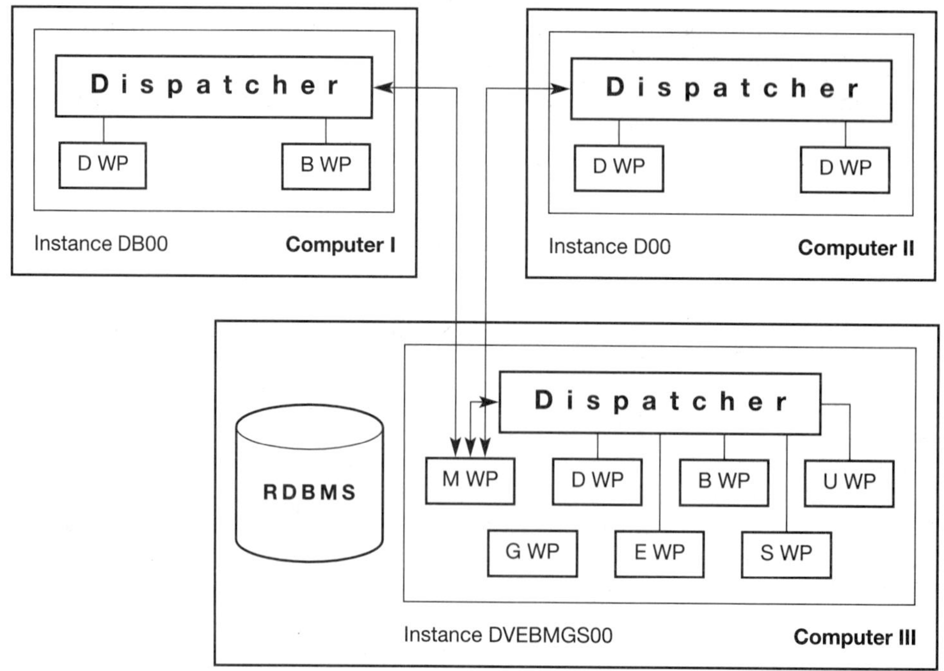

Figure 1.36 Distributed R/3 system, Example 1

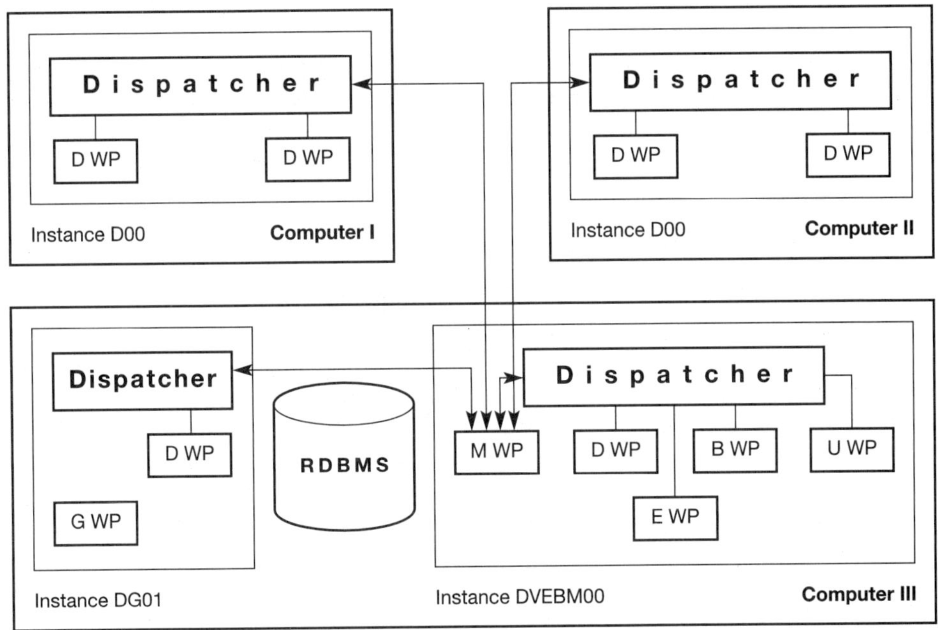

Figure 1.37 Distributed R/3 system, Example 2

1.5 Technical aspects of the computer environment

1.5.1 Client/server architectures in the R/3 system from a hardware viewpoint

The general comments made in Section 1.1.1 on the two possible ways of viewing client/server architectures also apply to the R/3 system. The R/3 environment, however, demands no highly specialized type of computer for a specific business task. Only the computer's efficiency and capacity for expansion constitute the criteria for hardware selection. R/3 applications determine the hardware chosen only in a broad sense.

Three R/3 applications are currently used to evaluate the efficiency of hardware components:

- Financial Accounting (**FI**),
- Material Management (**MM**),
- Sales and Distribution (**SD**).

Production Planning (**PP**) takes the place of Material Management (**MM**) in version 3.0.

In addition to the user profile, the number of users expected and a decision for a centralized or distributed system takes a very important place among the factors used in the evaluation process. In a distributed system one must distinguish between the performance requirements demanded by the application server and those of the database server. Appendix A contains the formulas used in evaluating requirements.

1.5.2 R/3 directory trees

The remarks that follow apply to most of the operating systems in the R/3 environment. They assume a plain UNIX operating system, without regard to specific types (HP-UX, SINIX, etc.) or versions (release 5.4). Unless otherwise noted, all comments referring to front ends presuppose X-terminals. Only a desire to restrict the size of this book makes such limitations necessary. Other operating systems enjoy no less importance.

The R/3 system defines an **SAP directory tree** based on a name and structure convention (see Figure 1.38).

Every configured instance of one or more SAP systems must mirror the SAP directory tree. The directory tree also logically divides the individual R/3 systems from each other. The division results from the unique choice of an SAP system name (**SID**) and the naming conventions given in Section 1.4.6. SAP system names currently consist of a chain of three alphanumeric characters: the first character must be a letter. Both identifiers (SID and instance name) must be unique to a local computer. The naming conventions and the information contained in the corresponding profiles create and guarantee the commonality between the instances and the SAP system. Appendix B provides an illustrative profile of a centralized R/3 system.

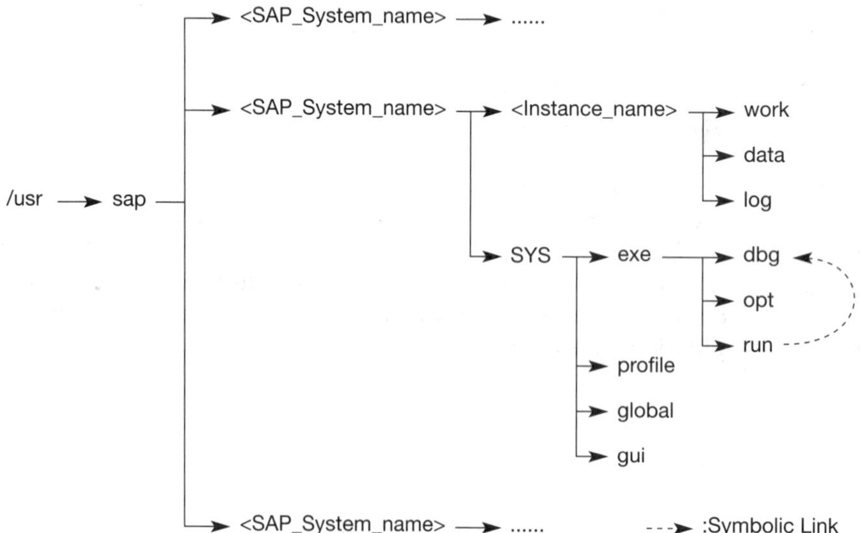

Figure 1.38 R/3 directory tree

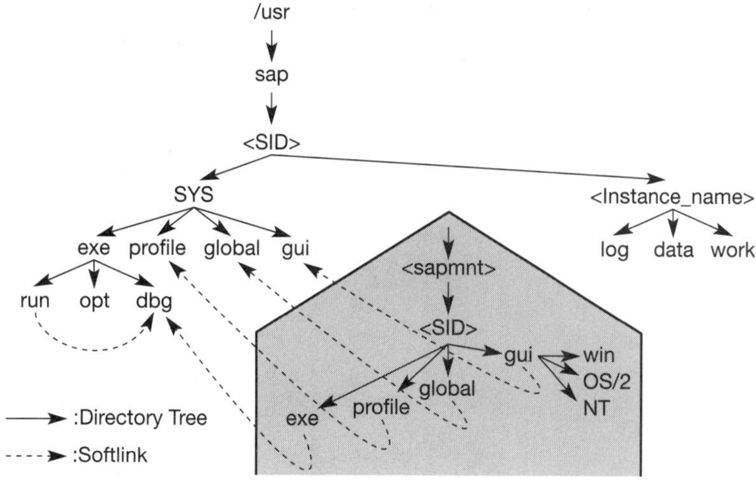

Figure 1.39 Logical and physical directory tree

Instance branches access only those processes belonging to the instance within a subdirectory. Within the **SYS branch** (see Figures 1.39 and 1.40) each instance belonging to a specific SAP system has access authorization. Because the non-local instances of the SYS branch must work within it, the branches of the subtree can be mounted on the external computer via NFS (Network File System).

The following describes the tasks and contents of the individual branches:

- *SYS*
  The **exe** directory and its subdirectories contain executable programs. The **dbg** directory stores programs that still contain symbol tables and, therefore, debug information. Optimized programs (without debug information and symbol tables) are held in the **opt** directory. The **run** directory stores those files immediately required by the application.

  All profiles (see Section 2.1) the R/3 system requires are stored in the **profile** directory.

  The **global** directory contains files (batch job logs, for example) accessible to all instances.

  SAPGUI programs for Windows, OS/2 and Windows NT are found in the **gui** directory.

- *Instance name*
  The **work** directory stores all trace and error information, start and stop messages, and data created by a system crash (see Section 2.6).

  Roll and paging data (see Section 1.4.1) of a given application server are stored in the **data** directory.

  The **log** directory contains the syslog entries for all processes belonging to the corresponding instance (see Section 1.4.5). When evaluating the logs, data is linked to R/3 texts administered by the RDBMS.

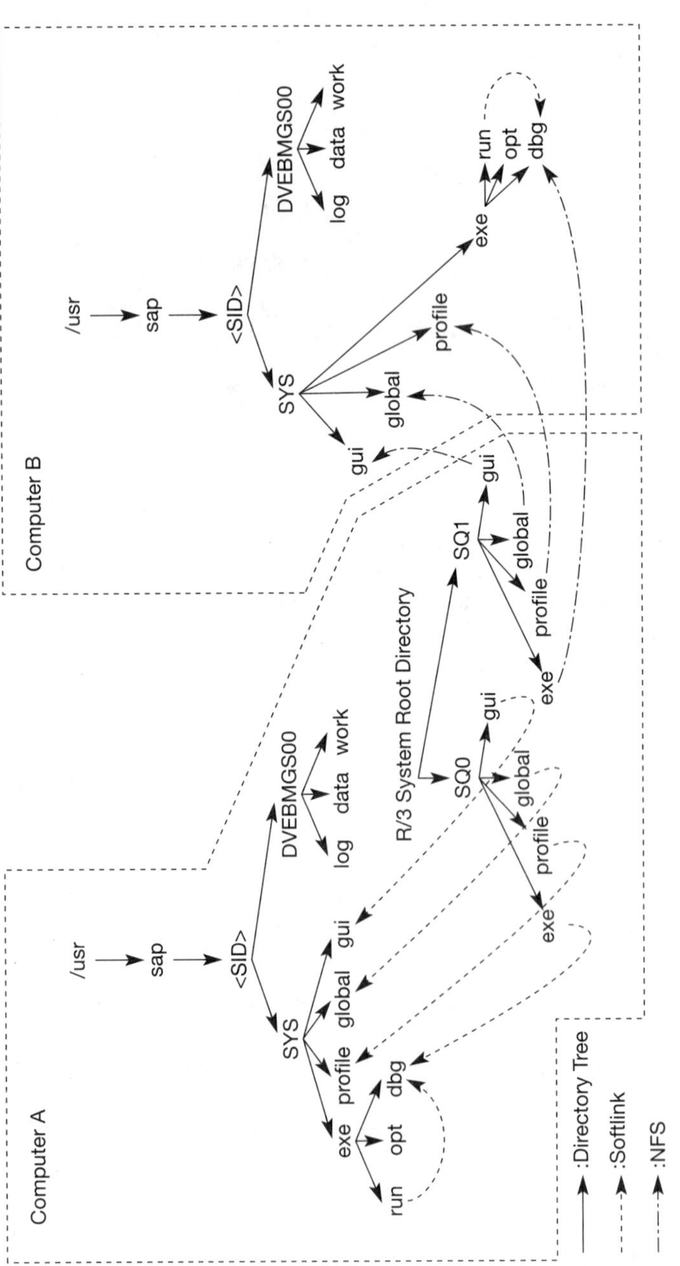

Figure 1.40 The use of Softlink and NFS

The directory tree described above illustrates only the logical viewpoint of the R/3 system. SAP defines this structure. Using NFS for a structure reaching beyond the boundaries of a specific computer or using links (generally softlinks) for a local computer allows the installation of the R/3 system in administratively better suited locations within the directory structure of a computer (**sapmnt**). Figure 1.39 depicts how the logical and physical structures relate to each other.

A link is defined as a branching of files or directory trees. A softlink reaches beyond the limits of a particular file system. A hardlink can be used only within a file system.

Figure 1.40 shows both alternatives (link and NFS). Two R/3 systems are installed on computer A; the first is used locally and the second is used on computer B.

Besides the general directory structures of the SAP system, certain tasks require additional directory structures. The correction and transport system, for example, uses its own directory. Chapter 7 discusses the corresponding directory trees.

In addition to the directory trees defined by the R/3 system, each RDBMS requires its own structure. One must distinguish between two subdirectory structures:

- A general tree, defined by SAP and
- A tree defined by each RDBMS manufacturer.

Depending on the RDBMS in use, some differentiation may exist in its general portion. All RDBMSs have the same general structure, presented in Figure 1.41.

```
/<DB-ID>/<SID>/sapdata/<device>
      ...      /saplog/<device>
      ...      /db/<DB-dependent_directory_structures>
```

Figure 1.41 An R/3 directory tree in an RDBMS environment

The SAP directory tree must exist on almost every server. The installation of a purely presentation server does not require it, however, because these servers run only SAPGUIs (see Section 2.1 and Appendix B). The SAPGUI must recognize the paths to profiles and programs.

1.5.3 Security considerations

The confidentiality and integrity of the entire system at the presentation, application, database, operating system and network level, constitute an extremely important aspect of system administration. The R/3 system therefore uses an **authorization concept** that permits the issue of both general and highly differentiated user authorizations.

Logging into the R/3 system requires a user name and a unique password. In addition, authorizations can limit access even at the level of transactions, fields and values. A master record, created for each user, implements central administration of authorizations.

User authorizations can refer both to working with specific data (e.g., project master data or company code data) and to specific operations (e.g., transactions or reports). The user generally must possess several authorizations to execute a particular action. Take, for example, the modification of user master record. Besides having the right to employ the 'change' transaction, the user himself must have access to the data. As one might easily imagine, the execution of complex actions can require the simultaneous possession of a large number of authorizations. To simply the administration of authorizations, the system organizes them on the basis of **authorization objects**. An authorization object is a collection of several system elements that require protection, such as transactions or user groups. See the following examples in Buck-Emden and Galimow (1996):

- 'Maintenance of any given material by only one transaction or within only one company code, or
- Maintenance of a specific group of materials by all transactions within one company code.'

The collection of authorization objects into **authorization profiles** represents the next level of the authorization concept. These collections, however, can also be joined to produce **composite profiles**. Composite profiles have particular importance for users who have a great variety of tasks to perform and therefore must work with several authorization profiles.

These sorts of broad authorizations cannot be managed for each user in her own master record. Such an approach would demand far too much effort. The profiles are instead centrally administered and maintained. An appropriate allocation of authorization and composite profiles provides a connection to the user. As a side effect, this procedure also changes the profile for all allocated users automatically.

Each R/3 administrator can create profiles specific to his firm. To simplify this task, the system includes several examples of extensive configurations.

The authorization concept implements a specific part of security considerations. Wherever access to the RDBMS takes place with R/3 tools (e.g., CTS) via defined interfaces (e.g., RFC), it comes into play. However, the other components involved must also contribute to data security.

The RDBMS offers its own mechanisms (e.g., passwords) for this purpose. R/3 applications can deal with the RDBMS only in this manner. Each operating system likewise has its own means of limiting access. In UNIX systems access authorizations can be configured at the level of the directory tree. Of all R/3 users, only the administrator possesses the knowledge and the right (or the need) to work at the operating system level. Various procedures exist to secure communications between the various servers. The services of the database manufacturer fulfill this function for data flow between the RDBMS and the R/3 system. The SAP system sends compressed data packets between the presentation and the application server. The user can also employ other security and authorization checks for networks and open systems (e.g., Kerberos).

1.5.4 Buffers

For communication between a computer's processes, the SAP system uses the capabilities of the operating system in use. UNIX uses shared memory segments (SHM segments) for this purpose (see Section 1.4.1). Entries in the instance profiles determine the size of the segments. The R/3 system buffers the following information in these SHM segments:

- Programs,
- Tables,
- Repository objects and
- Presentation objects.

The SAP system calls the organizational units of SHM segments 'pools.' If the size of the data requiring storage in the pools becomes greater than the size of the pools themselves, the size of the pool must increase accordingly. A given instance cannot start in the event of insufficient configured memory. Lack of memory can occur if, for example, more tasks have been assigned to the instance, requiring a higher number of work processes. The installation of additional instances on the same computer can also cause this situation.

1.5.5 Technical specifications and operating system resources

The installation of an R/3 system onto a computer requires the fulfillment of certain hardware-oriented, technical requirements. The following specifications represent the absolute minimum required for installation of a centralized system excluding a large number of users and applications, but including a database server. Experience has shown, however, that the system runs more efficiently when the specifications given below for each application (e.g., FI, SD, etc.) are increased by one level. The calculation rules in Appendix A provide some direction for this process, but they represent only approximations.

Versions 2.1 and 2.2 of the R/3 system (and R/3 exclusively) demand the following requirements:

- 64MB main memory,
- Depending on the RDBMS, 4.5GB (ADABAS D) to 6.5GB (Oracle) disk space; distribution onto physical hard drives differs from RDBMS to RDBMS,
- One or two CD-ROM drives,
- A tape drive (EXAByte or DAT), a multiple tape unit would be advantageous (for backups),
- Network software, X.25 (for support from SAP and the database manufacturer),
- NFS for a distributed SAP system,
- The correct release of the operating system,
- An appropriate window system (e.g., Motif),
- The appropriate code pages (e.g., to run a Japanese SAPGUI),
- Use of the appropriate keyboard driver (e.g., German or American),

- Installation of a printer (if desired),
- Installation of sufficient swap (approximately 400–500MB).

Many of the requirements demanded by the centralized system also apply for an application server. The size of the hard drive involved represents the decisive factor: an application server requires only 300MB disk space.

Because of the new main memory management, release 3.* of the R/3 system sets different values for the configuration of main memory (at least 256MB). See Appendix A for further information.

Files must store administrative information for the system to establish communications between the individual computers. Generally, these files are stored on local drives. UNIX, for example, uses the files '/etc/hosts' and '/etc/services.' Since the installation tool of the R/3 system generates the required entries automatically, we will not discuss them in more detail here.

Operating system tools must monitor not only the processes of the RDBMS, but also those of the SAP system (see Section 1.5.6). The following naming conventions serve to simplify recognition:

- dw.sap<SAPsystem>_<instance_name>
  the following processes run under this identifier:
  - Dispatcher
  - Dialog
  - Update
  - Batch
  - Enqueue
  - Spool
- sp.sap<SAPsystem>_<instance_name>
  Spool (no longer common; a dw-process usually performs this function)
- gw.sap<SAPsystem>_<instance_name>
  Gateway
- ms.sap<SAPsystem>_<instance_name>
  Message

The expected network communications rate is another important consideration. In a distributed R/3 system, network demands depend upon the application (FI, SD, etc.) and the number of users. Use a screen change (i.e., dialog step) as the basis for measurement. The following values serve as a model for the financial accounting application (FI):

- between the presentation server and application server: 1–2KB
- between the application server and the database server: 20KB

The following values are possible for the communications rate:

- 10 users 5KB/second
- 20 users 15KB/second
- 50 users 50KB/second

We emphasize yet again that these values represent approximations: do not apply them to future versions of the R/3 system as they stand.

1.5.6 Operating system tools

Experience has shown the following tools helpful to monitor the SAP system from the viewpoint of the UNIX operating system:

- ps: Monitoring the processes
- uptime: Monitoring the CPU
- vmstat: Motoring main memory and the swap area
- sar: Monitoring system activities
- iostat: Monitoring the hard drive
- bdf/df: Monitoring the file system
- netstat: Monitoring the network
- ping: Measuring network activity

See the manual of system commands or the operating system's on-line help for advice on the exact use of these tools. Both sources provide a description of the call parameters and output of the individual commands.

1.5.7 Practical experience

Deutsche Post AG

The authors wish to thank Mr Adam of the Deutsche Post AG for providing pamphlet number 11, 'Client/Server Solutions: R/3 on Windows NT,' June 1996, from which we have taken the information in this section.

The enterprise: With its 320,000 employees and an annual volume of 28 billion marks, Deutsche Post AG is the largest postal enterprise in Europe. Deutsche Post AG earns more than half its volume in open competition.

Innovative products, sales and distribution methods and logistical concepts have been developed for the divisions handling packages, letters and branch post offices. These improvements offer customers increasingly better quality and make Deutsche Post AG more competitive.

In mid-1995, Deutsche Post AG (DPAG) opened 33 new parcel post centers, creating the most modern European parcel-logistics system. Eighty percent of packages mailed in Germany to domestic address are delivered within 24 hours: the remaining twenty percent are delivered within 48 hours.

DPAG has also developed new systems for letters. Eighty-three highly automated centers for handling letters will open throughout Germany by 1999. These centers aim at processing letters more quickly, reliably and economically.

In the area of providing postal services (approximately 17,000 branch post offices and 3,000 postal agents), DPAG moves in two directions simultaneously. While post offices enjoy modernization, the number of postal agents (small businesses offering some postal services) increases.

A restructured accounting system builds the core of this future-oriented business organization. Flexible standard software and a high-performance data processing platform form the foundation of the new accounting system. These bases allow the divisions to produce an enterprise-wide, transparent depiction of financial and business data. DPAG can thus provide its customers with more effective, less costly payment transactions (debits and credits) – an important requisite for successful, long-term competition.

The problem: The old financial accounting system used by DPAG at the branch post office level no longer met the demands of modern accounting. The postal service used a proprietary dialog program developed for its own needs (NLB). The program, written in Micro Focus COBOL, did meet the requirements for which it had been conceived:

- Cash settlement,
- Stamp administration,
- Supplementary data entry (statistics, infopost),
- Entry and settlement of business clients,
- Accounting,
- Payroll.

The tasks of financial accounting were performed by 248 NLB systems. Data provided by the 17,000 branch post offices entered the NLB, where 1,000 PC systems running MS-DOS processed it. The 248 NLB systems provided decentralized customer maintenance. An R/2–based central accounting system then dealt with the data prepared and collected at the local level.

Regular and preventive maintenance of this system demanded a great deal of time and effort. As one example, consider an update to the program. The new version needed to be sent to all 248 locations, since the PC systems had no internal or external network connections.

The solution: To consider all the possible viewpoints involved in the choice of a new system, Deutsche Post AG used the services of external experts as early as possible in the process. In November, 1993, a consulting firm issued a study on the 'FiBu (NL) Project.' The study provided a cost estimate and recommended that the standard software of the SAP R/3 system replace the individual software of the NLB. At the end of 1993, DPAG decided for SAP R/3. At the time, no other manufacturer in the marketplace offered a product that could meet the required needs.

Project start: After careful consideration of the FiBu (NL) Project, the first concrete steps were taken in May 1994. DPAG arranged for office space for three experts in Darmstadt as well as a test and development environment. The consultants first needed to determine which hardware basis, system platform and database were best suited for R/3.

On **1 January 1996**, the future began with the on-time production start of 20 systems under SAP R/3.

What spoke for SAP R/3? No other manufacturer offered a product that could perform such a complex set of tasks. SAP standard software also had a great advantage (already present in R/2): the modular design of the solution it offered allowed for easy and as-needed expansion. This aspect took on particular important in a situation where the future functions required of the system had not yet been determined. SAP offered in R/3 the required investment safeguards, both because of the long-term availability of and support for its products and from the perspective of a continually developing product.

What spoke for ADABAS D? Convincing benchmarking results led to the decision for the ADABAS D database system. It offered the most rapid working speed and allowed for more simple administration.

Especially good and intensive contact with SQL Database Systems (a subsidiary of the firm that had developed ADABAS D) in Berlin enhanced progress on the project. DPAG had contact with a developer assigned to the project and therefore enjoyed prompt and wide-ranging support. ADABAS developers solved whatever problems appeared either on side or remotely.

Why Windows NT? At the very beginning, no one was completely sure of Windows NT. Particularly among those with mainframe experience, questions remained concerning this environment's suitability for large data processing solutions over and against a UNIX environment.

Several factors triggered the final decision for ADABAS D: an easier learning curve, less demanding maintenance, the desired high level of performance and system security and clearly lower overall costs.

Technical description: The large data volume involved means that the system architecture of the FiBu (NL) System rests on a combination of several R/3 systems. Task-specific interfaces for master and transaction data couple the systems, each of which operates with its own database.

The new combination system for FiBu (NL) contains the following five major areas:

1. The EKP system prepares uniform, truncated customer and product master data beyond the boundaries of the individual divisions. The proprietary ALE interface transfers the data to all R/3 systems.
2. Order entry and invoicing (SD) for parcels, letters and EPOS (postal counter transactions):

   EPOS data begins at the 18,500 counters (Front Office/FO) in the approximately 17,000 branch post offices of DPAG. Data is entered here with the EPOS point of sale system. The data entered at these front offices (from stamp administration to cash management) then moves to the 228 back office systems (BO). These PC-based systems complete the technical structure of financial accounting at the branch level as it existed before the implementation of R/3.

The back offices transfer the processed data to 53 concentrators. The central computer center in Darmstadt then calls up the condensed data by mailbox. Finally, the data enters the SD-EPOS system of the FiBu (NL) by batch input.

3. The central customer financial accounting system (FI) provides centralized administration of the customer and master data of the FiBu (NL). In addition, all local SAP R/3 systems (packages, letters, EPOS) deliver their data to the centralized system via the proprietary ALE interface. To this end, each local system creates a 'technical FI document' from the invoice data and then sends it to the centralized system.

   The centralized system performs payment and clearing runs. It directs the results of the payments runs to the post office bank via the PC software MultiCash. Money is transferred into the appropriate accounts at the post office bank. At the same time, an interface guides the accumulated FI data of the centralized FiBu (NL) system into the G/L accounting of the R/2 system. The centralized R/2 system, in turn, supplies the R/3 systems with current master data (G/L accounts, cost centers).
4. The FiBu HR system processes settlement of the payroll either outside of or at the request of the department handling cash salary transactions.
5. The customer and product information system (KPS) provides a general view of the revenues of customers, products and services.

SAP R/3 systems also run outside of the combined system for FRAMA (statistical system for freight) and Philately (FI data for mail-order stamps with approximately 730,000 customers).

Additional interfaces allow the SAP R/3 systems of the Deutsche Post AG to supply data to additional, external data-processing systems.

Hardware:

- The database servers consist of 20 Compaq computers (ProLiant 4500), each with a CPU consisting of four Pentium processors with a frequency of 100 MHz. Of these servers, 16 have 1GB working memory; the remaining four servers each have 512MB RAM. Combined disk space totals 1.8 terabytes: one system with 42 × 4.3GB, three systems with 28 × 4.3GB, 12 systems with 21 × 4.3GB (freight, EPOS, letters), and four systems with 14 × 4.3GB.
- Application servers: 42 Compaq ProLiant 450 systems (CPU: 4 × Pentium 100 MHz), each computer's main memory consists of 512MB RAM, disk space 2 × 4.3GB pro computer.
- Additional servers: (also Compaq ProLiant 4500): one printer server, one interface server, two servers for training, 11 servers for development and acceptance and seven servers for tests (kernel, benchmarks, etc.).
- Backup-server: seven Compaq ProLiant 4500 (each FDDI ring = one server) each with three Pentium 100 MHz CPU and 128MB RAM main memory; disk space: one system with 2 × 4.3GB, four systems with 6 × 4.3GB, two systems with 8 × 4.3GB.

Number of users: The entire environment of the R/3 FiBu (NL) system has 2,400 users, about 1,400 of them active. Users in local branch post offices make up the largest portion of users: about 2,000, with 1,200 of them active.

Data volume: The FiBu (NL) application was designed for a maximum capacity of 1,000GB (1 terabyte) to ensure sufficiency for long-term growth. The largest single application currently takes 36GB. The following are processed:

- Master data: 553,129 customers; approximately 320,000 personnel master data records, each with 12 infotypes,
- Transaction data (daily): FI postings, about 50,000; SD postings, about 84,000; payment run (daily average): debit memos of 42 million marks; credit memos of 1.1 million marks; dialog steps: about 1.5 million per day.

Software products in use:

- SAP version 2.2F for the production system; SAP version 3.x for project development and for production as of January, 1997; SAP modules: finance (FI), asset management (AM), the special business module SD-VIS and human resources (HR)
- Database: ADABAS D, Version 6.1.1.14.ZF (planned: 6.1.1.15)
- Administration: Computing Center Management System CCMS (SAP R/3), Insight Manager (Compaq), Resource Kit (Microsoft), R/3 Guard (proprietary development)
- Development tools: Microsoft Access and Visual C++ by Microsoft
- Electronic mail system: Microsoft Mail
- Client applications: Microsoft Office Standard/Professional
- Operating system: Microsoft Windows NT Version 3.51 with Service Pack 3; Windows NT Workstation 3.51

The configuration is designed for a growing number of users and the eventual installation of additional R/3 modules.

Data backup and fail-safe measures:

- The system uses Q47 Robots (Breece Hill Technologies, Inc.) for completely automated backup with Quantum disk drives (DLT 4000). NetVault (Version 4GK) AT&T was chosen for security after extensive test runs and revision phases. Close collaboration took place between the software manufacturers, Software AG and Deutsche Post AG.
- A high availability level was a decisive factor in determining which system to put into production. In the future, the use of an off-site backup and standby system will raise this level even higher. An external disk tower (1 terabyte) will store all the FiBu (NL) databases running under R/3. A second disk tower, located some 800 meters away in the clearing computer center, will mirror the database in real time. Only thus can we meet the requirement set by the consultants: the ability to restart the entire system within two days in case of an emergency.

External open system disk arrays make up the core of this fail-safe system. The arrays feature an especially large cache and special firmware with an optimized hit list. A remote copy function allows real-time mirroring over large distances.

C&L-Unternehmensberatung GmbH

We wish to thank C&L Unternehmensberatung GmbH for its generous help. Mr Helmut Krumm provided us with a description of the firm and the technical data of the SAP R/3 systems situated in Hamburg. This information serves as the basis of the following section.

'C&L-Unternehmensberatung GmbH is a subsidiary of C&L Deutsche Revision AG Wirtschaftsprüfungsgesellschaft, one of the largest auditing firms in the field.

The firm's headquarters are in Frankfurt. We are a member of Coopers & Lybrand International, a corporation founded according to Swiss law.

The member firms, operating in more than 130 countries, are legally and economically independent. They employ a total of 70,000 workers; about 7,000 of these provide consulting services.

Just some of the issues the firm deals with on a daily basis include internationalization, global services, the European domestic market, radical changes in eastern Europe, concentrations of economic power, the ability to compete effectively, cost pressure and the complexity of business processed.

We support our clients in their attempt to meet these challenges. We define "qualified consulting" as the ability not only to react, but also to recognize developments early and to implement practical solutions.

We base our consultations on a thorough knowledge of the industry, specialization and a large palette of services. Businesses and public administration engage our services in equal portions.

Three principles

- Independence – Impartiality – Quality

guide the activities of C&L.

These principles define our work from solving strategic questions of enterprise-wide reorganization tasks to the continual improvements in efficiency to organizational changes. Such changes often involve the installation of information systems.'

An R/2 system on BS2000 with ISAM files handles financial and accounting matters, controlling and personnel. The six R/3 systems in Frankfurt, Hamburg and Saarbrücken work most intensely on the following tasks:

- International training for the C&L Centre of Excellence,
- Training for SAP,
- Client presentations, workshops,
- Internal C&L training, independent study,
- Pre-customization for projects.

To complete these tasks properly, all available functions of the R/3 system are used. In addition to the standard modules, the C&L system also work with industry solutions: IS-B (Banking), IS-IS (Insurance) and IS-H (Hospital).

After introduction of the R/3 system C&L maintained users/consultant familiarity with the current status of the system by establishing permanent training and by requiring active independent study. Up to 32 parallel users currently work in Hamburg with all the functions offered by the R/3 system, although with an operating business. The system must provide an acceptable response time.

In addition to serving interactive users, the system also runs the following batch jobs:

- Standard jobs (EU_PUT, EU_REORG) daily, at night,
- Collector jobs (RSCOLL00) hourly,
- Batch inputs and client copy as needed,at night.

The R/3 systems run on Hewlett Packard and Compaq computers using ADABAS D. Experience with the system up to now can be summarized as follows:

- The combination of hardware and software allows the consulting business a high level of efficiency. Such a business requires high availability and good stability.
- A disadvantage was seen in the large number of SAP updates and manual corrections (hot packages). Maintenance efforts often lead to further demands, making the system temporarily unavailable.

The technical environment of the system:

- Network
  - Ethernet 10 Mbit (IPX/SPX, TCP/IP)
  - Connection via an ISDN Router
    - Branches in Frankfurt, Berlin, Essen, Düsseldorf
    - SAP Walldorf (via EUNET)
- 2 R/3 servers (central instances)
  - UNIX
    - HP9000/800–H40, 256MB RAM, HP-UX 9.04
    - SAP R/3 2.2F, IS-H 2.24/2, IS-IS 2.22F6
    - ADABAS D 6.1.1.14 (Size: 10GB/6.4GB full)
  - Windows NT
    - COMPAQ Proliant, 2 CPU (P90), 360MB RAM, NT 3.51 SP2
    - SAP R/3 3.0D, IS-H 3.01
    - ADABAS D 6.1.15 (Size: 10GB/5GB full)
- R/3 response time
  - UNIX, R/3 2.2F
    - Avg. response time: 259.5 ms
    - Avg. CPU time: 155.8 ms
    - Avg. wait time: 5.7 ms
    - Avg. load time: 38.7 ms
    - Avg. DB request time: 34.5 ms

- Windows NT, R/3 3.OD
  - Avg. response time: 739.6 ms
  - Avg. CPU time: 181.8 ms
  - Avg. wait time: 12.2 ms
  - Avg. load time: 83.5 ms
  - Avg. DB request time: 306.8 ms

- 200 Work stations
  - Intel PCs (DX4 66 – Pentium 100), 16MB RAM, 600MB–1GB hard drives)
  - local Windows installations (WfW 3.11)
  - central SAPGUI installation in the network

The ADABAS tool 'control' manages data backup for the database. Log saves are started automatically at the end of each log segment.

Backup media:

- *Windows NT*
  Four DLT tapes (manual feed)
  Two generations (each with one data and one log tape)
- *UNIX:*
  Four DAT tapes (with auto loader)
  Two generations (each with one data and one log tape)

KSB AG

KSB AG has made the following information available to us. It comes from the 1995 Annual Report (which we cite) and a telephone interview. We wish to thank Mr Hellmann and Mr Stephan for their help.

The KSB Konzern produces, sells and maintains pumps and fittings for water supply installations, power plants, construction and environmental technology in over 40 countries. In addition to producing pumps and systems, the group provides a service network. The firm employs some 800 workers 'in communal settings, industrial areas and power plants' to ensure the 'faultless operation of pumps and systems.'

Worldwide distribution of employees:

- Germany 38%
- France 13%
- Rest of Europe 6%
- America 10%
- Asia, Pacific, Africa 33%

The KSB Konzern employed an average of 15,351 persons (including trainees) in 1995; KSB AG employed 5,709. In the same year, the KSB Konzern had earnings of 1.9890 billion marks and KSB AG earned 1.1292 billion marks.

Earnings according to region:

- Germany 36%
- France 13%
- Rest of Europe 23%
- America 10%
- Near East, Africa, Asia Pacific 18%

To direct and administer the firm's procedures and structures, KSB AG uses the R/3 system. The decision to implement R/3 was based on the following particulars:

- Successful use of R/2 in enterprises,
- The international character of the R/3 product,
- R/3's available functions,
- The reputation of SAP AG,
- Use of the R/3 system's standard functions. The system required only limited modifications to company procedures to handle them well.

When its plan is fully implemented, KSB AG will eventually use all the components of R/3 in all its operations. At that time, about 3,000 employees throughout Europe will work directly with the system.

The introduction of the R/3 system is currently in a pilot phase. About 130 employees currently work with the system (Sales and Distribution, Production, Purchasing, Financial Accounting).

Both 'attractive price' and 'high performance' influenced choice of the database, ADABAS D. No noteworthy problems surfaced with ADABAS D during the pilot phase. System stability was regarded as good, and system unavailability remained within acceptable limits (e.g., downtime for upgrades).

The hardware/technical aspects of the project include the following options:

- PCs with Windows 3.11 and Windows 95 serve as work station computers.
- Three distributed R/3 systems currently run on RM600 computers from SNI AG. The database and application server run on the same computer in all three systems. The computers are equipped with six or eight CPUs. Main memory capacity lies between 0.5 and 1.5GB. An additional RM600 functions as a test and development computer (four CPUs and 0.5GB main memory).
- Network connections: TCP/IP and LAN/WAN connect all KSB locations in western Europe.
- Operating system: UNIX derivative Sinix 5.43.
- Database versions in use: ADABAS D 6.1.1.15 and 6.1.1.14.
- The current data volume of a production computer encompasses 1,796,197 data pages @ 4KB: approximately 7GB of data.

A complete backup to disk is performed daily, taking between 30 and 60 minutes. The SNI backup tool Networker then writes the data to tape. A variant scenario, using Hypertape backup software from Multistream may be implemented in the future.

VitraService GmbH

The authors wish to thank VitraService GmbH, especially Mr Thomas Braun, for help and support. The following section is based on material made available to us by the firm.

'We, VitraService GmbH, are a service company of a group of companies involved in the office furniture and store construction industries. The Vitra group consists of:

- Vitra GmbH,
- Vitrashop GmbH,
- Ansorg GmbH, Mülheim/Ruhr.

Vitrashop GmbH and Vitra GmbH each employ about 300 persons.

We are an international company (Switzerland and Germany, with branches in various other countries). Production takes place in Weil: essential services, such as sales, are performed in Switzerland.

After exhaustive tests with various database systems, the firm finally decided on Oracle. One reason for the decision was that SAP developed primarily for Oracle at the time.

SAP first became productive on May 1, 1995, as a pilot project in some divisions with the following modules: HR, FI, CO, SD, MM, PP. At the time, not all parts of the group were integrated in the SAP system: they will be by July 1, 1997. Ansorg GmbH has been completely integrated with the system since May 1, 1995. All divisions currently use the FI and HR modules.

The relatively quick decision to change our production planing system was caused by the bankruptcy of our previous software supplier in addition to limited functions. Other reasons included:

- Use of a modern, future-oriented PPS system,
- Return to standard programs; our old system continued a large number of proprietary programs.

Even before the start of production, the pilot project showed that the hardware configuration suggested by SAP and HP (Hewlett-Packard) was insufficient. We eventually installed three application servers and one database server.

Within the first six months we purchased larger, more powerful computers.

Starting configuration:

- E55 (DB)
- E55 (Application server, leased computer)
- 735 (Application server, leased computer)
- G40 (Batch server and development system)

Today:

- K200 (DB server, 1GB main memory)
- K100 (Application server, HR, CO, FI; 512MB main memory)
- K200/2 (Application server, MM, SD, PP; 1GB main memory)
- G40 (Batch server and development system; 384MB main memory)

Planned configuration (3/97):

- T520/3 (DB server, 1GB)
- K200/2 (DB server, 1GB)
- K420/2 (DB server, 1GB)
- K420/4 (DB server, 1GB)
- K220/2 (DB server, 1GB)
- K100 (FI server, 512MB)
- G40 (Batch server, 384MB)
- Symmetrix (EMC) drive with 40GB initial capacity)

The planned configuration applies to version 3.0 of the SAP R/3 system; we also plan the integration of all firms. Our current R/3 release level is 2.2F.

Users are currently divided as follows:

- SD 30 users,
- FI 25 users,
- CO 9 users,
- MM 15 users,
- HR 12 users,
- PP 20 users.

Except for FI, CO and HR, the number of active users will double.

After some initial performance problems and problems caused by out special applications, our system is currently stable. Temporary problems regularly arise when we change releases, since Vitra usually belongs to the first group of users upgrading to a new release.

The SAP system computers are networked via FDDI; users have PCs connected via a LAN.'

2 Getting started

2.1 Installation of the R/3 system on the host system

2.1.1 SAP profile

The various profile categories

Profiles start, stop and configure R/3 systems. In the SAP environment, two categories exist:

- The **start profile** and
- The **system profile**.

Note the two subdivisions of the system profile:

- The **instance profile** and
- The **standard profile**.

The start program of the R/3 system, sapstart, reads the **start profile** to start the processes needed for a given instance. The entries in the system profiles configure the elements of the SAP system.

The **instance profile** (named DEFAULT.PFL) contains parameters for the processes of a given instance. The information includes:

- The total amount of a given type of process (e.g., update),
- Entries for the size of buffers,
- The unique (to the computer) instance number, also called SAPSYSTEM.

Besides those parameters specific to the instance, others apply to the entire R/3 system. The **standard profile** contains these parameters. Some examples include:

- Entries indicating the computer running special work processes (e.g., the message server),
- An entry indicating the computer working as the database server.

An SAP system contains approximately 500 to 600 configurable parameters. All of them contribute significantly to the flawless functioning of the system. The profiles delivered with the R/3 system do not contain all the possible parameters. Many of them

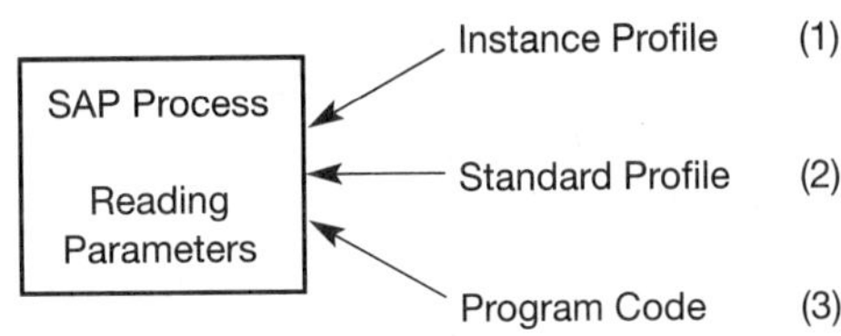

Figure 2.1 Reading parameters

have only secondary significance to the administrator, as they serve SAP-internal needs (e.g., for performance analysis).

A three-level hierarchy of information procurement provides an SAP process with all required parameters. Figure 2.1 illustrates the procedure. The first level, the instance profile, contains all the profiles needed to start an instance. If the system cannot find a given parameter there, it then searches the standard profile. If it still cannot find the required parameter, it takes them from the program code itself. The code lists every possible parameter and supplies it with an unchangeable default value. Accordingly, profiles must maintain and administer only those parameters for a given configuration that deviate from the default values. Appendix B provides an example of the most common parameters.

SAP parlance provides individual types of profiles with fixed naming conventions. Consider the following:

- The standard profile always uses the name **DEFAULT.PFL**. Users often call it the system profile or (depending on the naming environment) the default profile.
- The instance profile consists of the name of the SAP system and the name of the application server. Take an example from R/3 releases 2.1 and 2.2: **SQ0_DVEBMGS00**.

  The naming convention has changed as of version 3.0: it now adds the name of the host system. Assume 'hw1453' as the computer name. The instance profile would now use the name **SQ0_DVEBMGS00_hw1453**.
- The word 'START' and the application server name constitute the name of the start profile. Take **START_D15** as a possible example. In special cases, when, for example, the same server names apply to different computers, an administrator can expand the naming convention to differentiate the start profiles uniquely. The administrator might choose the following two profiles: **START_D02_host1** and **START_D02_host2**.

CAUTION: The naming environment has a quite legitimate basis. The start procedure as of release 3.0 first looks for profile names ending with an indication of the host system. Only after completing this search does it look for profiles corresponding to the old naming convention. The procedures thus ensure that versions 2.1/2.2 and release 3.0 do not block each other.

Figure 2.2 illustrates an example in a distributed system. To provide a better overview, the figure depicts a logical view of the allocation of profiles to computers. The sketch represents the profiles as external to the SYS/profile directory rather than their actual, physical locations within it.

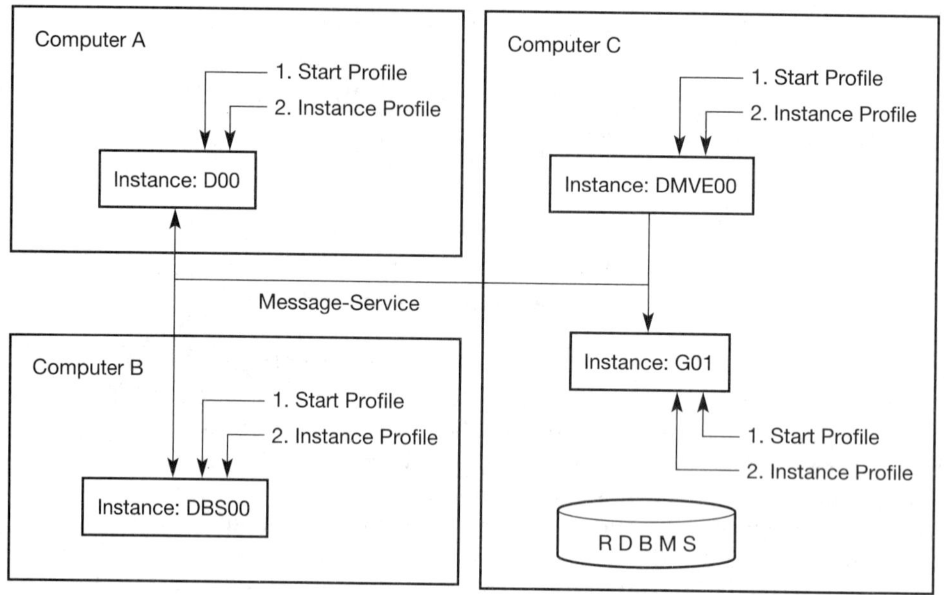

Figure 2.2 Reading the parameters in a distributed R/3 system

So far we have not mentioned the type of profile for the SAP front end, SAPGUI. In a distributed system with separate presentation servers, the SAPGUI program must start with information indicating which application server to which it should establish a connection. The program call might contain this information directly. For example:

```
../sapgui <application_computer_name> name=<SAP_system> nr=<instance>
```

Alternatively, a **temu profile** might contain the information. See Appendix B for an example. The program call for the SAPGUI would then appear as follows:

```
../sapgui <application_computer_name> pf=<temu_profile>
```

The SAPGUI must also know the paths to the programs of the SAP system and to the profiles.

Editing the individual profiles

The origin of the various profiles for the R/3 system is interesting. The installation program 'R3INST' (see Section 2.1.2) normally creates the start and instance profiles automatically. The system profile (default profile) is generated only at the very first installation of an R/3 instance. Later installations simply modify and update it.

The installation program assumes the presence of a host system prepared for the SAP system. That system normally possesses the highest level of performance and a great deal of main memory. If, however, these presuppositions remain unfulfilled, the R/3 system just installed may not start. In this case, modify the default profiles, primarily the instance profile. The following procedure has proven itself:

- Save the original profile by copying it,
- Modify all the parameters in the instance profile that influence the size of shared memory segments. The names of many of these parameters contain 'shm.' Appendix B describes the most important parameters.

This sort of manual intervention in the world of parameters has its own dangers. It should remain an exception, used only in case of necessity. Many parameters contain mutual dependencies that may suffer from such manipulations. When the need to change parameters arises, always use the profile maintenance tool provided in CCMS. (In version 3.x: *Tools → Administration → Computing Center → Management System* and then *Configuration → Profile maintenance;* in version 2.1 or 2.2: *Configuration → Profile maintenance → Easy mode.*)

As of release 3.0C, the installation program, 'R3INST,' allows for a recalculation of the profiles in light of the conditions existing on the host system. The situation describes above should, therefore, no longer arise.

The following circumstances list the situations requiring a change in the profiles:

- The number of application servers has changed.
- Performance is inadequate and requires improvement.
- The R/3 system requires reconfiguration.

Besides its ability to modify the profiles, the profile maintenance tool also offers examination tools to test the correctness of the profiles. First, however, the profiles must be transferred into the R/3 profile database. Use the menu path: *Tools → Administration → Computing Center → Management System* and then *Configuration → Profile maintenance.* The read and check functions are stored there.

As a reference version, the R/3 profile database has an advantage. Using the host system, it can immediately determine a change to the profiles during a check. The authorization profile 'S_RZL_ADM' links manipulation of profiles with the profile maintenance tool to a user.

Just as the profile maintenance tool allows for the examination of profiles, the sappfpar program checks the accuracy of instance profile parameters. Call it as follows:

```
sappfpar pf=<Instance_profile_name> check
```

2.1.2 Configuration of an R/3 system

The installation of an R/3 system generally takes place in three steps:

- Installation of the R/3 programs,
- Installation of the RDBMS,
- Creation of the instances.

To provide the user as much ease as possible, an interactive installation program (R3INST) performs all the steps necessary for a successful installation. To create the directory tree, for example, the installation tool calls two programs:

- **saproot** and
- **sapinstance**.

The saproot program must run exactly once on each computer belonging to an SAP system. It accomplishes the following tasks:

- Creation of the standard directory tree (SYS branch) on the application server in a SAP system,
- Creation of the default profile used by all servers of an R/3 system.

The sapinstance program must be called for every instance created in an R/3 system. The program fulfills the following tasks:

- Creation of the instance-specific directory tree,
- Supplementing the required entries in the default profile,
- Creation of the instance profile and
- Creation of the start profile.

When installing an SAP system, every installer can choose between a distributed and a centralized system. A centralized system can be changed into a distributed system at any time. The following parts comprise the **centralized system configuration**:

- Dialog, update, lock, batch and spool services,
- Message server,
- Gateway server,
- RDBMS.

The first step in distribution is normally the storage of dialog services on the dialog server. The system can use the server for the time-intensive tasks requested by users. The computer running the RDBMS thus has a lightened load: the resources that have become free are now available to other services. Each individual circumstance will determine if additional services should be distributed to other computers. The following points play an important part in making this decision:

- To maximize performance,
- To maximize availability of the system,
- To aim for the optimum performance of the individual components,
- To minimize the level of communications – individually:
  - Access to the RDBMS,
  - Communication over the message server,
  - Access to central buffers.

To achieve an optimal division of labor within the entire system, consider the following recommendations:

- PCs or front ends should offer presentation services,
- Work stations or dedicated dialog servers can provide dialog services,
- Batch processing should be installed on its own computer only in cases of extremely high work-load (e.g., in dialog processing).
- To achieve a minimum level of communications, install the following services on the database server:
  - Message server,
  - Update server,
  - Lock management server.
  - Store files used centrally here as well.

2.1.3 Starting and stopping the R/3 system

The RDBMS must be up and running before the SAP system can be started. This usually occurs by using shell scripts (e.g., UNIX control files for the shell interpreter). In broad strokes, these files appear as follows:

```
Starting the RDBMS.
Is the RDBMS ready for operation?
   Yes:    Starting the SAP system (sapstart).
   No:     Issue error message and stop the start process.
```

The alias **startsap** lets the RDBMS and the R/3 system start in the correct order. The alias is located in the administrator's HOME directory. It is a reference to the file **startsap_<host_name>_instance**. The <sid>adm home directory stores the startsap_<host_name>_instance. The 'startsap' alias is defined in the file sid<adm> '.cshrc' (C shell) or, if a korn shell is used, in the file '.profile'. By default, SAP uses the UNIX C shell.

Starting the SAP system means activation of at least one instance. The other instances (in a distributed system) and the application server (with its processes) are started afterward. In the event that one instance is already running on a distributed configuration, the Computing Center Management System (CCMS) enables other instances to start.

Figure 2.3 illustrates the collaboration between the start programs and the profiles. To clarify the principle involved, the example assumes a centralized system. The actual start takes place via the shell script startsap. The naming convention follows the form of versions 2.1/2.2. For version 3.0 and above, the profile name adds the host name to the names of the instance and start profiles (see Section 2.1.1).

The start shell script calls the **sapstart** program. To provide the start program with all the information necessary for the start, the script is called with the following syntax:

```
sapstart pf=< START_profile >

Example for R/3 system versions 2.1/2.2 and from 3.0:
   sapstart pf=/usr/sap/SQ0/SYS/profile/START_DEVBMGS00
   sapstart pf=/usr/sap/SQ0/SYS/profile/START_DEVBMGS00_hw1453
```

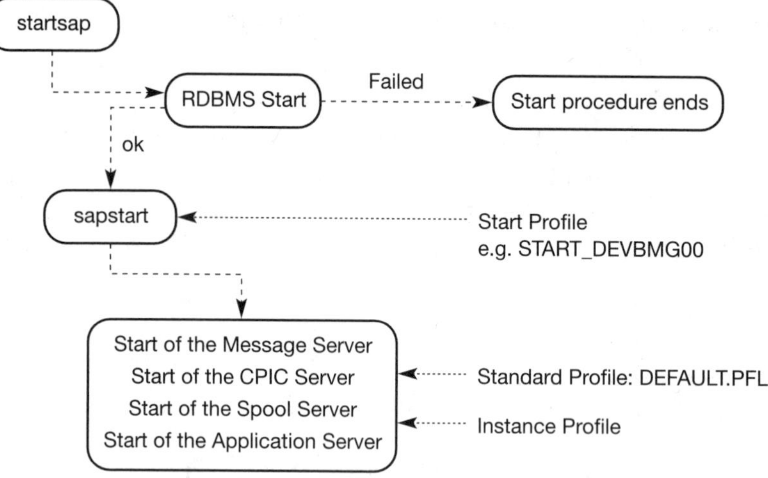

Figure 2.3 Starting the R/3 system

Because the system's central profile directory contains all the start profiles of all instances belonging to a distributed SAP system, every server must have access to the directory (e.g., via NFS). Two kinds of entries in the start profiles are particularly important:

- 'Execute_' commands and
- 'Start_Program_' entries.

The system first performs the commands contained in the lines marked 'Execute_'. These operating system commands (not supported in Windows NT) prepare the computer(s) for the actual start of the R/3 system. The entries contained in the lines marked 'Start_Program_' start the processes used by the R/3 system. The numbering assigned to the entries determines the order in which the system executes them. The start program process does not wait for any status messages from the individual processes: it starts the asynchronously. A log record is written for each process started (see Section 2.6).

When the start program process has completed the task of starting the R/3 system, it deactivates itself. It then waits until the system is to be shut down. At that time the start program process ends all processes in the same order it started them. Accordingly, the process ought to be called the start/stop program process. These actions do not affect processes started with the 'Execute_' statement.

Both the start and stop procedures work asynchronously. To enable follow-up processing of the stop procedure, 'Stop_Program_' statements can be added to the start profile. The system executes these commands sequentially, according to their numerical order. When the last command ends, the start program process ends itself. Both the start and stop procedures are logged.

Examples of the start and stop procedures are given below. Examples of start and stop logs follow. The naming environment orients itself toward the name of the host and the instance number of the R/3 system. Assuming a computer named 'axp' and an instance number '88,' the start and stop logs of an R/3 system would be called:

- startsap_axp_88.log or
- stopsap_axp_88.log.

The logs written at the start or stop of the RDBMS would be called:

- startdb.log or
- stopdb.log.

The following lists the logs created at the start and the stop of an R/3 system with an instance named '88' on a computer named 'axp' and a database named 'FST.'

startdb.log

```
------------------------------Tue Jul 2 13:42:35 MET DST 1996 LOGFILE
FOR STARTING ADABAS

------------------------------Tue Jul 2 13:42:35 MET DST 1996
checking required environment variables

DBNAME  is >FST<
DBROOT  is >/adabas/FST/db<

------------------------------Tue Jul 2 13:42:35 MET DST 1996
starting vserver

vserver: socket address already in use, probably a vserver is already
running!

------------------------------Tue Jul 2 13:42:36 MET DST 1996
Connect to the database to check the database state:

R3trans: connect check finished with return code: 12
Database not available

------------------------------Tue Jul 2 13:42:46 MET DST 1996
starting database

Restart Database ...

------------------------------Tue Jul 2 13:43:25 MET DST 1996
Connect to the database to verify, that the database is now open
R3trans check finished with return code: 4
Database is now running
*** WARNING: Transport system not initialized
```

startsap_axp_88.log

```
Trace of System startup of R/3 System FST on Tue Jul 2 13:42:32 MET
DST 1996

Starting SAP-Collector Daemon
------------------------------
 saposcol on host axp started

Starting SAP R/3 FST Database
------------------------------
 Startup-Log is written to /usr/users/fstadm/startdb.log
 Database started

Starting SAP R/3 Instance
------------------------------

SAP-R/3-Startup Program V1.7 (92/10/21)
---------------------------------------

Starting at 1996/07/02 13:43:28
Startup Profile: "/usr/sap/FST/SYS/profile/START_DVEBMGS88_axp"

Execute Pre-Startup Commands
----------------------------
(5333) Local: /usr/sap/FST/SYS/exe/run/sapmscsa -n
pf=/usr/sap/FST/SYS/profile/FST_DVEBMGS88_axp
/usr/sap/FST/SYS/exe/run/sapmscsa: make new mode. SCSA currently non
existent.
sapcscsa: SCSA defined. sapscsaId == 1507363 == 00170023
sapcscsa: SCSA attached at address 00010000
sapcscsa: SCSA initialized.
rslgwr1(21): Searching for overlap point in pre-existing SysLog
file...
/usr/sap/FST/SYS/exe/run/sapmscsa: finished.
(5333) Local: ln -s -f /usr/sap/FST/SYS/exe/run/msg_server

ms.sapFST_DVEBMGS88
(5333) Local: ln -s -f /usr/sap/FST/SYS/exe/run/disp+work

dw.sapFST_DVEBMGS88
(5333) Local: ln -s -f /usr/sap/FST/SYS/exe/run/rslgcoll

co.sapFST_DVEBMGS88
(5333) Local: ln -s -f /usr/sap/FST/SYS/exe/run/rslgsend

se.sapFST_DVEBMGS88

Starting Programs
-----------------
(5359) Starting: local ms.sapFST_DVEBMGS88
 pf=/usr/sap/FST/SYS/profile/FST_DVEBMGS88_axp
(5497) Starting: local dw.sapFST_DVEBMGS88
 pf=/usr/sap/FST/SYS/profile/FST_DVEBMGS88_axp
```

```
(2224) Starting: local co.sapFST_DVEBMGS88 -F
 pf=/usr/sap/FST/SYS/profile/FST_DVEBMGS88_axp
(5577) Starting: local se.sapFST_DVEBMGS88 -F
 pf=/usr/sap/FST/SYS/profile/FST_DVEBMGS88_axp
(5333) Waiting for Child Processes to terminate.
 Instance on host axp started
```

stopsap_axp_88.log

```
Trace of System shutdown of R/3 System FST on Wed May  8 09:05:00 MET
DST 1996

Stopping the SAP R/3 FST Processes
----------------------------------


Stopping SAP R/3 FST Database
Shutdown-Log is written to /usr/users/fstadm/stopdb.log
Database stopped
```

stopdb.log

```
------------------------------ Wed May 8 09:05:01 MET DST 1996 LOGFILE
FOR STOPPING ADABAS

------------------------------ Wed May 8 09:05:01 MET DST 1996
checking required environment variables

DBNAME  is >FST<
DBROOT  is >/adabas/FST/db<
------------------------------ Wed May 8 09:05:01 MET DST 1996
Connect to the database to check the database state:

R3trans check finished with return code: 4
Database is running
Continue with stop procedure
*** WARNING: Transport system not initialized

------------------------------ Wed May 8 09:05:01 MET DST 1996
Forcing a log switch and then stop the database

Shutdown Database...

------------------------------ Wed May 8 09:05:02 MET DST 1996
Connect to the database to check the database state:

R3trans check finished with return code: 12
Database not available
Shutdown successful
```

2.2 R/3 user concept

2.2.1 User master records and authorizations

The R/3 administrator must fulfill an important task. She uses the **user** and **authorization concept** to create users, to grant rights for certain actions to some users and to limit rights for some actions to other users.

A user can work productively with the system after the creation and activation of a **user master record** containing the user's authorizations. The R/3 system distinguishes between two types of authorizations. One type allows the definition of users having an **authorization profile**. Possession of this profile grants these users the right to grant authorizations to other users by making appropriate entries in the user master record. The second type of authorization allows the user only to work with the system. As part of the standard system, SAP delivers varied authorization profiles for individual applications. The administrator can view these profiles with the following menu path (from the administration menu): *Maintain users → Profiles → Information → Overview*. The system allows for the use of these profiles to grant authorizations or to create individual profiles and authorizations. So that customer-specific profiles do not employ the same names as SAP profiles, those created by users may not contain an underscore in the second position of the profile name.

Authorization object

The **authorization object** permits the definition of complex authorizations in the R/3 system. As a first step, the administrator grants the authorization object a name. Here we will use the authorization object *S_USER_GRP* (see Figure 2.4) to explain the individual components of an authorization.

The *CLASS* field limits the maintenance of authorization to specific groups. The *ACTVT* field can determine the type of maintenance activity. An **authorization check** always checks both fields in an AND combination: both fields must pass the check to allow access to an R/3 object. Only fields defined in the *AUTH* table can function as **authorization fields**. An authorization object can contain the definitions of up to ten fields. The system uses authorization objects to join fields together for combined authorization checks.

An authorization object can contain any desired number of defined **system access authorizations**. The administrator must define the amount of permissible values for the

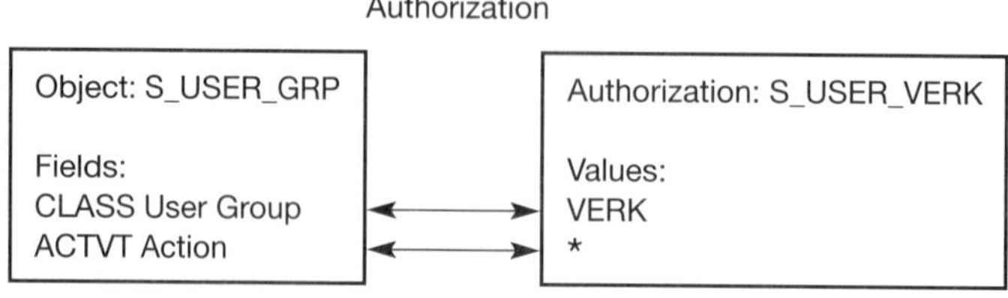

Figure 2.4 Components of an authorization

fields of the authorization object (*CLASS* and *ACTVT*) in an additional **value set object**, also called an **authorization**.

The above example shows the creation of an authorization named *S_USER_VERK*. A user with this authorization can create and maintain user master records for all members of the *VERK* group (*). The system allows the definition of as many authorizations as desired to an authorization object. The system bases its check of the individual authorizations on an OR relationship. The system requires a unique authorization name and the corresponding object name to check an authorization. An ABAP program can also perform authority checks; it uses the *AUTHORITY CHECK* command.

Authorization profile

To keep maintenance requirements to a minimum, administrators do not enter authorizations directly into user master records. Individual authorizations (several objects and their values) are allocated instead to **authorization profiles**. This profile has its own unique name that is entered in the user master record. When these profiles change, the changes affect all users having the profile in their user master records. The system distinguishes between an **individual** and a **composite profile**.

- *Individual profile*
  An individual profile is an authorization profile that has been entered into a user master record. The profile contains an object name and the object's value set (authorizations).
- *Composite profile*
  Several individual profiles can be joined to form a composite profile. The user master record then contains an entry with the name of the composite profile. Composite profiles contain nothing but individual profiles. All the individual profiles in the composite profile are loaded together into the roll area. Should composite profiles give users too many profiles (more than they actually require), system performance will suffer. When the roll area is too small, it must occupy disk space.

Activating authorizations

The administrator must activate new and changed authorizations so that they take effect in the system. An activation copies the update version to the active version. The authorization becomes active immediately.

Using *Authorization* → *Activate* or *Authorization* → *Activate all* will activate either individual authorization or all authorization currently without an active version.

2.2.2 The superuser SAP* and the user administrator

As delivered, the SAP standard system includes the superuser SAP*. This user possesses all the authorizations needed to administer the entire system.

For security reasons the user SAP* should have a new password after the installation. Afterward define a user (by copying SAP*) who has all the authorizations granted to SAP*.

To protect the superuser, the new user should belong the SUPER user group. The user profiles **SAP_ALL** and **SAP_NEW** grant rights for all components of the R/3 basis system and for all applications. If, in addition the rights granted in SAP_ALL, the superuser needs authorization to maintain and activate the user master record, profiles and authorizations, he must also have the **SAP_SUPER** profile. Note that nothing requires any individual user to have both authorization profiles.

For security reasons, three users can be created. They would then divide the following tasks among themselves:

- The **authorization administrator** can create and maintain authorization profiles and authorizations.
- The **activation administrator** activates the authorization profiles and authorizations created by the authorization administrator.
- The **user administrator** creates only the user master records and enters the profiles into the user master record.

Table 2.1 illustrates the rights of the individual administrators.

See the table in Appendix C for an overview of the authorizations of basis administration (including the transport system and ABAP/4 development).

Table 2.1 Profiles for user administration

Administrator	*Objects*	*Fields*	*Values*
Authorization administrator	S_USER_PRO	Profile name Action	Names of the profiles for the profile: create, change, display, delete, display change document
	S_USER_AUT	Object name Authorization name Action	Names of the permissible objects Names of the permissible authorizations Authorization: create, change, delete, display
Activation administrator	S_USER_PRO	Profile name Action	Names of the profiles for the profile: delete, activate
	S_USER_AUT	Object name Authorization name Action	Names of the objects Names of the authorizations Authorization: delete, activate
User administrator	S_USER_GRP	User groups Action	Names of the user groups User master records: create, change, display, delete
	S_USER_PRO	Profile name Action	Names of the profiles Display profiles and enter them in the user master record

2.2.3 Creating users

Administering the user master record

Use the menu path *Tools → Administration → Maintain users → Users* to create users. The system provides two methods of creating user master records: create a new one or copy an existing record. Enter the user's name and choose the function *Create/Change* (or *Copy*). The screen for maintaining users will appear (see Figure 2.5).

As the first step, enter an **initial password** for the new user's first log on: enter the password twice. When the user himself logs on for the first time, he can (or must) change this password to work on the system. Some restrictions exist for this password. It may not be PASS or SAP*, may not begin with a question mark (?) or exclamation point (!), must contain no fewer than three and no more than eight characters. New users can be, but need not be, allocated to a **user group**. The entry for **user type** determines the sort of user involved in the transaction: a normal **dialog user** or a special type of user. The latter would include users limited to **batch input**, **normal batch processing** or those who access the system over a remote network.

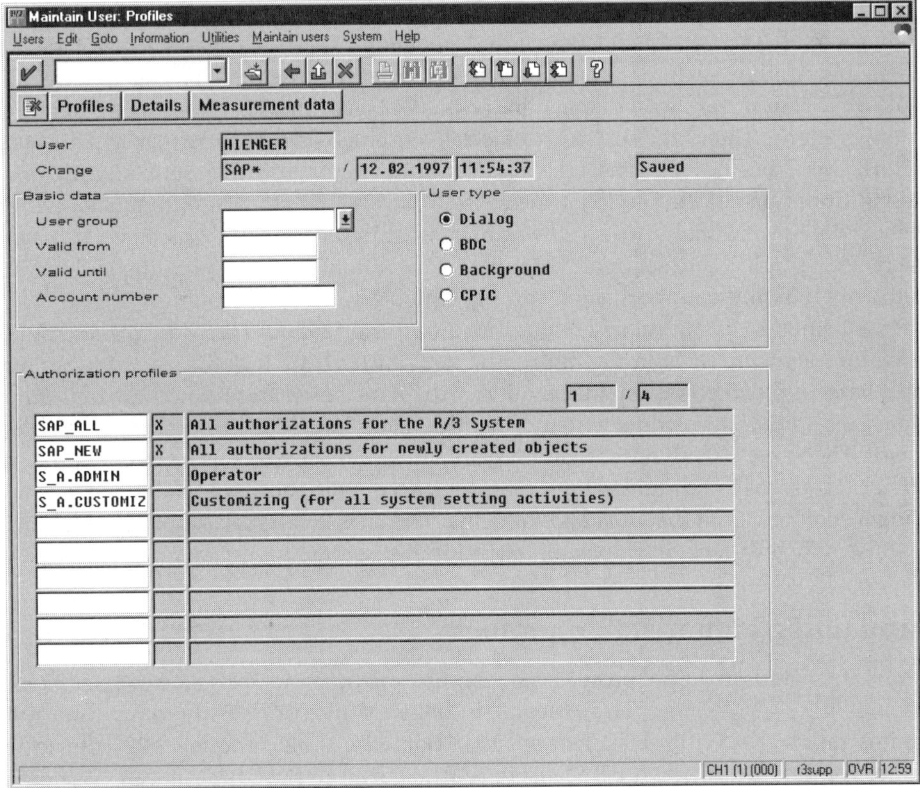

Figure 2.5 User master record

Entries in the *Valid from ... Valid until* fields enable the administrator to limit the validity period available to a given user. Enter individual profiles in the column *Profile*: this entry grants access authorization to the system.

Changes made to a user master record take effect only when the user logs on to the system again. The function *Lock/unlock* in the *Users* menu allows the administrator to grant or prohibit access to the system to a given user. This action, too, takes effect only when the user performs another log on.

The user administrator can grant a user a new password by choosing *Change password*. Password changes take effect immediately.

The functions *Information* and *Overview* permit display of user master records, authorization profiles, authorization objects authorizations.

To simplify administration of the user master record involving several changes, use the menu path *Utilities* → *Mass changes*.

Delete all users erases all the user master records for a given client.

The function *User profile* allows the administrator to delete a profile from all or part of a client's user master record, or to add it to part or all of that record.

Maintaining authorizations

The menu path *Tools* → *Administration* → *Maintain users* → *Authorization* (see Figure 2.6) creates new value sets for an authorization. First choose one of the object classes displayed. The screen will display individual objects in the object class (e.g., basis administration). Then choose which object (e.g., batch input) to which to allocate the authorization. Further options create, delete and activate value sets. Use the menu options *Create* or *Utilities* → *Copy* to create a new value set. Use *Utilities* → *Delete* to delete a value set. Finally, use *Authorization* → *Activate* or *Authorization* → *Activate all* to activate a single value set or all value sets. The system requires a unique authorization name only within the authorization for a given object.

The function *Maintain values* creates the new authorization; enter individual values in the menu *Maintain Fields*. In the figure, the new authorization defines a value set for an object batch input. The system automatically displays fields that require the definition of fields. Here the administrator enters the value *Lock* for the field *Batch input monitoring activity*. The values for all authorization fields must be entered consecutively in the same manner. To assign individual values, make entries only in the *From* field. For entries with a range, complete both the *From* and *To* fields. The user given the authorization shown in the illustration can lock or unlock all batch input sessions.

Maintaining authorization profiles

To maintain authorization profiles, choose the menu path *Tools* → *Administration* → *Maintain users* → *Profile*. Here, too, SAP delivers the profiles required for system administration with the installed system. Sometimes, it is quite difficult to give the appropriate privileges to R/3 users. Particularly at start time it can happen that required privileges are missing. Then it is recommendable to set the R/3 profile parameter auth/check_value_write_on to 1. If the R/3 system has been started with this

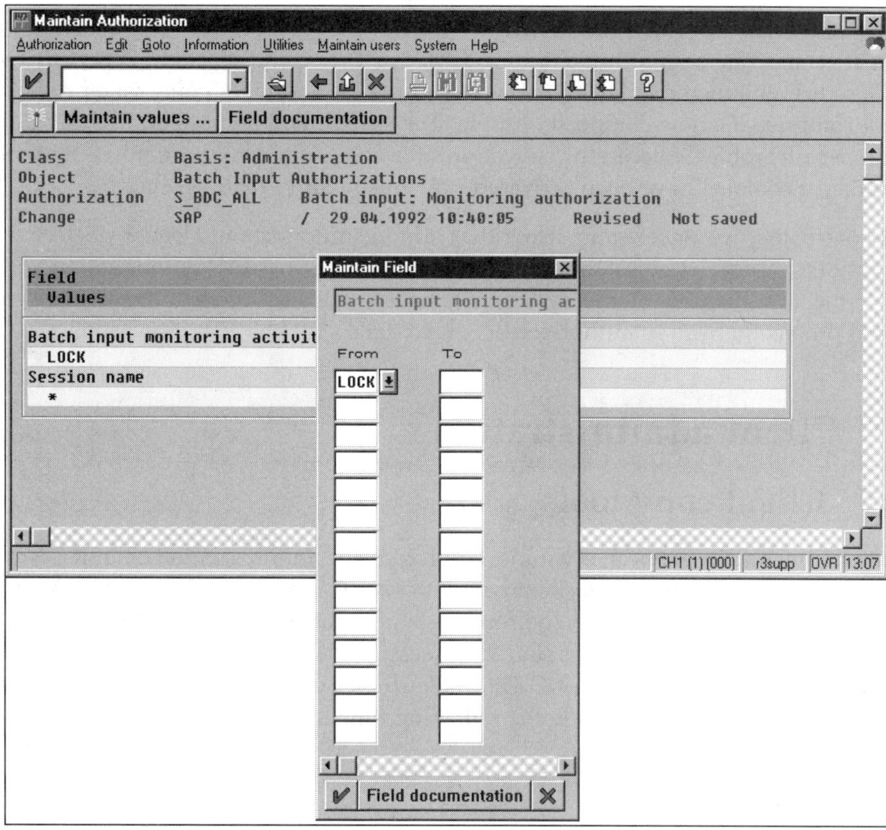

Figure 2.6 Maintain authorization

parameter and privileges are missing, transaction su53 can be called to execute certain tasks and to display the authorization object that caused the abnormal termination.

- *Individual profile*
  To create customer-specific profiles, we recommend beginning with SAP profiles. Copy the profiles supplied by SAP and adjust the copies to individual requirements. Step one involves finding the appropriate profile among those provided. The SAP naming convention makes the determination of the correct default profile a simple task. Assume that the administrator for batch processing requires the profile S_BTCH_ADM. Copy this profile under a different name (e.g., SBTCH_ADM), and adjust the authorizations contained in the copy. Remove any unnecessary authorization by deleting the appropriate lines from the profile. The function *Add* permits the addition of further authorizations. If SAP authorizations within the profile require changes, copy them under their own names, perform the changes and then enter them in the new profile. This procedure avoids overwriting the authorizations during an SAP version update. All new and changed authorizations must be activated before the profile itself can be activated.

- *Composite profile*
  Create composite profiles by choosing *Profile → Create* and marking *Composite profile*. The screen will then display all the names of the individual or composite profiles that will comprise the new composite profile. The system will accept entry of any desired number of profiles. Successful activation of a composite profile requires that all the profiles it contains have been activated previously with *Profile → Activate*.

In conclusion, we once again stress that administrators should never neglect a well thought-out approach to system security by examining the SAP authorization concept during the introduction of the system. Doing so will ensure that the system enjoys optimal protection from unauthorized access to data.

2.3 Client administration

2.3.1 Client copy tools

Client administration plays a very important role in the administration of an R/3 system. As of version 3.x, SAP provides client copy tools for this purpose. The tools provided in this version enable much more comfortable and error-tolerant execution of administrative activities than those of version 2.x. Access the tools via the menu path *Tools → Administration → Administration → Client administration* or via the appropriate transaction code. The client copy tools include the following functions to administer clients:

- Client maintenance (transaction `scc4`)
- Client copy (transaction `scc0`)
- Client transport (transaction `scc2`)
- Delete client (transaction `scc1`)
- Copy individual customizing settings with transport requests (transaction `scc1`)
- View logs (transaction `scc3`)

The rules of the authorization concept, of course, apply to client administration. The user SAP* has all the authorizations necessary to allow a complete client copy. If another user wishes to copy clients, she must have the proper authorizations to do so. The required authorizations depend on the type of data to be copied (see Table 2.2).

Table 2.2 Authorizations for client copy

Action	*Required authorization*
Maintenance of tables of all clients	S_TABU_CLI
Maintenance of table CCCFLOW (control table for client copy)	S_TABU_DIS
Copying user masters	S_USER_GRP
Copying user profiles	S_USER_PRO

2.3.2 Client maintenance

Before starting a copy, make sure that the system recognizes the target client. Table T000 contains a directory of all the clients in a given system. The table administers a short description and the characteristics of each client. Access the maintenance of this table either via the function *Client maintenance* of client copy (transaction scc4) or via direct table maintenance (transaction sm30) of table T000. The process allows the user to determine, for example, if the Customizing Organizer should record customizing activities in the client or if the client under examination is a productive client. The transfer of customizing settings into another system cannot occur unless they have been recorded.

2.3.3 Client copy

Once table T000 contains the target client, transaction scc0 (client copy) can copy client within a system or beyond the boundaries of a system. Start transaction scc0 in the target client as user SAP*. The destination of the client defines it as a:

- Local copy, or a
- Remote copy.

Note that in the event of a remote copy, the system's RFC interface handles all exchange of data. That means that the file system does not provide any intermediate storage of the data being transferred. For both local and remote copies, make sure to record all changes to the largest of the tables being copied. Recording can take place, for example, in the rollback segments (Oracle) or the transaction log (ADABAS D) of the database. This restriction exists because the copier works in blocks (of data). The copier transmits a database commit only after the transfer of a complete table. Should it prove impossible to determine if recording has taken place, use the following procedure.

The system offers a subgroup of the copy operation to transport a source client into several systems or if the copy procedure approaches the limits of a direct client copy (scc0). To access this feature, use the function *Client transport* of the client copier (transaction scc2). Once the data intended for transport has been selected, the system will export it from the source client. The client copier offers copy profiles (see Table 2.3)

Table 2.3 Default copy profile of the client copier

Copy profile	*Selected data*
SAP_UPRF	User master records and profiles
SAP_CUST	Customizing tables, user profiles
SAP_UCUS	Customizing tables, user profiles, user data
SAP_APPL	Customizing data, application data, user profiles
SAP_UAPP	Customizing data, application data, user profiles, user data

to simplify the choice of data to be copied. Files in the central transport directory (see Section 7.9.5) temporarily store the data.

Two object lists manage the execution of the export. The contents of the lists are determined at the beginning of the export operation; the names of the lists are displayed at the end of the export operation. The objects being transported with the transport control program `tp` are recorded in the list `<SAPSID>KTXXXXX`, where `XXXXX` represents a consecutive number.

The ABAP/4 program `RSTXR3TR` transports SAPScript objects (forms, styles, SAPScript texts); it takes the information it requires from the list `<SAPSID>KXXXXXX`. A client export from system P01 would then produce the following command files:

P01KT00004 → Input for `tp`

P01KX00004 → Input for `RSTXR3TR`

After the successful import of all the data exported from the source client into the target client, call transaction `scc2` in the target client to provide follow-up processing of the imported data.

When configuring the new client, the system first deletes (in the target client) those table entries from the source client that are not to be transferred. This process debugs the target client and prepares it for the transfer of data from the source client. After the successful preparation of the target client, the system copies the selected data from the source client to the target client. Depending on the volume of data in the source client, this can be a lengthy and write-intensive process. The copy should therefore take place as a background (batch) process, so that no dialog process becomes tied up for too long. If desired, the user can check the progress of the copy procedure with the function *Copy logs* of the client copier (transaction `scc3`).

During the copy procedure, the system prohibits users from performing any work in either the source or the target client. Only this restriction ensures that no inconsistencies will appear in the target client.

When transporting clients into other systems, note that a transfer of client-independent tables is possible only when no customizing settings have been made in the target system. If this restriction is ignored, the customizing previously performed in the target system will be destroyed.

During any client copy, users should always employ the restart abilities of the client copier. Long runtimes and heavy system load increase the probability that a copy procedure will terminate. For exactly this situation, users should always plan on running a second background process in restart mode that becomes active only when an actual restart situation occurs. The client copier can thus execute the function *Recopy for errors* to recopy unsuccessfully copied tables. The log of the copy procedure in `CCCFLOW` allows for monitoring, restart and subsequent transports.

The limitations noted above make it advisable to examine alternatives to copying clients between systems. If the client transport will serve only as a backup measure, copying the entire database may serve as a better solution. The copy tools offered by database manufacturers rest on a much deeper foundation. They are far superior to the SQL-based copying techniques for client copy in R/3.

2.3.4 Delete client

The function *Delete client* in the client copier deletes a client (transaction `sccl`). This function might apply to the configuration of a system by copying the database and then debugging it. While deleting, the user can determine if the affected client should also be removed from the directory of clients (table `T000`). Although difficulties that arise while deleting may be unpleasant, they have no negative impact on operations, unlike error situations that occur during a client copy.

2.4 Printers

2.4.1 General introduction

What applies to the performance level of the R/3 system as a whole also applies to the system's individual components. Conceptual planning must take an important place in the foreground of planning an implementation. The following questions require answers to allow for the planning and proper administration of a printer configuration:

- Will the system handle print requests that are
  - **Time-critical**, or
  - Must meet **high security requirements**, or
  - Demand a **high availability** of output options?
- Will **batch print requests** require processing?
- Will **non-critical print requests** require processing?
- Which users of the R/3 systems must execute which print requests?
- Who must initiate the various types of print requests? When and where?
- What maximum print volume must the R/3 system be able to process?
- Is it possible to create groups of output devices that can be dedicated to one of the types of print requests noted above?
- Would a number of small printers be advantageous, or would a centralized printer division make more sense?
- Are print requests sent to remote printers via networks?

The answers to these basic questions determine a general direction for the configuration and administration of printing at the most optimal level. In addition, placing a limit on the monitoring options will improve the performance of the printer(s).

- If the R/3 system uses several application servers, each of them should also function as a spool server, provided that sufficient output devices are available.
- Only one spool work process can exist on one application server. The server running the spool work process is also called the **spool server**.

- Each spool server should administer only one type of print request. This setting avoids collisions entirely or limits their occurrence (especially important for time-critical output).
- Consider the capacity of the network when connecting output devices remotely. Under some circumstances, it must process a high volume of data.
- Performance is generally better when an output device is connected locally (SAP connection types L and C (see Section 2.4.3)). Performance is generally poorer when data must be transported over network components, although it is possible with SAP connection types U or S (see Section 2.4.3). For time-critical print requests, we recommend the choice of a local printer. Exceptions are permissible only when the network consistently provides stable and high-level performance.
- Print requests that must meet high security requirements should, obviously, use a local connection to the printer.
- For the output of large documents we recommend use of a high-capacity printer. The connection can be made via the network, although doing so will not rule out performance problems caused by the transfer of data. However, as mentioned frequently, an individual spool server should handle these sorts of print requests to avoid blockages caused by other print requests. This is especially true of time-critical output. Do not overlook the availability aspects of networks and remote computers.
- Non-critical printers can be connected to the R/3 system via networks without problems.
- When users can avoid making inquiries about the status of the print request at the operating system and print manager level, the speed of the printer will likely increase.
- Printer output will also generally accelerate by deactivating the immediate deletion of correctly executed print requests. This action, of course, must take place at a later time (see Section 2.4.4).
- For critical print requests, we recommend configuration of a backup spool server. Doing so will increase the availability of the R/3 systems, the system software and the computer hardware.
- To avoid bottlenecks during output, it is important to limit access opportunities to an absolutely necessary group of users (selective granting of access authorizations).

2.4.2 The SAP spool system and its associated components

The R/3 system features an integrated, proprietary spool system to guarantee the uniform processing of print requests. Defined and configurable interfaces make its use possible in almost every hardware and software environment. Figure 2.7 provides an overview.

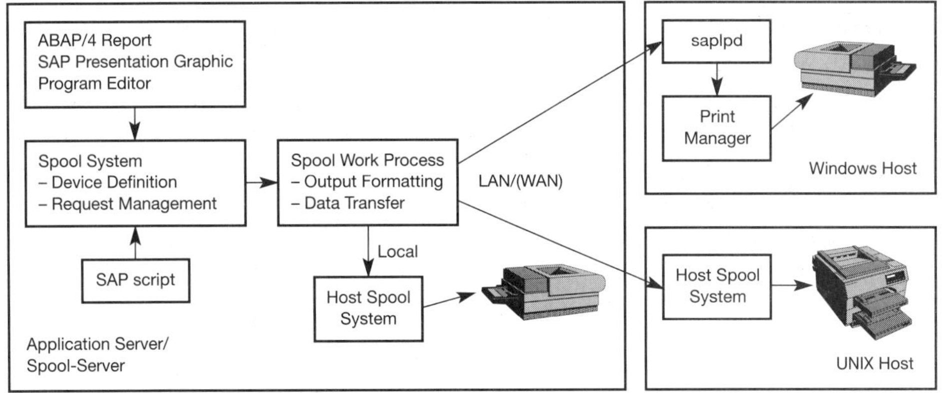

Figure 2.7 SAP spool system architecture

Various possibilities suggest themselves as the source and **originator of a spool request**: an ABAP/4 program, a program editor, the proprietary SAP text editor SAPScript or the presentation graphics systems of the R/3 system. The creators can be divided into two categories:

- SAPScript documents and
- The other sources.

The **SAP spool system** manages spool and output requests. A request primarily consists of the data generated at the source. The spool system processes the data, enabling the request to arrive at an output device. To do so efficiently, the spool system knows the SAP device definitions used to identify the output devices and the device interfaces. As far as possible, the device definition corresponds to the output driver of the host system.

Spool requests originate either in on-line or in background processing. The required information (which printer, output format, etc.) is written to a spool database. The output data, however, is stored in a temporary, sequential file (TEMSE or TemSE). The actual print request originates only when the data is to be output.

Besides ensuring that data is output in the proper form, the SAP spool system also stores output data that other R/3 components (such as the SAP communications server) process. The SAP communications server is described in Section 1.2.4.

The SAP archiving system, mentioned for the sake of completeness, comprises an additional component. It allows for reading data directly from the RDBMS. Data is returned to the archiving system in file form.

As presented in Sections 1.2.2, 1.2.3, 1.2.4 and 1.4.5, specific work processes handle the tasks of spool control. The **spool work process** converts the output data into the form required by the output medium and redirects it to the computer's spool system or the proprietary SAP processor saplpd. The following actions may then be necessary:

- Conversion of the print controls of the SAP system into the print commands used by a given printer.
- If necessary, device-specific initialization and event sequences such start-of-page or start-of-line must be added. The spool work process would then integrate the required escape sequences into the output's character string.
- Sometimes a conversion between the character sets of the two components (R/3 system ← output device) becomes necessary.
- When using SAPScript the corresponding SAPScript driver for formatting the output must be activated.

The R/3 system utilizes two procedures to transmit output requests. It can use either the capabilities provided by the spooler of the operating system for remote communication or proprietary, SAP capabilities. The following lists the variations that result from use of the functions provided by the spooler of the operating system. Note that the spool work process should run on a local computer.

- The spool work process transmits the output request to the local system spooler (client). The client then addresses the remote system spooler (server) and directs the request to it.
- The system spooler on the local computer cannot be used. In this case, the spool work process sends the output request directly to the remote spool system on the print server. This procedure functions only when the remote spool system supports the Berkley lpd protocol.

The system uses proprietary, SAP features when the system spooler cannot or should not be used (see Figure 2.7). Section 2.4.3 describes the possible connection types used for communication between the R/3 system and output devices.

Today more and more computers in the client/server environment of the R/3 system use Windows NT or Windows for Workgroups. To enable connection of locally attached output devices to these systems (e.g., using a PC as a printer server), SAP offers the **SAPLPD work process** (also written as saplpd). SAPLPD communicates both with the print manager of the Windows system and with the spool work process. It directs the output data and status messages to the appropriate recipients.

Before data can be output to a physical output device, it must pass through the **host spool system** or the **print manager**. This procedure is the current standard.

2.4.3 Connection types on the R/3 system

Good planning and configuration of components fulfill the prerequisites for problem-free output operations. This task includes the correct installation of output devices on the host system. The R/3 system must also be provided with the necessary internal definitions of the output devices. On its own, the system neither knows the specifics of a device nor can it request them from the host spool system. The system cannot leave output formatting completely up to the host spool system. Most important, however, the system must have the correct type of connection types to allow further transmission of output data. The R/3 system provides five such methods:

- **Local print** offers the quickest and most secure type of printing. The system sends formatted output data to the local host spool system. Note the distinction between the following two types:
  - *Connection type L (valid for UNIX systems only)*
    At the operating system level, the R/3 system (the spool work process) generates a regular file. The system commands 'lp' or 'lpr' (depending on the UNIX version) transmit the file to the host spool system. The R/3 system can receive status information on the print requests from the host spool system.
  - *Connection type C (valid for Windows NT systems only)*
    The print manager is addressed directly here. No temporary storage at the operating system level, as is the case in UNIX, takes place. Unfortunately, this method does not permit a query of the status of the print request.
- Under **remote print**, data is output to a remote system: this is **connection type U**. All operating systems that support the LPD protocol (primarily UNIX systems) can handle this connection type.

  For performance reasons, only local networks (LANs) should be used The use of wide area networks (WANs) can cause bottlenecks; the spool work process cannot process any additional tasks while output data is transmitted.

  Note that the receiving host system must be active during this type of transmission. If, for whatever reason, the remote system cannot accept data, the sender (host spool work process) remains blocked. The system becomes free only when it can reestablish a connection or the print request times out. Such a situation has obvious negative effects on efficient and high-performance processing of output requests.
- The SAP processing program saplpd enables use of the possibilities offered by **PC Print**. Note the distinction between the following two types:
  - *Connection type S*
    This connection uses a special SAP communications protocol with several special functions, data compression among them. In addition, the title of the spool request is transmitted to identify the output request under Windows. Future plans include the addition of a feature providing data encryption.

    The SAP processing program redirects the output data either to the Windows GDI interface (for the proprietary device type SAPWIN) or to the print manager in file-form (for all other device types).
  - *Connection type U*
    This connection type transmits the output data to saplpd via the 'Berkley Standard Distribution UNIX lpr-Protocol.' It functions more quickly than connection type S.

Connection types influence not only how much data, but also which character sets can be transmitted. They are the key to double byte character sets. The SAP system can output these characters (Cyrillic, Japanese and Chinese among others) when using connection type S with device types saplpd or SAPWIN.

2.4.4 Installing printers

General information

The R/3 system has a very limited **name range**. Unfortunately, only four characters can designate the name of a printer. Administrators must therefore think through the naming environment very carefully. If the names clearly identify the printers, granting authorizations or determining who or which group may use which printer or class of printers can become much easier. SAP suggests, but does not require, the following naming convention for printers.

- 'X' for critical output devices,
- 'R' for remote output devices
- 'Y' for batch output devices.

The next letter can classify the application more precisely. For example, 'F' might identify financial accounting. Consider using a number for the last two characters. The number would identify an individual printer when using multiple devices. Accordingly, printer 'XF07' would be the seventh, critical output device for financial accounting.

Creation of an **access profile** for an output device can take place most easily with two steps:

- Copy the general template 'S_SPO_DEV_AL' and
- Adjust the settings with transaction 'SU03.'

Use the option 'SET/GET PID' in the user profile to enable the choice or allocation of output devices.

To control output from within SAP applications, turn off the access authorization for the output device. Doing so allows the system to handle the access control independently of the application.

The R/3 system contains several pre-defined output devices. These default settings ease the installation of devices decidedly.

The following rule applies to the connection of output devices to the R/3 system and the system's ability to drive them:

An output device connected to the R/3 system function without problems when the device, in and of itself, can be driven without difficulties at the operating system level.

Installing local output devices

Execute the following steps to install local output devices:

- Install the output device, generally a printer, on the host system that will drive the device. If necessary, request help from the system administrator; installation of an output device on the host is a task specific to the host system.
- Install the application server as a spool server (see also Section 3.2). Use the menu path *Tools → Administration → Computing Center → Management System → Configuration →*

OP-Modes/Servers → Operation mode → Maintain instances → Profile view. Choose the instance, then execute *Instance → Maintain → Instance → General data.*

- Use the following menu path to install an output device: *Tools → Administration → Spool → Spool Administration.* Mark the selection *Output devices,* then make the appropriate entries.

– Output device	e.g., XF07,
– Device type	if necessary, use the pull-down menu to see possible entries (e.g., SAPWIN),
– Spooler server	Host name: e.g., rm600_spool,
– Host printer	taken from the device definition of the host system: for Windows it is the interface (e.g., LPT1),
– SAP title page	choose only when a cover page should precede every output request,
– Connection type	see Section 2.4.3 and below, under device pools,
– LPQ-Format	Status messages on the print request: B Berkley compatible format S System V compatible format 2 BS2000 format

  In addition, output devices can be locked or unlocked. The status query to the operating system can be switched on and off in the same manner.

- To install a device pool, use the menu path *Tools → Administration → Spool → Spool Administration* (mark Output devices, choose Change, then choose Create). Enter a 'P' at the menu option 'connection type.' Then press 'ENTER,' followed by the push button 'Pools.' Finally, enter the name of the pool.

- The definition of device types becomes necessary only when using the several device type definitions in the SAP system is impossible. Creating a user-specific device type can be accomplished most easily by copying a definition already present in the SAP system. Use the menu path *Tools → Administration → Spool → Spool Administration* and then execute *Utilities → Copy device type.* At 'Copy device type,' enter the name of a standard device type. Then, enter the name of the new device type in a manner that prevents conflict with an existing name in the SAP environment. It has become the custom to use a 'Z' or a 'Y' as the first letter of the new name.

Local device type may have to process time-critical output requests or those which must meet high security requirements. Accordingly, the following points must also be considered.

- Delete successfully completed output requests immediately after execution (security).

- Setting the profile parameter 'rspo/store_location = db' will avoid storage of the output data in the file system of the host system. This will also protect the data from unauthorized access by other users. Note that the TemSe database table is not intented for archiving output requests for a long time. It has a maximum storage limit of 32,000 output requests.

- Installing a backup spool server will further increase an already high availability of output data. To change a spool device of a spool server to a backup spool server, use the menu path *Tools → Administration → Spool → Spool Administration → Utilities → Output devices → Assign Server*. When using a network printer, nothing beyond making this switch need occur: the device is already known to the backup server. However, when using a local output device, it must be installed physically. Also, define the same spool queues on the backup spool server that exist on the primary spool server.
- If a terminated output request is still available (either in a TemSe file or in a file system file and automatic deletion is not in effect), it can be restarted manually and then output.

Installing remote device drivers

The procedure used to install remote output devices generally corresponds to the installation of local output devices. Please note the caution we have mentioned several times in this section: the connection type must be 'U' or 'S' to avoid dangerous complications.

Installing a PC output device

Administrators should perform the following steps during installation:

- The processing program saplpd must be installed in the Windows system. The program is normally installed during regular installation of the SAPGUI front end software.
- The print manager must recognize the output devices.
- The CCMS must prepare the application server to function as a spool server.
- Output devices must be made known to the R/3 system, as described in the section on 'Installing local output devices,' above.
- In most cases, use connection type 'S' (along with device type SAPWIN). For other device types or when using the Berkeley protocol, use connection type 'U.'

2.4.5 Helpful notes for the administrator, authorizations, transactions, tables and background jobs

Administration of spool requests

Tools → Administration → Spool → Output controller or System → Services → Print requests

- Output spool requests:
  - immediately
  - to other devices on the host system
- Display or change spool request attributes and information

Deleting spool requests

Tools → Administration → Spool → Spool Administration → Administration → Delete spool request

Terminate and restart spool process

Tools → Administration → Monitoring → System monitoring → Process overview; Mark the Process, then *Process → Cancel without core* or *Restart after error*

Checking the consistency of the spool database

Tools → Administration → Spool → Spool Administration → Administration → Check consistency

Transactions

SP12	Administration of TemSe files,
SM37	Job selection,
SU03	Admin user authorization object.

Authorization

S_SPO_DEV_AL

Tables

NAST	Output control status,
TNAPR	Processing of output control,
TNAST	Store messages from application for further processing.

Background jobs

- RSNAST00
  Calling the output program
  This program should run occasionally to prevent the jamming of too many outstanding output requests.
- RSPO0041
  Monitoring the growth of the spool data
  Run this job every 24 hours when demands on the system are light. It deletes already executed output requests and frees the space they occupy.

2.4.6 Special aspects of output requests

Printing from within applications

Output control consists of some tables (e.g., TNAST) and programs (e.g., RSNAST00). The administrator can adjust it to the special circumstances of clients (Application Customizing: Display View 'Output Types': Details). The following parameters, for example, can be entered:

- Where to print?
- When to print?
- How much to print?
- Must security guidelines be followed?

Batch printing

Unless security considerations demand something to the contrary, set the profile parameter 'rspo/store_location = G.' This setting changes the location of output data storage from the R/3 system to the host file system (/usr/sap/<SID>/SYS/<SID>SPOOL). If it is not set, the RDBMS must have enough room to archive the output data until it is deleted.

Data output is slower when the spool system receives prepared output from the RDBMS. It is fast when the spool system can read it directly from a file in the host file system.

2.4.7 System profile parameters

The SAP system allows a large number of settings for various functions. To understand the interdependence between them, SAP recommends using the CCMS to manipulate profiles (*Tools → Administration → Computing Center → Management System and Configuration → Op modes and Servers*).

Here we introduce some of the parameters. They apply only to the UNIX environment. Since the official user interface is addressed in Windows systems, changing parameters on that platform is meaningless.

Most parameters begin with 'rspo' and lend themselves to easy recognition within the profile. Many parameters contain special variables that allow processing of the most varied kinds of information or transmission of information to programs that call for it. A detailed description of each would explode the scope of this book. See the on-line documentation or training materials for this information.

- `rspo/host_spool/print`
  This command instructs the host system to execute the output request.
- `rspo/to_host/data_file`
  The file to be output.
- `rspo/host_spool/query`
  Query status at the time of the output request.

- `rspo/host_spool/answer_format`
  Answer format of the status information on the host system.
- `rspo/rspoget2_daemon/tcp_block_size`
  This parameter gives the block size of the TCP/IP communications between the editing and the processing programs.
- `rspo/store_location`
  This entry determines the location of the data: either in the SAP database or in the host file system.

The following four parameters and their settings (time and repetition factors) apply to all output devices that the system can reach. It is not possible to define times or repetition factors for individual devices.

- `rspo/tcp/timeout/connect`
  This parameter sets the timeout value for establishing a connection.
- `rspo/tcp/timeout/read`
  Timeout parameter for reading and writing during network communication.
- `rspo/tcp/retries`
  This parameter determines how often to repeat an attempt to read, write or connect.
- `rspo/tcp/retrytime`
  The time interval between new attempts.

The following parameters describe the environment of the character set:

- `rspo/ccc/max_sapcode`
  The number of characters defined in the SAP character set. If new characters are defined, increase the value.
- `rsts/ccc/cachesize`
  This parameter indicates the size of memory available for the table conversion of character codes.
- `rsts/ccc/max_sapcode`
  The highest SAP number in the SAP character list.
- `install/codepage/appl_server`
  Entry for the system character set (code page).
- `abap/local_ctype`
  This parameter must contain the same entry for the character set as the parameter 'install/codepage/appl_server.'

2.4.8 Error analysis

What opportunities does the administrator have to analyze and solve an error in the output aspects of the system? This section provides some general guidelines: SAP documentation provides further details. In difficult and 'insoluble' situations, call SAP for support.

- First question: has the output request been executed for not? An answer requires examination of the status of the request. Perform the following steps:
  1. *Tools → Administration → Spool → Output controller*
  2. Enter all the information required into the screen template
  3. Possible status conditions and their meaning:
     - **--**
       This indicates that the spool request has not yet been sent to the output device. In this case the spool request should be executed immediately to check whether or not output is possible.
     - **in process**
       The output request is being processed right now (formatting/transmission to the host spool system). The administrator now needs patience. If the status does not change in a reasonable time, undertake further investigation (see below).
     - **waiting/completed**
       If no output has appeared, determine why the system has not fulfilled the request (see below). Check the attributes of the requests marked 'completed.' To do so, mark the output request under examination and use the menu path *Goto → Attributes Attributes II*. A display of the requests already processed will appear. Each one marked 'Processed ... Without printing' requires further analysis (see Section 2.4.6).
- The output request was processed, but it
  - Omits some characters, or
  - Replaces some characters with the pound sign (£), or
  - Outputs graphical elements, such as colors, symbols, lines, boxes or backgrounds incorrectly or not at all, or
  - Did not output the desired graphics.

  SAP defines these situations as 'minor errors.' Check the SAP 'Notes' system: it describes several error conditions and their solutions.
- The output request was processed, but it
  - Used an incorrect character set, or
  - Has an incorrect text sequence incorrect: e.g., incorrect line or page breaks, or
  - Contained control commands for the output device, or
  - Output no characters at all.

  These 'serious' error conditions require further analysis. Check the following settings:
  1. Does the entry for the device type in the device definition agree with the setting used for the output device addressed? Perform a check as follows:
     - *Tools → Administration → Spool → Spool administration*
     - Mark 'Output devices' to check the device type.
  2. To examine the settings on the output device itself or its direct environment (e.g., driver software), see the description of the device.

Solving an error often requires consideration of other questions. Does the error occur because of settings in the R/3 system itself or in the output device? Where does one best correct the problem: at the R/3 level or the device level? How can correcting the error prevent occurrences of other errors in the future?

- Execution of the output request did not occur, although the spool request was generated. Check the generation of the spool request as follows:
  1. Follow the menu path *Tools → Administration → Spool → Output controller.*
  2. Fill in the entries as completely as possible. The user who wishes to print and the output device are the most important entries.
  3. The beginning of this section provided a first look at the interpretation of status entries. When examining a status, determine which of the following applies:
     - The status 'waiting' indicates a processing delay. The end of this section describes possible causes and their correction.
     - The status 'completed' is displayed. This status should indicate the successful completion of the output request. Because this has not occurred, various elements require examination. Does the host system (spool system or print manager) recognize the output request? If yes, the problem most likely lies in the host system. In this case, continue with the error analysis. If the output request is present on the host system, check if the correct output command was used.
       1. *Tools → Administration → Computing Center → Management System*
       2. *Configuration → Profile maintenance*
       3. Search for the profile of the application server sending the output request
       4. Choose 'Extended maintenance' and check the parameter 'rspo/host_spool/print.'
       5. Execute the host system command determined in point 4 at the host system level. This procedure will determine if the command is correct in and of itself.
       6. If the command is correct but the data still not output, examine the output files themselves. The files may contain control sequences preventing output.
       7. If the command is incorrect, it must be changed in the DEFAULT profile. Use the menu path provided above. Restart the application server after making the correction. Otherwise the change will not take effect.

- The status indicates 'problem.' Analyze the problem by examining the error log (*Tools → Administration → Spool → Output controller*):
  1. Select 'Spool request'
  2. Mark the last incorrect output request
  3. Analyze the error log

     The error log may contain the following sources of messages:
     - The **spool work process** issues an error when the output data itself contains errors. Possible causes:
       1. Incorrect ABAP/4 program
       2. Problems in the host system
       3. Problems in the RDMS
     - The **saplpd processing process** logs errors in its own area of activity. The error log also contains errors from the host system or the print manager if these errors produce responses that the R/3 system can recognize.

  If the output log does not allow an analysis of the error situations, switch to a log for output data. Before re-attempting to output the data, follow the menu path

(*Tools → Administration → Spool → Spool → Administration*). Mark 'output device' and choose 'Change.'

Activating a trace in the R/3 system or using ABAP/4 debugging also provide information. See Section 2.6 and Chapter 3.

- Execution of the output request did not occur because no spool request had been generated in the R/3 system. This situation causes the R/3 system to write a spool dump (ABAP/4 short dump). Analyze the dump by using the menu path *Tools → ABAP/4 Workbench → Test → Dump analysis*. See Chapter 3, p. 117 for further information on dump analyses.

To close this discussion of error analyses, we present additional circumstances that may lead to delayed execution of output requests:

- The status of the message server is to be buffered. Transaction 'SM51' can cause this situation.
- The status of the spool work process must be buffered. Since this environment holds several possibilities that may lead to slow execution of output requests, we present only some general remarks. See the R/3 system documentation for further details.

  Use transaction 'SM50' to gain access (as an example). A solution also requires an examination of the environment of the output request. The examination includes:
  - Identification of the output device
  - (*Tools → Administration → Spool → Output controller*, choose 'Attributes'),
  - Identification of the spool work process
  - (*Tools → Administration → Spool → Output controller*, mark 'Output device,' choose 'Display' and note the information in the field 'Formatting server,'
  - Check the formatting server
  - (Transaction 'SM51'),
  - Check the spool work process
  - (Transaction 'SM51,' choose 'processes,' search for type 'SPO' and note the name of the user)
  - Activate the developer trace. See Section 2.6 for further information.
  - Determine the users executing the output request (see 'check the spool work process,' above): the user 'SAPSYS' indicates the execution of internal R/3 output requests,
  - Check the setting of the time parameters,
  - Check the messages in the system log (see Section 2.6),
  - Determine and avoid wait queues.

2.4.9 List of supported printers

The following list provides a small selection of the default printers in the R/3 system:

Honeywell Bull Compuprint 960 or 4/66
C.ITOH CI-1000/CI-500 Printer
Digital Equipment LN07, DEClaser1100, or DEClaser22
Hewlett-Packard HP256x Printer (HP256...series)

Hewlett-Packard Laserjet (SAPscript Driver STN2)
Hewlett-Packard Laserjet II
Hewlett-Packard Laserjet IIIP, III, IIID, or IIISi
IBM 4232-302 Printer
Lexmark/IBM 4226 Printer
Kyocera F-1200 or F-1200S
Kyocera P-2000
Mannesmann Tally MT 600 Printer
OKI ML 3410 Lineprinter
QMS-PS 410
SEL Alcatel 4440XT Lineprinter
SNI 4009 Lineprinter
SNI 9014-12 Lineprinter
Siemens/Nixdorf 9021
Siemens/Nixdorf 9026

2.5 Customer support

SAP's concept of customer support rests on establishing a network connection to every R/3 installation. Accordingly, the network connection for the computer running the R/3 system is best planned, if not actually established, before installation of the system. Customers provide SAP colleagues with access to their own, local systems by establishing a connection to the central SAP computer, sapserv3. For best results, use the menu path *System → Services → SAP Service*. This connection provides SAP with access to a customer's computer via a SAPGUI. Executing the command 'ping' at the operating system level will also establish a connection (via telnet) to the SAP computer. If required, SAP can also log onto the operating system.

2.5.1 SAProuter

If the customer site uses several R/3 systems or if a third instance should regulate access centrally, we recommend use of the SAProuters. Ultimately, SAProuter functions as a switching program for a given computer. It

- Separately protects access to the customer's network,
- Serves as a central collection point for WAN input and output data,
- Establishes connections with the customer's system.

Without the SAProuter every R/3 system would have to establish its own connection to the outside world (SAP). With the SAProuter, only one connection exists between the local R/3 system and the SAProuter. The router itself, rather than the system, creates a connection to the WAN. The use of SAProuters has the following advantages:

- Less traffic on the WAN,
- Higher network security,

- Increased log-possibilities for network traffic,
- Centralization of administrative network tasks.

SAProuter works in conjunction with the SAP Network Interface-Layer (NI Layer): it needs to handle various hardware platforms separately.

The SAProuter program starts with

```
saprouter -r
```

and stops with

```
saprouter -s
```

To log onto one system from another with the SAPGUI, the route string must be provided. Adhere to the following syntax:

```
/H/<saprouter>[/H/<saprouters>][/S/<service_no.>][/P/<password>]
```

The route string can, of course, consist of several SAProuters. The route string describes the access path to the target system. Include the service number only when it differs from the default value of 299. If a password protects access, enter the password with the /P/ parameter.

The file ./saprouttab determines which non-SAP systems have access to the customer's network. It also controls access to specific computers with specific passwords. The routing table contains entries made along the following pattern:

```
[P|D] <non-SAP_system> <target_computer> <password>
```

The letter `P` stands for permit (access) and `D` for deny (access). Comment lines begin with the number (or pound) sign (£). Allocate the routing table to the SAProuter with the option -R <saprouttab>. If no explicit entry for the routing table exists, the system uses the default file ./saprouttab. SAProuter also accepts the following options:

-l	list of all connections made on the SAProuter currently running.
-c <id>	terminate the connection with password <id>; the password must be recognizable with the option -l.
-n	reread the routing table
-t	write the log file (default): dev_rout
-T <file>	name of the log file
-d	write technical information to the log file

2.5.2 Online Service System

Customers' network connections come into play for their consultations and the Early Watch Service (see Section 3.7.7). In addition, all customers have access to the central SAP system and its OSS (Online Service System). Each R/3 license holder is also an OSS user and can request additional users at any time. The OSS contains all error reports generated by customers, problem notes, development requests and other important material.

Customers no longer need to report their difficulties orally via the SAP Hotline. Instead, they describe the problems and provide the required supporting information in the OSS. The OSS allocates the problem to a topic area and automatically sends it to those responsible.

For their part, SAP employees use the system to describe already-existing problems and errors. Developers assign numbers to solutions so that customers can access previously resolved difficulties.

Customers can also receive solutions to their problems directly, via fax, from the OSS. The importance of OSS becomes even more clear when customers wish to change or create an object. To make these types of changes, customers must request an access key and register the installation number of their SAP systems to the OSS. SAP then registers the customer as a developer and issues the first key number. The following step registers the object to be created or changed under the key number. OSS grants a new access number for each of these objects. Changes take effect only after entry of the access key in the customers' systems. SAP thus has an exact record of any objects that customers have created or changed.

2.6 Traces and logs

2.6.1 Traces

The R/3 system offers a large variety of diagnostic tools, tracing among them. We present here a broad summary of commands used in tracing. The R/3 system allows for an examination of the following operations with tracing:

- SQL accesses to the RDBMS, for example, directly entered programs or test instructions,
- ABAP/4 programs,
- Internal operations of the R/3 system,
- The flow of processes in the SAP system (e.g., the system's start procedure).

Both the R/3 system itself and profile settings activate individual variants. If required, define the paths and names of the log files in the profiles (see Appendix B).

The path *Tools* → *Administration* → *Monitoring* → *Traces* leads to a submenu offering the following traces:

- SQL trace,
- ABAP/4 trace (reachable via the path only in version 2.1/2.2; as of version 3.0 use *Tools* → *Administration* → *Monitoring* → *Traces* → *SQL trace*, then choose *Monitor* → *Traces*),
- System trace,
- Developer traces.

Under **SQL trace** two alternatives present themselves for subsequent action. Either activate an SQL trace by choosing *Trace on* or simply examine a given command more closely. In the latter case, click on the function *Explain*. The system will return an analysis of the SQL statement including which strategies the RDBMS would use to execute the command.

SQL trace can be switched on for one or all users of the R/3 system. To store the trace information, the R/3 system overwrites a file in cycles. The information contains the following particulars for each SQL command executed:

- The time of the RDBMS access,
- The duration of the access,
- The type of access (static or dynamic),
- The tables addressed,
- The data records accessed and
- The SQL statement.

The system highlights anomalies, such as longer than average execution times, in color, on the screen. Figure 2.8 illustrates an excerpt from an SQL trace.

A double click on such a statement provides further details, such as where-conditions and the corresponding parameter values. See Figure 2.9 for an example.

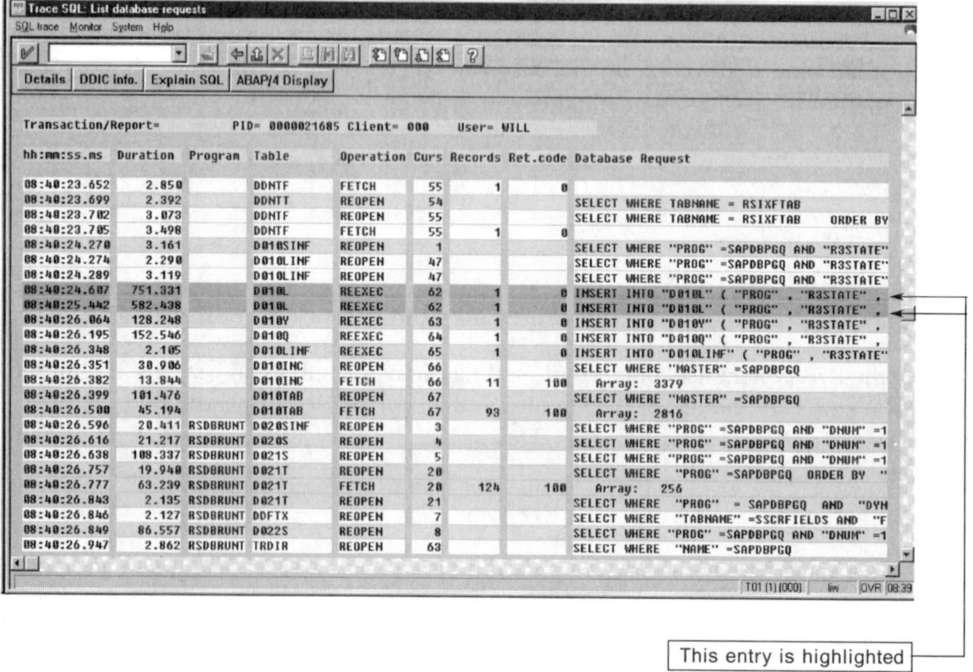

hh:mm:ss.ms	Duration	Program	Table	Operation	Curs	Records	Ret.code	Database Request
08:40:23.652	2.850		DDNTF	FETCH	55	1	0	
08:40:23.699	2.392		DDNTT	REOPEN	54			SELECT WHERE TABNAME = RSIXFTAB
08:40:23.702	3.073		DDNTF	REOPEN	55			SELECT WHERE TABNAME = RSIXFTAB ORDER BY
08:40:23.705	3.498		DDNTF	FETCH	55	1	0	
08:40:24.270	3.161		D010SINF	REOPEN	1			SELECT WHERE "PROG" =SAPDBPGQ AND "R3STATE"
08:40:24.274	2.290		D010LINF	REOPEN	47			SELECT WHERE "PROG" =SAPDBPGQ AND "R3STATE"
08:40:24.289	3.119		D010LINF	REOPEN	47			SELECT WHERE "PROG" =SAPDBPGQ AND "R3STATE"
08:40:24.607	751.331		D010L	REEXEC	62	1	0	INSERT INTO "D010L" ("PROG" , "R3STATE" ,
08:40:25.442	582.438		D010L	REEXEC	62	1	0	INSERT INTO "D010L" ("PROG" , "R3STATE" ,
08:40:26.064	128.248		D010Y	REEXEC	63	1	0	INSERT INTO "D010Y" ("PROG" , "R3STATE" ,
08:40:26.195	152.546		D010Q	REEXEC	64	1	0	INSERT INTO "D010Q" ("PROG" , "R3STATE" ,
08:40:26.348	2.105		D010LINF	REEXEC	65	1	0	INSERT INTO "D010LINF" ("PROG" , "R3STATE"
08:40:26.351	30.906		D010INC	REOPEN	66			SELECT WHERE "MASTER" =SAPDBPGQ
08:40:26.382	13.844		D010INC	FETCH	66	11	100	Array: 3379
08:40:26.399	101.476		D010TAB	REOPEN	67			SELECT WHERE "MASTER" =SAPDBPGQ
08:40:26.500	45.194		D010TAB	FETCH	67	93	100	Array: 2816
08:40:26.596	20.411	RSDBRUNT	D020SINF	REOPEN	3			SELECT WHERE "PROG" =SAPDBPGQ AND "DNUM" =1
08:40:26.616	21.217	RSDBRUNT	D020S	REOPEN	4			SELECT WHERE "PROG" =SAPDBPGQ AND "DNUM" =1
08:40:26.638	108.337	RSDBRUNT	D021S	REOPEN	5			SELECT WHERE "PROG" =SAPDBPGQ AND "DNUM" =1
08:40:26.757	19.940	RSDBRUNT	D021T	REOPEN	20			SELECT WHERE "PROG" =SAPDBPGQ ORDER BY "
08:40:26.777	63.239	RSDBRUNT	D021T	FETCH	20	124	100	Array: 256
08:40:26.843	2.135	RSDBRUNT	D021T	REOPEN	21			SELECT WHERE "PROG" = SAPDBPGQ AND "DYN
08:40:26.846	2.127	RSDBRUNT	DDFTX	REOPEN	7			SELECT WHERE "TABNAME" =SSCRFIELDS AND "F
08:40:26.849	86.557	RSDBRUNT	D022S	REOPEN	8			SELECT WHERE "PROG" =SAPDBPGQ AND "DNUM" =1
08:40:26.947	2.862	RSDBRUNT	TRDIR	REOPEN	63			SELECT WHERE "NAME" =SAPDBPGQ

Figure 2.8 Trace SQL

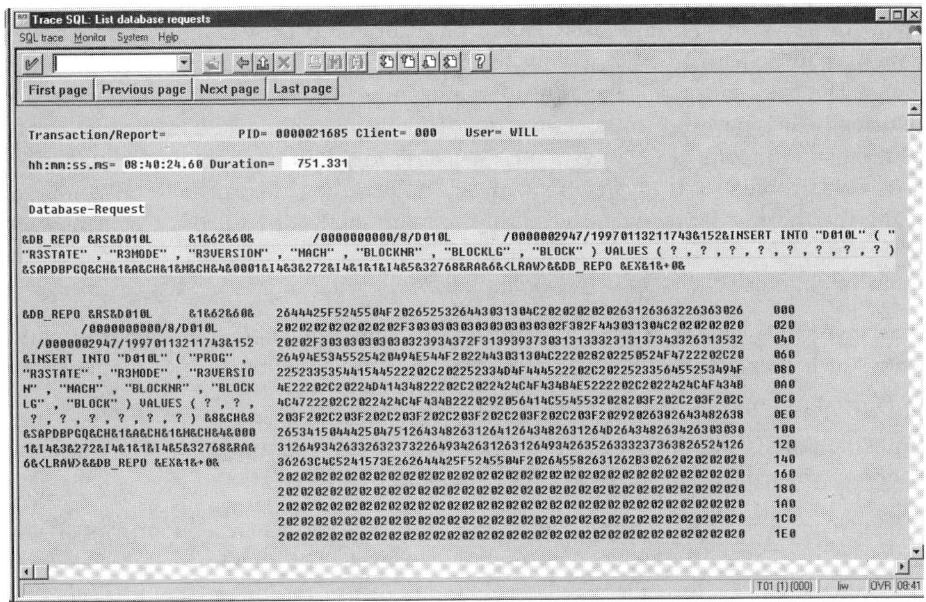

Figure 2.9 Trace details

Since every user of the SAP system can activate an SQL trace, the system shows the user if any other user has already activated the same trace. In this case, starting the trace again has no value: the sets of information written to the log files can overwrite and delete each other. Always start the trace on the server running the application to be traced.

Start an **APAB/4 trace** to perform a runtime analysis of an ABAP/4 program. In versions 2.1/2.2 of the R/3 system, the trace output includes runtimes of:

- ABAP/4 operations,
- Operations on the RDBMS and
- Organizational R/3 system operations.

In release 3.0, activate the ABAP/4 trace as follows:

Tools → *Administration* → *Monitoring* → *Traces* → *SQL trace*, then choose *Monitor* → *Traces*.

After choosing the ABAP, start the analysis with the button 'Execute.' At this point, a multiplicity of evaluative possibilities become available (see Chapter 4).

If a user follows the menu path given above, but chooses *Internal traces* rather than ABAP/4 trace, the screen for Developer traces appears.

Choose the **SAP system trace** whenever internal R/3 system activities require logging. Such is always the case for the application server on which the trace is activated. The process flows for analysis can be activated in two ways. Use the menu function *Switch, edit*... or choose the desired switch in the trace switch menu (*Traces* → *System trace* → *Trace switch* → *Switch, edit*...). Note that SQL tracing does not become active when the system trace is switched on via the menu path provided above. We recommend using the menu path to activate SQL tracing when limited, specific programs or users require tracing.. The trace must be started (use the button 'Standard options') for trace analysis.

Normally, it is best to turn traces on and off with the menus *SQL trace* or *System trace*. This method automatically allows the R/3 system to set all trace options automatically.

To avoid problems with system load, deselect the options for normal evaluation before starting the trace. If *Switch* was chosen in the main menu, the trace is performed for all active users.

An evaluation of a system trace contains the following data:

- **Last Sync** or **time since last sync** is the accumulated time between the performance of two synchronizations (program starts, task switches or work process changes).
- **T.(Trace)** or **ent T.(Trace)** repeats the type of entry.
- **Specific part** is the message text of the trace. It can contain a list of activity codes. Choose a specific entry to see a short explanation of the text.

The system stores internal trace information by writing it to a file in cycles. If several traces require display, the system shows the user the start of each trace. If the user wishes to write trace entries to a file (for later evaluation: use the menu option *Evaluate file*), versions 2.1/2.2 of the R/3 system can do so in three ways:

- **Buffered** (menu option *Write to disk*): the internal buffer must be full before writing to disk,
- **Unbuffered** (menu option *Unbuffered write to disk*): all trace entries are written directly to disk, although this may affect performance negatively,
- **Write** the contents of all buffers **to the file** (the option *Write now* must be checked).

As of release 3.0 the system provides even more possibilities. Use the menu path *List* → *Save* for the following variants:

- *Office*
  Lists can be stored in the SAPoffice environment. The system allows storage in various folders (e.g., Personal) or can send the list to other users of the R/3 system.
- *Reporting tree*
  Here the administrator can save the lists within the R/3 system. Remote connections to other R/3 and R/2 systems remain open to the administrator.
- *File*
  Use this option to perform various conversions: enter a file name at the end.

All processes of an SAP system have their own buffer for the output of trace information.

Clicking on the menu option *Stop trace* will stop the trace. Choosing the menu option *No trace* terminates the trace completely.

Developer tracing means following the flow of individual processes in the SAP system. **Developer traces** provide technical information on an SAP system. Such traces assume thorough knowledge of computers, the operating system and the R/3 system.

When information from the system logs no longer helps diagnose error situations, developer traces can provide the required data. Currently four variants of traces exist:

- Trace = 0; no trace written.
- Trace = 1; only error messages are written to the trace file (default).
- Trace = 2; a full trace is written. Entries in the file vary according to the SAP process involved.
- Trace = 3; data blocks are logged in addition to the information provided in a full trace.

As a rule, enter the **trace level** in the start profile of the instance (e.g., rdisp/TRACE=1). The instance's working directory (work) stores the trace files. Their names always begin with the character string 'dev_' followed by an abbreviation indicating the type of process. Typical examples of abbreviations follow:

- disp dispatcher,
- w<n> nth work process (task handler),
- dy<n> nth screen (screen processor),
- ro<n> nth roll,
- pg<n> nth paging,
- db<n> nth database interface,
- ab<n> nth ABAP/4 processor,
- eq<n> nth enqueue service,
- lg<n> nth log process (logging),
- w spool,
- ms message server,
- st<login_name> SAPGUI,
- appc APPC server (CPI-C gateway),
- digr graphic actions (e.g., up/download),
- rfc<n> RFC calls per work process,
- tp tp process (transport/correction),
- rd gateway-reader process,
- dpmon dispatcher monitoring process.

Entries indicating an error always begin with that word. The operating system provides tools that enable a user to search for 'ERROR' in the trace files.

Starting an instance automatically actives the trace according to the level set in the start profile of the instance.

2.6.2 System logs

System logs provide a record of events and problems that might develop on individual SAP servers. As a default, a local file on the server stores the logs in /sapmmnt/<SID>/global (see also Appendix B: rslg Parameters). Appropriate entries in the profiles allow the administrator to configure additional, centralized logging. Such a logging procedure allows the system to collect all messages from the various servers of the R/3 system into a central location. Figure 2.10 shows the relationships between local and centralized log files. The system stores the information contained in the local system log in a file that it overwrites in cycles. Two procedures exist for storing data relating to the flow of the SAP system in a central file. First, when a file that is currently being written to reaches its configured size, the newer file overwrites the older one. In other words, the current file is copied to the name of the older file. Second, when storing current data, the system uses a new file created for this purpose. Logging continues only when this procedure has concluded. By copying a file that is not, at the moment, current, the administrator can save it for archiving.

One SAP system can have several centralized system log files. Note, however, that a server can write its data to only one of the possible centralized files. Two processes must be active for communications:

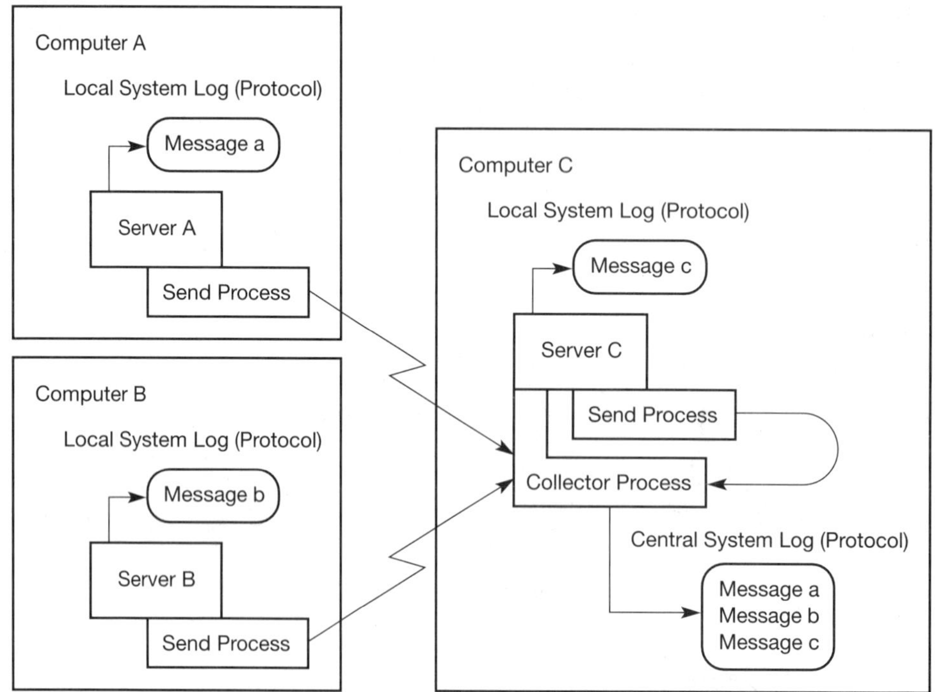

Figure 2.10 Syslog

- The **send process** (**rslgsend**) transmits the data collected up to the send time in intervals. The process then rests until the next scheduled transmission, thus avoiding an unnecessary burden on the system. The intensity of logging activity on the server determines the period of time between transmissions.
- A **collect process** (**rslgcoll**) must be started on the computer writing the centralized log file. This process is required in addition to the send process. It becomes active only when the send process transmits data.

All the parameters in the system profile that control system logging begin with '**rslg/**'. To start both the send and the collect processes, make or activate the appropriate entries in the start profiles of each instance. The entry for a send process might have the following form:

```
_SE                    = se.sap<SID>_DVEBMGS00
Execute_06             = local ln -s -f  $(EXE-DIR)/rslgsend $(_SE)
Start_program_06       = local $(_SE) -F pf=$(PROFILE-
                                               DIR)/<SID>_DVEBMGS00
```

The first line, according to the naming convention, names the send process. The second line uses the operating system (UNIX in the example) to make the executable 'rslgsend' available under then symbolic name given in the first line. The command in the third line starts the process. An almost identical command starts the collect process. Simply substitute the characters '_CO' and 'co' for '_SE' and 'se.'

Evaluation of the system logs takes place via the menu path *Tools → Administration → Monitoring → System log*. The administrator then chooses an analysis of the local or the centralized log file. To limit the information further, consider the following search parameters:

- *from Date/Time*
  to Date/Time
  Date and time entries
- *User*
  Messages referring to a specific user
- *Transaction codes*
  e.g., 'SM31'
- *SAP process*
  SAP processes (e.g., dispatcher), external tasks
- *Problem classes*
  Message types (e.g., status messages, system-kernel messages, etc.)
- *Instance name*
  Messages from a certain instance (for a centralized system log only)
- *Number of pages for individual entries*
  Limitation to the number of pages to be presented: had no bearing on the leader and the format of the display

- *With statistical evaluation*
  Statistical analysis

Additional limitations can be activated by resetting the expert mode via *Setting* → *Expert mode* and then *Setting* → *Wide*. Choose criteria for:

- *Problem classes*
  Additional message types
- *From file/position to file/position*
  Limitations to the log segments (internal to SAP)
- *Terminal*
  Messages from (for example) PCs (single disk computers)
- *Message format (type)*
  Sorting according to system-specific message formats (e.g., for the ABAP/4 processor)
- *Development class*
  Limitation to messages from modules of a development class (e.g., user maintenance)
- *With internal syslog entries*
  Messages from the send and collect processes.

In addition to the search parameters noted above, the administrator can choose other information and options. The menu *Settings* allows for the selection of sorting attributes for messages and the layout of the display. The menu *Environment* offers the following options:

- Check the system clock: used for time-stamping the messages (clocks).
- Authorization check for use of system logs (show authorizations).
- Check values of the system log parameters in the system profile (show SAPPARAM).
- Display status of the collect and send daemons (daemon status).

3 Computing Center Management System

3.1 Tasks and purpose

The **Computing Center Management System (CCMS)** exists as the central tool of the R/3 administrator.

An R/3 administrator must perform complex tasks. She must manage a database containing several gigabytes of data and the R/3 system. She must master not only the typical tasks of database management, but also the entire range of functions offered by the R/3 system.

This section presents the primary responsibilities of the R/3 administrator. It considers the typical tasks of database management only insofar as they affect the R/3 system. Other works handle questions relating to database management independently of R/3 much more thoroughly. See, for example, Hagen and Will (1993).

Chapter 1 presented the architecture of R/3 as well as the structure of and collaboration between the various components of the R/3 system. The RDBMS, of course, plays a key role in the architecture. The functionality and performance of the database ultimately determine the productive value of the entire system. Database management clearly belongs to the essential tasks of an R/3 administrator. As the control station of the R/3 administrator, the CCMS offers tools for database administration and significant additional functions.

The CCMS includes the following areas:

- Performance
- Flow control and optimization (job scheduling)
- Distribution of system resources
- Controlling working modes
- Monitoring of instances
- Scheduling and control of database and log backups
- Background processing
- Event triggering

Performance

An administrator must possess the ability to glean a view of the level of system performance and, if necessary, to regulate the system manually. Both selected parameters and statistics aid him in this task. The R/3 environment uses the term 'monitoring' to describe such activities. Various components determine the response time of an R/3 system: operating system, network, RDBMS and, last but not least, the R/3 software itself. Specific tools permit observation of individual components.

Flow control and optimization (job scheduling)

The administrator recognizes possible bottlenecks during the operation of the R/3 system and must intervene appropriately. The coordination of job flows and the subsequent evaluation of the runs form the central elements of this task.

Distribution of system resources

The R/3 environment requires a relatively high level of system resources such as memory (in every form), disk capacity, backup media, etc. The administrator must have immediate access to information about the load on all instances and the ability to regulate the load manually. An analysis of the work load and its rhythms allows the administrator to configure even the buffer settings (in version 3.x) from the R/3 system. The system reads these settings directly from the profiles.

Controlling working modes

The defined number and type of R/3 processes determine a working mode. In relation to the tasks noted above, an administrator can drive the R/3 system in various modes. Different demands on the system at different times (e.g., day and night) decide the need for working modes. The administrator can define various operating modes that automatically determine the distribution of system resources. Depending on the requirements of users, this process can influence the number and type of R/3 processes.

Monitoring instances

As R/3 systems become larger and larger, more and more distributed systems come into play. The administrator takes responsibility for distributing users among the servers as evenly as possible.

Scheduling and control of database and log backups

Backups increase in importance along with the volume of data in a given system. The R/3 system distinguishes between various types of backups. Complete backups include all the data in a system: they form the starting point for recreating the data in case of loss. Periodic log backups, or incremental backups, contain only the changes made since the last backup. Each RDBMS provides its own tools for additional backup options.

R/3 contains its own planning tool for database backup and other maintenance activities. The tool provides for automatic execution of the backup tasks; R/3 can evaluate the results.

Background processing

R/3 allows system activities to run in the background. By scheduling and processing jobs during periods of light load on the system, the administrator can avoid peak load periods for certain tasks.

Event triggering

The event concept supports triggering runs when previously defined events occur.

To work with the CCMS, a user requires at least the authorization S_RZL_ADM, where the value 1 grants the right to change parameters and 3 allows only display.

Users reach the CCMS via the menu path *Tools → Administration → Computing Center → Management System*. All topics originate at this point. Figure 3.1 displays the menu structure of the CCMS.

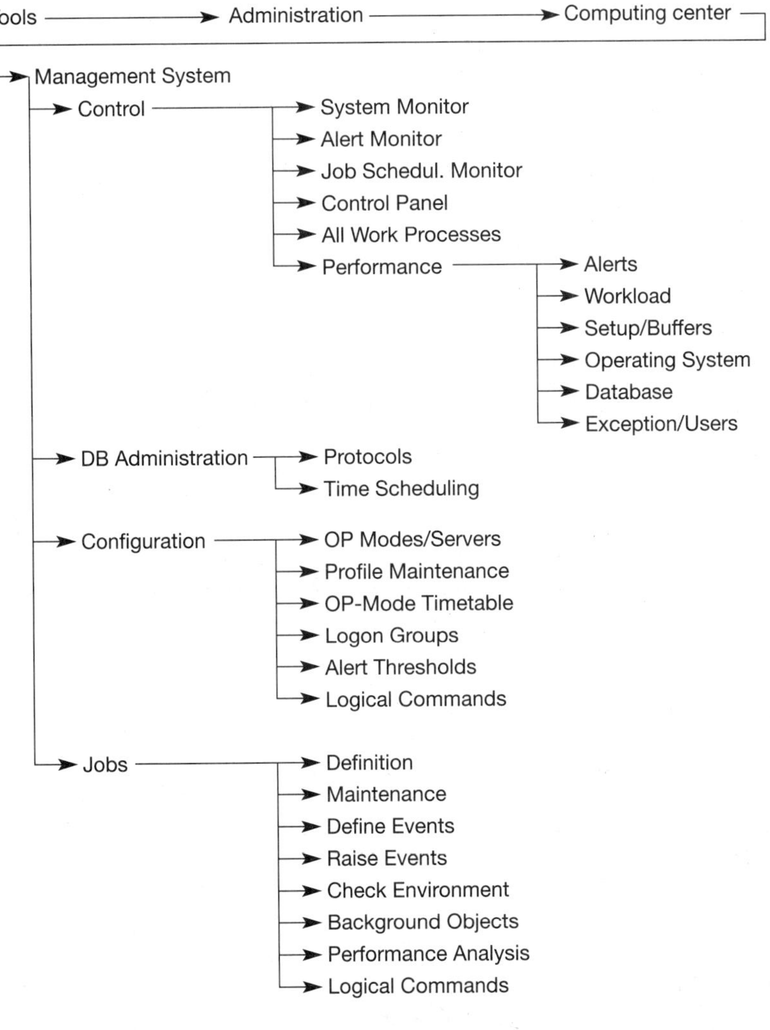

Figure 3.1 Menu tree

3.2 Instances and operation modes

3.2.1 Operation modes

The R/3 system understands an operation mode as the total quantity of all dialog, background, spooler and other processes that the administrator defines for a specific period of time. The administrator can establish various operation modes, depending on the number of tasks required. A distributed system allows allocation of processes to the corresponding servers independently of the tasks involved.

In most cases, defining one operation mode for days and one for nights makes the most sense. A high level of dialog activity characterizes the day mode; a high level of background processes typifies the night mode. The number of processes available to fulfill these tasks mirror this division of labor.

Create operation modes via the menu path *Configuration → Op Modes/Servers* or with transaction code `rz10`. The system displays an exact listing of the defined processes for each mode and computer. Define an operation mode by choosing a unique name for it; the text should describe the purpose and important characteristics of the operation mode.

Permissible types of operation modes:

- M Maintenance,
- P Production,
- T Test.

The entry for the class controls the inclusion of specific instances:

- A all,
- E exclusive.

Always choose 'exclusive' whenever a demand exists for various, time-dependent operation modes for the instance. Time-independence characterizes instances of type A: it supports the same services at all times.

3.2.2 Defining instances

An instance includes all the servers and their processes that belong to an R/3 system and access the same database. Each server represents an instance. The allocation of a host name and an SAP system number identify an instance. The active R/3 processes, as determined in the appropriate profile, define an instance.

Define instances by starting with the menu path *Configuration → Op Modes/Servers*, and continuing with *Instance → Create a new instance*. After entering the name of the computer on which the instance works and the SAP system number, choose *Current Settings* to accept the current settings or, if necessary, to change the settings. Enter a user (normally SAPSID>adm) for starting and stopping the system (*Startup User*) to create the preconditions for automatic starting and stopping of the instance processes.

Storage of these settings completes the definition of an instance's specifications. The system displays a dialog box to allocate the specifications to previously defined operation modes.

The menu option *Consistency Check* helps the user to define operation modes and instances by checking important logical correlations.

With the menu option *OP Modes/Server* the user can display and change the distribution of processes for a given operation mode on each server. Please note that:

- The number of dialog processes derives from the total number of processes allowed, reduced by all other types of processes.
- The total number of background processes for job class A is a true subset of all background processes. Other job classes (see Section 3.6) exist in addition to job class A. Otherwise no background processes would be available to execute the other job classes.
- Lock processes are allocated to exactly one instance, the enqueue server: they cannot be changed in on-line mode.
- The number of spool processes cannot be changed in on-line mode.

3.2.3 Changing the operation mode

A user can change between operation modes either automatically or manually. A time-controlled method provides the most elegant means of changing the operation mode. This method requires allocating the operation modes to a schedule, reached via the menu path *Configuration* → *OP mode timetable*. The available choices include normal and exception operation. For nomal operation allocate the desired operation mode within the 24-hour table displayed.

User the same method to declare exceptions: users must specify the day (date) exactly. Using exception operation modes becomes necessary when, for example, monthly settlement runs require only background processing.

Automatic switching from one operation more to another occurs when a defined point in time has been reached. The system completes processing of all transactions that began before the switch. It allows processing of new transactions only after the switch has taken effect.

Manual switching from one operation mode to another occurs via the menu path *Control* → *Control Panel* → *Choose operation mode*. The display *Control Panel* shows the occurrences and types of problems for each server belonging to the system. It provides the administrator with an overview of the active operation modes, allowing analysis of the problems to begin (see Figure 3.2).

Use *Control* → *System Monitor* to see a graphical overview of the configuration at the present moment. The system displays the active dialog, background and spooler processes and the database server (see Figure 3.3). The display uses various background colors to present the database (plain green) and the individual instances (red = inactive, hatched = active).

```
------------------------------------------------------------------------
| Active op. mode: DAY OPERATION                                       |
------------------------------------------------------------------------
| Standard view                      Sorted by server name             |
------------------------------------------------------------------------
| Server name    |Services| Status   | Alert    | Alert Text           |
------------------------------------------------------------------------
| lw0401_T01_17 | D       | active   | RED      | Freespace Problems   |
| hs0412_T01_17 | D       | active   | YELLOW   | Collector process    |
|               |         |          |          | SAPOSCOL not running |
| hs4001_T01_17 | DBS     | active   | RED      | SQL error 904 occurred |
|               |         |          |          | when executing AB    |
| hs4002_T01_17 | D       | active   | RED      | SQL error 3113 occurred|
|               |         |          |          | when accessing p     |
| hs4003_T01_17 | D       | active   | RED      | SQL error 6110 occurred|
|               |         |          |          | when accessing t     |
| hs4004_T01_17 | DS      | active   | RED      | ArchiveLink (Error from|
|               |         |          |          | the Archive system   |
| hs4005_T01_17 | D       | active   | RED      | SQL error 6110 occurred|
|               |         |          |          | when accessing t     |
| hs4006_T01_17 | D       | active   | RED      | ArchiveLink (Error from|
|               |         |          |          | the archive system   |
| hs4007_T01_17 | D       | active   | RED      | SQL error 6110 occurred|
|               |         |          |          | when accessing t     |
| hs5001_T01_17 | D       | active   | RED      | ArchiveLink: Error from|
|               |         |          |          | the SAP-Kernel &     |
| hs5002_T01_17 | D       | active   | GREEN    | Work process non-standa|
------------------------------------------------------------------------
```

Figure 3.2 Control panel display

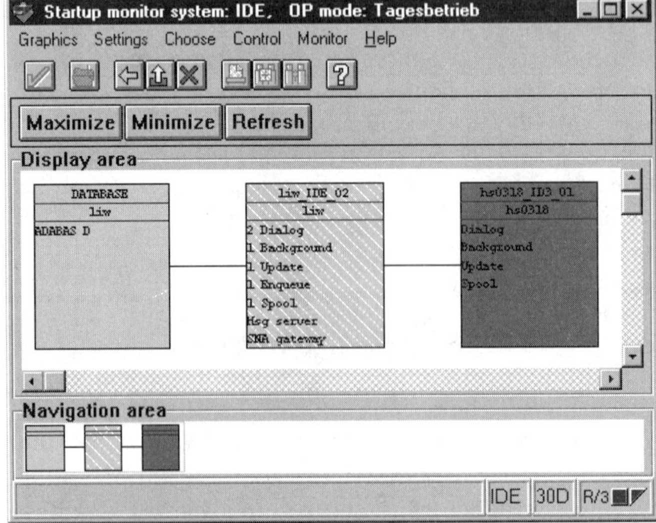

Figure 3.3 Network graphic

3.2.4 Maintaining instance profiles

The instance profile controls the type and size of buffers in addition to the number and type of R/3 processes. Correct buffer settings have extremely important ramifications for system performance. Version 3.0 allows for the configuration of important parameters via menus. A profile maintenance tool also exists. Find the tool via the CCMS menu path *Configuration → Profile Maintenance.*

The profiles created for each instance during installation of an R/3 system require importation and activation before the profile maintenance tool is ready for use. They must be read from the operating system files, stored in the database and made available to the profile maintenance tool (see Figure 3.4).

Use the menu path *Utilities → Import Profiles → Of active servers* as the easiest method of importing all the instance profiles created during an installation. Import individual instance profiles into the database by entering the appropriate file name and directory. Before making any changes to these files, make copies of them. In addition to the profile name, the administration data contains a short description, the name of the operating system file (from which the profile was read), the server and the type and creation date of the profile (see Figure 3.5).

Choosing *Basic maintenance* displays the screen for maintaining the basic parameters of the R/3 system (see Figure 3.6). *Extended maintenance* displays the settings of all parameters that can be changed.

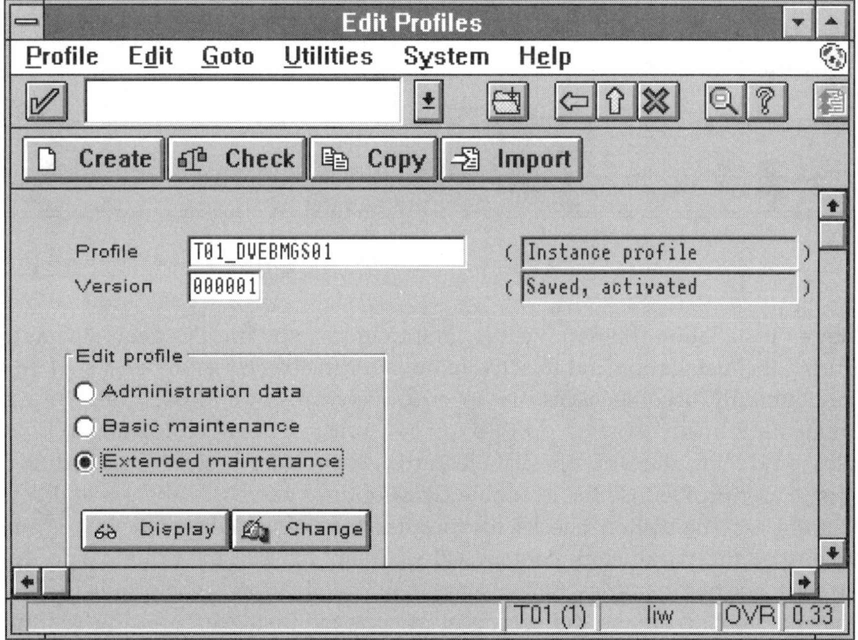

Figure 3.4 Display profiles – initial screen

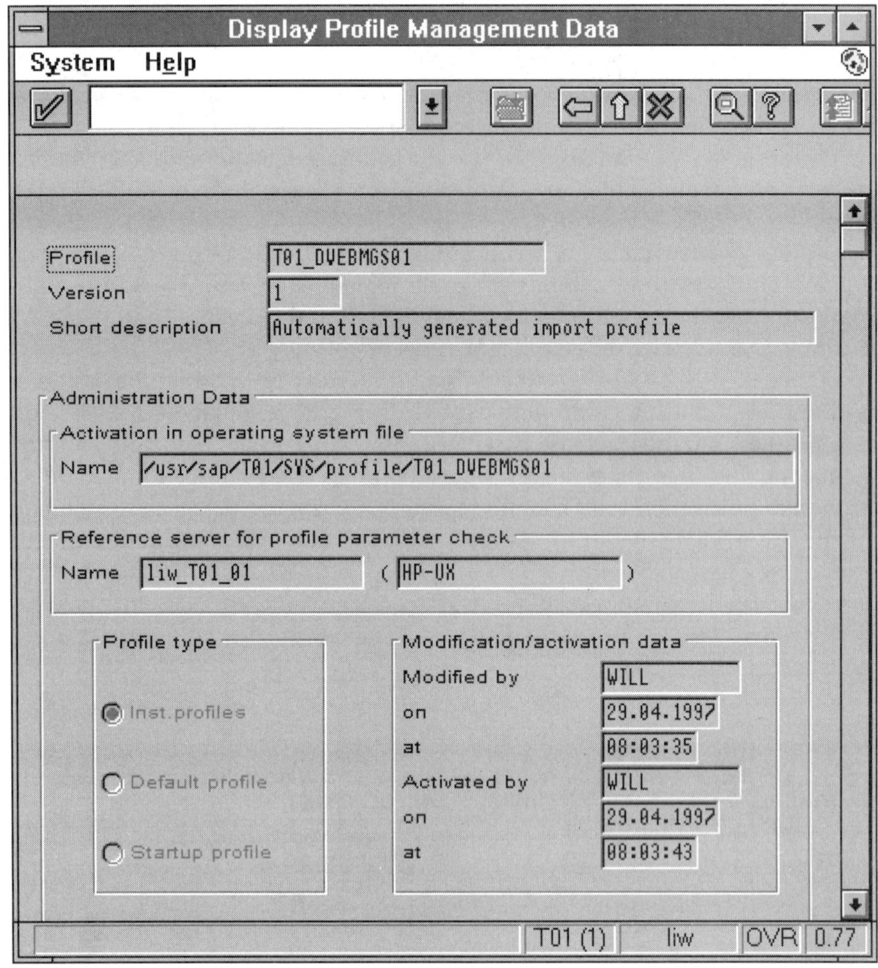

Figure 3.5 Maintenance of administration data

After an installation (R3inst) it is best first to import the profiles generated automatically during the installation and to activate them for the basic maintenance tool. In time, it will undoubtedly become necessary to create special, individual profiles for specific requirements. Already existing profiles can be copied or changed (*Maintain*). *Create* also includes producing the appropriate files at the operating system level. After making changes to any profile, use the available *Check* option to exclude the possibility of basic inconsistencies. The option checks the profiles for logical consistency: it ensures, for example, that the parameters contain values from the correct value range. It checks for the existence of directories. Such features allow activation of the profile for the profile maintenance tool. To make the setting active for the instance currently running, shut down the instance and restart it with the appropriate profile. Perform the shutdown/ restart process manually or from the menu *Control Panel* and the corresponding menu

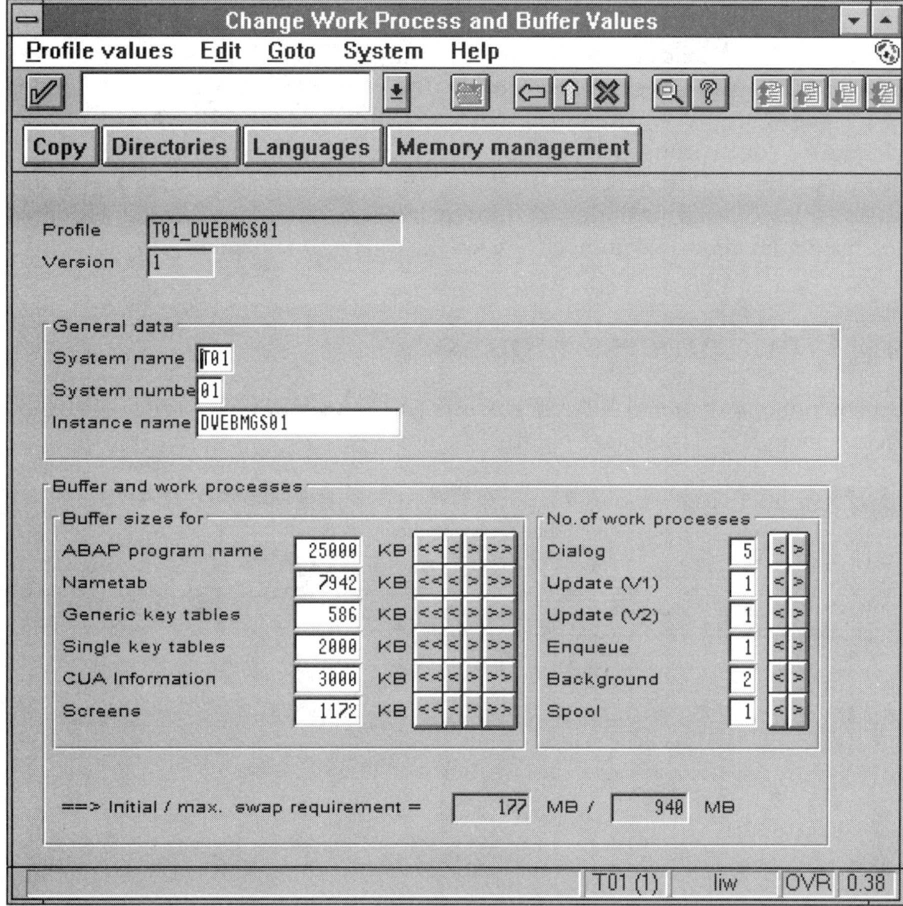

Figure 3.6 Basic maintenance

options. Windows NT drives R/3 as a service: start and stop R/3 via *Control Panel → Services* in the main program group.

Run report RSPARAM to determine the parameters currently active most easily. Chapter 6 describes starting the report.

3.3 Logon groups

Only systems with several application servers require logon groups. These groups allow for the most equitable distribution of user load on the servers. Use the menu path *Configuration → Logon Groups → Goto → Load distribution* or transaction code `smlg` to see a list of the current load on each server. Use the menu path *Goto → User list* to view the distribution of users more exactly.

The servers with the lowest response time are underlayed in color. A system should have as equitable a load as possible as it affects response time. The creation of logon groups joins specific servers into a group. The user chooses a logon group, and the system chooses the server (from the group) best suited for the connection.

Define new logon groups via *Configuration → Logon Groups*. Unique names are given to each group; servers are allocated to those names. Use *Group allocation → Format → Extended* to determine a maximum load for each server (determined by the response time) or the maximum allowable number of users.

3.4 Work process monitor

The menu options *Control → All work processes* (`sm51`) provide an overview of all the work processes in an R/3 System (see Figure 3.7).

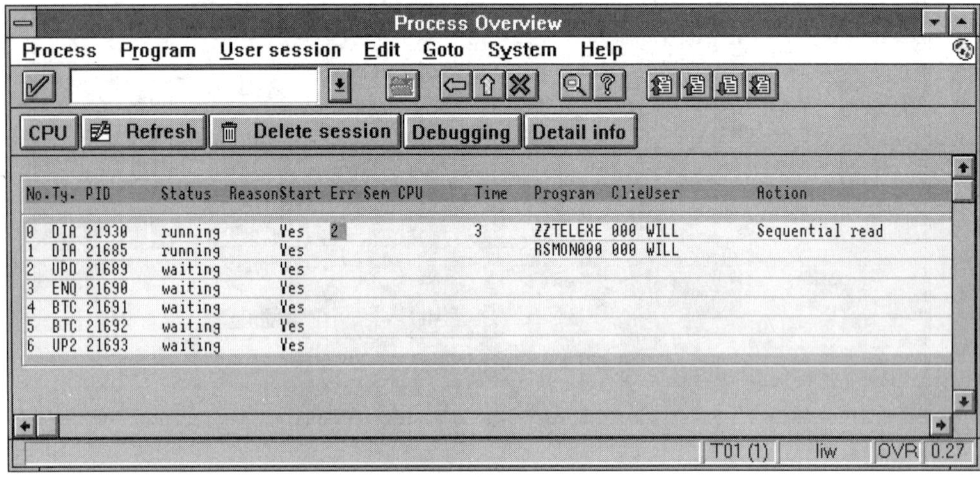

Figure 3.7 Process overview

Choose specific instances with a double click. The system then displays all users logged on to the instance, the report and any critical actions (e.g., table scan) currently running. The CPU time used for the job can also be requested. This information allows the identification of jobs that require long runs and may therefore be critical.

3.5 Handling user exceptions

The registration of irregularities in the R/3 system constitutes an important part of the administrator's work. System parlance defines exceptions as unexpected terminations of transactions caused by system errors, database errors, hardware errors, etc. The R/3 system log keeps track of such occurrences so that the administrator can research their

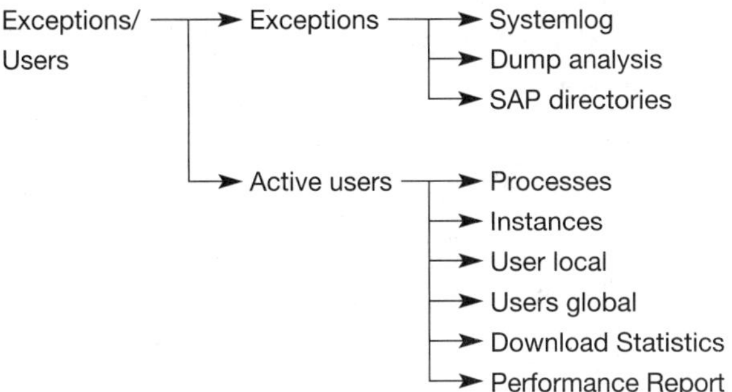

Figure 3.8 Menu tree Exceptions/Users

causes. Section 2.6.2 discussed the system log and its contents. Reach the system log via the menu path *Control → Performance Menu → Exceptions/Users → Exceptions → System log*.

Figure 3.8 displays additional topics dealing with user exceptions and an overview of users.

The following section of a system log (see Figure 3.9) indicates a program termination.

```
--------------------------------------------------------------
|Time     |Ta|User |Tcod|C|Text
--------------------------------------------------------------
|15:59:56|D1|WILL |SE38|K|Database error -3008 at
                            PRE access to
|        |  |     |    | |table SYSMONITOR
|15:59:56|D1|WILL |SE38|K|> INVALID KEYWORD OR MISSING
|15:59:56|D1|WILL |SE38|K|> DELIMITER
|15:59:56|D1|WILL |SE38|W|Perform rollback
|15:59:58|D1|WILL |SE38|T|Run-time error "DBIF_DSQL2_SQL_ERROR"
|15:59:58|D1|WILL |SE38|K|> Short dump "960509 155958 liw WILL "
                          generated.
```

Figure 3.9 System log

A double click on any line provides further details on runtime errors.

To analyze problems, the log displays the error number, the program called (and possible subprograms), termination point and register contents for each runtime error. The system also manages runtime errors separately under the menu option *Dump analysis*.

The menu option *SAP directories* displays information on the R/3 directories the system uses for log or roll files.

Active Users contains various statistics on the activities of logged on users and processes, differentiated according to local and remote systems. These statistics allow the administrator to estimate the load on the entire system and the types of transactions involved. In case of emergency, the administrator can intervene in a specific case and terminate individual reports with the push button *End session*.

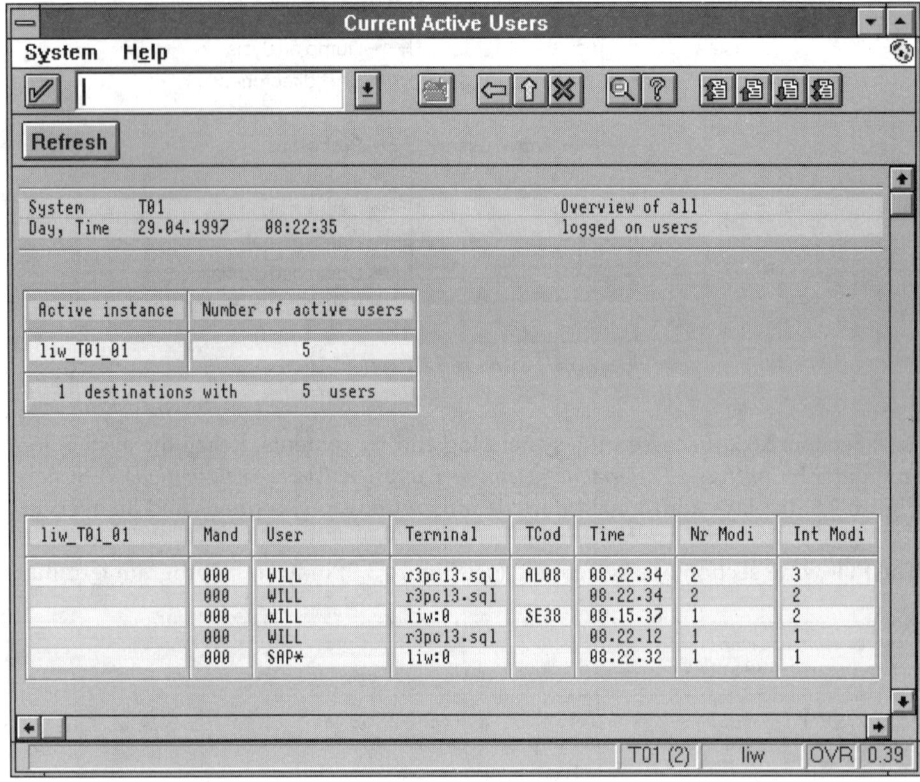

Figure 3.10 User overview

Figure 3.10 displays statistics for a global overview of users, chosen for the computer `liw`. The administrator can thus see which users currently work on which computer and with which transaction. This display can help tremendously to identify a job when searching for performance-critical applications.

3.6 Background processing

3.6.1 Scheduling

The analysis and control of background processing constitutes an essential element of the CCMS. The administrator can run all jobs either on-line or in the background. Allowing jobs to run in the background has an advantage: they can run asynchronously.

The CCMS provides tools for the control and evaluation of background processes. The user must have the appropriate authorizations to use the tools; the administrator, for example, must possess the authorization S_BTCH_ADM. To understand and execute operations such as planning, releasing, projecting and logging, the user must possess at least the authorization S_BTCH_JOB. The special user SAP*, seen by SAP as the administrator for all clients, possesses this authorization as a matter of course. Please note that the required authorizations depend on the version; consider the possibility of change from version to version.

The administrator can choose between time-dependent or event-triggered run activation. R/3 has its own job scheduler to implement these options. Schedule jobs via the menu path *Jobs* → *Define* or with transaction code `sm36`.

A unique name identifies a job throughout the system. The job class determines its priority for processing. Choose from the following job classes:

- A Highest priority
  For jobs ensuring the ability of the R/3 system to function
- B Medium priority
  For periodic jobs
- C Lowest priority (default)
  For single programs to create lists (for example)

The administrator can change the priority of jobs as desired. Other users work with priority C as a default value. Within each job class, processing takes place first for those jobs with an established, specific target system (computer name). The priority also determines distribution of system resources. If several jobs require processing at the same time, the system first works on the job with the highest priority.

The administrator can also determine whether a given time or an event triggers processing of a job. The system establishes time-triggers according to date and time or as *Immediate*. Entry of an interval permits the periodic repetition of time-controlled jobs. Enter the desired start date, then check on *Periodic job* and define the repetition period. If, for example, the next scheduled run would occur on a holiday, the definition of periodic jobs allows for exception rules. Define exceptions with the SAP factory calendar, reached via the menu path *Tools* → *Business Engineering* → *Customizing* → *Implement. Projects* → *SAP Reference IMG* → *Global Settings* → *Maintain Calendar* then check *Factory Calendar*, or use transaction code `sft3`. The system allows definitions that cause execution of the job regardless of the holiday, process the job a working day earlier or later or omit execution altogether. To choose one of these options, enter the start date, the repetition period and then the type of behavior desired at an exception for the specific SAP factory calendar.

A job can consist of multiple steps; define each step with the push button *Steps*. Definition of a step requires entry of the program to be executed and its classification. Both ABAP programs and external programs (those running in the operating system) can be scheduled. User allocations can be changed during creation of the steps. The system allocates job runs to the user and client who performed the scheduling as a default. Note that schedules created by user DDIC under client 000 do not use this default. Those schedules are valid for all clients. Consider collectors, which gather information about the entire system, as a typical illustration.

An example:

In the operating system, the process saposcol holds responsibility for collecting data used in the creation of statistics about the load on computer resources. The background process COLLECTOR_FOR_PERFORMANCEMONITOR performs a similar function within the R/3 system. Because the job is client-independent, it must be planned under client 000 as DDIC. In the broadest sense, the system cannot function completely without the job. It therefore belongs to job class A. Use the push button *Steps* to allocate the corresponding ABAP program (rscoll00 for the performance monitor). After storing the data, choose and save the start date (*Immediate*) and the repetition period (1 hour). Job scheduling is complete when the job has been saved.

3.6.2 Event triggering

R/3 provides event triggering of background jobs in addition to time-dependent scheduling. A typical example is the event-triggered job RDDIMPDP, particularly important during import and update runs. With event-triggering, a job runs when a defined event has occurred, rather than at a particular time. For example: the event SAP_TRIGGER_RDDIMPDP triggers job RDDIMPDP.

Additional pre-defined events are shown in Table 3.1.

Table 3.1 Pre-defined events

Event identifier	*Description*
SAP_BRANCHE_IMPORT	Industry sector import
SAP_DBA_ACTION	Data copying completed
SAP_EIS_DATA_IMPORT	EIS data copying completed
SAP_END_OF_JOB	
SAP_LANGUAGE_FILL	Language filling
SAP_LANGUAGE_IMPORT	Language import
SAP_NEW_CONTROL_RECIPES	New control recipes created
SAP_NEW_PROCESS_MESSAGES	New process messages received
SAP_OPMODE_SWITCH	Switch operation mode
SAP_QEVENT	Event at the start of a batch job via QAPI
SAP_SYSTEM_START	
SAP_SYSTEM_STOP	
SAP_TEST	
SAP_TRIGGER_RDDIMPDP_CLIENT	
SAP_TRIGGER_RDDIMPDP	Event to start transport program RDDIMPDP

Use the menu path *Jobs → Define Events* to see an overview of all events known to the system. Starting at this menu option the user can define other events and thus trigger individual actions.

A table stores the defined events. When scheduling jobs, bear in mind that just such an event can trigger a job. When defining the job, enter the name of the event, as given in the table, as the trigger. The event scheduler registers the occurrence of an event and causes the required actions.

Start the event scheduler on the computer within the R/3 system given in the parameter rdisp/btcname in the start profile.

Initiation of an event must occur with the help of the program sapevt. Find the program in the directory /usr/sap/<SID>/SYS/exe/run (default location). Calling this program informs the R/3 system that a specific event has occurred. The call uses the following syntax:

```
sapevt <event_name> [-p <parameter>] [-t] [pf=<profile_name>
      | name = <SID> no = <instance>]
```

The option `p` enables the transfer of parameters that classify the work area, such as FI, for example. The option `t` creates a log named dev_evt in the calling directory. The log contains further information on the circumstances of execution. The R/3 system affected can be determined by a profile (TPPARAM file) or by the name of the database <SAPSID> and the instance number. Within the R/3 system the call of the function BP_EVENT_RAIS triggers an event (see Section 6.10.3 on function modules).

The menu system also integrates a function named *Raise Event*, which triggers a given event immediately.

The transport system, for example, activates the event-triggered job RDDIMPDP. To trigger the job the program tp calls sapevt with the event SAP_TRIGGER_RDDIMPDP.

3.6.3 Starting external programs

Job administration also enables calls of external programs. We will examine this method is detail, as it forms the basis of database backups from within the R/3 system.

CPIC calls start external programs. During job scheduling, the parameters and the target system are transferred along with the name of the program to be started. It is also possible to run external programs on a specific computer, for example the database server. Several preconditions must be met for this mechanism to function properly. The user must provide the complete path to the program to be run at the start of the job. If the path of the R/3 user <sid> contains the access path, full entry is not required. On the SAP side, the program sapxpg controls runs of external programs. Accordingly, make sure that the search path of <sid>adm contains the path to this program (/usr/sap/<SID>/SYS/exe/run).

The most important precondition for the ability of CPIC calls to function is an active gateway. Make sure that the installation program R3inst has installed the appropriate software. The installation program also makes the corresponding entries in the services files (for UNIX systems /etc/services and wint35\system32\drivers\etc \services for

Windows NT systems) such as

```
sapgw<instance>    33<instance>/tcp
```

For example:

```
sapgw00          3300/tcp
sapgw01          3301/tcp
sapgw02          3302/tcp
```

If the entries are not present, add them with an editor. Although the first versions of 2.2 required an explicit release of the gateway process in the parameter file START_DVEBMGS<instance>, it is now started automatically. Define it in the default profile, DEFAULT.PFL. A check of the processes and the start protocol of R/3 in the root directory of user <sid>adm determines whether or not the gateway is actually active (i.e., has been started). The gateway process is called gwrd.

In the event of an error, the gateway process writes a message in the log file. For example, the file /usr/sap/<SID>/DVEBMGS<instance>/work/dev_rd might contain the following entry:

```
--------------------------------------------------------
trc file: 'dev_rd', trc level: 1, release: '30C'
--------------------------------------------------------
***LOG S00=> GwInitReader, gateway started () [gwxxrd.c 0801]
*** ERROR => R3ALLC: timeout, partner LU: sqlram2, TP:
  sapxpg [gwr3cpic 1359]
*** ERROR => R3ALLC: conv ID: 69083521 [gwr3cpic 1361]
```

3.6.4 Analyzing the logs

The menu path *Jobs* → *Maintain* (sm37) provides an overview of which jobs are scheduled for which user. All jobs have a specific processing status:

- Scheduled — All job data saved.
- Released — Data has been checked or, if necessary, changed. The job can be executed.
- Ready — Waiting for system resources to begin execution.
- Active — Is currently being processed.
- Cancelled — Processing terminated because of an error.
- Finished — The job was completed successfully.

A double click with the left mouse button on a given job displays the job log for active, finished or cancelled jobs. The log contains important information used to identify the causes of any errors.

Follow the menu path *Control* → *Job Scheduling* to obtain a graphic presentation of the processes related to specific computers or times. The graphic allows the administrator to see the status of individual jobs on the server (see Figure 3.11). The chart uses various colors to highlight different conditions. Use the menu or a mouse click from within the graphic to see the job logs and the properties of individual jobs.

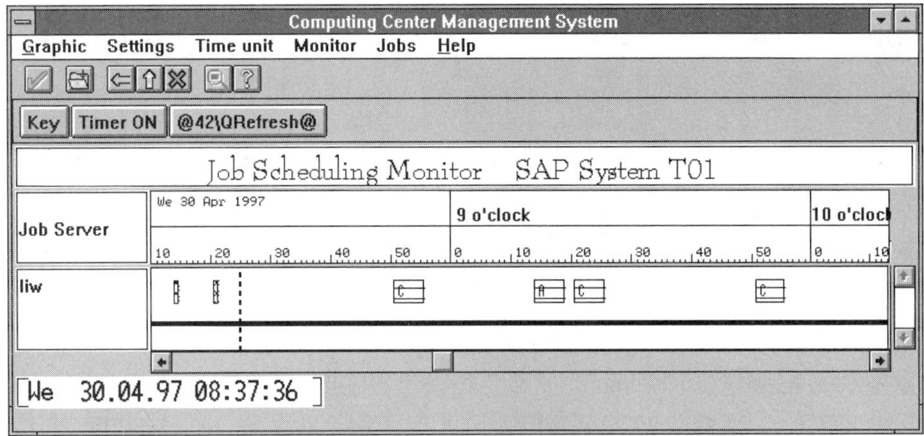

Figure 3.11 Graphic job monitor

```
Job selection   on    05.06.1996  at  11:02:47

Number of jobs read             86
Displayed                        5

Display Criteria

Job name: *           from  05.03.1996    00:00:00
   Active             : X
User: *               to    05.06.1996    11:02:47
Ready                 : X
Cancelled             : X

-------------------------------------------------------------------
|User Job Name                                |Status
|Start                          |Length       |Delayed        |
|Date                 | Time    |in sec       |in sec         |
-------------------------------------------------------------------
|COLLECTOR_FOR_PERFORMANCEMONITOR|DDIC        |Ready
|05.03.1996           |11:00:34   | 1         |  34           |
|COLLECTOR_FOR_PERFORMANCEMONITOR|DDIC        |Ready
|05.04.1996           |17:00:12   | 11        |  12           |

|COLLECTOR_FOR_PERFORMANCEMONITOR|DDIC        |Ready
|05.04.1996           |20:00:19   |  0        |  19           |
|DBA:SAVEALL__________@12:00/5007|WILL        |Ready
|05.03.1996           |12:02:03   | 63        | 123           |
|DBA:SAVELOGSEG_______@00:00/6007|WILL  |Cancelled
|05.04.1996           |00:03:01   |  0        | 181           |
-------------------------------------------------------------------
```

Figure 3.12 Performance analysis

3.6.5 Performance analysis for background jobs

The job menu also provides the administrator with tools to evaluate statistically the length, status and delayed start of the background jobs currently running. Especially for periodic jobs, these statistics make it much easier to search for temporary bottlenecks. The excerpt from these statistics in Figure 3.12 displays the collector for statistical data and two save jobs. It indicates that on May 4, at 17:00, the collector ran for a longer than average time.

3.6.6 External commands

As of R/3 version 3.0, two methods of starting external programs exist: directly by program name or by external commands. An external command contains not only the name of the program to be started on the operating system, but also parameters and other properties. Table SXPGCOTABE controls the required allocations between the logical command and the external program. Delivery currently includes the commands shown in Table 3.2.

Table 3.2 Pre-defined logical commands

Command name	*OS*	*Type*	*OS command*	*Last changed by*
ARCAUTO	ANYOS	public	arcauto	DDIC
BRARCHIVE	ANYOS	public	brarchive	DDIC
BRBACKUP	ANYOS	public	brbackup	DDIC
INFARCEXE	ANYOS	public	infarcexe	DDIC
INFUPDSTAT	ANYOS	public	infupdstat	DDIC
SAPDBA	ANYOS	public	sapdba	DDIC
UPDCOL	ANYOS	public	updcol	DDIC
XBACKUP	ANYOS	public	xbackup	DDIC

These programs find their primary use during weekly planning of periodic, administrative actions. One typical use of external commands is data backup; note that the commands are specific to a database. Use the menu path *Jobs → External Commands* directly to execute the commands; the database documentation provides information on the effects of the commands and their parameters.

3.6.7 Maintenance jobs

Evaluating the performance and maintenance of the R/3 system requires regular execution of a reorganization report. The report usually runs in the background. Among other matters, these jobs ensure that the system deletes unneeded logs. These

Table 3.3 Reorganization jobs

Report	*Meaning*	*Period*
RSBTCDEL	Deletes all logs for jobs executed successfully. The variant determines the number of days after which logs are deleted.	Daily
RSBPSTDE	Clears the runtime statistics for background jobs.	Monthly
RSBDCREO	Deletes the logs of batch input processes.	As required
RSPO0041	Deletes spool objects.	Daily, depends on printer load
RSSNAPDL	Deletes runtime entries.	Daily
RSM13002	Deletes update requests if automatic deletion has been deactivated.	Daily

jobs often have pre-defined variants. Table 3.3 shows the most important, application-dependent jobs.

These jobs are all client-independent and do not require any special authorizations.

Every R/3 system should also regularly schedule RSBPCOLL and RSCOLL00 (see Table 3.4).

Table 3.4 Statistics collectors

Report	*Meaning*	*Period*
RSBPCOLL	Maintains the statistical data for jobs that run periodically. Determines the average runtime.	Daily
RSCOLL00	Collects general system statistics; scheduling requires user DDIC in client 000.	Hourly

An important job for the SD (Sales and Distribution) application is RSNAST00. This job allows printing of messages sent within the application. If necessary, make sure that RSNAST00 runs regularly: every half hour, for example.

3.7 Performance

3.7.1 Basics

Any judgment of system performance must include the following factors:

- Performance cannot be evaluated apart from transactions,
- Performance is a property with its own history,
- Only relative comments can be made.

Within the R/3 environment, several interrelated components contribute to the runtime speed of the system: the operating system, the network, the RDBMS and the R/3 software. Determining which component causes problems at any given time can therefore often demand difficult and intensive research. This section clarifies the most important and generally valid criteria.

To deal with the historical aspect of performance, various collectors work within the R/3 system. The collectors run at defined intervals to accumulate data and store it in a special table. The program saposcol collects data on the load to operating system resources (main memory, CPU, etc.) and the network. The program starts automatically when the R/3 system is first started. It remains active even when the R/3 system has stopped. Servers without R/3 work processes use the program rfoscol as a substitute for saposcol.

Report rscoll00 runs within the R/3 system as a background job. Under the name COLLECTOR_FOR_PERFORMANCEMONITOR or SAP_COLLECTOR_FOR_PERFORMANCE, it collects data on the load to system resources. In the process it starts other reports coordinated in table TCOLL. Maintain the table TCOLL with the menu for table maintenance, `sm31`.

The report collects data at regular intervals and writes it to the table cluster (see Section 5.3.3) MONI. Only R/3 tools can read these table structures. The table MONI always grows and therefore requires regular reorganization (clearing). Use the menu path *Control* → *Performance Menu* → *Workload* → *Analysis* → *Goto* → *Parameters* → *Performance database* to maintain parameters that reorganize the table MONI. The user can override the default settings and determine how many and which should be cleared or saved after a given time. The reorganization essentially means deletion of obsolete statistics. It has nothing to do with the technical database reorganization required by some RDBMS.

3.7.2 Workload

According to its configuration, the R/3 system offers various tools for evaluating performance. Use the option *Performance Menu* within the CCMS (transaction code `stun`) to reach all the tools. A general examination of performance will probably always begin with a check of the overall workload. The concept of workload includes statistics on the general and specific use of buffers as well as on response time as seen from various viewpoints. Accordingly, the menu tree for these functions is very complex. Figure 3.13 seeks to make navigation easier for the user. The figure illustrates access only via the menus. Separate push buttons often make indirect access to different branches possible.

The following remarks treat the most important statistics for the 'normal' needs of the administrator.

The menu option *Workload* contains two functions. The first, *Analysis*, provides for the evaluation of various work areas for a given server. The second, *Statistics records*, presents the response time for the local system.

Analysis displays all the servers belonging to a system. It supports calls for statistics taken at variable times on all the computers comprising the system. The function first

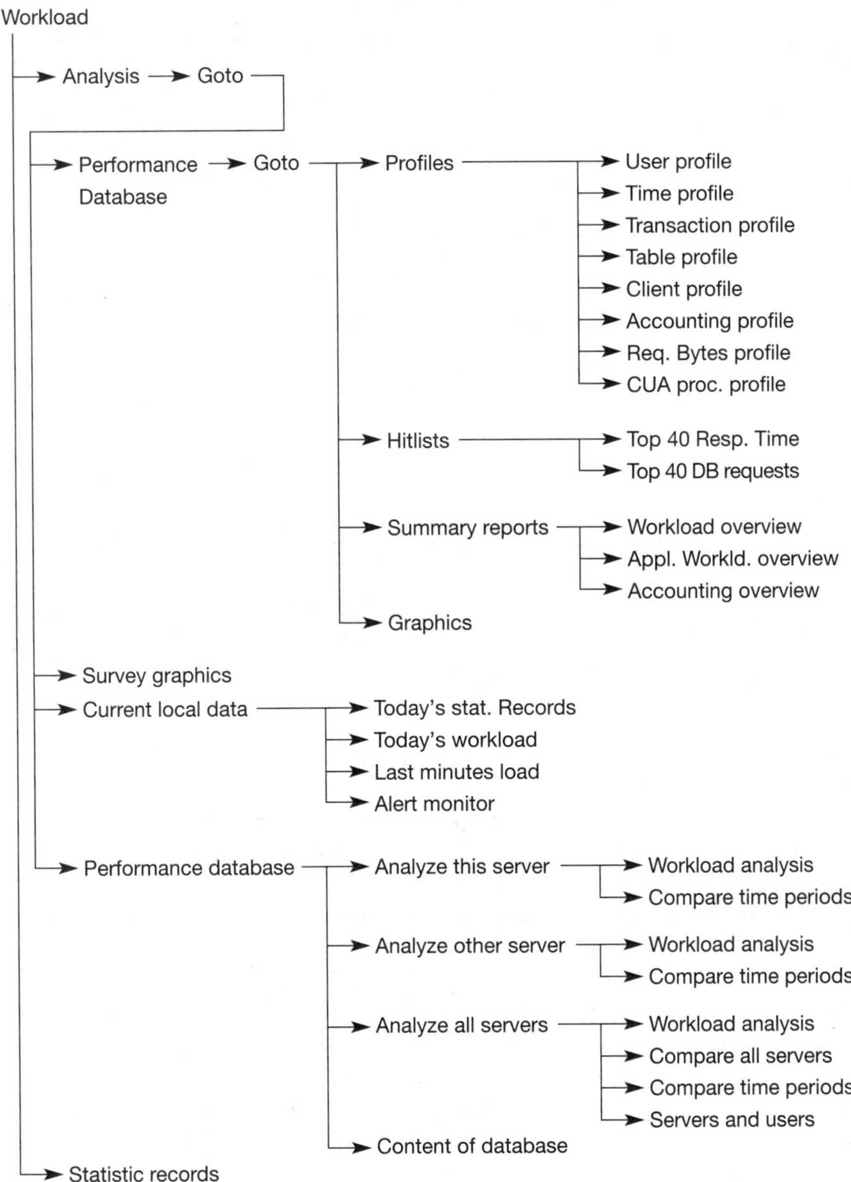
Workload
Analysis
Goto
Performance Database
Goto
Profiles
User profile
Time profile
Transaction profile
Table profile
Client profile
Accounting profile
Req. Bytes profile
CUA proc. profile
Hitlists
Top 40 Resp. Time
Top 40 DB requests
Summary reports
Workload overview
Appl. Workld. overview
Accounting overview
Graphics
Survey graphics
Current local data
Today's stat. Records
Today's workload
Last minutes load
Alert monitor
Performance database
Analyze this server
Workload analysis
Compare time periods
Analyze other server
Workload analysis
Compare time periods
Analyze all servers
Workload analysis
Compare all servers
Compare time periods
Servers and users
Content of database
Statistic records

Figure 3.13 Workload menu tree

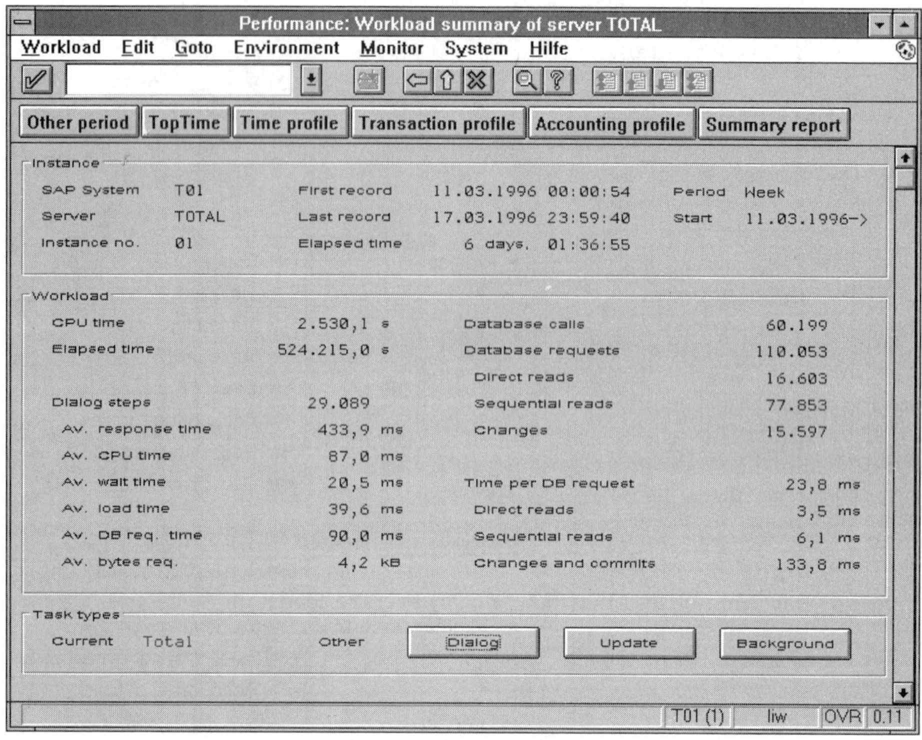

Figure 3.14 Workload analysis (transaction st03*)*

displays the average response time of the components. Figure 3.14 shows the statistics for one month.

An R/3 system should have an *average response time* of about 1 second. This value, of course, depends on the computer, the operating system and the system load. Regard the values given here only as approximations.

The relation between the individual components plays a decisive role in the analysis. The *average DB request time* should not make up more than 40% of the average response time. In a well-functioning system a further 40% of the average response time consists of CPU time. The *average wait time* indicates how long the user had waited for the allocation of a dialog process. If this value seems high (especially in relation to the other value), start another dialog process to reduce it. The time it takes to load and generate the corresponding ABAP and CUA programs in addition to the screen elements determines the *average load time*. If not already loaded during installation (*ABAP Loads*) or manually by generating a report, the system generates an intermediate code (see Section 6.1) before processing any transactions. A newly installed system can therefore have longer load times. The system needs some time to become stable. If developers use the system to develop new programs, the load time increases. These programs frequently require regeneration during development. In any case, however, the average load time should not make up more than 10% of the total response time.

These statistics can be produced for any server in the system. When comparing various servers, deviations from the average often appear. The analysis provided here allows for a more thorough examination of time allocations. The statistics provide a first impression of the system performance.

The push button *Top Time* produces a list of the 40 transactions or programs with the highest response times in the R/3 system. By analyzing the context of the response times for the slowest transactions, the administrator can limit the scope of the problem and find hints for better performance. The function *Transaction profile* provides the context of the execution times for the forty most frequently used transactions.

The function *Time profile* uncovers time-dependent bottlenecks. It displays the average response and wait time for specific periods of time. This analysis provides a view of times of the day that have a particularly heavy type of load. If the differences are particularly large, reduce them by splitting the work among various operation modes with different profiles. Running certain processes as background jobs when the load is lighter, at night, for example, can also contribute to a solution to the problem.

The function *Task type profile* displays how the individual services work. Consider some rules for the user's most obvious service, dialog. The average response time should be about 1 second. The CPU and RDBMS should each make up about 40% of that time. An average wait time of less than 1% and an average load time of less than 10% are acceptable. Large deviations from these values indicate problems.

In a well-functioning system, the average response time for the database lasts about 10 milliseconds. *Direct reads* should take place in less than 10 milliseconds. Sequential read-processes take more time by definition: values under 40 milliseconds are acceptable. For *Changes/Commits* times under 25 milliseconds are admissible.

The *Summary Report* activates a summary of the essential aspects of statistics. Figures 3.15 through 3.17 display excerpts from this list that contain the statistics created for a one-week period. The display of these values over a given period of time provides a good view of system load throughout the course of a day. If the times regularly peak at certain times of the day, the use of various operation modes may help solve the problem. Figure 3.15 clearly indicates the lower system load at night. These times would provide reserves for background processing.

After the summary, the report lists the values according to instance, to allow identification of the 'weakest' instance. Figure 3.16 shows that the response times for background processing are above the average for the entire system.

The display of system load over time provides information helpful to the definition of operation modes. The excerpt in Figure 3.17 shows heightened activity between 6 and 7 o'clock. Late night hours have a much lighter load. The statistics therefore indicate that the response time is much longer between 6 and 7 o'clock in the morning than in the late hours of the night.

The *Transaction/Report Profile* shows that in addition to background spool activities, editing required a good portion of system resources. It follows from this information that development activities took place on the system.

The report then lists in descending order the 20 jobs and transaction with the longest response time and highest database activity. The ABAP collector program rscoll00, for example, collects data for database statistics (see Section 3.7.1). This program is

```
System 00 E25    Server sqlhp9    Analyzed period      Week 04.19.1996->
---------------------------------------------------------------------
SUMMARY FOR TASKTYPE     *TOTAL*
---------------------------------------------------------------------
Dialog steps                 7,334        First record time        00:00:15
   with DB calls             4,122        First record day       01.09.1995
   waiting > 50 ms             746        Last record time         18:06:43
   with roll in              1,238        Last record day        01.11.1995

                                          Elapsed time          208,510.0  s
Avg response time          1,294.7  ms    Response time          10,228.6  s
 CPU time                    301.1  ms     CPU time               2,208.1  s
   wait time                  99.1  ms       wait time              727.0  s
   load time                 217.2  ms       load time            1,592.9  s
   DB request time           255.5  ms       DB request time      3,340.3  s
DB calls                   171,291
DB requests                190,621       Time per DB request         17.5  ms
   Dir. reads               27,956          Dir. reads               14.9  ms
   Seq. reads              117,898          Seq. reads                6.6  ms
   Changes                  44,767          Changes/Commits          48.0  ms
----------------------------------------------------------------------
Response time distribution --Cumulated dialog counts by time of day in %
sec.       <0.1    <0.2    <0.3    <0.4    <0.5    <1.0    <2.0    <3.0    <10
----------------------------------------------------------------------
|00--06     24.7 | 73.7 | 74.4 | 74.4 | 74.8 | 94.4 | 99.4 | 99.8 |100.0
|06--07     24.8 | 74.0 | 74.8 | 74.8 | 75.2 | 95.0 | 99.2 |100.0 |100.0
|07--08     24.2 | 73.8 | 74.2 | 74.6 | 75.0 | 95.5 | 98.0 | 99.2 |100.0
|08--09     23.4 | 65.6 | 72.9 | 74.0 | 76.0 | 87.5 | 94.3 | 94.8 | 98.4
...
|21--24     42.0 | 83.8 | 84.0 | 84.0 | 84.0 | 97.7 | 98.1 | 98.6 | 99.5
----------------------------------------------------------------------
Response time distribution -- Dialog counts by time of day and resp.time
sec.       <0.1    <0.2    <0.3    <0.4    <0.5    <1.0    <2.0    <3.0    <10
----------------------------------------------------------------------
|00--06      347 |  689 |    9 |    1 |    5 |  275 |   70 |    6 |    3
|06--07       60 |  119 |    2 |    0 |    1 |   48 |   10 |    2 |    0
|07--08       59 |  121 |    1 |    1 |    1 |   50 |    6 |    3 |    2
|08--09       45 |   81 |   14 |    2 |    4 |   22 |   13 |    1 |    7
...
|21--24      179 |  178 |    1 |    0 |    0 |   58 |    2 |    2 |    4
----------------------------------------------------------------------
```

Figure 3.15 Excerpts from the weekly summary report – Part 1

particularly slow in terms of both database requests and response time. The report allows for the determination of critical flows in a production system.

Starting with these statistical overviews, analysis in individual areas can proceed more thoroughly. The overviews have already identified certain weaknesses that serve as the starting point for a more exact analysis. In all cases, however, check the R/3 buffers and their loads.

```
System 00 E25    Server sqlhp9    Analyzed period     Week 04.19.1996->
-----------------------------------------------------------------------
SUMMARY FOR TASKTYPE     BCKGRD
-----------------------------------------------------------------------
Dialog steps                   3,532     First record time      00:00:15
   with DB calls               3,531     First record day       01.09.1995
   waiting > 50 ms               377     Last record time       18:05:35
   with roll in                  774     Last record day        01.10.1995

                                         Elapsed time           208,510.0  s
Avg response time          2,289.0  ms   Response time            8,084.9  s
 CPU time                    508.0  ms    CPU time                1,794.2  s
   wait time                 108.9  ms      wait time               384.8  s
   load time                 305.2  ms      load time             1,078.0  s
   DB request time           856.5  ms      DB request time       3,025.1  s
DB calls                   160,912
DB requests                173,087       Time per DB request        17.5  ms
   Dir. reads               25,440          Dir. reads              14.7  ms
   Seq. reads              103,281          Seq. reads               6.7  ms
   Changes                  44,366          Changes/Commits         44.2  ms

-----------------------------------------------------------------------
SUMMARY FOR TASKTYPE     DIALOG
-----------------------------------------------------------------------
-----------------------------------------------------------------------
SUMMARY FOR TASKTYPE     SPOOL
-----------------------------------------------------------------------
```

Figure 3.16 Excerpts from the weekly summary report – Part 2

```
System 00 E25    Server sqlhp9   Analyzed period    Week 19.04.1996->
Sorted by  Time of day
-----------------------------------------------------------------------
TIME PROFILE
             Dialog  Resp.     CPU       Wait      DB req.   Req.    DB
Time         steps   time      time      time      time      kByte   req.
                     avg(ms)   avg(ms)   avg(ms)   avg(ms)
-----------------------------------------------------------------------
|*TOTAL*     7,291|  1,398|      302|     100|     457|        190,227 |
-----------------------------------------------------------------------
|00--06      1,405|    329|      148|      13|     101|          9,939 |
|06--07        242|    313|      150|       9|      99|          1,719 |
|07--08        244|    347|      151|      11|     105|          1,729 |
|08--09        192|  1,559|      238|      50|     171|          1,782 |
...
|21--24        426|    353|      127|      25|      60|          2,021 |
-----------------------------------------------------------------------
System 00 E25    Server sqlhp9    Analyzed period      Week 19.04.1996->
Sorted by Dialog steps
-----------------------------------------------------------------------
```

Figure 3.17 Excerpts from the weekly summary report – Part 3

```
TRANSACTION/REPORT PROFILE              sorted by dialog steps
Program or   Dialog  Resp.      CPU       Wait       DB req.  Req.     DB
Tcode        steps   time       time      time       time     kByte    req.
                     avg(ms)    avg(ms)   avg(ms)    avg(ms)
---------------------------------------------------------------------------
|*TOTAL*     7,291|    1,398|      302|    100|       457| 137,421|190,227 |
---------------------------------------------------------------------------
|Bckgrd      3,494|    2,304|      511|    110|       864| 104,297|172,693 |
|Spool       1,861|      373|       14|    162|        24|      58|     31 |
|Rep_Edit      835|      287|      139|      2|        19|   5,337|  1,840 |
|RSSQD006      299|      429|      205|      5|        31|   3,246|  1,565 |
|DB13          203|      737|      130|     44|        68|   1,545|  2,548 |
|SE01          125|    1,331|      309|     51|       292|   4,340|  7,951 |
|SE38          115|      455|      158|     31|        31|   1,144|    723 |
...
---------------------------------------------------------------------------
System 00 E25     Server sqlhp9    Analyzed period    Week 19.04.1996->
Sorted by Dialog steps
---------------------------------------------------------------------------

TOP DIALOG STEPS BY RESPONSE TIME     ( out of 7334 )

                                                Response Dispatch CPU
 End time Tcode  Program  T Scr. Wp User        time(ms) time(ms) time(ms)
---------------------------------------------------------------------------
|09.01          (B)STRTR B 4005  5 SAPSYS     |1748503 |1748128 |339,770 |
|10.01          RDDDIC1L B 4005  5 DDIC       |863,524 |863,524 |249,130 |
|10.01          RDDEXECL B 4005  5 DDIC       |585,689 |585,689 |145,050 |
|09:30:06       RSCOLL00 B 4005  4 DDIC       |279,860 |279,860 | 17,720 |
|10.01          RDDMASGL B 4005  5 DDIC       |275,906 |275,906 | 72,960 |
|10.01          RSCOLL00 B 4005  4 DDIC       |210,870 |210,870 | 12,900 |
|10.01          (B)STRTR B 4005  5 SAPSYS     |154,496 |154,492 |  8,740 |
|16:41:11       (B)SCHDL B 4004  0 SAPSYS     |124,529 |     171 |     50 |
|09.01 SE38     RSUMOD01 D 0120  0 SAP*       |121,179 |121,178 |  2,070 |
|10.01          SAPMSSY6 B 1100  0 SAPSYS     |115,670 |115,595 | 36,800 |
|10.01          (B)EVDRI B 4007  0 SAPSYS     | 87,051 | 87,049 | 32,100 |
|10.01          RSCOLL00 B 4005  4 DDIC       | 85,366 | 85,366 | 13,160 |
...
---------------------------------------------------------------------------
.... only top 20 entries are displayed

TOP DIALOG STEPS BY DATABASE REQUESTS

 End time Tcode  Program  T Scr. Wp User          DB time Readtime Chg.time
---------------------------------------------------------------------------
|18.04       (B)STRTR B 4005  5 SAPSYS      1164318 |291,623 |817,159  |
|18.04       RDDEXECL B 4005  5 DDIC        107,463 | 79,782 | 13,008  |
|10.04       RDDDIC1L B 4005  5 DDIC        757,127 | 18,750 |708,537  |
|09:30:06    RSCOLL00 B 4005  4 DDIC         77,879 | 71,512 |  2,291  |
|10.04       RSCOLL00 B 4005  4 DDIC         63,400 | 62,066 |      0  |
|01          RDDVERSL B 4005  5 DDIC         31,849 | 28,966 |  1,085  |
|10.04       RDDMASGL B 4005  5 DDIC         65,726 | 33,071 | 25,940  |
```

Figure 3.17 Excerpts from the weekly summary report – Part 3 (cont.)

```
|17.04      (B)STRTR B 4005  5 SAPSYS      10,900 |  7,602 |  2,662  |
|10.04 SE01 RDDM0005 D 1100  0 WILL         6,811 |  6,742 |     33  |
|18.04 SE01 RDDM0005 D 1100  0 WILL         4,961 |  4,900 |     30  |
|18.04 SE01 RDDM0005 D 1100  0 WILL           272 |    239 |     11  |
|18.04 SE01 RDDM0005 D 1100  0 WILL           257 |    225 |      6  |
...
---------------------------------------------------------------------
Time values are in milliseconds
.... only top 20 entries are displayed
```

Figure 3.17 Excerpts from the weekly summary report – Part 3 (cont.)

3.7.3 Buffers

If the buffers in the R/3 system have displayed bottlenecks, use the *Setup/Buffers* option from the performance menu or transaction code `st02` to continue analysis in this area. Figure 3.18 shows the menu structure.

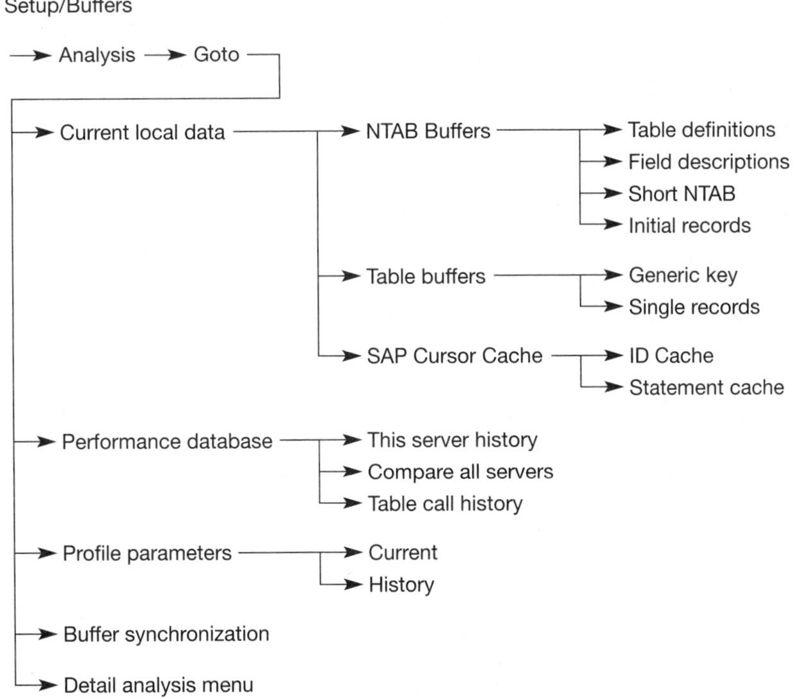

Figure 3.18 Buffer menu structure

The following functions are available for analysis:

- *Analysis*
  Summary of access statistics for the buffer areas.
- *Performance database*
  The contents of table MONI serve as the database for performance. This function provides a look at the unedited data in this table.
- *Table call history*
  Listing of the most frequently used tables and the required resources.
- *Profile parameters*
  Buffer parameters and change history.

The summary presentation of the quality of buffer accesses in *Buffers* provides the most information for a preliminary estimate of buffer size (see Figure 3.19).

The settings in the instance profile <SID>_DVEBMGS<instance> determine the size of the individual buffer areas. Chapter 1 already discussed the architecture of the R/3 system. A number of parameters regulate the size of the individual areas. When setting the values, consider whether the computer runs other applications or if R/3 can use all of the main memory.

The display indicates the size, the number of entries and the number of *Resets* (re-initializations) for each buffer as well as the quality of the accesses. As a rule of thumb, the effectiveness of buffer accesses, i.e., the ratio of successful to unsuccessful accesses, should be about 95%. Consider enlarging the appropriate buffer if the value falls below this figure.

The column marked *Swaps* shows the number of required removals from storage in main memory. Such removals cost time. The chart therefore highlights these actions in another color. Even with a satisfactory hit ratio, removals from storage indicate temporary bottlenecks that enlarging the main memory areas will reduce.

After changing the profile of an instance, stop and restart it so that the changes can take effect.

Actions such as transports or increased development activity play an influential role in assessing the buffer load. A transport, for example, resets all buffers, as does the special transaction `$sync`. The buffers return to normal use only afterward.

3.7.4 Operating system

Continue analysis of the operating system with the option *Operating System* in the performance menu. Figure 3.20 shows the functions available for analysis of the operating system.

System configuration

Displays the start profile parameters of the local R/3 system and the remote application server.

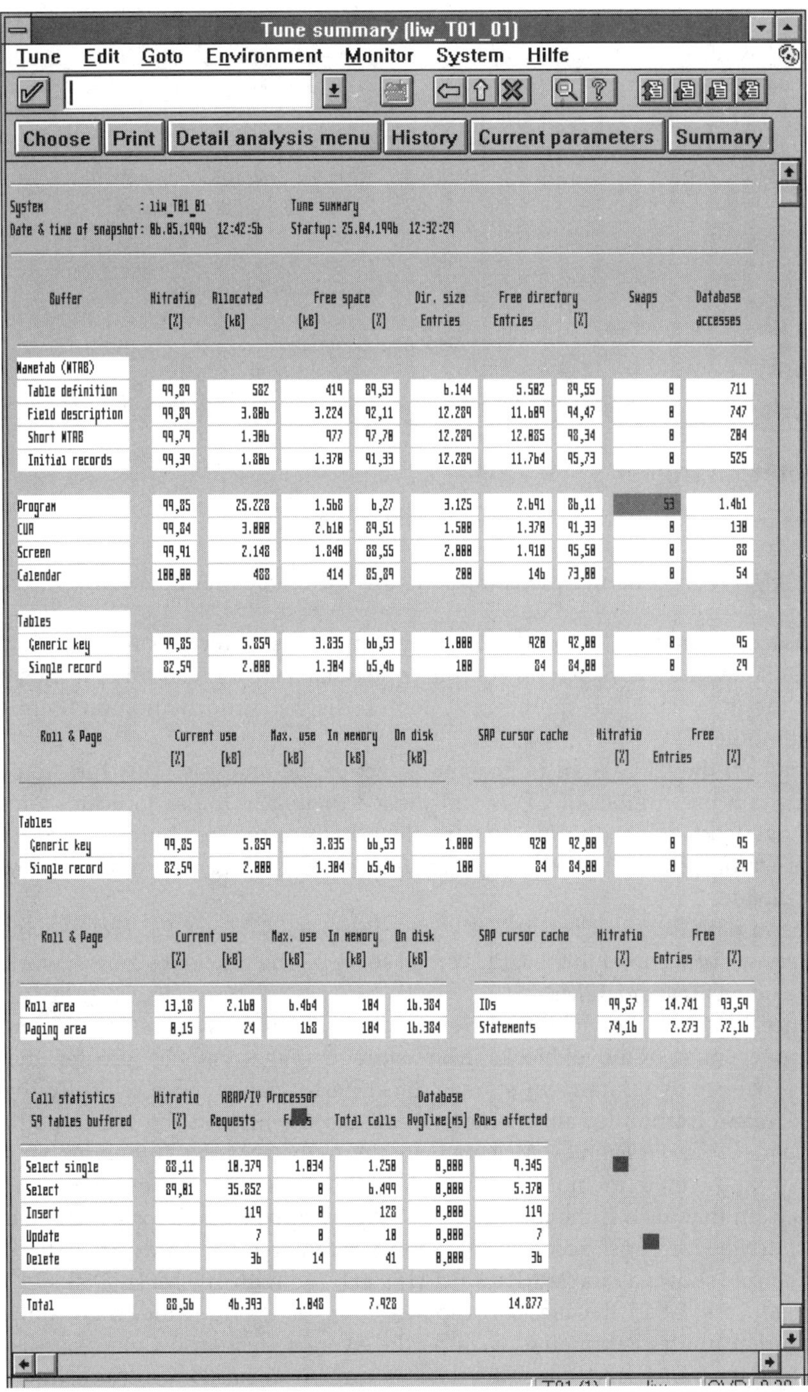

Tune summary (liw_T01_01)

Tune Edit Goto Environment Monitor System Hilfe

Choose | Print | Detail analysis menu | History | Current parameters | Summary

System : liw_T81_81 Tune summary
Date & time of snapshot: 8b.85.199b 12:42:5b Startup: 25.84.199b 12:32:29

Buffer	Hitratio [%]	Allocated [kB]	Free space [kB]	Free space [%]	Dir. size Entries	Free directory Entries	Free directory [%]	Swaps	Database accesses
Nametab (NTAB)									
Table definition	99,89	582	419	89,53	b.144	5.582	89,55	8	711
Field description	99,89	3.88b	3.224	92,11	12.289	11.b89	94,47	8	747
Short NTAB	99,79	1.38b	977	97,78	12.289	12.885	98,34	8	284
Initial records	99,39	1.88b	1.378	91,33	12.289	11.7b4	95,73	8	525
Program	99,85	25.228	1.5b8	b,27	3.125	2.b91	8b,11	53	1.4b1
CUA	99,84	3.888	2.b18	89,51	1.588	1.378	91,33	8	138
Screen	99,91	2.148	1.848	88,55	2.888	1.918	95,58	8	88
Calendar	188,88	488	414	85,89	288	14b	73,88	8	54
Tables									
Generic key	99,85	5.859	3.835	bb,53	1.888	928	92,88	8	95
Single record	82,59	2.888	1.384	b5,4b	188	84	84,88	8	29

Roll & Page | Current use [%] | [kB] | Max. use [kB] | In memory [kB] | On disk [kB] | SAP cursor cache | Hitratio [%] | Free Entries | [%]

Tables									
Generic key	99,85	5.859	3.835	bb,53	1.888	928	92,88	8	95
Single record	82,59	2.888	1.384	b5,4b	188	84	84,88	8	29

Roll & Page	Current use [%]	Current use [kB]	Max. use [kB]	In memory [kB]	On disk [kB]
Roll area	13,18	2.1b8	b.4b4	184	1b.384
Paging area	8,15	24	1b8	184	1b.384

SAP cursor cache	Hitratio [%]	Free Entries	Free [%]
IDs	99,57	14.741	93,59
Statements	74,1b	2.273	72,1b

Call statistics 59 tables buffered	Hitratio [%]	ABAP/IV Processor Requests	ABAP/IV Processor Fails	Database Total calls	Database AvgTime[ms]	Database Rows affected
Select single	88,11	18.379	1.834	1.258	8,888	9.345
Select	89,81	35.852	8	b.499	8,888	5.378
Insert		119	8	128	8,888	119
Update		7	8	18	8,888	7
Delete		3b	14	41	8,888	3b
Total	88,5b	4b.393	1.848	7.928		14.877

Figure 3.19 Tune summary

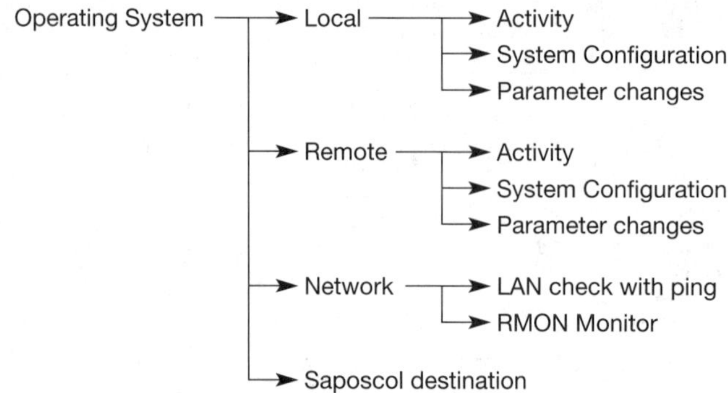

Figure 3.20 Menu tree for operating system analysis

Parameter changes

Displays the history of the changes made to the parameters.

Activity

Use transaction code `os06` for the local system or `os07` for the remote system. The function displays the demands on computer resources for a given time. It thus provides the basis for analysis of the operating system. It displays information on both local and remote computers.

The load on the CPU is an important aspect of the analysis. This function displays information on the number of CPUs and the load on each. It also indicates a maximum load (or overload) when the *idle time* of the CPU approaches zero or the number of processes waiting for CPU time is greater than three. Figure 3.21 displays a computer with little load.

The menu path *Goto* → *Current local data* → *Snapshot* → *Top CPU-Processes* provides a quick overview of the load to the CPUs on all servers. The resident size of a work process should be between 9 and 12MB.

Bottlenecks occur if the remaining physical main memory area is smaller than 10MB or the computer must remove blocks from storage (*Pages out/s* is greater than zero). Activities that remove data from storage affect performance more critically than lower buffer hit rates. Examine main memory more thoroughly via the menu path *Goto* → *Current data* → *Previous hours* → *Memory* from the Activity Menu. If the number of blocks removed from the main memory area normally is over 30,000 per hour, one can speak of a bottleneck in that area. If the indicators noted here appear, look for ways to reduce the numbers. In the worst-case scenario the computer may require hardware enhancements.

The example shows a Hewlett-Packard HP9000/715 with 100 MHz. Disk `c0t3d0` with the SCSI address 3 had the highest response time. The values indicated, however, lie within normal limits. Parameters such as the average response time of a disk or the amount of data transferred depend, quite naturally, on hardware. Accordingly, make decisions on a case-by-case basis. However, if the number of queued processes (*Queue*) steadily lies above zero, a physical bottleneck has indeed occurred. Check major

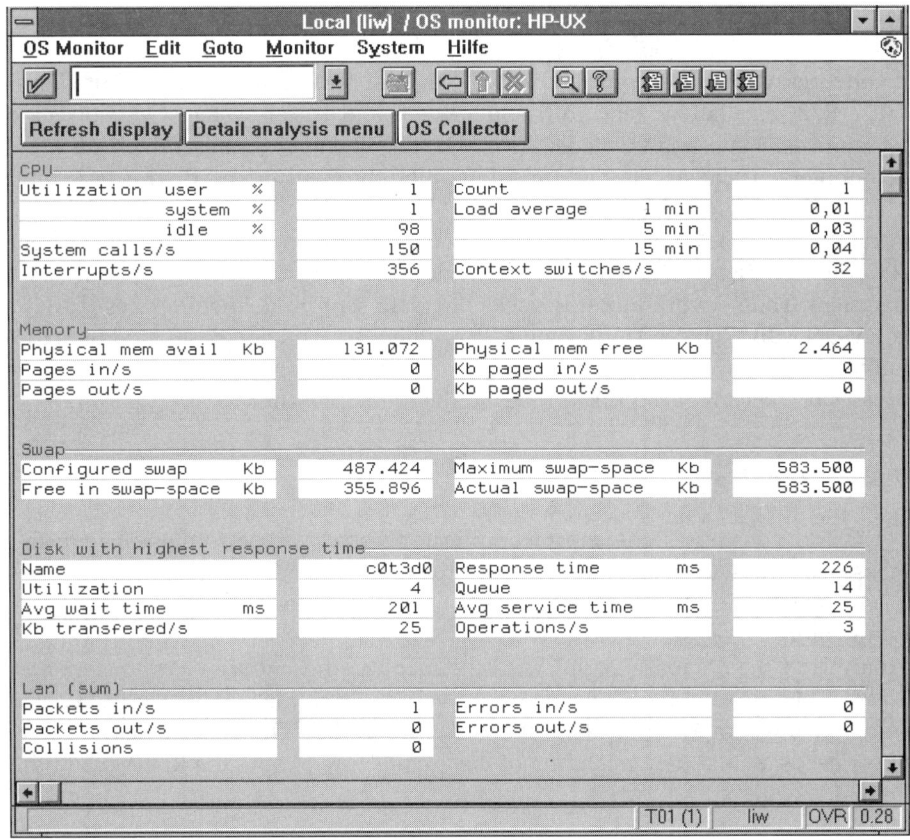

Figure 3.21 Overview of operating system activities

deviations in any case, to see which function has taken over the disk area. (Perhaps some activities can move to another, faster disk.)

An examination of memory utilization is an important aspect of an analysis of the operating system. If available memory drops below 5MB, consider it a clear indication of a bottleneck. Detailed analysis provides further information on individual components. For example, this function allows an examination of main memory utilization at various times of the day.

Top CPU processes also allows analysis of the operating system area. The processes displayed there relate closely with the architectures of the R/3 system and the RDBMS. The R/3 work, SAP frontend, transport, network and database processes normally range in the upper area. Check the necessity of all other processes.

The program saposcol, which runs parallel to R/3 on the computer, collects the values displayed in the operating system statistics. If, instead of the expected statistic, the message `Collector not running` appears, use operating system tools to determine if saposcol is running properly. The menu option *saposcol destination* determines where the program writes the information it provides.

Network

The network in operating contributes to the overall performance of distributed systems. Because R/3 installations tend to become larger and larger systems, version 3.x offers much more extensive analysis tools. As in the past, version 3.x can send test packets to all the computers on the system and thus determine the transfer speed. This test can find a bottleneck that might exist in the network.

A new feature is the network monitor that provides an overview of the current and past traffic on network segments. Install the network monitor on exactly one server in the R/3 system. The network monitor tracks test data sent by defined devices (LANProbes on a RMON MIB (Remote Monitoring Management Information Base)) and uses the echo to judge the quality of the network load. The directory /usr/sap/tmp stores the internet addresses of the configured LANProbes in the file R3net_conf.

3.7.5 Database

The RDBMS constitutes the most complicated aspect of performance analysis. The database software ultimately determines the performance level of the R/3 system. Inspection of the RDBMS therefore forms one of the most essential tasks of the R/3 administrator.

Analysis of the database begins with the menu path *Control → Performance Menu → Database*. This menu node allows access to various evaluations (see Figure 3.22) which provide the most important statistics on activities in the RDBMS. To assess these values the user needs a good understanding of the architecture of both the RDBMS and the R/3 system.

Basics of RDBMS architecture

Various database systems have established themselves within the R/3 environment: ADABAS D, Informix and Oracle. The individual systems all operate in essentially the same manner. More exactly, the systems differentiate themselves in minor details that ultimately affect operations and runtime properties. Accordingly, the evaluation lists offered under the menu option Database are specific to the database software and differentiate themselves in certain fine points.

RDBMS use separate space on the disk for data storage. Depending on the software used, the system uses either raw devices or files in the operating system. Oracle systems

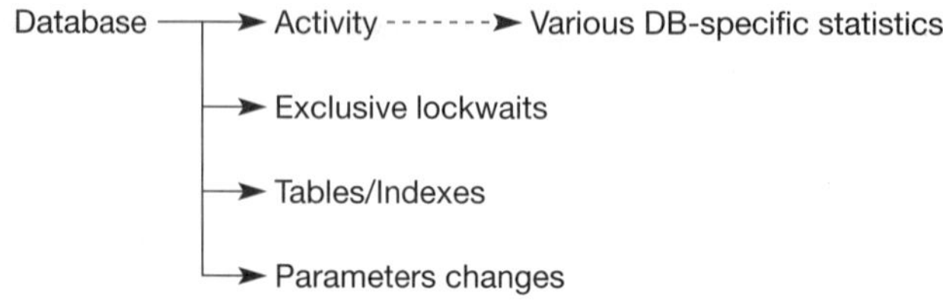

Figure 3.22 Database evaluation

use files to store data in what Oracle calls **tablespaces**. Informix and ADABAS D function in the most advantageous manner with raw devices in UNIX systems. Performance and security considerations often lead to this choice of data storage.

High data security is one of the most essential demands made on an RDBMS. A separate area, the log area, serves this purpose by documenting every change to data records. It makes repairs possible when data within the data area has become lost. Complete backups of all data records provide only a snapshot of the data at a particular time in the data's life-cycle. The log area, however, documents the development of the data. Starting from a complete backup of the DB, the actions stored in the log area can be repeated. This process allows reconstruction of the database as it existed at the point of loss. Experts call the process **recovery of the log** or a **redo of the log**. An operational system also uses the information in the log areas to roll back cancelled transactions.

All these possibilities presuppose an unbroken backup of the log area and management of the backups created. Since the DB registers in the log area every change to the data so that all changes can be recreated, remember the following important considerations.

The log area

- Is the most active write area among the disk areas assigned to the DB,
- May never become full,
- Must undergo regular backups and
- Must enjoy as much protection as possible from a total breakdown.

The high level of write actions to the log area requires, during configuration of the DB, the choice of a disk area that provides high performance. The area should have its own disk controller, and not exist on the same disk with other I/O areas such as SWAP in UNIX systems. We recommend a separation of the data and log areas so that in the event of a disk crash only the data or the log area would require reconstruction. Mirroring the log area at the operating system level or by the database can further heighten protection against breakdowns. Today's technology often prefers hardware mirroring to that provided by software. RAID systems add another step in increasing the level of security.

After saving the data in the log area, the system releases the space for new write actions. Should the backup fail to take place, the log area can easily overflow. Given the importance of the log information, the critical nature of such a situation should be clear. An unavailable log area makes it impossible to continue work reasonably. The RDBMS reactions to this situation range from blocking all further work to allowing only read actions.

Depending on the RDBMS in use, the system requires other files on the disk in addition to the areas noted above. In all cases, Oracle needs control files that contain the most important information on the structure and control of the DB. A loss of this information would lead to a breakdown of the entire RDBMS. The system therefore stores this file twice during normal operation.

To provide the high data performance expected of an RDBMS, the system occupies other memory areas in the main memory of each computer.

Each RDBMS generally has its own name for the memory areas it usually occupies:

- SGA System global area (Oracle)
- Shared memory (Informix)
- DB cache Database cache (ADABAS D)

The same reality exists behind all these memory areas: storage of important data in main memory significantly shortens access time. Each RDBMS distinguishes several essential areas within the main memory area. These additional areas are classified according to their use:

- *Database buffer pool*
  All database applications use this memory area; it contains data pages taken from the DB's data area on disks. One data page is a block in the RDBMS sense. A page is normally 2KB (Oracle, Informix) or 4KB (ADABAS D) large. Processing of DB data does not take place directly on disk but in the database buffer pool of the RDBMS. During every access to data, the system first checks if the required data page is present in the database buffer pool. If not, a copy of that page is copied to the buffer pool. For pages undergoing frequent processing, the probability that the cache already contains the required is rather high. This process also reduces the number of required disk accesses, which, in turn, improve runtime. Compared to memory access, disk access remains rather slow. This mechanism also allows one to conclude that enlarging the main memory available to the RDBMS can contribute significantly to improved performance.
- *Data dictionary buffer*
  A cache for the management of data in the database also exists; it functions much like the database buffer pool. The term data dictionary refers here only to the metadata for the data in the database. Each RDBMS creates its own data dictionary for a database.
- *Redo log buffer*
  All changes to data pages first take place in the database buffer pool. The system transfers the changes to disk only at certain times: savepoints or checkpoints. Another main memory area records the information that led to the change so that the changes can be repeated. Each RDBMS has its own name for this memory area: redo log buffer (Oracle), physical log buffer (Informix) or log cache (ADABAS D).

  Every RDBMS recognizes a *Checkpoint*. At this point the system writes a new, consistent condition of the DB to disk: it transfers all the pages marked as changed from the cache to disk. In normal cases the system initiates the checkpoint when about 75% of the redo log buffer is full or when a specific period of time has elapsed. Special actions also cause most RDBMS to trigger a checkpoint: a change between areas (segments) within the log area, a shutdown or a startup. The term checkpoint might lead to confusion. Most exactly, it is not a point in time but a point that triggers certain actions. Execution of a checkpoint in the R/3 system can take some time because of the volume of data.

- *Procedure cache*
  An additional area in the main memory of the database processes user commands (SQL commands). Typical names for this area include shared SQL buffer of procedure cache. This area contains execution plans of SQL commands, triggers, functions and procedures created by a syntactical analysis. If a command is transmitted repeatedly, the analysis of the execution plans (parsing) becomes unnecessary.

In addition to the area noted above, the RDBMS has additional, currently database-specific areas for queues, administrative lists and other internal purposes.

DB processes execute RDBMS activities. Note the following processes, divided by task:

- *Database writer*
  The process responsible for the interplay between the database buffer pool and the data area on disk.
- *Log writer*
  Documents changes to the data pages and the information in the redo log buffer to the log area on disk.

The RDBMS software may also classify other processes. For example:

- *Checkpoint-Process*
  Coordinates the actions necessary for a checkpoint.
- *Archive*
  Saves the log areas to a specified medium (Oracle).

Obtaining an understanding of the processes and their allocation, from the point of view of the operating system, is usually quite difficult. Each RDBMS, however, offers tools for observation and, if necessary, repair of error (SQL*DBA for Oracle, onmonitor for Informix, Control for ADABAS D). Figure 3.23 presents the architecture in simplified form.

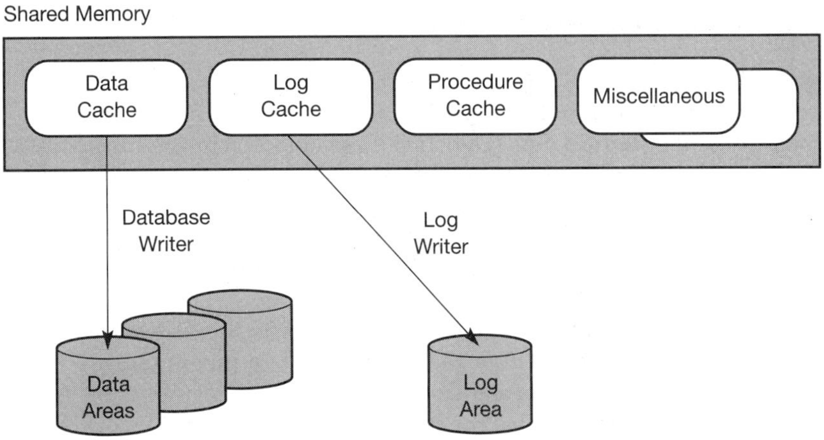

Figure 3.23 Basic architecture of an RDBMS

Various finer points of each database complete the presentation of the basics of RDBMS architecture. The following section briefly discusses the most significant RDBMS in the R/3 environment.

- *Oracle*
  Original development of R/3 software took place with the Oracle system. Even during the development phase, however, an attempt was made to limit specifics of the RDBMS and deviations from or additions SQL standards as much as possible. Nonetheless, complete independence from any specific database appeared only in version 3.0. Oracle versions with R/3 are available for both UNIX and Windows NT systems.

  Complexity is a particularly noteworthy characteristic of Oracle's architecture. As one of the first RDBMS available, it has reached a certain maturity and contains proprietary elements. The numbers of parameters reflect the complexity of the archictecture. The type and size of the data involved determine parameter settings. Ajusting the parameters, however, requires a great deal of knowledge and constant observation of the system.

- *ADABAS D*
  Software AG makes ADABAS, the only RDBMS developed in Germany that has an international following. The database packet offered by the firm contains two components: ADABAS C and ADABAS D. Only ADABAS D supports R/3. The system is also known by its earlier names, Reflex, DDB/4 and Entire SQL-DB. ADABAS D runs with R/3 on the UNIX and Windows NT platforms.

  ADABAS D understands various SQL query dialects, Oracle mode among them. This ability made it relatively easy for ADABAS D and R/3 to work together; the first versions became available in 1993.

  Administration of ADABAS D is especially free of problems. Its dynamic memory management requires almost no reorganization runs as do earlier RDBMS. The RDBMS processes these tasks mostly by itself.

- *Informix*
  Informix, sold by Informix Software Inc., also runs on UNIX and Windows NT. Informix uses the term DSA (Dynamic Scaleable Architecture) to describe its architecture. The system's ability to be configured provides it with independence from hardware. Just like Oracle, Informix uses tablespaces. In that regard, administrative tasks are similar among both vendors.

- *SQL Server*
  The RDBMS sold by Microsoft, SQL Server, is based on the database server from the firm Sybase. The variant for Windows NT has played a role in the R/3 environment for some time, based on the porting from R/3. As the use of Windows NT grows, so will that of SQL Server. The actual functionality of the server is identical to the Sybase Server. Tools developed by Microsoft provide seamless integration into the world of Windows at the front end.

Database performance

The general task of an optimization of RDBMS runtime is to tune the common efforts of the processes and the memory areas as well as possible. Since the architecture of the most commonly used RDBMS is basically the same, R/3 offers the same type of analytical tools. From the CCMS Performance Menu chose the option *Database* to enter this area. The menu option *Activity* (transaction code `st04`) provides an overview of the most important parameters. Figure 3.24 shows a list for an ADABAS D system.

```
Database E25 Day, Time  01.10.1995  19:28:06     Database summary
DB Server    sqlhp9  Startup/Reset   22.12.1994   19:43:45
---------------------------------------------------------------------
|Cache activity |    Size Kb |      Accesses |      Hits |    Hitrate% |
---------------------------------------------------------------------
|Data           |    12,000  |     781,283   |  766,394 |         100  |
|Converter      |    14,000  |     423,385   |  421,769 |         100  |
|Catalog        |     4,000  |     779,293   |  612,068 |          79  |
|Temporary      |       120  |           0   |        0 |           0  |
---------------------------------------------------------------------
|Commands                                                            |
---------------------------------------------------------------------
|SQL commands   |   136,231  | Create        |        8 |
|Rollbacks      |         0  | Alter         |        0 |
|Commits        |     8,381  | Drop          |    1,115 |
|Prepares       |     2,597  |               |          |
|Executes       |    75,528  |Catalog scans  |   11,129 |
---------------------------------------------------------------------
|I/O activity                                                        |
---------------------------------------------------------------------
|Physical reads  |14,889      |Logical reads    |   14,781,274   |
|Physical writes |29,348      |Logical writes   |    4,165,893   |
---------------------------------------------------------------------
|Locking activity                                                    |
---------------------------------------------------------------------
|Entries available   | 20,400 |Row locks    |      22,589 |
|   Max. used        |  4,007 |Table locks  |      22,608 |
|   Avg. used        |     40 |             |             |
|Lockholder          |      0 |Collisions   |          62 |
|Lockrequester       |      0 |Escalations  |           0 |
---------------------------------------------------------------------
|Logging activity                                                    |
---------------------------------------------------------------------
|Logpages written       |  19,916 |  Group commits          |     5 |
|Waits for logwriter    |  13,375 |  Log queue overflows    |     0 |
---------------------------------------------------------------------
|Scan and sort activity                                              |
---------------------------------------------------------------------
|Table scans   |  19,327   |Sorts (Sort cache)   |     5    |
|Index scans   |        0  |Rows                 |   368    |
---------------------------------------------------------------------
```

Figure 3.24 Database activity (transaction code `st04`*)*

Although the details of the information provided and some of the terms vary among the different database manufacturers, general similarities exist. A count of certain events and the calculation of the percentage rate of positive and negative incidents over a period of time provided the following results.

The very beginning of the figure illustrates one of the most important aspects of evaluating RDBMS performance: the statistics for the main memory used by the database. The value for the data cache hit rate is decisive. A figure that lies near 100% means that the data requiring processing was already present in main memory. A value under 90%, however, means that some data had to be read from disk and placed in memory. A rate lower than 90% also indicates that increasing the size of the main memory available would improve database performance.

The same principle determines calculation of access rates for the remaining main memory areas. These rates also indicate a required size for the main memory area. Unlike the data cache hit rate, these values should be set in relation to completed activities in the database over the period of time under observation. If, for example, this period saw the creation of new tables, a lower catalog or data dictionary hit rate should cause no concern. Table creation, like modification and deletion of table structures, requires intensive processing in the data dictionary. If, however, such activities are the rule rather than the exception, and the hit rate in the main memory area of the database permanently lies significantly below 100%, enlarge the affected area in any case.

Another section of statistics describes what kinds of and how many SQL commands were executed. In RDBMS parlance, the number of completed transaction equals the number of *Commits* and *Rollbacks*. The number of rollbacks shows how many transactions did not complete successfully. Before drawing any rash conclusions from this value, however, consider some possible causes. Did the period under examination see any transport requests with option `t` (test)? Transport requests end with an explicit rollback that cancels all actions on the database. Nonetheless, if the value seems high, especially compared to other periods, examine the system log `sm21` to search for possible error messages.

Another entry describes logging activity. The log area of the RDBMS holds every change to the database so that, if needed, it can recover the data. The statistics for the log area indirectly show the level of change activities in the period under examination. The number of log pages written indicates if a large average number of changes took place. If so, the log area requires backup.

This initial overview presents a summary of all important aspects of the RDBMS. As such, it provides only preliminary indications of possible bottlenecks. Branch to submenus from this information to perform a more exact analysis. The following aspects have particular importance for database analysis:

- *Database performance*
  This function provides an overview of the requests made of the database on previous days. This statistic shows when the RDBMS had a particularly high load. Depending on the RDBMS software in use the display categorizes the calls according to SQL commands, read requests or write requests. The excerpt in Figure 3.25 comes from an Oracle system.

```
Oracle call statistics  Sun 15.01.1995 12:13:43 -Mon 16.01.1995 08:22:45
-------------------------------------------------------------------------
|   |           |          |   user    |recursive | user   |user  |parses |
|day |  date     | endtime |   calls   |  calls   |commits|rollb.|        |
-------------------------------------------------------------------------
|Tue| 10.01.1995| 14:13:11| 2,502,689| 6,916,598| 77,841|   234| 137,870|
|Mon| 09.01.1995| 18:11:46| 3,502,075| 0,525,215| 86,865|   305|  77,859|
|Thu| 05.01.1995| 16:15:52| 9,192,606|   956,781| 18,120|    61|  86,177|
|Wed| 04.01.1995| 16:12:30| 3,650,131| 3,760,626| 19,118|1,863| 258,463|
|Tue| 03.01.1995| 18:11:52|   576,659|   425,664| 11,463|   028|  12,691|
|Mon| 02.01.1995| 18:44:38| 7,317,556| 5,760,147| 90,696|   839| 203,926|
|Sat| 31.12.1994| 16:12:22| 7,241,299| 3,906,196| 71,968|    15| 788,180|
...
```

Figure 3.25 Database performance in an R/3 system with Oracle

- *Devspaces, file system*
  The statistics displayed show, for each unit of memory, the input and output activities that have run since starting the database. For an Oracle system the statistics indicate the read and write accesses for each tablespace; for ADABAS D the display presents the accesses for each devspace.
- *Sessions, DB processes, session monitor*
  All processes that affect the database are displayed. These include the database processes (database writer, log writer, archiver, etc.) and the R/3 user processes (work processes, message writer, etc.). This information allows the administrator to check if all the processes required are present and active. The activity of each process displays its status (see Figure 3.26). Wait conditions that exist for longer periods may indicate blocks or other conflicts among the processes.
- *Tables/indexes*
  The memory required for all tables and indexes that exist in the database is displayed. Lists of all the tables contained in the database can also be called.

```
01.10.1995   19:38:29      INFORMIX Session/Thread Monitor
------------------------------------------------------------------------------
|Host    |Process|Session|Thread|  Thread                     |  Owner    | RSAM    |
|name    |   id  |   id  |  id  |  status                     |  name     | calls   |
------------------------------------------------------------------------------
|hs1303 | 27436 | 2712  | 2763 |cond wait (0x84CE6370)|informix | 70,021  |
|hs1303 | 16771 | 3590  | 3643 |cond wait (0x84DE5488)|sapr3    | 35,104  |
|hs1303 | 16768 | 3591  | 3644 |cond wait (0x84DEEA70)|sapr3    |     315 |
|hs1303 | 16767 | 3592  | 3645 |cond wait (0x84DF8058)|sapr3    |389,920  |
|hs1303 | 16770 | 3593  | 3646 |cond wait (0x84E011640|sapr3    | 20,021  |
|hs1303 | 16766 | 3594  | 3647 |running               |sapr3    |180,197  |
|hs1303 | 16772 | 3595  | 3648 |cond wait (0x84E14210)|sapr3    |     579 |
|hs1303 | 16769 | 3596  | 3649 |cond wait (0x84E1D7F8)|sapr3    |     32S |
```

Figure 3.26 Informix: process overview

The administrator has particular interest in the comparison of the indexes known to the repository and those actually present in the database (*Missing Indexes*). Any apparent deviations are displayed. Missing indexes often indication installation error. Check them in all cases.

- *Exclusive lockwaits*
  The RDBMS have a broad lock concept to allow for parallel processing in the database. Various types of locks guarantee the consistency of the database. If a user reads a particular record, the system normally locks the record against any attempt by another user to change it. Other users may still read the record. Exclusive lockwaits prohibit every sort of access by other users. The system uses this type of lock when changing records. Because exclusive locks prohibit every other access, they can certainly inhibit the performance of the system. When activated, the function `Exclusive Lockwait` displays all waiting situations in which a user must wait for the release of an exclusive lock.
- *Configuration*
  This function provides an overview of the most important configuration parameters for the RDBMS in question. This functionality is particularly dependent on the RDBMS in use. The display here indicates both the possibilities and the difficulties individual RDBMS offer the user.
- *Operating messages, database log*
  When working, all RDBMS write important messages to a log file. In the case of errors, this file often contains indications of the causes. If, for example, the log area begins to approach critical values for its capacity, the system writes warnings to the log file. If for no other reason, therefore, examine these messages frequently.

Additional, database-specific functions exist to observe and evaluate various aspects of the individual RDBMS. R/3 thus provides all the essential criteria for evaluating the performance of the database. Nonetheless it may be necessary to use proprietary tools offered by each RDBMS in critical situations. Depending on the database software in use, the user may have to become familiar with these tools.

3.7.6 Alert monitors

As the previous sections indicate, monitoring individual aspects of the CCMS is rather complex and difficult to grasp in one look. To simplify this difficulty, R/3 offers alert monitors under the menu option *Performance*. A graphic displays the most important information for each work area. One glance thus indicates gross bottlenecks. Alert monitors are available for both global and local evaluations (see Figure 3.27).

Figure 3.28 displays the alert monitor for the entire SAP system. The left half of the display contains a number of push buttons that, when activated, provide information on the most important parameters in each topic area. The alert monitor for SAP operations offers an additional function: double-click on a topic in the left side of the display to provide more specialized information.

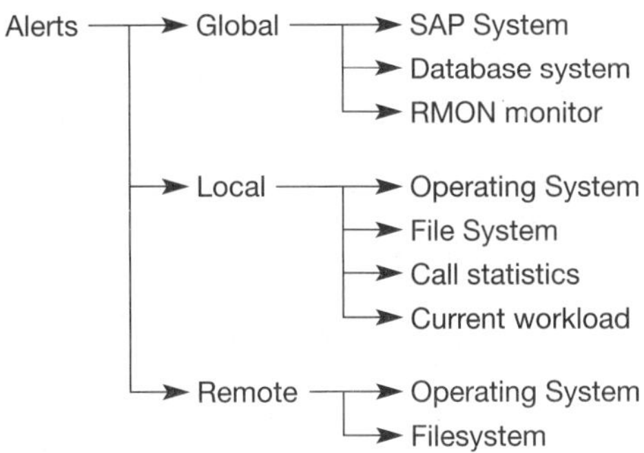

Figure 3.27 Alert monitors

Reset all Alerts deletes old information; `Acknowledge all` simply resets all errors as known. The latter choice becomes important when an error does not require an immediate solution, but should no longer affect the alert monitor.

Because of its importance, the status of the RDBMS has its own alert monitor. Figure 3.29 illustrates the performance monitor for the database. A change in color, from green to red, indicates critical situations. In the local area the monitor displays important

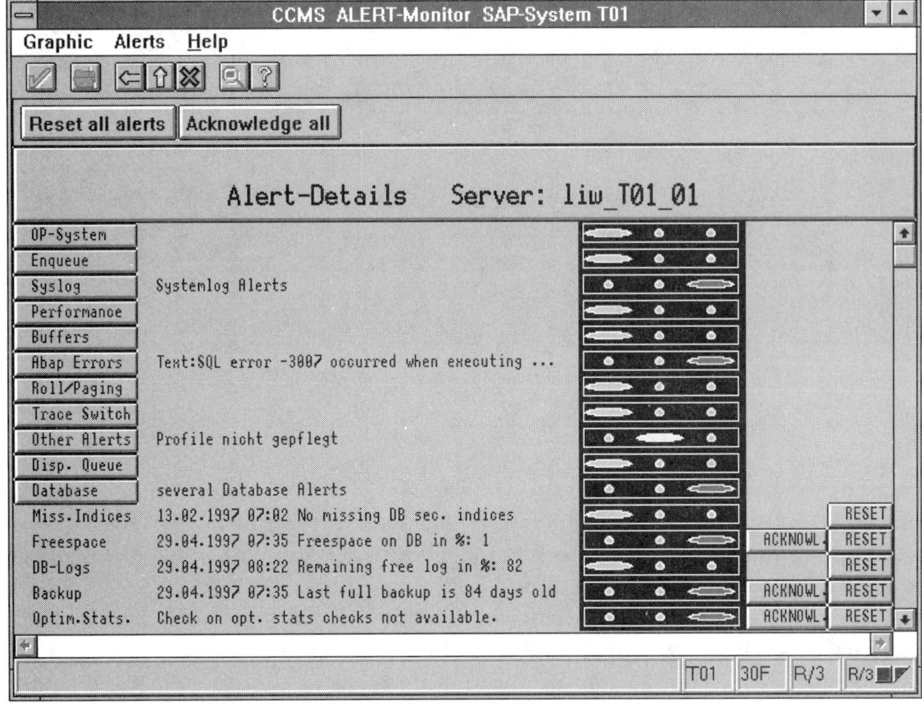

Figure 3.28 SAP system alert monitor

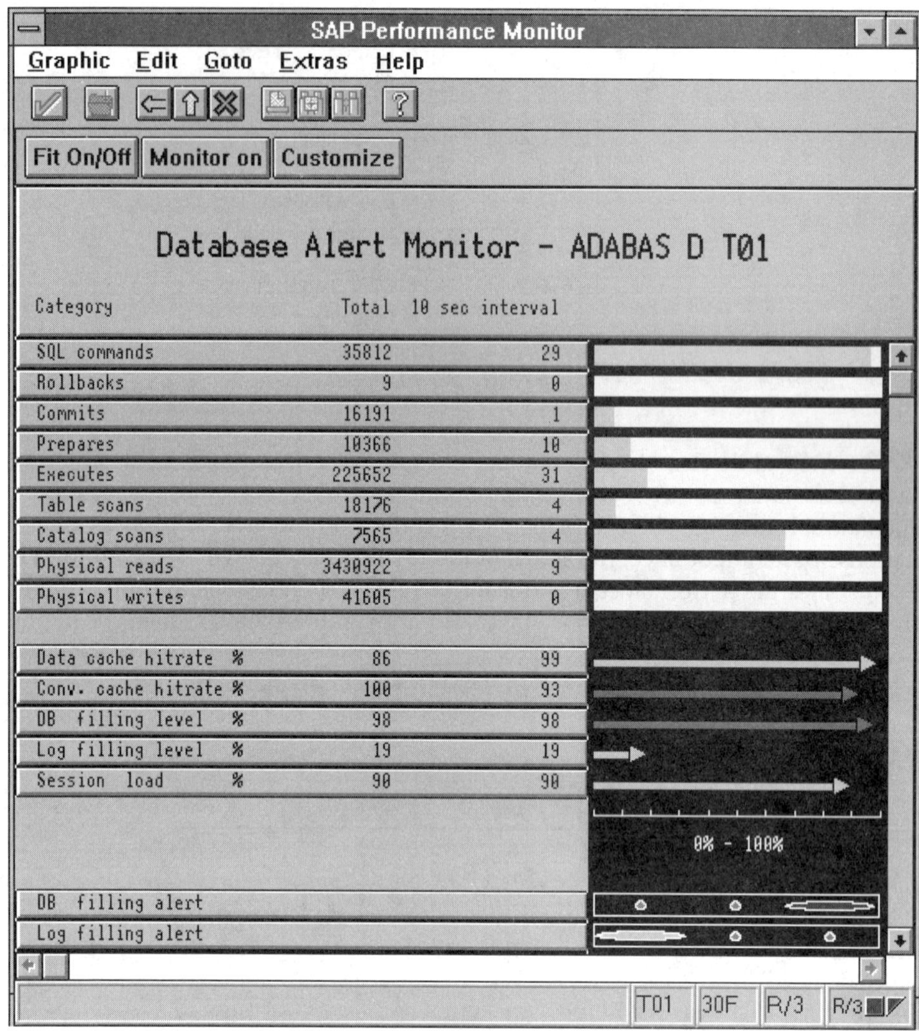

Figure 3.29 Database alert monitor

aspects of the operation system (`OS`), statistics on calls and participating components (`Call statistics`) and an evaluation of the load to various work areas (`Current workload`). Color changes, from green to red, allow rapid recognition of critical situations (see Figure 3.30).

The threshold values set for each area determine when the colors change. The R/3 system has its own default values, but these rarely meet the circumstances and needs of local operating conditions. After an appropriate break-in period, adjust the setting to meet local requirements. For normal, i.e., usual, loads, the displays should be green. Adjusting the setting for individual needs is normally called `Customizing`.

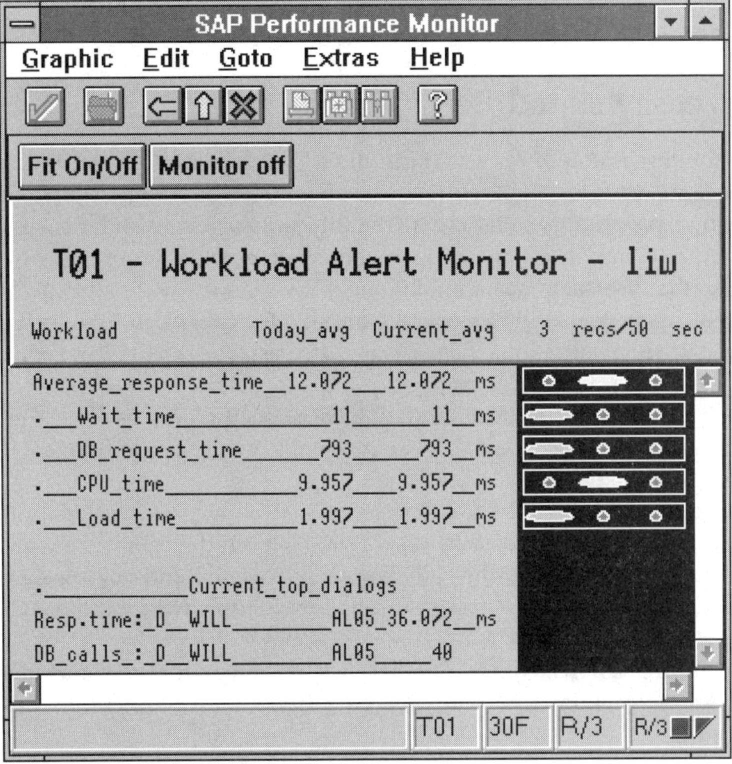

Figure 3.30 Workload alert monitor

Use the menu path *Configuration → Alert Thresholds* (transaction `rz06`) to adjust the settings. Appropriate templates are available for each topic area and, therefore, for every alert monitor.

3.7.7 Early Watch

The previous sections have surely provided an impression of the complexity of the R/3 system and the many layers involved in analyzing its performance. Using the tools provided is one thing. Evaluating the statistics and arriving at conclusions based on them is another matter; it requires a great deal of knowledge and understanding. An R/3 administrator with a thorough knowledge of these topics has a distinct advantage. Such knowledge, however, is not absolutely required.

SAP and other service providers offer users detailed performance analysis under the name Early Watch. The purchase of a service contract provides customers with regular access to this service. SAP checks the total performance of the system within this context. If necessary, it examines certain system flows individually. It also provides the results of the examination to the customer as concrete suggestions to eliminate bottlenecks (parameter settings, indexes, hardware upgrades, etc.).

3.8 Backups and DB-specific actions

3.8.1 Weekly schedule

Up to now the discussion of topics within the CCMS has limited itself to evaluations of runtime. Backing up data is a central task of an administrator's work. Each RDBMS provides its own proprietary tools to perform this function on a regular basis. Data backup has a particularly important meaning when dealing with several gigabytes of data. Consider also that user data has a much longer life than software and special hardware. Unfortunately, many users fail to recognize the significance of careful data backup. Errors can then produce fatal situations. Backups are the basis for repairs to the database.

Most RDBMS offer a proprietary backup tool, specific to each RDBMS. R/3 provides its own tool to schedule backups and database-specific actions. Use the menu path *DB Administration* → *Time Scheduling* to reach the weekly schedule, as illustrated in Figure 3.31.

The menu path *Time Scheduling* → *Calendar display* allows setting the number of weeks displayed and the number of actions displayed for each day. Both logs for background processing and the RDBMS can be called at each executed and completed action. Issue the calls either directly with the push buttons provided or with a double click followed by a choice.

Schedule future actions with a double click on either the weekday desired or the work area for a weekday. Actions can be scheduled for execution on a one-time

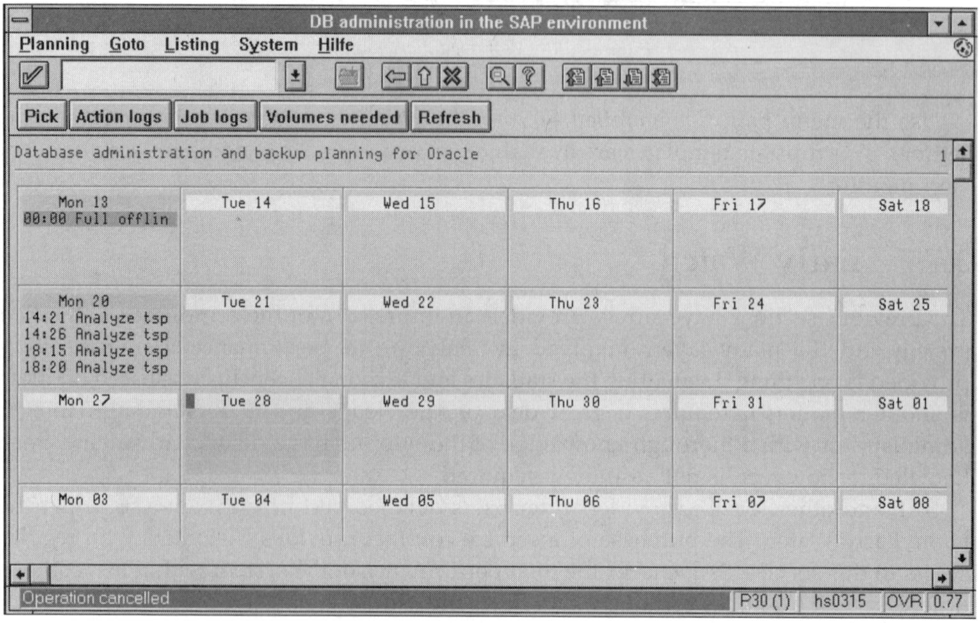

Figure 3.31 Weekly schedule

or weekly, periodic basis. Technically, the scheduling process triggers a job named DBA_<aktion_name> in the background. Find the logs for these background jobs at the push button *Job logs*. The scheduled background jobs use external commands to start the appropriate, database-specific backup program: Oracle: brbackup; Informix: onarchive; ADABAS D: xbackup. After execution of the external command, find the log of the RDBMS at the push button *Action protocols*. A positive message from the RDBMS is decisive for the successful completion of an action.

The RDBMS strongly determines which actions can be performed with R/3 weekly scheduling. What each RDBMS offers depends mostly on the architecture and the backup strategy.

Table 3.5 provides an overview:

Table 3.5 Options for scheduling actions

Action	*ADABAS D*	*Informix*	*Oracle*
Complete data backup during system operation	Yes and consistent	Yes, but not consistent	Yes, but not consistent
Complete data backup with an automatic stop and restart of the RDBMS	No	Yes	Yes
Incremental backup	Yes	Yes	No
Data and log backup	No	Yes	Yes
Log backup	Yes	Yes	Yes
Automatic log backup	Yes	Yes	Yes
Update of statistical data for the query optimizer	Yes	Yes	Yes
Control of RDBMS structures	Yes	Yes	No

- *Complete backup*
  This option saves the entire contents of the database. In the case of a recovery, the last complete backup is the starting point for the recreation of the data. Except for ADABAS, systems differentiate between a complete backup while the database is active or stopped. A complete save while Informix or Oracle are operationally ready is not consistent. Consistency requires an additional step, restoration of the log backup. These RDBMS therefore offer the options of performing a backup while the system is stopped or of performing a data backup followed by a log backup.

  In ADABAS D no difference exists between a complete backup with the RDBMS in either a warm or cold condition.

- *Log backup*
  The log area contains all the changes made to the database since the last log backup. In the case of a recovery, log backups are used after importation of the last database backup to recreate all the changes.

- *Automatic log backup*
  Log backups can also be automated. Whenever a certain log area becomes filled with data, the area is automatically saved to a pre-defined medium and the area released for new data. This process protects the user from overflows in the log area – a definite advantage.
- *Incremental backups*
  This process backs up all the pages of the database that have changed since the last complete or incremental backup. In the event of a recovery, import the last complete backup and then the incremental backups (in order). In principle the incremental backups can serve as alternatives to log backups, although log backups are more common. Incremental backups are preferable whenever the user assumes that only already existing data has changed and that less new data has been added or old data deleted. Unlike log backups, which register every action, including all intermediate changes to the same data pages, an incremental backup saves only the true, last status of all changed data pages. The contents of the log area mirror the development of the data. An incremental backup represents the exact status of development. The ability to use this status can have its advantages: some databases use log backups to restore consistent intermediate statuses of the database.
- *Updating the optimizer statistics*
  Although not a backup activity, this action can be scheduled just as the ones noted above. This procedure updates the internal statistics on the structure and contents of tables. The RDBMS uses this information to develop the best search strategy (cost-based optimizer) for SQL queries. The relevance of the statistics therefore has direct relevance to the performance of the R/3 system.
- *Control of the RDBMS structures*
  This action checks the logical correctness of the tree structures used by the database to store data.

The user can create a strategy for the week from the options offered for specific actions or can use a pre-defined pattern. Use the menu path *Time Scheduling* → *Time Scheduling* to choose and implement a model.

3.8.2 Logs

In addition to the weekly schedule, a separate menu option, *DB Administration* → *Protocols* is also available. This function supports the observation and evaluation of scheduled actions and offers additonal alerts that point to certain exceptional situations. A history allows study of actions that have already run (see Figure 3.32). Flow logs for the actions can be requested and evaluated. One alert, for example, notes the age of the last successful complete backup. If the date of the last complete backup of the database lies more than seven days in the past (the value can be adjusted), a warning is issued when calling the monitor function. A similar warning appears if the last complete backup ran with errors.

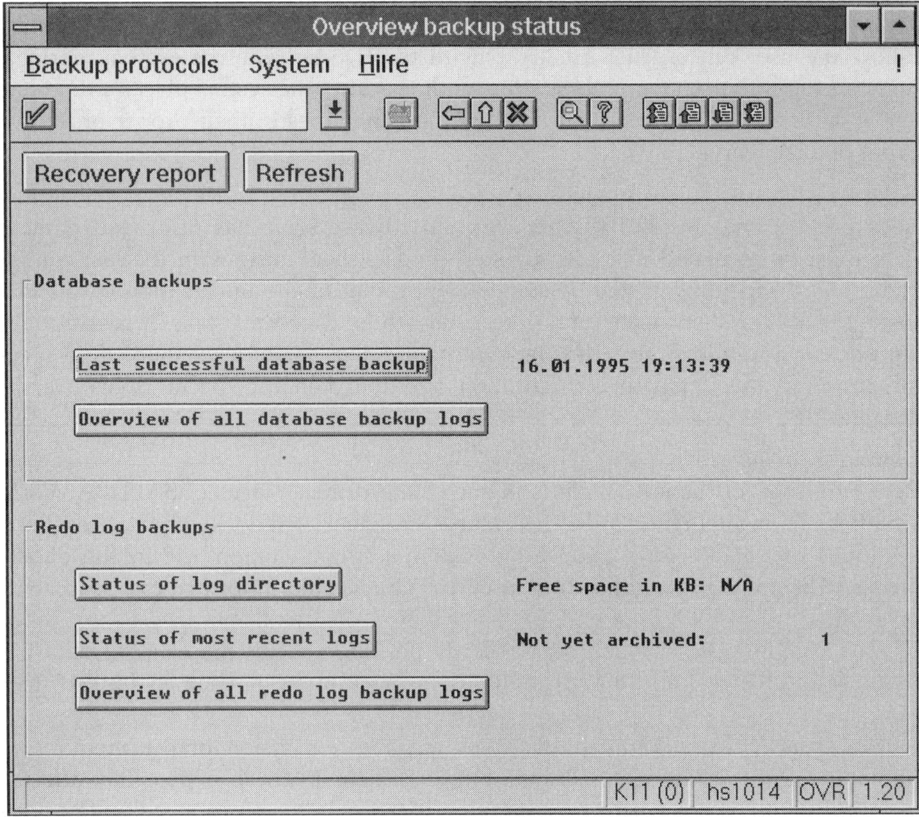

Figure 3.32 Oracle backup report

3.9 DB-specific tools

3.9.1 SAPDBA

SAP developed the tool SAPDBA for Oracle and Informix to simplify and to control backup activity better. The actual RDBMS software, therefore, does not contain SAPDBA. ADABAS D does not require the tool because its functions are already contained in the RDBMS.

The tool SAPDBA generally performs the following tasks:

- Starting and stopping the RDBMS.
- Expanding the database areas.
- Export and import of database objects.

- *Backup*
  Before the user can execute a backup with the R/3 system, the system marks and registers tapes used in the process. During the backup, the system places a time stamp and a mark on each tape so that it can request the tapes in their proper order in the event of a recovery.
- *Recovery*
  Recovery becomes necessary whenever a hardware error has destroyed data. The data must be recreated in a step-by-step process, beginning with the last complete backup and including a step-by-step incorporation of the information saved in the logs. The R/3 system itself cannot be used while a recovery takes place. SAPDBA supports the administrator during a recovery: the database contains R/3-specific structures in the database configuration and the database-specific tools are quite complex.
- *Database reorganization*
  Reorganization of the data records is one of the primary tasks of SAPDBA. Various situations make reorganization necessary. Frequent deletions of, changes to and additions of data records can lead to internal fragmentation within the database blocks. The memory organization user by Oracle and Informix can lead to this problem.

  Data chaining exists when data records no longer fit in the original data block (because of changes) and an additional data block must be chained (linked) to the record.

  The steadily rising number of tables requires expansion of the memory area (table space) by additional memory blocks (extents). These expansions affect the technical setting made during the definition of tables in the repository (see Chapter 5). As a result, tables or indexes distribute themselves across several, non-contiguous extents.

  In the final analysis, all these factors affect the performance of the database negatively. When the level of changes made to the database is high (certainly the case in a start-up installation of R/3), the factors have a correspondingly high negative effect. In this case, use database-specific means to determine the table spaces or tables causing the problem. Then export the data to another storage medium. Finally, create sufficient contiguous memory for the data and re-import it.

  This simplified overview of a reorganization should show how much the procedure requires a thorough knowledge of the RDBMS and the operating system. The tool SAPDBA offers welcome support in the process.

3.9.2 Control

In a certain sense, the tool control (xcontrol) of ADABAS D is the counterpart of SAPDBA. It contains, however, no reorganization functions, as the software itself manages it automatically. The various RDBMS have divergent philosophies: ADABAS D requires no reorganization of the entire system. The software itself recognizes and repairs any fragmentation affects. ADABAS D uses no table spaces.

The tool's tasks include:

- Starting and stopping the database
- Expanding the database area
- Evaluation functions for activities and performance
- Backup
- Recovery
- Weekly scheduling of activities.

3.9.3 Enterprise Manager

SQL Server provides its own graphic tool for administration. Enterprise Manager covers all administrative tasks, just as other RDBMS are familiar with them. In the Windows NT environment, use of the mouse can accomplish all tasks. Just as Oracle and Informix use table spaces, SQL Server uses segments. With R/3 no segments are currently used, so they require no administration. Backup actions can be scheduled within the Enterprise Manager, but the interfaces to the CCMS are still being developed. SQL Server will have to prove itself in the future.

The tools discussed here cover only one part of the database-specific tools available. The RDBMS offer additional possibilities for administration, including the development of individual applications. Processing business matters, however, remains the central purpose of an R/3 system. These matters play a subordinate role in the administration of an R/3 system.

4 ABAP/4 workbench

The ABAP/4 workbench functions as a collection of all the working elements required to create an R/3 application. An R/3 transaction comprises:

- Repository objects such as tables, structures and data elements,
- Templates (screen images),
- Menus, GUI status,
- Program source text in the ABAP/4 programming language.

The tools used to create these objects include:

- Repository,
- Screen painter,
- Menu painter,
- ABAP/4 editor and function library.

The correction and transport system completes the ABAP/4 workbench. The system serves as the transfer mechanism between various R/3 systems and coordinates development activities. The applications are divided into individual development objects. Reach the workbench via the menu path *Tools → ABAP/4 Workbench*. The push buttons located here allow comfortable access to all required development tools.

4.1 Object browser

The ABAP/4 workbench integrates the various development tools needed for each object. The developer can branch to the development tool by entering the object to be processed explicitly. That assumes, of course, that the developer has a rather exact overview of the project; he must know what templates are allocated to what program, etc.

The object browser, however, provides another route for the developer. Figure 4.1 illustrates the initial screen for the object browser for development class ZZ01 from Appendix G.

Starting with the choice of object (e.g., the development class), the system presents the developer with a tree representing the hierarchical structure of the sub-objects (see also Figure 4.2). A double click on the individual nodes of an object divides the object into its component parts. Once the developer reaches the smallest unit (the template, for example), he can automatically branch to the corresponding tool (the screen painter,

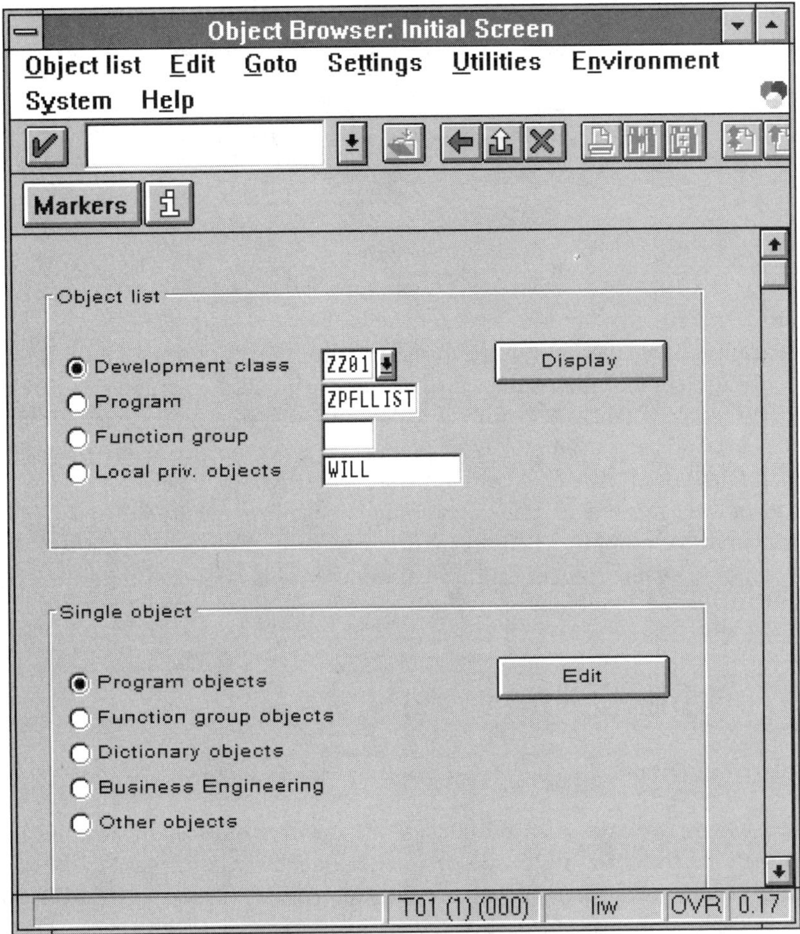

Figure 4.1 Object browser

for example). The advantage here is clear: the developer always has an overview of the context of the sub-objects and can navigate to the proper tools easily.

Objects within the R/3 system are interrelated. These correlations almost completely exclude examination or application of an individual tool or object outside of R/3. The clearest presentation of the SAP software development environment would show interplay between the R/3 repository, the screen painter, the CUA painter and pure ABAP/4 instructions. The workbench organizer manages changes to objects and transports between R/3 systems (see Figure 4.2).

The repository provides the required information on R/3 data. It forms the connection between the world of R/3 data and ABAP/4 programs. The screen painter supports the creation of data masks that allow interactive data processing. It also permits attaching check procedures to the individual input/output fields. Along with a basis in ABAP/4

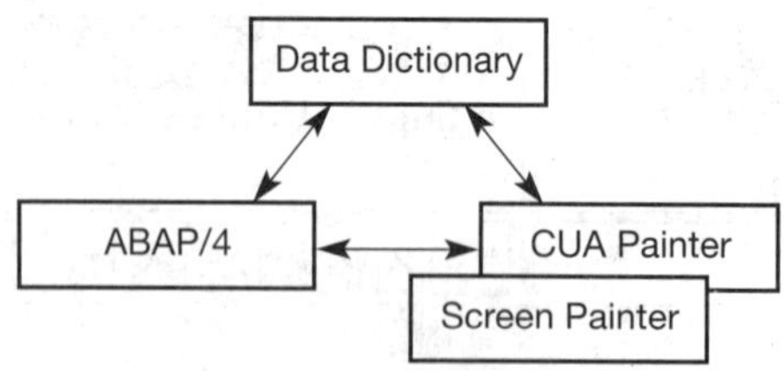

Figure 4.2 Interplay of objects

instructions, the screen painter also determines the flow logic. The object created is a screen program, often called a dynpro (dynamic program) in the R/3 environment.

Menus usually control the sequence of screens. The CUA painter aids in the design and flow of menus. The CUA painter creates and controls menu bars, functions and buttons. CUA stands for Common User Access. The screen processor provides central control of the flow of all ABAP/4 programs and their components.

The information system of the development environment includes all modules of ABAP program development. The information system in the repository allows branching to the information system in program development. This connection permits queries to all the information on ABAP objects.

4.2 Workbench organizer

4.2.1 Function

In the R/3 system, an enterprise purchases a software product whose complexity and range of functions trigger a multitude of smaller data processing tasks within the firm. Customizing tailors the system (as delivered) to enterprise-specific needs. R/3 also allows modification of the business applications as delivered and development in ABAP/4.

The coordination and regulation of development efforts play an increasingly large role in software development. Successful efforts in this regard can certainly contribute to lower costs. Some of the most important requirements in software development include: the ability to read and maintain software; to replicate modifications by recording their change-histories; and tuning parallel developments in a multi-user development environment.

Managers normally subdivide development work into projects, so that a project encompasses a closed part of the development process. A project group, consisting of several developers working together, holds responsibility for a project. Tasks and responsibilities within the project group can take various forms. Consider the following possible configurations:

- One fixed set of development objects are allocated to each developer. Other developers have no access to these programs.
- One fixed set of development objects are allocated to each developer. If necessary, other developers may maintain these programs.

- Several developers work on the same development objects. Each developer should have access to the all the programs.

R/3 can manage these, or similar, organizational plans for development work. The correction system, the **workbench organizer** (transaction `se09`), offers the user a tool that satisfies requirements for efficient, easily managed coordination of development.

In R/3 version 3.x, SAP has succeeded in fully integrating the correction system into the ABAP/4 workbench. The workbench organizer differentiates itself from the correction system in version 2.x in its completely updated interface. The use of hierarchical lists (a double click opens and closes folders) not only improved movement within the workbench organizer itself, but also allowed a much wider overview. Version 3.x also permits management of customizing settings in the **customizing organizer**. The organizer can switch automatic recording of customizing activities on or off.

Integration of the workbench organizers and the ABAP/4 workbench permits navigation from the development environment to the workbench organizer and from the workbench organizer back to work on individual objects within various development projects.

The workbench organizer offers control, identification and documentation of developments and changes in the system. It provides software to implement and monitor various organizational forms of development work. It also prohibits simultaneous work on the same object by several developers.

4.2.2 Development environment objects

An R/3 system consists of numerous component parts. These include, among others, ABAP/4 programs, repository objects, contents of tables, screen definitions, documentation and texts. There exist between the elements some dependencies, which require attention during processing. For example, an ABAP/4 program can run only when the repository objects it needs to access actually exist, or when screen definitions for the screens it calls are available. It would make matters much easier to work on related components as a unit, especially during processing or transport. The correction and transport system (CTS) addresses this development wish with its view of system components.

The correction and transport system consists of development environment objects: **DE objects**. A DE object is defined as the combination of connected or mutually dependent system components for a particular object. A DE object, therefore, consists of several components. This consideration makes it much easier to process components of the R/3 system. The CTS determines, based on the object type **object type**, if all or part of a DE object requires processing. For example, the DE object `R3TR PROG` represents the source code of an ABAP/4 program, the program's CUA definition, graphics, accompanying text and documentation as a unit. Figure 4.3 shows the most important pre-defined object types for the development environment.

The object type `R3TR` addresses complex objects such as an ABAP/4 program and the system components dependent on the program. The object type `LIMU` identifies subcomponents of a complex object. The specification `LIMU DYNP`, therefore, creates a single

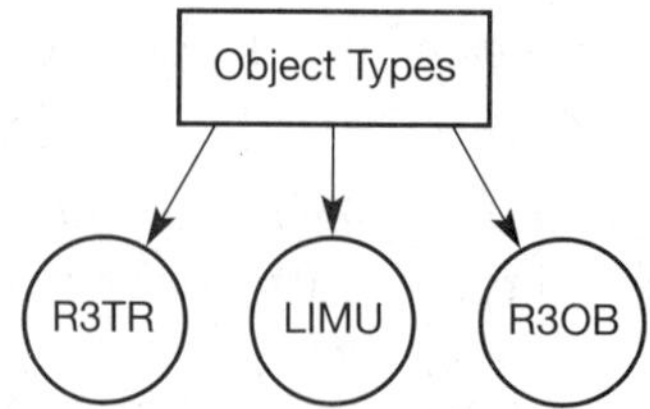

Figure 4.3 Pre-defined object types in the development environment

screen under the correction request. Most DE objects can be allocated the object type `R3TR` or `LIMU`. SAP application development uses the object type `R3OB` (e.g., forms, styles). The object type and the DE object name provide system-wide identification of a DE object.

Pre-defined `LIMU` objects often exist for complex objects of object type `R3TR`. The pre-defined objects permit targeted access to sub-components of the complex objects. Note that when `LIMU` objects are used the responsibility for modifications of complex objects generally lies with the user. Section 7.8.2 presents the pre-defined object types most frequently used.

The correction and transport system is based on the assumption that every object possesses exactly **one original**. All other versions (with changed characteristics) of the object in other systems are merely copies of the original. R/3 parlance designates the system in which the object was first created as the **original system**. The object itself is called **original**. The workbench organizer stores changes to originals and copies in various administrative units (see Section 4.2.6).

SAP introduced the term **object category** with version 3.x. The expansion of the correction system required this concept. As of version 3.x, the correction system could administer customizing settings, which made the transfer of completed customizing activities into other systems significantly more simple. The object category indicates if the object comes from the SAP repository or is a customer-specific customizing object (see Table 4.1).

Table 4.1 Object categories

Object category	*Meaning*
SYST	SAP repository object or customizing object beyond the limits of one client
CUST	Customer-specific customizing object

4.2.3 Object types

The correction and transport system distinguishes between three object types. The allocation of an object to a particular object type determines how the CTS will treat it. The development class to which the object belongs defines the object type. A **normal object** belongs to either a system development class or a customer development class (see Section 4.2.5). All the rules of the correction and transport system can apply to normal

Table 4.2 Treatment of object types in the CTS

Object type	*Processing registered by the workbench organizer?*	*Transport into other systems allowed?*
Normal objects	Yes	Yes
Private objects	Adjustable	Yes
Local, private objects	No	No

objects. The CTS treats two object types, **local objects** and **local, private objects** as special cases. Objects of local development classes are called local objects. Objects of private test development classes are called local, private objects. Table 4.2 summarizes how these categories affect CTS treatment of these objects.

It is, however, possible to change a private or a local, private object into a normal object. Simply create a change request for the affected object that allocates the object to a development class for normal objects.

4.2.4 Naming conventions for DE objects

To avoid conflicts with objects of the SAP development environment, use the naming template illustrated in Table 4.3 for any newly developed DE objects. When creating names, `Z` can stand for `Y`. Replace `X` with any character. The convention ensures that updates to R/3 application software will not overwrite customer objects.

Table 4.3 Naming convention for Customer-DE objects

Development environment object	*Name template*
ABAP programs	ZaXXXXXX
ABAP module pools	SAPZXXX
Repository objects	ZZXXXXXXXX
Pool/cluster names	ZXXX
Function modules	Z_XXX...
Function groups	ZXXX
Development classes	ZXXX
Transaction codes	ZXXX

4.2.5 Development classes

Gathering dependent or closely related DE objects into logical units creates a **development class**.

Development classes join the DE objects of a functional area. Classes allow correction or transport of a large number of complex DE objects (see Figure 4.4). They greatly

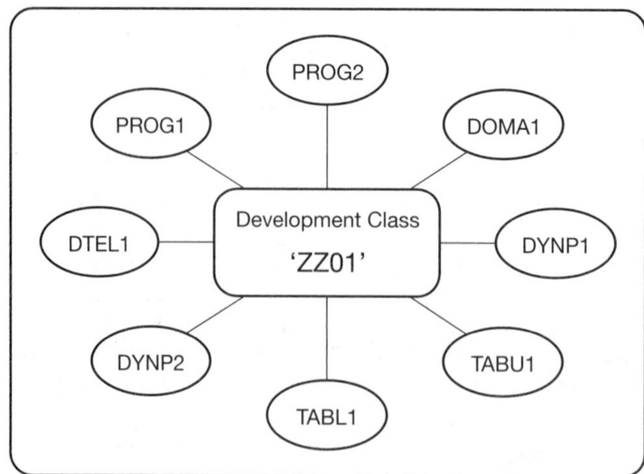

Figure 4.4 DE objects of development class ZZ01

ease the processing of objects by way of the correction and transport system. On the one hand, they provide a clean structure for development activities; on the other hand, they avoid the danger of forgetting individual objects during a transfer. They thus provide an example of teamwork and the use of software to support projects. The features make development classes in the ABAP/4 workbench an aid in creating structures.

Attributes can be assigned to a development class. The attributes will affect how the workbench organizer treats Euobjects in the development class. As of version 3.x, for example, a development class includes a fixed transport layer. The transport layer determines which system functions as the recipient of transportable change requests (see Section 7.5.3).

The name ranges divide development classes into four categories (see Table 4.4). Each category has its own functional properties that determine how the correction and transport system treats the category.

The workbench organizer does not register changes to objects of a local development class. These objects cannot be transported. A connection to the workbench organizer can be chosen as an option when establishing private test development classes. Such objects, however, cannot be transported.

Table 4.4 Naming conventions for development classes

Name range	*Meaning*
Name begins with `A-S` or `U-X`	System development classes (for SAP standard objects)
Name begins with `Y` or `Z`	Customer development classes (for objects of individual application development)
Name begins with `T`	Private test development classes
Name begins with `$`	Local development classes

Customer and system development classes include a connection to the workbench organizer by their very definitions. The objects they encompass can be transported according to the rules of the CTS.

4.2.6 Tasks

The R/3 system permits individual development as an addition to the basis system as delivered. Development work in the R/3 environment is defined as the new development of individual DE objects or the modification of extant objects. The workbench organizer registers processing of an DE object as a **task**. The correction system understands a task as the smallest and lowest level administrative unit that the development coordination of the workbench organizer can drive. The task stores information on the current level of processing of the DE object it contains for **one developer**. A task can process several objects simultaneously.

The DE objects contained in a task create an **object list**. A term from the world of R/2, `command file` is often used here. The first object contained in a task determines the characteristics or type of the remaining objects. The task can administer all the other objects only if they possess the same task type. A characteristic, however, can be allocated to an empty task; doing so prevents misuse.

The workbench organizer distinguishes between the task types shown in Table 4.5:

Table 4.5 Task types

Task type	*Meaning*
Development/correction	Administers only those objects originally created in the system (originals).
Repair	Registers changes to copies (not originals).

A task is addressed by name, as seen in the following:

```
<SAP_system_name>K<ID_number>    Example: T01K900001
```

The system automatically grants names to tasks. Because task names are numeric, they are sometimes called **task numbers**. Both terms have exactly the same meaning. Along with archiving information about who edited a DE object when, a task has a second important function. It serves as an instrument to coordinate competing access attempts to DE objects. Tasks and requests implement a multi-layer lock concept that informs one user of another user's attempt to work on the same object simultaneously or refuses parallel access. Section 7.7 displays the lock mechanisms involved.

4.2.7 Requests

A request represents the next highest administrative unit in the correction system. A request combines the tasks of a given development project. The efforts of one or more developers come together here. Each developer, of course, can work on all the objects of a

Table 4.6 Request types

Request type	*Meaning*
Transportable change request	Administers DE objects whose development class allows transport into other systems. Development classes beginning with `A-S`, `U-X`, `Y`, `Z`
Local change request	Administers DE objects from development classes beginning with `T`. Transport into other systems is possible only with special transport requests, not with the workbench organizer.

request. Tasks allocated to a request (development/correction or repairs with entries in their object lists) are always coupled directly to the request. The workbench organizer uses the development class of a DE object in a task to determine which request type to allocate to it. The workbench organizer recognizes the request types shown in Table 4.6.

The correction and transport system classifies requests according to category besides request type:

- `CUST` (to administer customer-specific customizing settings),
- `SYST` (to administer changes in the SAP repository or customizing setting beyond the limits of a particular client).

The workbench organizer administers requests in the category `SYST`. The customizing organizer administers requests in the category `CUST` (transaction `se10`). Both tools are used almost identically; Chapter 7 discusses the workbench organizer almost exclusively. The functions discussed here also apply to request administration in customizing.

Please note two special cases when recording customizing activities. First, customizing allows switching the automatic recording of settings made during customizing on or off according to client. The user can also decide whether customizing settings can be transported or not, and set the system accordingly. In the category `CUST`, therefore, the transportability of requests does not depend on the objects contained in the request.

4.2.8 Work methodology

The preceding sections introduced the elementary components of the workbench organizer. This knowledge provides an easy understanding the basic work methodology of the correction system.

An SAP R/3 system comprises numerous DE objects. The objects would be all the more numerous when customers perform their development work. Requests register any work done on DE objects. For their part, requests do not exist as independent administrative units. The requests are always coupled to a change request. In a certain sense, a change request represents a project in itself, a project that is subdivided into several smaller development activities (tasks).

The workbench organizer allows the organization to function as a one-person project or as a development team. In any case, it prohibits parallel and uncoordinated or unauthorized access to the DE objects of a change request.

The combination of tasks into requests grants the workbench organizer responsibility for administering the registered and documented development work contained in the request as a unit.

A project can end only when all the tasks associated with it have been completed. If desired (e.g., for transportable change requests), the workbench organizer triggers the export of the objects into the file system of the transport server at the end of the project (see Section 7.9). In any case, it removes object locks at the end of a successful project so that these objects become available for new development projects.

4.3 Repository tool

4.3.1 Concepts

The following section discusses the terms **data dictionary** and **repository**. It begins with a general definition of the term and then develops the special aspects of the R/3 repository.

Data dictionary

The data dictionary of a relational database

Two-dimensional tables store all the data in a relational database and the interrelationships between the data.

Data dictionary means `data description`. A data dictionary describes the database model upon which the database is structured. It contains data about the data: the **metadata**. This information includes data definitions, tables, table relationships, access rights to tables and the integrity conditions of a database (see Figure 4.5). A database's data dictionary, also called a data catalog, exists independently of the type and meaning of the data held in the database. The information contained in a database-internal data dictionary provides no reverse access to the data or how a business application uses it.

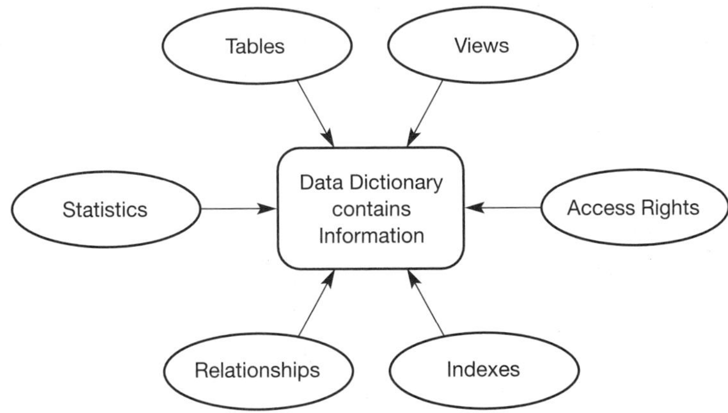

Figure 4.5 Information-delivery structure of the data dictionary (internal to the database)

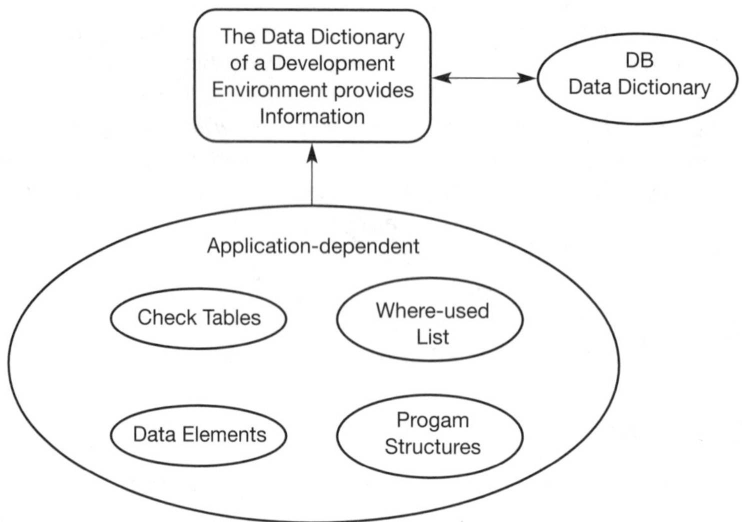

Figure 4.6 The information of the data dictionary in a development environment

The data dictionary of a software-development environment

Software development environments require metadata on the use of the data within a program package just as much as database systems themselves do. In this case the requirements include a description of the program elements used within a program, such as data structures. Nevertheless, the function of a data dictionary of a development environment goes far beyond that of a database-internal data dictionary.

Program developers should have an uncomplicated ability to determine where data structures are used. The data dictionary provides this function. The data dictionary contains a description of all the objects and checks them before they become active in a program. It also stores conventions, whether determined during program development or later during the use of a software package. The use of data elements (described exactly in Section 5.1), allow the data dictionary to create a logical relationship between a pure description of a field and its later use in an application. The data dictionary in a development environment forms the central information source about the data of a software package (see Figure 4.6).

R/3 data dictionary

The **ABAP/4 development environment** (workbench) works with metadata, as do all 4GL development environments. The metadata describes all the data structures used in an ABAP/4 program. These structures include table, field definitions and relationships between tables. The task of the R/3 data dictionary is to create and administer information on these objects. The R/3 dictionary also describes the internal structures of program modules and their interfaces. Domains and data elements help to define

Table 4.7 The R/3 data dictionary

Which data objects does the database contain?	Tables, views...
What properties do these objects have?	Name, format, length, type, fixed values, logical names
How are the individual objects related?	Foreign key

the field properties of relational tables. It uses foreign keys to illustrate the relation of the individual tables to each other and declares external views for tables. The R/3 data dictionary thus presents an 'information base for users and various software components' (SAP Data Dictionary). It provides the information given in Table 4.7.

The R/3 data dictionary combines the concepts of an integrated and an active data dictionary.

- *Integrated R/3 data dictionary*
  Integration means the complete embedding of data dictionary information in the R/3 development environment. The data dictionary creates and administers each piece of information given above only once. Each user has access to the information always and at every point in the system. The ABAP/4 editor, for example, can directly display table definitions from the data dictionary. Internal program structures can refer to table or field definitions of the ABAP/4 data dictionary. Chapter 6 describes the possibilities open to the developer.

- *Active R/3 data dictionary*
  An active data dictionary means that changes to dictionary objects can take effect in the application programs automatically and immediately. The interpretative work methodology of the R/3 system makes this possible. The ABAP/4 processor does not work directly with the original coding of an ABAP/4 program. Rather, it interprets a generated, intermediate code: the runtime object. Since runtime objects relate to the status of the data dictionary at the time of their creation, they may not reflect current values when they actually run. When a program starts, it checks the time stamps of all the affected objects for exactly this reason. If the check determines that the information in the data dictionary has changed since the generation of the runtime object, the system automatically regenerates the program's runtime objects based on the current status of the data dictionary.

  At what point a changed object becomes active depends on two factors. First, it depends on the type of data dictionary object involved. Second, objects can be activated explicitly. If, for example, a new value is entered in a value table, it becomes active immediately. Only then can all the screens containing a field with this value table immediately display the help function listing the value among possible entries. The data dictionary, however, offers the developer another possibility. She can determine the activation point (Section 5.7) by first saving the change in an inactive version.

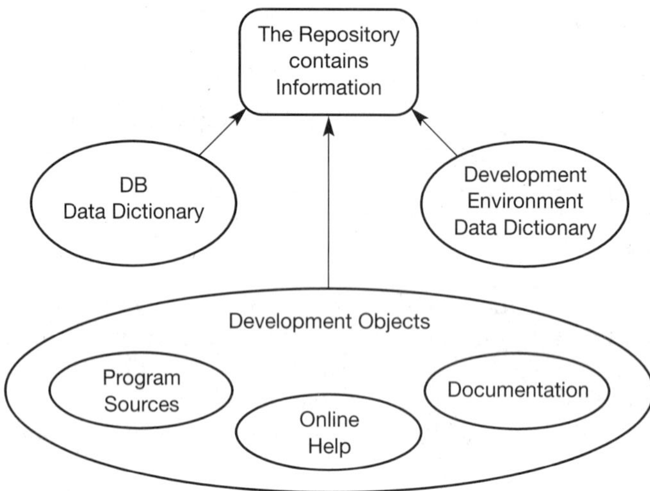

Figure 4.7 Information in the repository

Repository

Along with the information noted, a repository (see Figure 4.7) holds all the objects created during the development process centrally. This would include program source texts, function modules, documentation and help texts.

R/3 repository

The R/3 repository stores all development objects created within the ABAP/4 workbench during the development process. These development objects include all ABAP/4 programs, screens, reports, masks, data models, documentation, help texts and data in the data dictionary. Please note that the R/3 system stores the data dictionary itself in the R/3 repository (see Figure 4.8). Although SAP looks at both components separately, it is possible to consider them as one component. The remainder of this book speaks only of the R/3 repository.

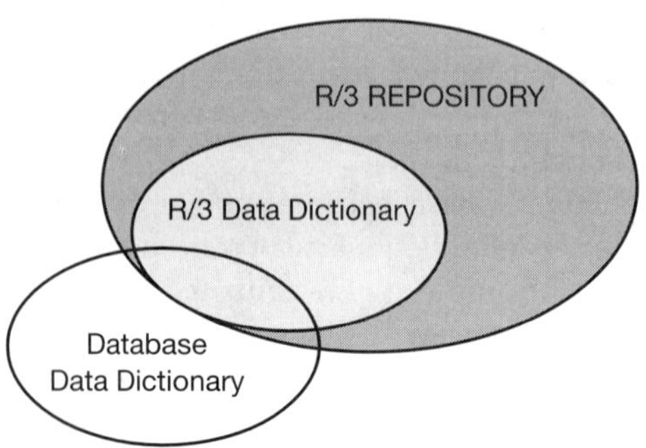

Figure 4.8 Information base of the R/3 system

Purpose

One purpose of a repository is to store information about an enterprise. However, central data storage is not the only function of a repository. It is not a passive structure that simply delivers a status report. The information it contains should flow into the enterprise actively and introduce improvements. If information from the repository data makes regulating access necessary, the changed data becomes active in the repository immediately. The repository, therefore, has the following purposes and goals:

- *Central administration of metadata*
  As its first and primary purpose, the R/3 repository serves as a tool for the creation and administration of information about data. Data storage is free of redundancy because, by their very definition, data objects are created and described centrally and only once. Every authorized user has access to this data within the system. To ensure that all changes to the repository take effect immediately in all system components, the repository is integrated into the other R/3 software components such as program development or the database interface.

- *Support for the software development process*
  The quality of standard software exhibits one hallmark: the ability to meet the special conditions of an enterprise by easy adaptation to those needs. This stipulation requires adherence to certain guidelines as early as possible in the development phase. At best, this occurs during the analysis and design of the software. The repository can support this process actively both during the development of software and when maintaining extant programs. The system generates data declarations from the information contained in the repository to prevent a developer from creating her own field names and types for her own program. Unlike inactive, isolated repositories, the R/3 repository takes an active role in the development environment. Programs such as the ABAP/4 language interpreter, reporting functions or the mask generator can always call current information from the R/3 repository via the defined interfaces.

- *Support for documentation*
  The effort involved in maintaining programs depends greatly on their documentation. The metadata of the R/3 repository can serve as a basis for current system documentation. To a large extent, data from the repository creates help texts in the R/3 environment.

- *Retrieval of information for analysis*
  Repositories also make available information on the relationship between the individual data elements. Relationship refers both to the relationship of individual tables to each other and the where-used list of tables or table fields in ABAP/4 programs. A user can obtain information reports on the use of special fields at any time. This information provides ready answers to questions such as: '`which table contains this field`' or '`which application contains this table?`' The report immediately shows if the data corresponds to the current status. This information also shows whether the data needs new or changed organizational requirements. Section 5.6 treats the R/3 information system in greater detail.

- *Performance*
  As a direct consequence of the requirements noted above, R/3 applications require permanent access to the repository and the data contained in the database. Flexibility and currency can thus lead to larger disk space, higher CPU load and longer wait times during database access. Accesses to the repository can be held to a reasonable number by storing all the information affecting performance in the runtime objects. In addition, SAP uses a special buffer mechanism to keep the I/O rate as low as possible.
- *Presentation of the enterprise data model*
  An enterprise combines three production factors: productivity, operating resources and materials. Productivity means both the objective work itself and the work that drives business, dispositional productivity. Its functions include planning, monitoring and organizing business processes. Information plays an ever larger role in the decision-making process that results from an attempt to master these functions. It is the task of information management to observe business realities and to describe an enterprise data model exactly. The R/3 repository describes this enterprise data model, formalizes it and stores it in the database, thus integrating it into the data processing system.

4.4 ABAP/4 editor

ABAP/4 programs are created in dialog. To reach the tool used to create programs, the ABAP/4 editor, use the push button of the same name (transaction `se38`). Reach the transaction with the menu path *Tools → ABAP/4 Workbench → Development → ABAP/4 Editor*. This transaction, like all others in the R/3 system, consists of a series of menus, screens and ABAP/4 modules.

A specific name range is available for customer programs. Use `Y` or `Z` for the first letter, then a letter that specifies the application area. Choose the remaining six characters at will.

Create the program before composing the actual source text; program creation involves maintaining the characteristics. Unless otherwise specified, the title of a program serves as the standard title of lists and documentation.

The type classifies the program according to the following:

- 1 Report
- I Include program
- M Module pool

Allocation to an application supports the system when it presents business topics.

An existing authorization group can be allocated to the program. Doing so means that only those users whose profiles make them part of the authorization group can execute the program. Make additional limitations to the program being created via *Editor lock* and *Start via variant*. A check on Editor lock means that no other users can edit the program. Start via variant allows program starts only with already-defined variants. Specify a

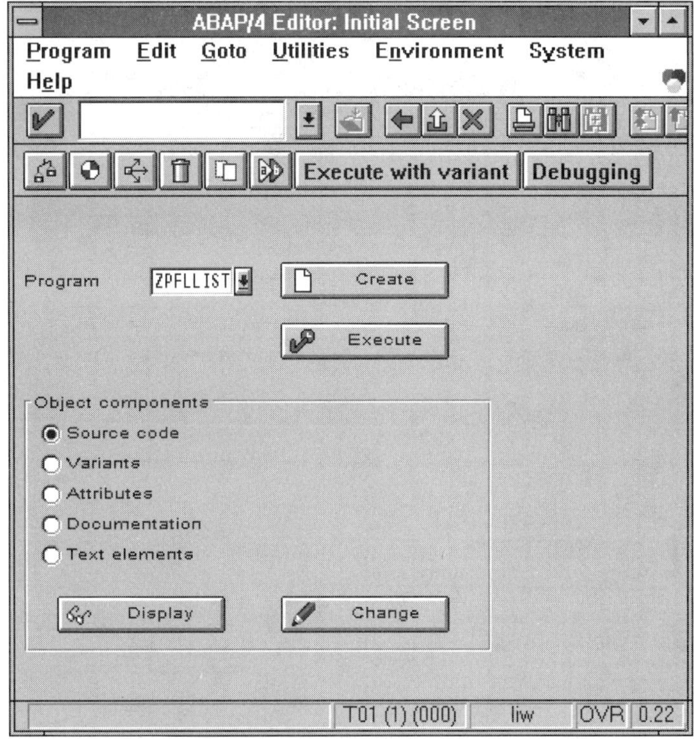

Figure 4.9 Initial screen

logical database if working with one (see Section 6.8) along with the corresponding application.

A check on *Upper/lower case* characters suppresses automatic transposition of the characters into uppercase during editing. The characters remain as entered. *Fixed point arithmetic* affects the display and calculation of fields with type P. These fields are rounded according to the number of defined decimal places. Choose the option *Source code* and use the appropriate push buttons to activate *Change* (see Figure 4.9) to enter the editor.

R/3 offer various working modes for the editor in version 3.x. The modes depend on the hardware used at the front end. Choose among the following:

- PC mode,
- PC mode with line numbering,
- Command mode.

Use the menu to choose the editor mode. The setting remains in effect until the next choice. In PC mode the editor works much like other PC-based editors: use of the mouse is available.

The editor mode with line numbering provides numbers for each line. The editor does not permit entry of a command in the numbering column. Use the command mode if

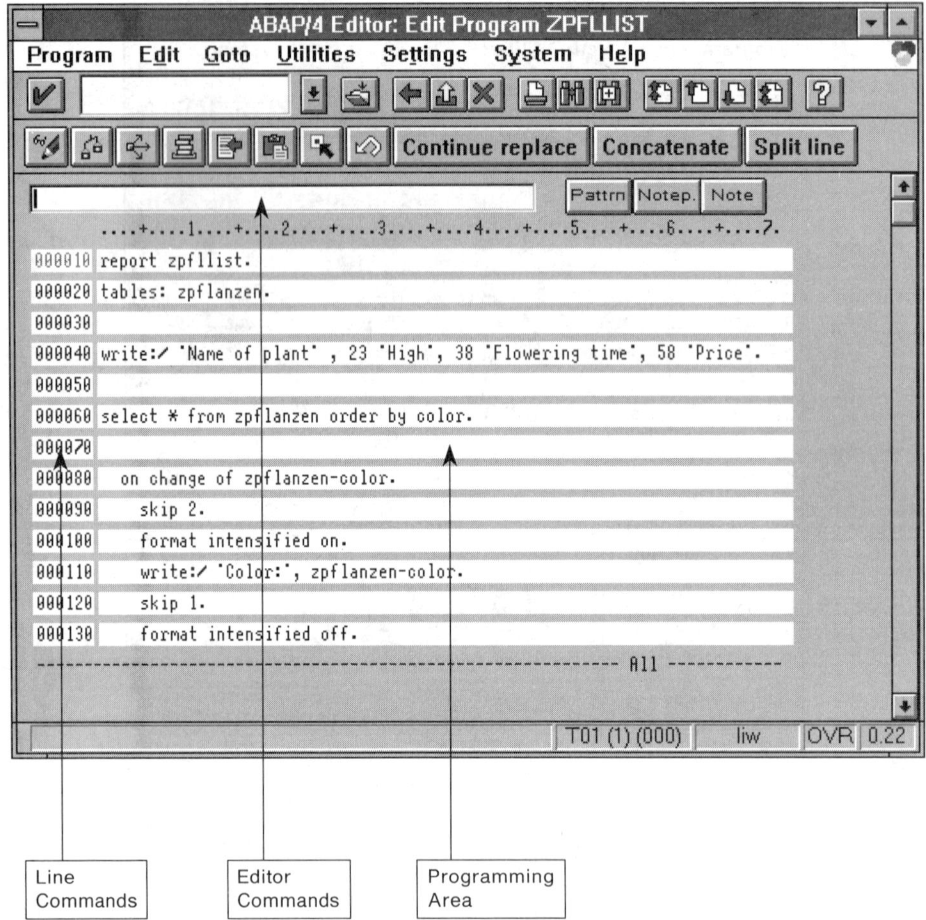

Figure 4.10 Editor

entering commands. Becoming familiar with the command mode will take some time, especially if the user has already worked with a PC editor. Command mode, however, is consistent and, after some use, comfortable. The editor's command mode is available on X-terminals without any limits. It therefore deserves a closer look.

At the moment, it is impossible to include another editor (e.g., one specific to the operating system) in the R/3 system. The editor must perform almost all work on programs, modules, documentation, etc.; it provides additional special functions for individual areas. A basic outline follows.

The ABAP/4 program editor is line-oriented. It grants each line a number internally (see Figure 4.10), and distinguishes between line commands and editor commands. The editor permits entry of line commands only in the line numbering column. These commands allow positioning the cursor and editing blocks and lines (copying, intermediate storage, moving). The command *I*, for example, inserts a blank line after the current line. *I*<*n*> inserts <n> blank lines after the current line. Note that overwrite mode (OVR) is active (insert key on/off); no insertion in the line number column is possible. Line numbering is adjusted automatically every tenth step.

Use the line command *m* or *c* to move or copy a line. The editor marks the line with an *m* for move or *c* for copy in the line number column. Then move the cursor to the target line and mark it with an *a* (for after) if the line is to be inserted after the target line. Mark the target line with a *b* (for before) if the line is to be inserted before the target line. If moving or copying entire program blocks, mark the beginning and end of the block with *mm* or *cc* and use the line commands *a* or *b* to determine the target. Delete a line or block with the commands *d* or *dd* according to the same principle. Appendix D contains an overview of all line commands.

Unlike line commands, editor commands affect the entire program. Appendix D also contains a list of all editor commands. Most are completely normal and require no explanation. Command *ic* is a special case. If *ic* is entered in the command line, followed by the beginning key word of an ABAP instruction, the editor inserts a sample of the instruction after the current line. If, for example, *ic case* is entered, the editor inserts the following program module which must then be adjusted to current requirements.

```
CASE F.
  WHEN W1.
  ...
  WHEN W2.
  ...
  WHEN OTHERS.
  ...
END CASE.
```

The commands *show* <table_name> or *show function* <function_name> display the structure of the table or a description of the I/O parameters and the functionality of the output parameters of the module to help the user. Double click on an object in the program to display all the places in the ABAP/4 program that use the object.

Note the command *pp*, which calls the 'pretty printer.' The pretty printer structures the program automatically. Whenever it recognizes the beginning key word of an instruction, it adds an indent; at the end of an instruction it does the opposite.

The last few commands significantly simplify and speed up programming with R/3. The following sections treat other commands when required.

Use the ABAP/4 editor to create and maintain variants of already-existing programs. A variant is a defined allocation of values for report parameters. Background processing frequently uses variants. Create a variant from the *Initial Screen* via *Variants* → *Create*.

4.5 Menu painter

In the broadest sense, the CUA painter creates and allocates the menus and push buttons for a report or transaction. Maintain the CUA interface with the push button *CUA Painter* or with transaction code `se41`. Every CUA interface mirrors the status of a program.

To provide a certain level of uniformity within the R/3 system, each CUA interface features some standard buttons. These buttons require only activation or assignment of a return code. Which buttons function and whether a menu can be created at all depend on the type of CUA interface chosen.

Note the following types of CUA interfaces:

- Screen
  The CUA interface will be used with a screen program. Menus, push buttons and function keys are appropriate.
- Dialog window
- Lists

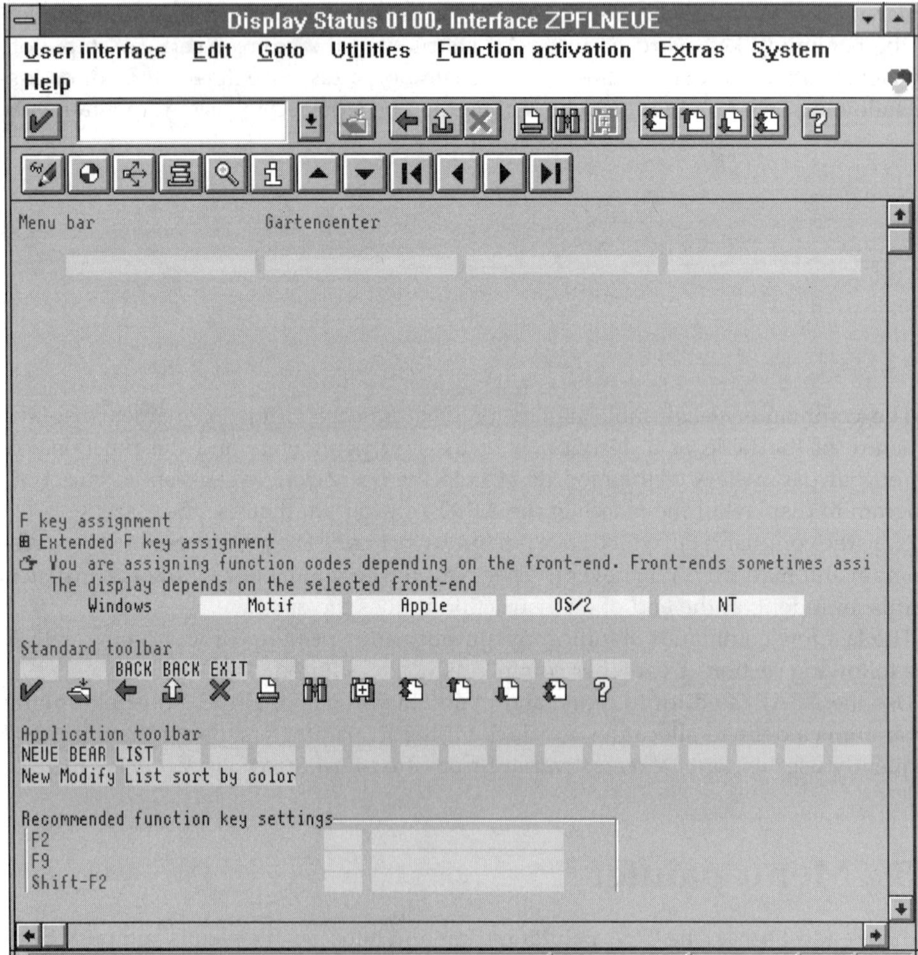

Figure 4.11 Menu painter

Status types do not affect runtime behavior. They serve solely to control the standard allocation of buttons and help functions.

Use the CUA interface to display a list. Lists frequently require a user to make choices, an option mirrored in the default settings for F2, *Choose*.

Figure 4.11 shows the working area of the CUA painter. The lower portion edits the allocation of push buttons and function keys. A default allocation exists for function keys, depending on the type of CUA interface being created. The use of icons is a new feature in version 3.x. The icons apply to standard functions. The developer has additional icons at his disposal.

The working area also shows the default setting for a normal screen program. Enter the function code that a key should return in the four character field to the left of the field naming function keys. Chapter 6 discusses the event AT USER-COMMAND. Whenever a user pushes a key, the event USER-COMMAND appears in the report. The system field SY-UCOMM is assigned the code allocated to the key. This procedure permits the system to react to the key according to the field SY-UCOMM.

The menu is designed in the upper area. The white fields maintains the menu bar. The painter adds the options *System* and *Help* to every menu as a default. After entering the top-level menu options successfully, enter subordinate options and their function codes by double clicking the left mouse button. Follow the same procedure to create additional subordinate menus for any menu option.

Titles can be created for program status. From the CUA painter, choose *Title list*. The desired titles are entered with a number. Control the header for the screen mask in the appropriate program. This closes a preliminary discussion of the maintenance of the CUA interface. Save the interface and then generate it.

4.6 Screen painter

The screen painter is the tool used to maintain screen masks for a transaction or report. R/3 systems also call screen masks dynpros (dynamic program). Navigate to the screen painter via the push button of the same name or with transaction code `se51`. No significant differences exist between PC and X-terminals.

A four-digit number, allocated to an existing report, identifies a screen.

Execute the following individual steps to create a screen:

- Define the screen attributes,
- Determine the repository fields,
- Define the screen,
- Create field lists,
- Program the flow logic,
- Generate.

4.6.1 Attributes

- *Determine next screen*
  If no definition exists for the next screen, the transaction process continues according to the program defaults. With the function the user can go to the next defined screen at the end of this screen.
- *Screen type*
  - normal (entire screen)
  - selection screen (automatically created by ABAP/4 according to the standard settings)
  - modal dialog window (secondary window)
  - sub-screen (corresponds to the new mode)
- *Cursor position*
  The name of a screen field sets the starting point for the cursor.
- *Screen group*
  This entry groups screens (four-digit number).
- *Size*
  An entry here is regarded as the upper limit during design of the screen.

4.6.2 Repository fields

To display or edit a mask administered by the R/3 repository, arrange them on the screen with this function of the screen painter.

4.6.3 Fullscreen editor

Use the fullscreen editor to create internal fields and to `paint` the screen. Internal fields are used only within the transaction and not administered in the repository. Fix the length and position of the internal fields with underscores (_). For this purpose, the editor also allows use of all the characters typical of building a mask (%, . , etc.) besides underscores (see Chapter 6).

- *Graphic elements and groups*
  Graphic elements include borders, check boxes, push buttons and radio buttons: the number of possibilities available increase from version to version of the R/3 system. Radio buttons are special fields that allow the choice of exactly one possibility from a group of options. By establishing groups (mark, group), the creator of the group can ensure that only one choice can be made from the group of possible options. The initial screen of the screen painter, for example, follows this organizational principle. The radio button, represented by a field with the length of 1, permits a choice. The menu makes available both round buttons, activated by a click, and check boxes, chosen with an `x`.

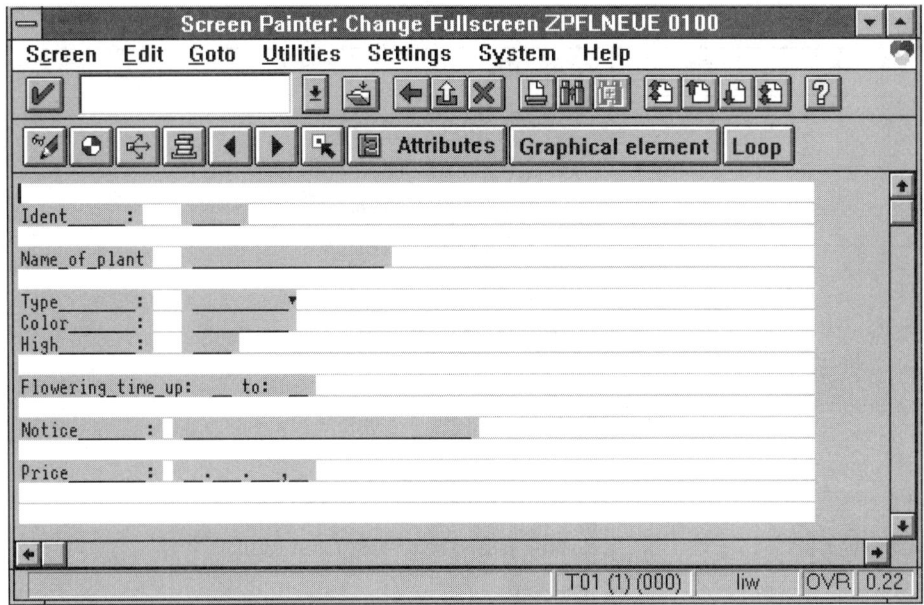

Figure 4.12 Screen in fullscreen display

A border combines groups visually. Create a border for a particular field by choosing the option *Graphic*. Then choose `Border` from the options presented. A click on the opposite corner or the desired border will create the border.
Figure 4.12 shows a screen in fullscreen editing.

4.6.4 Field list

The field lists displays all existing fields, including those in the repository. It allows maintenance of properties and return codes (push buttons).

A field has the following properties:

- *Name*
  The field name identifies the field within the module pool. The module pool must contain the name of the field with the corresponding data type. Accordingly, a field name can be assigned only once. A field name can contain a maximum of 30 characters.
- *Line, column and length*
  Fix these values with `Drawing` in the fullscreen editor.
- *Form*
  This property allocates a field format linked to a simultaneous plausibility check. See the R/3 documentation for a list of all valid field formats. Table 4.8 shows the most important field formats.

Table 4.8 Field formats

Data type	*Internal format*	*Description*
CHAR	C(n)	Character string with length <n>
DATS	D(8)	Date in DDMMYYYY format
TIMS	T(6)	Time in HHMMSS format
DEC	P	Numeric field with separators and possibly a plus/minus sign
INT1	X(1)	Integer, one byte long
INT2	X(2)	Integer, two bytes long
INT4	X(4)	Integer, four bytes long
NUMC	N(n)	Numeric field with length <n>
CUKY	C(5)	Currency key
CURR	P	Currency field, displays a field of type CUKY
ACCP	C(6)	Posting period with YYYYMM format
UNIT	C(n)	Unit key
BIT	B	Binary string: only 0 or 1 as permissible entries

- *E,A, Only*
  E identifies fields that allow entries.
  A identifies fields that allow output.
  Only identifies fields that represent pure output templates.
- *Dic*
  The system fills this field automatically, depending on whether it contains a repository reference (x) or not (-). The keyword shows which field description from the repository it uses:
  - without repository reference
  0 modified repository reference
  1 short keyword
  2 medium keyword
  3 long keyword
  4 header
  - Mod
  The intended use of repository fields are designated for this field.
  - Original
  If changes are made in the repository, they are presented on the screen (if possible).
  x Modified
  After generation of the screen, changes in the repository are no longer taken into account.

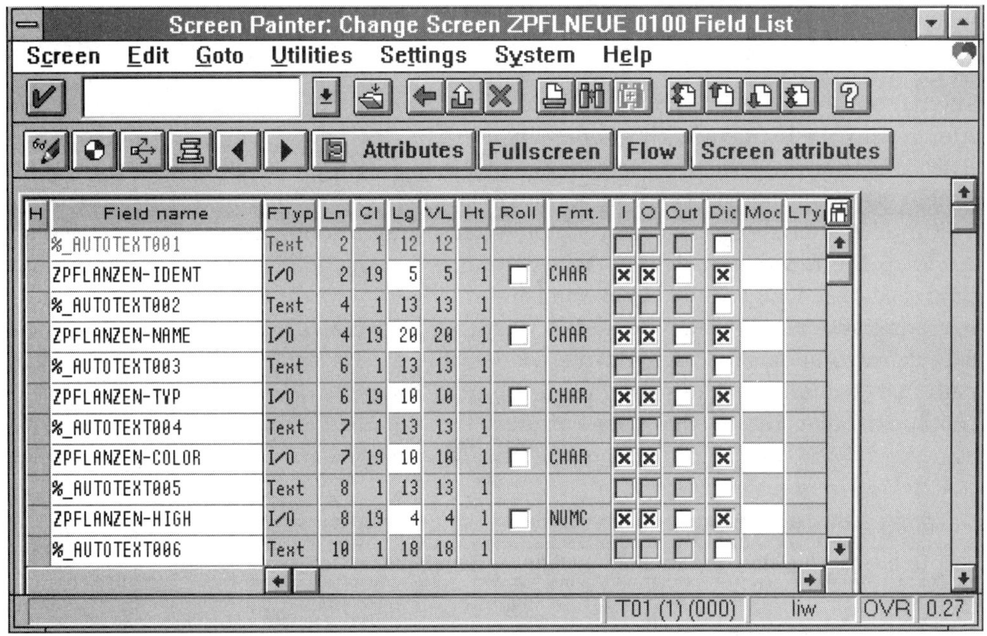

Figure 4.13 Field lists

- *Ltyp, Lanz*
  Both fields determine the characteristic of the screen during looping.
  Ltyp Size change, variable or fixed
  Lanz Number of loops for the entry of several records of the same type (e.g., tables).

  Each screen possesses an OK-code field, automatically added to the field list (see Figure 4.13). At every activation of a function key or push button, the applicable return code is sent to this field. Use the field names allocated to the OK-code to query the value of the field. Texts within the mask are also treated as fields without input or output options and thus require assignment of a name. %_AUTOTEXT<n> stands as a bookmark for fixed text-outputs.

4.6.5 Flow logic

Flow logic allocates two events to every screen mask:

- Process before output (PBO) before output of the screen,
- Process after input (PAI) after confirmation of the entry.

Modules can be assigned to these events. The modules are processed in order when the event occurs. Define modules in the module pool. Calling a module transfers control from the dialog processor to the ABAP/4 processor.

The keyword `OUTPUT` or `INPUT` is assigned to a module in the module pool, depending on whether it should be processed as PBO or PAI.

4.7 Testing

The ABAP/4 workbench provides special tools for testing under the menu option *Test*. Along with the syntax check offered by the ABAP/4 editor, the menu path *Test* → *Extended prog. check* provides a wide range of checks for programs. Both limited checks of certain elements and checks for important symbols or characters can be performed.

Runtime analysis is particularly noteworthy and recommended (*Test* → *Runtime analysis*). The function analyzes a specific transaction or report; it examines how much time each command requires to execute and the distribution of the runtime between the operating system, the database and R/3. Although the analysis at first requires some experience to understand the returned values, the reward is worth the effort. The menu path *Test* → *Runtime analysis* and the push button *Tips and Tricks* provides various ABAP commands that return the same results. The commands can be executed on an as-needed basis to determine the runtime on the system. The results very clearly

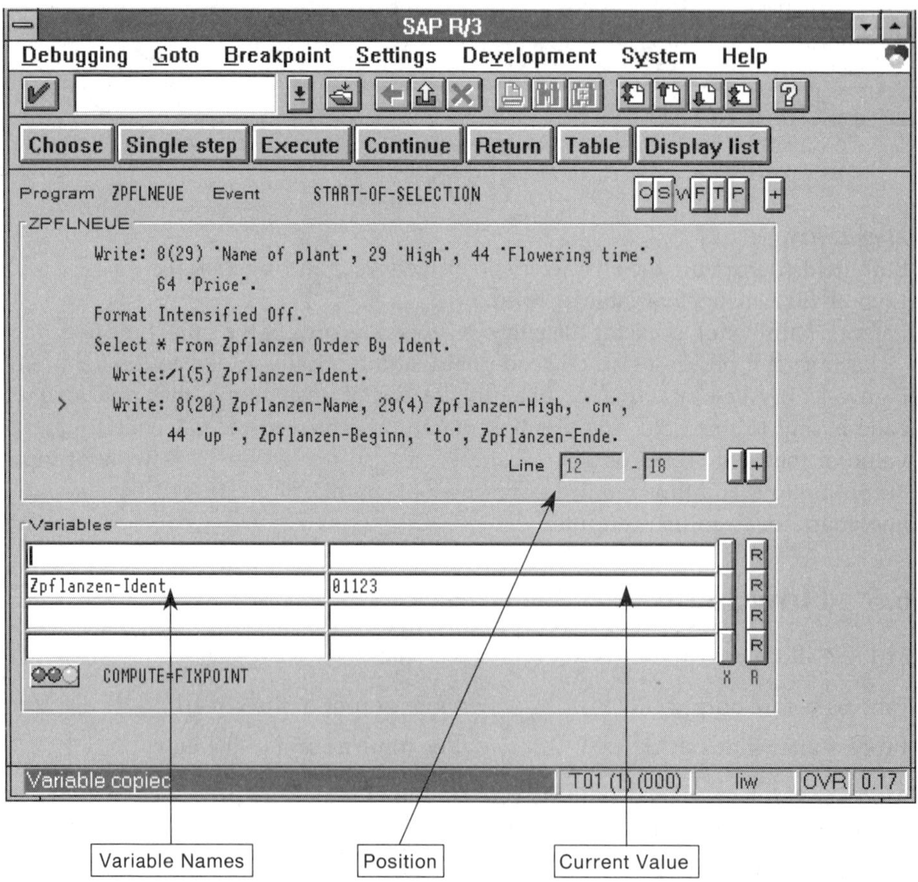

Figure 4.14 Execution in debugging mode

show that both `good` and `bad` variants exists to perform the same task. ABAP/4 is so complex that it offers several solutions to the same task. The runtime is a better determining factor than are the types of commands.

Debugger

We recommend use of the debugger for testing ABAP programs. To do so, start the ABAP/4 editor (transaction `se38`) with the push button *Debugging*. Execution of the report begins instruction by instruction.

The character > identifies the next instruction to be processed.

The push button *Single step* triggers execution of the next instruction. If the instruction calls a sub-program, the debugger branches to it and continues processing single steps.

The push button *Execute* executes the next instruction as a whole. If the instruction calls a sub-program, the debugger executes the entire sub-program without branching to debugging mode for the sub-program. After execution of the sub-program the debugger continues with the next instruction in the calling program. The push button *Continue* ends the debugging run and executes the report to its end. Figure 4.14 shows a screen during testing. The lower section displays a table.

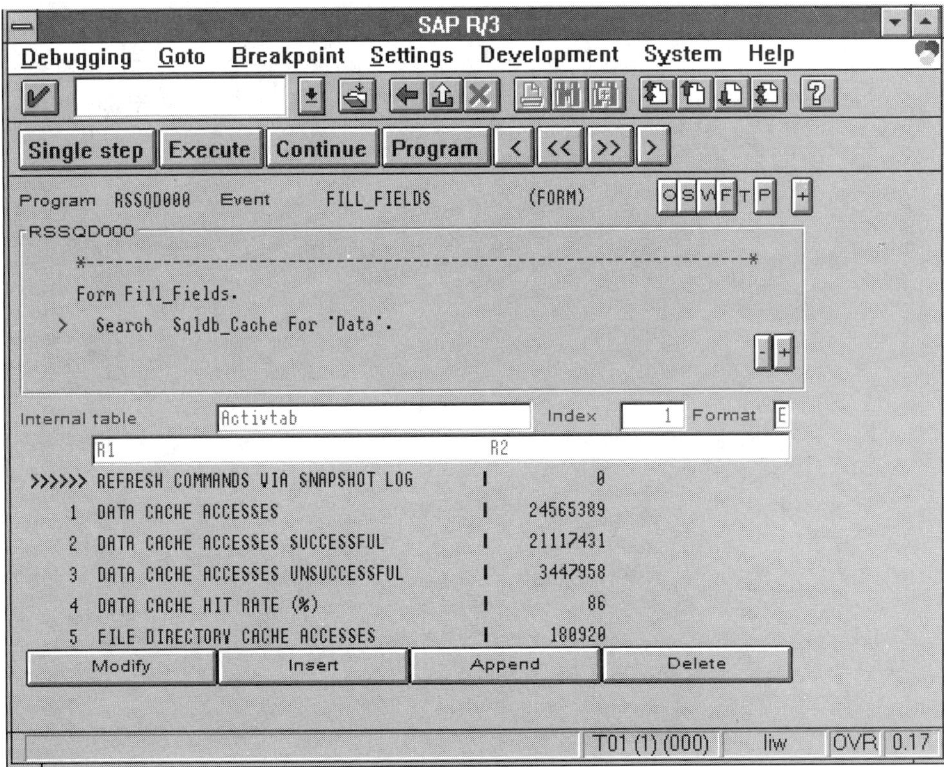

Figure 4.15 Table display in debugging mode

During a test, double click on a field or position the cursor on a field and use the push button *Choose* to include the field in the table and display the field's current value.

The display of table contents functions similarly with the push button *Table*. Figure 4.15 illustrates the screen display for a table. The display of fields, tables and their values can also be changed for the continued run of the program. In this case, the debugger overwrites the current values, marks them in column R and confirms them. The new value is then assumed as the current value and processing continues with that value. Reach an exact field description in debugging mode via the menu path *Goto* → *Fields* (see Figure 4.16).

Running each instruction of a program step by step can involve a great deal of time and effort. The test system therefore allows the user to set temporary breakpoints (by double clicking) at any line in the program. The debugger then automatically pauses before these lines during execution. Add permanent breakpoints with the instruction

```
BREAKPOINT.
```

in a program. Execution of the program will always stop when such an instruction is encountered.

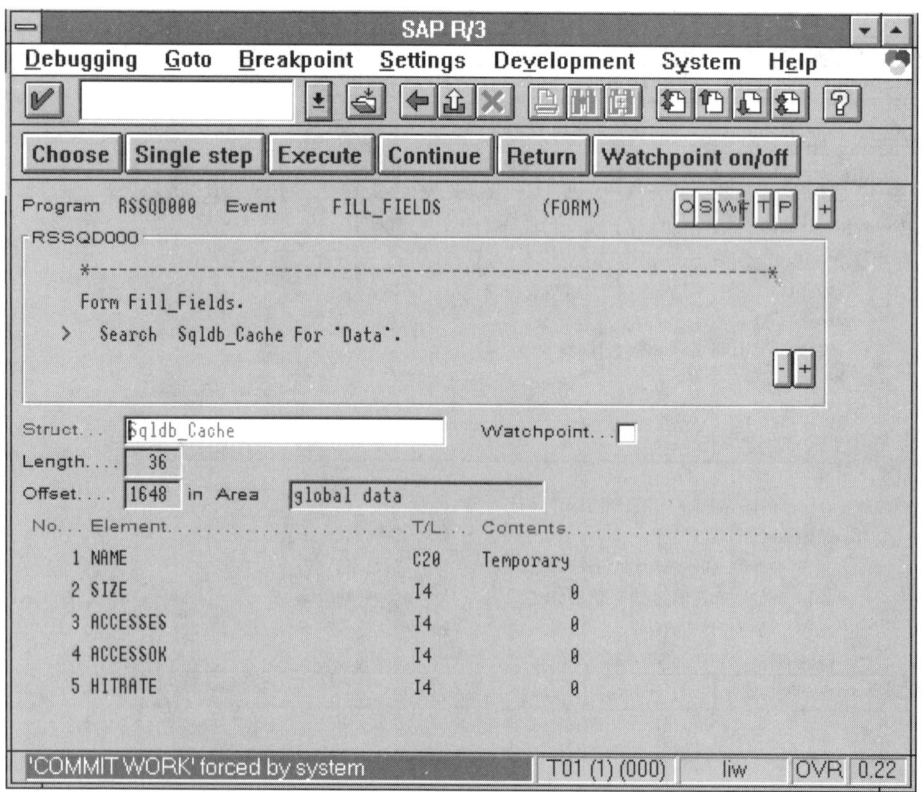

Figure 4.16 Field definition

R/3 version 3.x offers a new feature: the ability to add permanent breakpoints with a push button in the display mode of the ABAP/4 editor. An advantage of this procedure is that the user does not have to change an existing program when using it. Users are not required to create change requests and request access keys. After testing, remove the breakpoints in display mode with the menu path *Utilities → Breakpoints → Display*.

Continue in normal debugging mode, e.g., single steps, after the program has stopped.

Switch on debugging at any time during the run of any transaction by entering the code `/h` in the OK-code line.

5 Repository

The storage of all data in the form of tables (relations) constitutes the basis of a relational database model. All operations that choose or change data from tables create, in turn, more tables. In the R/3 repository a logical level overlays the physical organization of the data in the database. The logical level describes the data in a unified manner. It is created in the R/3 repository and reflects the relational data model.

5.1 Basis objects

Basis objects in the R/3 repository primarily contain all the field-related metadata required for the definition of a table. A table is a combination of fields defined by the hierarchical classification of domains and data elements.

5.1.1 Tables

The central object in the R/3 repository is the **table**: a two-dimensional matrix of columns and lines that represents a relation within the database system. A **primary key** ensures the unique identification of each record (table line) within a table. The definition of a primary key prohibits the insertion of several data records with the same key values in the same table. Every database table in the R/3 repository has its own primary key. Figure 5.1 illustrates the structure of a table.

In a table named *Customer Master* the user might define the field *KDNR* as a key field. With that definition it would be impossible to enter other customers with the same customer number in the table. Note, however, that the key field in the example (Figure 5.1) cannot guarantee unique identification. Accordingly, the system also allows several fields of a table to define a primary key. If an enterprise consists of several companies and the customer master is administered centrally, a given customer number might well be issued several times. In that case, include the field *COMP* in the primary key to ensure unique identification. The key to a table in the repository can consist of a maximum of 21 key fields.

5.1.2 Fields

The intersection of a line and a column within a table is called a **field**. Fields do not reside as independent objects in the R/3 repository because they can exist only with or as a constitutive part of a table. All the fields in a table column have the same characteristics: they can contain only data that corresponds to those characteristics. Set field character-

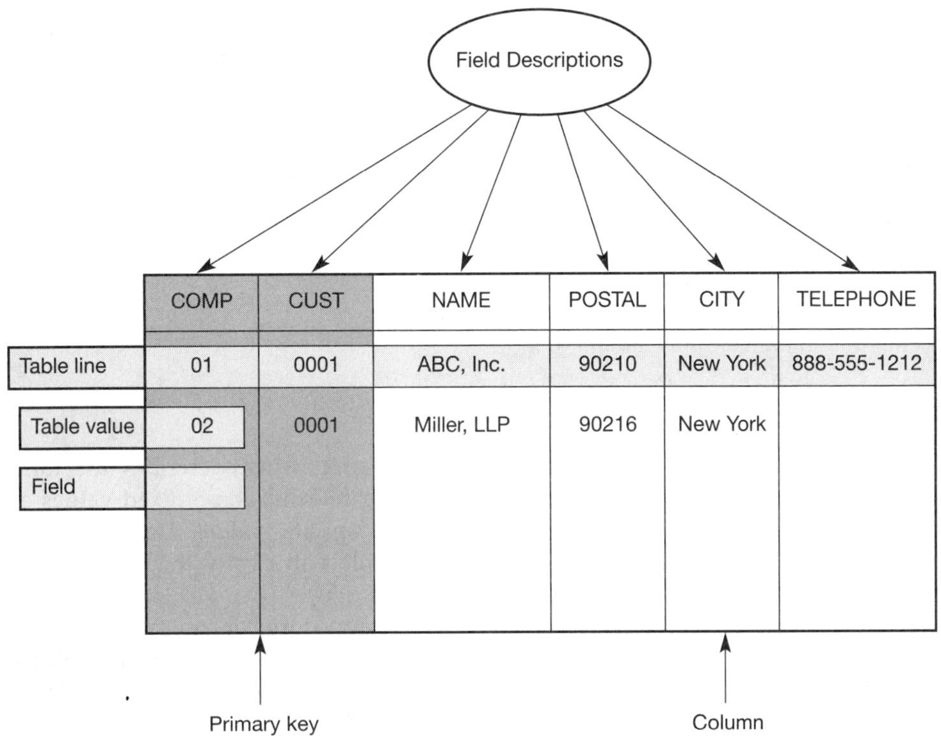

Figure 5.1 Example of a table

istics during definition of the table. The characteristics are also known as **field types** or **data types**.

The CREATE TABLE command defines the format, length and possible key assignment for every table field at the database level. At that level, **basis data types** determine the format of table fields within the table. The databases supported by SAP recognize various basis data types. Accordingly, applications dependent on the database must use superordinated, **logical** (**abstract**) **data types** for table definition. In business applications, for example, the fields 'company code' and 'client' might appear in several tables. The R/3 repository uses a two-level **domain concept** for two important reasons. First, it prevents different development areas from assigning different formats for the same field or similar fields. Second, it guarantees database independence during table definition. The R/3 repository thus allows the user to create formal and functional (semantic) dependencies. In their turn, the dependencies force common, standard field and table definitions.

A description of the table must exist in the R/3 repository before the system permits creation of a table in the database. Section 5.2 describes the exact procedure. After the user has assigned the table name, she can name and describe the individual table fields. The basis data types of the various database systems do not describe the formal characteristics of the field in the R/3 dictionary: the system uses **domains** for these definitions. The domains are automatically translated from the database interface into the basis data types of the database system. The description of fields with domains in the R/3 dictionary is independent of the database.

5.1.3 Domains

Domains form a second, independent basis object type in the R/3 repository. The repository has a two-level domain concept:

- Technical domains.
- Semantic domains (data elements).

Technical domains

A **technical domain**, abbreviated as domain in the following, describes the formal characteristics of a table field, such as format and length. Provision of **fixed values** or a **value table** enables the user to limit value areas to specific values. Domains use an 'external format' to describe a table field. An example will clarify the term 'external format.'

The table field KDNR consists of eight digits. The repository contains an allocation of the external format NUMC for this field. The provision of the external format (abstract data type) NUMC (not a basis data type in the database) describes the field as containing any number of digits; it is therefore not a calculation field. Allocation of a format (NUMC) and a length (here eight) describe a domain with a name, e.g., NUM8. Section 5.2.3 describes the allocation of a format and length within a domain. Users can employ the logical name (NUM8) to depict a field physically for all fields that correspond to that format, an employee number for example. This ability permits the combination of various fields of the same type into one domain. Accordingly, fields that refer to the same domain have a logical relation to each other. Their formats and lengths cannot change independently of each other. Chapter 6 pp. 238–40 presents details on abstract data types in the R/3 system.

The R/3 repository offers the means of setting the value areas of domains shown in Table 5.1.

The R/3 system joins fixed characteristics to external formats. For example, 'DATE' limits valid values to eight numbers in a date format. Listing individual values, or **fixed value** (e.g., 1, 2, 3, etc.) creates additional limitations for certain value areas. Setting the quantity of valid values must take place at the domain level. If using fixed values to limit the value area is too complicated, we recommend the use of **value tables** (see Figure 5.2).

Table 5.1 Options for setting the value area

Specification of the external format (e.g., NUMC, DATE, etc.)
Listing the valid values (fixed values)
Specification of a value table

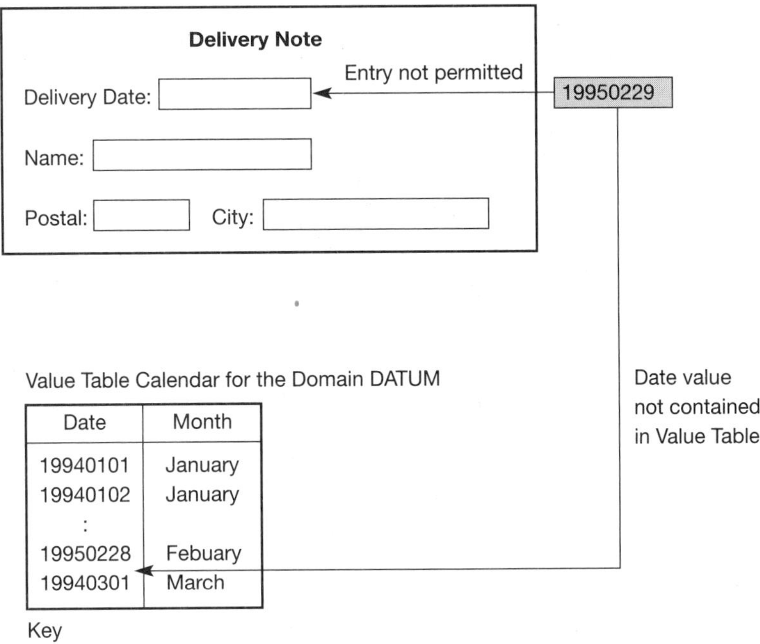

Figure 5.2 Value table

In theory, users can define every table as a value table by allocating the domain to a key field in the table (value table). The key values of the value table determine the possible values of the domain.

The table *Calendar* contains all possible date values and names of the months. The field *Date* is a key field for the table; the domain DATE defines the field. The R/3 repository also includes the mask field *Delivery Date* in the domain DATE. Both fields have the same value table. If the user tries to enter '19950229' in the mask as the delivery date, the system checks the value against the value table. The table does not contain the date, since 1995 was not a leap year. The system rejects the entry. Display all the valid values for an entry field with the *F4* key. A value table can be allocated to a maximum of one domain. All fields referring to the value area of this value table use the same domain.

Users can limit the contents of a value table to specific value. Produce these limitations in a **check table**. Rather than the domain, check tables are allocated to a data element.

Semantic domains: data elements

Although a domain can possess the same formal characteristics, it can have various properties because of semantic differences. Semantic domains are known as **data elements**. A data element describes the meaning of a technical domain in a business context. Figure 5.3 shows the correlation between data elements and domains. The example displays the object types: table, data element and domain. As discussed, the table fields do not form their own object type in the R/3 repository. A number identifies

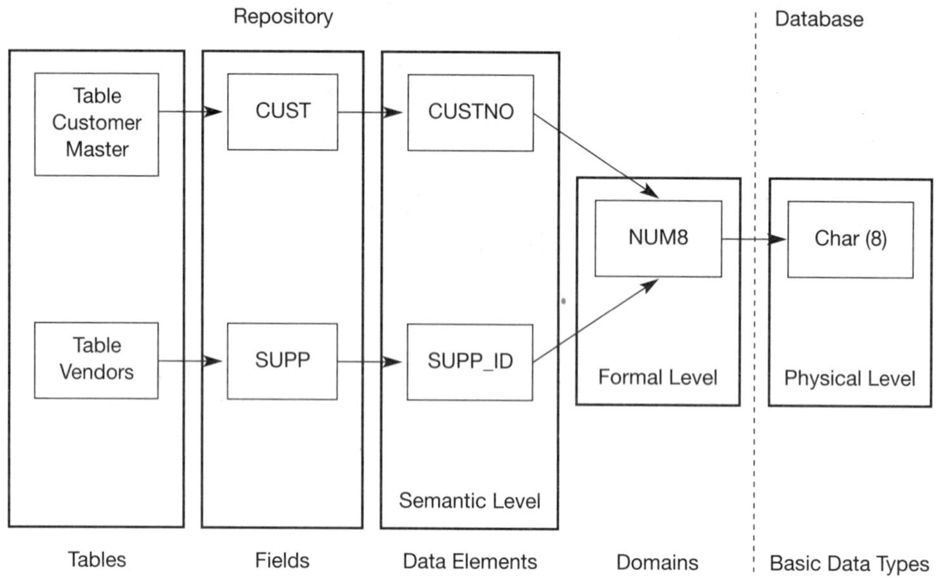

Figure 5.3 The correlation of data elements and domains

the customer and the vendor in the tables *Customer Master* and *Vendors*. The number consists of eight digits in both cases. From a formal standpoint, the user can allocate both fields to the technical domain NUM8. However, each field is used in a different business context. To clarify this semantic difference, different data elements (LIEFNR, KUNDNR) are assigned to each field.

A data element, therefore, carries field information; it produces a logical relation to the corresponding field. The field information is valid for every field referred to by the data element. The semantic information includes the external presentation of the field along with key texts in the screen mask. The data element also contains assigned column headers.

Consider the following closing remarks on domains and data elements:

- A domain can appear in as many data elements as desired.
- Various tables can use the same data element to describe a field.

5.1.4 Include procedure

When defining a table, the user records the individual table fields in the R/3 repository. He can also transfer or include fields from other tables as **substructures** in the newly defined table. The procedure has an obvious advantage: if the table inserted substructures later change in the basis table, the changes automatically take effect in **all** the tables containing the substructure. Individual fields and substructures can be combined as desired, as long as *all* the fields of *one* substructure are defined as key fields or non-key fields. The user can also nest substructures. A table, for example, can include another table that, in its turn, includes yet another table. The system allows a nesting level of up to nine tables.

5.1.5 Customizing SAP standard tables

Both new object types, **customizing includes** and **append structures**, enable customers to adjust SAP standard tables to their needs. However, both object types can be used only for transparent tables and structures, not pool and cluster tables. The use of these methods of object modification ensures that a later system upgrade will not overwrite the changes. An upgrade will preserve the modifications and use them along with the new version of the standard tables.

Customizing includes

If it becomes clear when planning an R/3 installation that the customer will have to customize standard tables to meet specific company requirements, SAP delivers empty customizing includes with the system. Customizing includes are created for tables or structures and can be integrated into several tables or structures. Customizing transactions enable the customer to enter new fields in these includes. Empty customizing includes cause no errors. Find customizing includes in the customer name range: they all begin with the prefix `CL_`. It therefore becomes possible to customize tables without having to modify the table itself. This procedure has its advantage. The insertion of new fields into a transparent table does not require a conversion of the table by the database. The sequence of fields in the repository does not have to correspond to the one in the database.

Append structures

Append structures also expand the SAP standard. However, SAP does not support these expansions from the outset. Append structures enable customers to devise their own developments. Customer fields can be added to any tables desired.

Unlike customizing includes, append structures apply to exactly one table, although several append structures can be defined for one table. Storage of all defined append structures in the customer name range ensures that a later upgrade will not overwrite them. Figure 5.4 shows the menu for creating an append structure.

All append structures are added to a table at activation of a table with defined append structures. If a user creates or changes an append structure, it must then be activated. The activation triggers automatic reactivation of all the tables related to the structure. Append structures differentiate themselves from substructures in the manner they refer to tables. If a table contains a substructure, the table must also contain an `include` statement. The reference begins in the table. An append structure, however, refers to a table. The table itself remains unchanged.

Note, however, the special situation that arises when copying a table with an append structure: the fields of the append structure become `normal` fields in the target table.

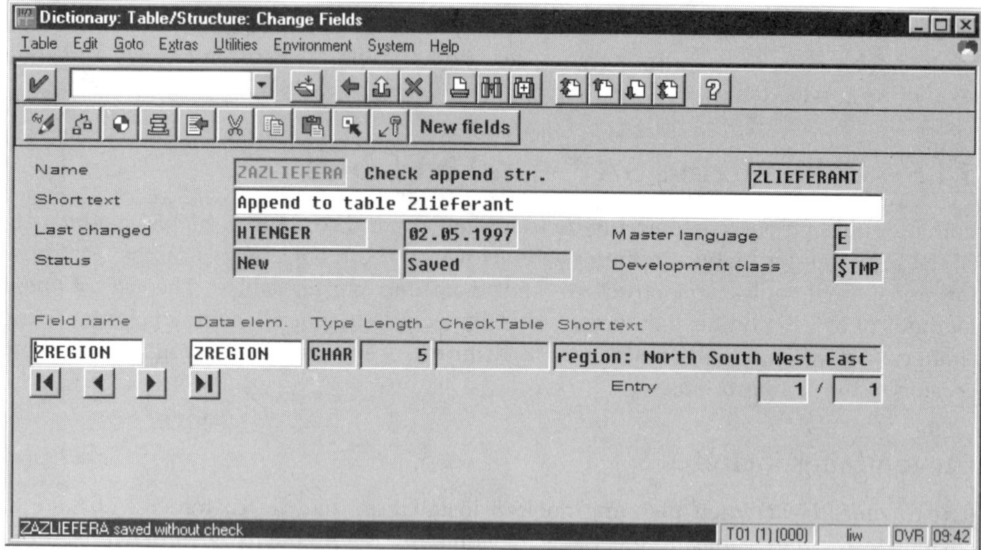

Figure 5.4 Append structure for a table

Users must convert pool and cluster tables into transparent tables before attempting to define append structures for the pool and cluster tables.

5.1.6 Index

An index to a table decreases access time for data that meets certain search criteria. The system allows definition of an index by certain extremely selective fields in the table. A separate index tree stores the values generated by this choice of fields in sorted order. The sort enables rapid access to the data. The index also contains a pointer to the corresponding table record so access to the remaining fields (i.e., those not contained in the index) can occur. An index, therefore, is a reduced copy of a table.

The system distinguishes between the **primary index** and the **secondary index**. The primary index always consists of the fields marked as key fields in the repository. Creation of the table automatically generates the primary key and stores it in the database. All other indexes defined for a table are termed secondary indexes.

An index entry can refer to several table records. If each entry should refer to exactly one table record, the index is defined as a **unique index**. Primary indexes are always unique indexes. Definition of an index as unique, or lack of such a definition, has no effect on access speed. A unique index simply means that the user can determine that data records with certain field combinations occur uniquely in the database.

Assign an index ID before creating an index (see Figure 5.5).

Index IDs can consist of both letters and numbers, although ID 0 is reserved for the primary index. The index name in the database combines the table name (max. 10 characters) and the three-character index ID. The index ID always makes up the

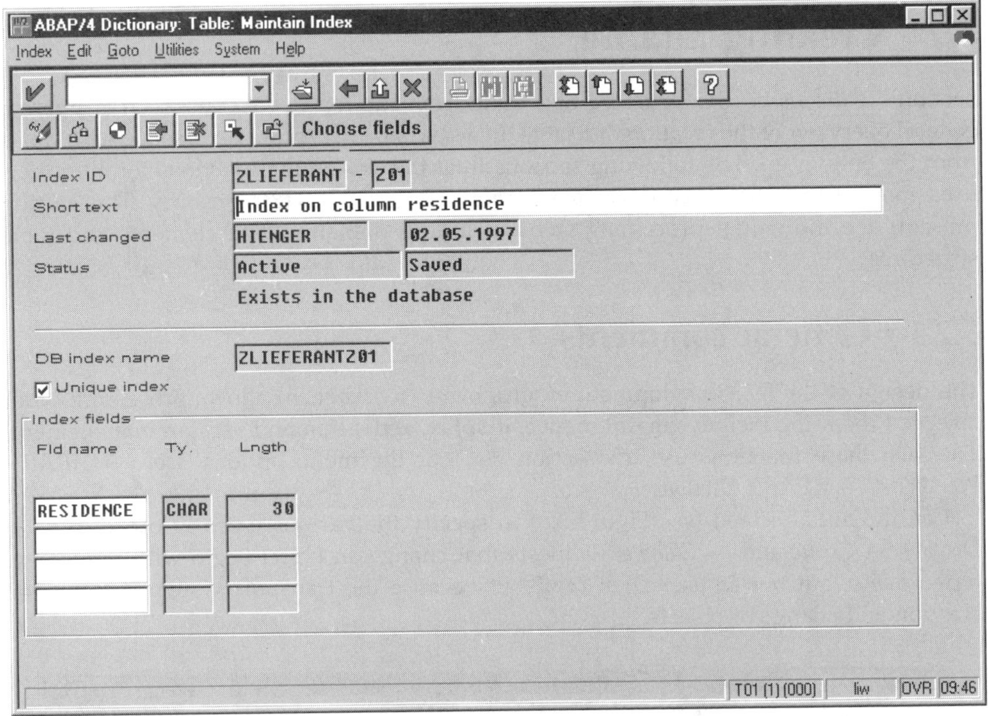

Figure 5.5 Index of tables

11th to 13th positions. If the table name consists of less than ten characters, the name is padded with underscores.

Access commands and the database system in use determine which table fields can define indexes. Access speed, in turn, depends on the order (sequence) of fields in the index. The most selective field should always begin the definition. An index should include only those fields that significantly limit the volume of results returned.

The access speed of an index also depends on how much the volume of data selected with the index corresponds to the volume of data the user actually desires. The use of pointers in a search to access the tables also influences the speed. These factors, however, should not lead the user into temptation: do not include all fields with a WHERE specification in an index. Updates to tables require the simultaneous maintenance of defined indexes. More rapid access, therefore, may cause longer update and insert times. The following principle applies: create secondary indexes when the primary index cannot process frequently made selections.

Also note that the use of an index by the optimizer depends on the database system. Perform a test to determine if using index for a selection makes productive sense. Test with the SQL trace (see Chapter 2); the push button *Explain* displays access strategies.

The basis objects described above provide developers with the means to design objects that can be used repeatedly. The objects remain consistent in meaning and type, allowing optimization of access to the data.

5.2 Creating a table

Section 5.1 discussed the structure of a table from the top down. This section offers a general overview of the creation of a table. In actual practice, however, users create tables from the bottom up. The following sections treat the processing functions for all objects used to create a transparent table (see Section 5.3.1) in the R/3 repository. This section presents the individual processing steps including domains, data elements and table structures.

5.2.1 General comments

The design of the R/3 development environment (workbench) allows processing of all objects. Processing includes **maintenance**, **display**, **activation** and **version management**. To reach these functions use transaction `se11` or the menu options *Tools → ABAP/4 Workbench → ABAP/4 Dictionary.*

Use the initial screen (see Figure 5.6) to specify the various types of processing: → *Display,* → *Create* and → *Change.* Requests that change an object begin with processing type *Change,* but not as user DDIC or SAP* because the transport system controls the creation and change of objects.

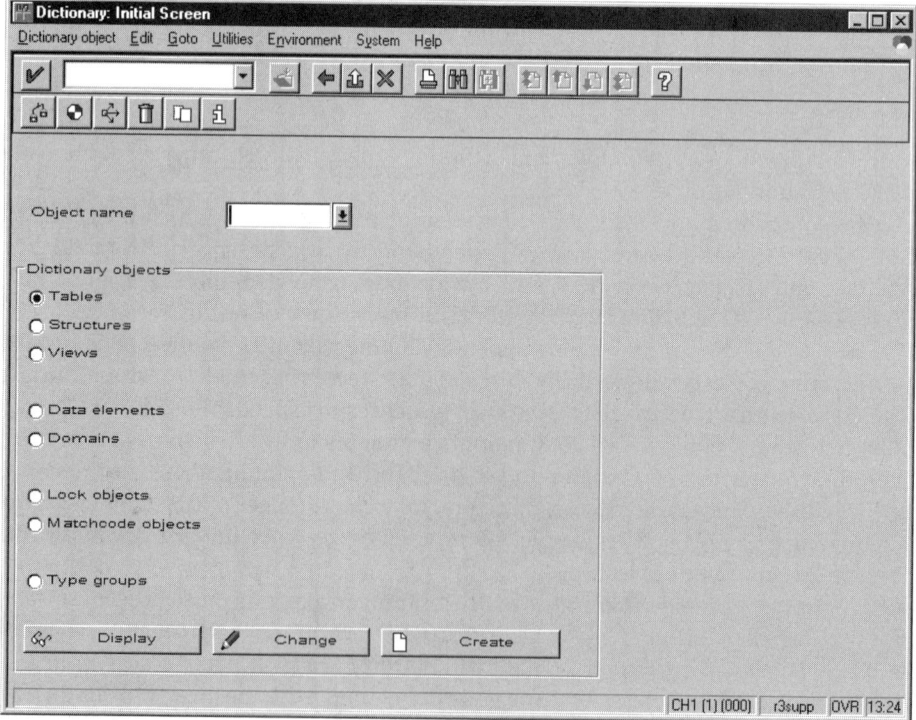

Figure 5.6 Repository: initial screen

- *Maintain existing object*
  Enter the name of the object to be processed (e.g., KNA1) in the field *Object name* and choose the corresponding object class with a click of the mouse. Use the push button *Change* to arrive at the maintenance menu. If the name of the object to be processed is unknown or only partially known, enter an asterisk (*) in the field *Object name* instead of the name. The user can also enter the beginning of the name followed by an asterisk (generic identifier KN*, for example). The system also requires choice of the appropriate object class here. It then returns a list of objects to the user. Choose any of the objects listed for further processing. After entry of the name of an existing object, the system performs an authorization check. The check permits maintenance of only those objects that other users have not locked for correction (see Chapter 7). Only original objects can be changed in a system group (e.g., production and test systems).
- *Create new object*
  To create a new object in the R/3 repository, enter the name of an object that does not yet exist and choose an object class. The maintenance menu for creating an object will then appear. Users must adhere to SAP naming conventions when assigning a name to the new object. The length of an object name is limited to ten characters. Do not use names that the database system uses as key names. Customer-specific repository objects should always begin with the letters `Y` or `Z` so that a later upgrade recognizes them as such.
- *Save object*
  Choosing the menu options *<Object>* → *Save* saves an object. When a user processes an object for the first time, the dialog window for the workbench organizer (see Chapter 7) appears. The workbench organizer ensures that no other user can work on the object. Saving creates a temporary version of the object. At this point the object is not yet active: it is not yet available to the runtime system.
- *Documentation*
  Users can create documentation for every object in the R/3 repository. Documentation consists of two types: **online help** (data element documentation) and **technical information** (table documentation, domain documentation). The program RSSDOCTB outputs the technical table documentation to a table handbook. Provide documentation for objects directly in object maintenance with the menu options *Goto* → *Documentation*. From the object maintenance menu, users can branch to the SAP editor and enter the documentation text there. If the text will be edited later, save it temporarily with *Document* → *Save* → *In raw version*. Save the final documentation with *Document* → *Save* → *In final version*. The various ways of saving documentation play a role in the transport of documentation modules: a transport includes only the final versions of texts.

5.2.2 Common processing options

A maintenance screen appears after the entry of an object and choice of an object class in the initial screen. All objects have certain processing options in common. The maintenance screen offers the following options.

- *Maintain affiliated objects*
  The maintenance screen for an object directly allows maintenance of an affiliated object. For example: maintenance of a table allows maintenance of a data element. The process creates a new data element name for a table filed. A double click on the data element will branch directly to data element maintenance.
- *Reset*
  The menu option *<Object>* → *Reset* returns all changes made to an object to the current (active) version. It deletes the edited version and any temporary versions.
- *Delete*
  From the initial screen, delete objects with the menu options *Dictionary Object* → *Delete*, as long as no other objects relate to this object. Deletion of table descriptions or indexes in the R/3 repository also deletes them automatically from the database (unlike version 2).
- *Copy*
  Choose *Dictionary Object* → *Copy* from the initial screen of the ABAP/4 dictionary to copy an existing object. The copy can serve as the basis for a new object.
- *Where-used list*
  Other objects can use tables, data elements or domains. The menu path *Utilities* → *Where-used list* provides a list of list of all objects that use the indicated object.
- *Print*
  From the initial screen of the dictionary, use the options *Dictionary Object* → *Print* to output an object to a printer.

5.2.3 Creating domains and data elements

Before creating a domain in the R/3 repository, use the **information system** (`se15`) to check if a domain with the same technical properties exists already. In this example, we will create a domain for a three-character field with numeric values. The domain will function as an identification field, not a calculation field. Enter the name of the new domain, `ZNUM3` (for number), in the field *Object name* and choose the object class *Domains*. Mark the push button *Create* to branch to domain maintenance (see Figure 5.7).

To simplify later identification of the domain, enter an explanatory text in the field *Short description*.

The system automatically fills the field *Status* (not an entry field) with the object's current status. A new object receives the status `new`. In addition, every maintenance mask provides the name of the person making the last change and the date of the last change to the object.

Specify the format of the domain with the fields *Data type* and *Field length*. Place the cursor on the field *Data type* and push the *F4* key to receive a list of permissible external data types. Specify field length in numeric form without commas or decimal points.

The domain can be saved after specifying the entry fields described thus far.

All the parameters described in the following are optional.

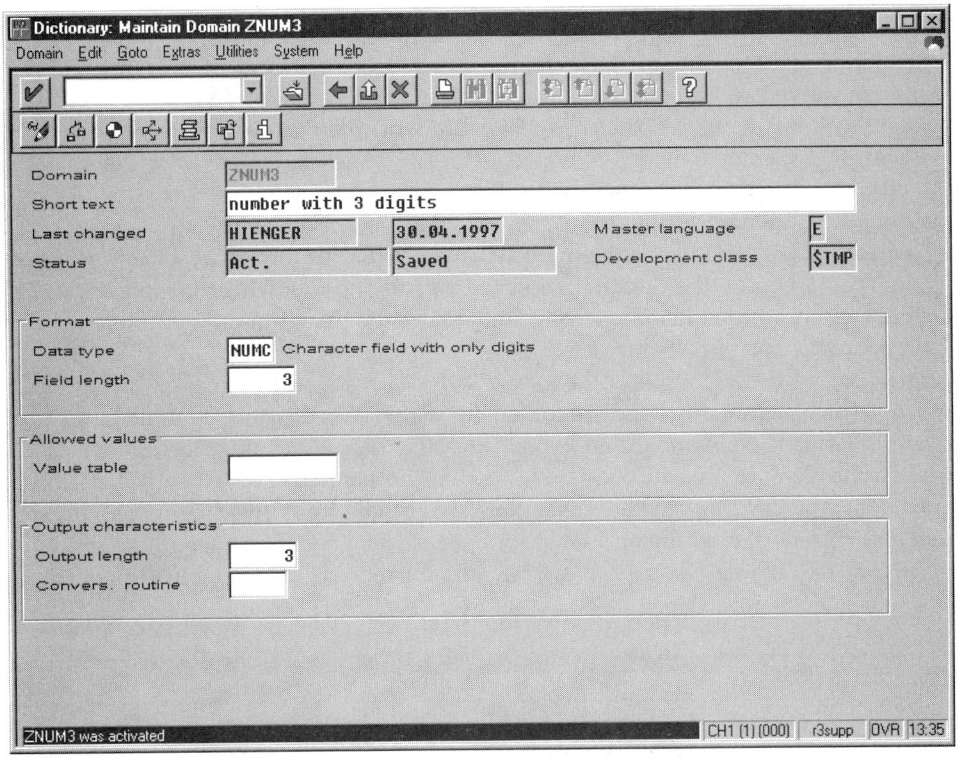

Figure 5.7 Creating a domain

If allocating a value table to the domain, enter the name of any existing or new table in the field *Value table*.

Optional output properties determine the format of the field owned by this domain.

Enter a number in the field *Decimal places* to set the number of places after the decimal point. The field *Output length* calculates the maximum field length, including the formatting characters (period and comma). Overwrite the default value if desired.

If a domain requires processing different from standard conversion, the system requires specification of the name of a **conversion routine**, generally called a **conversion exit**. This routine or exit ensures, for example, that in the transport of the contents of a screen field from display format into the internal SAP format and vice versa, according to the field type, a conversion takes place. Every conversion routine has a five-character name and is stored as a function module. Two function modules always exist for a conversion routine: one for input and one for output. The name of the function module integrates the name of the conversion routine:

```
CONVERSION_EXIT_xxxxx_INPUT
CONVERSION_EXIT_xxxxx_OUTPUT
```

The input module effects the conversion from display format into internal format. The output module does the opposite.

In the case of a character field, an additional parameter, *Lower case*, appears. If the parameter is marked, the output matches the case of the input. If no mark is made, the system converts all letters entered (regardless of case) into uppercase characters.

Save the domain with *Domains* → *Save* after maintaining all the necessary fields. However, the domain must be activated before it becomes available for other objects. After saving, use the push button *Activate* to activate the domain. See Section 5.7 for more detailed information on activation.

To create a new data element, enter its name (ZLIEF) in the initial screen of the data dictionary and choose the object class *Data element*. The following example creates the data element for a three-place vendor number. Use the push button *Create* to reach data element maintenance (see Figure 5.8).

Enter a short description and the name of the corresponding domain. If the domain does not yet exist, position the cursor on the field *Domain name*. A double click will branch to domain maintenance and create the new domain as described above. In this example the domain created above, `ZNUM3`, will be entered. For existing domains the field's data type, field length and value table are automatically filled. Enter short texts in three lengths (short, medium and long) with a *Field description*. The length specifications can be changed. If a field is used as a table field for record entry in table form, a column

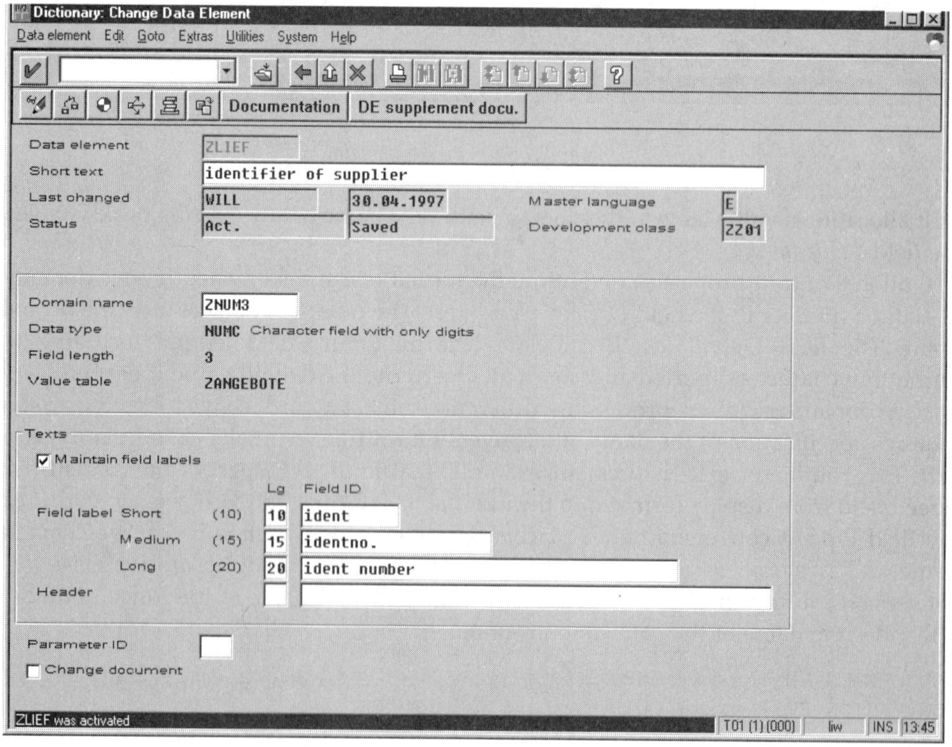

Figure 5.8 Data element maintenance

heading can be set at the data element level in the field *Header*. If no field descriptions require maintenance, switch off the flag *Maintain field labels*.

The menu options *Goto* → *Documentation* lead the user to documentation. As a rule, omit documentation for a data element only when the data element does not appear on the screen. Because data elements carry semantic field information, documentation is very important. Users can request the documentation created for a data element by using the FI key on every field to which the data element refers. All the necessary entries are now present to save and activate the data element.

The parameters *Parameter Id* and *Change document* are optional maintenance fields.

The field *Parameter ID* allows the definition of default values for a field. If, for example, a user has authorization only for a specific company code, the system can automatically enter a certain value in the fields that display the company code.

When the field *Change document* is marked, the system writes a change document for every change to data related to the data element. The document helps to recreate every change made to an object.

5.2.4 Table properties

Enter the name of the new table to be created in the field *Object name* of the initial screen of the data dictionary. Choose the object class *Tables*. Use the push button *Create* to display the menu *Table/Structure: Change Fields*.

The system allocates table type `TRANSP` to every table created with this menu. Section 5.3 presents all the possible table types in the R/3 repository. The following example creates a transparent table, depicted 1:1 in the database. If the table will require late maintenance, its name may not contain more than five characters. Mark the field *Table Maintenance Allowed* and use transaction `sm31` for later entry of data in the table. We do not, however, recommend this procedure for system tables or tables maintained by application programs. Enter the short description and then maintain the **table properties**. These properties set the permissible access types for a table (e.g., transaction `sm31`) and the person responsible for table maintenance.

The **delivery class** indicates who (SAP or the customer) enjoys responsibility for table maintenance and at what level.

The delivery class defines the table type; Table 5.2 provides an overview of the delivery classes. Use the *F1* key to query all valid delivery classes directly. Take great care to choose the correct delivery class. An incorrect choice can lead to data loss during an **upgrade**, **transport** or **client copy**.

An upgrade never overwrites tables of class A, C and L. Upgrades do not affect customer entries in tables of class G and E.

Client copy within a system copy only the contents of tables of class C, E, G and S to the new client. The rule also applies to client-dependent tables. Client copy does not copy tables of class L and W. Client-dependent tables of class A are copied in part; client-independent tables of class A are copied in full.

Transports and upgrades do not import tables of class L. An upgrade imports tables of class C, G and A only to client 0.

Table 5.2 Delivery classes

Delivery class	*Table type*	*Example*	*Maintained by*
A	Application tables, master and transaction data	Customer master	Customers, with application transactions
C	Customizing tables	Company code	Customers
L	Tables for storing temporary data	Employee group	Customers
E	System tables	Special stock identifier	SAP, expandable by customers
G	Customizing tables with protected contents	Number ranges	SAP and customers
S	System tables with program characteristics	Codes for SAP transactions	SAP
W	System tables for system operation and maintenance	Function module tables	Transport system

Normal import applies to all other classes for upgrades and transports between customer systems. In this context, import means both the insertion of new records and the overwriting of records already present.

Tables of the runtime environment can have additional specifications for the activation type. The activation type determines which mechanism activates an object.

The value `01` generates the runtime object (see Section 5.7) of an object with a C program. Activation of such an object requires the use of the repository. This activation type prevents direct change to and activation of system tables.

C programs can use tables that have an entered value of `02`. The structure, however, must be adjusted in the C program.

Assign the value `10a` for initial tables that must exist before the transport program `R3trans` can be triggered.

If the table does not require classification, assign no value or the value `0`. Such tables can be activated directly from the repository.

5.2.5 Specifying table structures

After describing the table properties, the user can specify the table structure (see Figure 5.9).

The column *Field name* lists all the table fields. If a table field belongs to a primary key, enter a check in the field *Key*. The menu options *Fields* → *Save* stores the table structure. After saving the structure, specify the table-specific attributes at the field level. Allocate field properties to individual fields with the data element. Enter the name of the corresponding data element in the column *Data elem.* for every table field. If no data element exists, double click on the name to branch to data element maintenance and

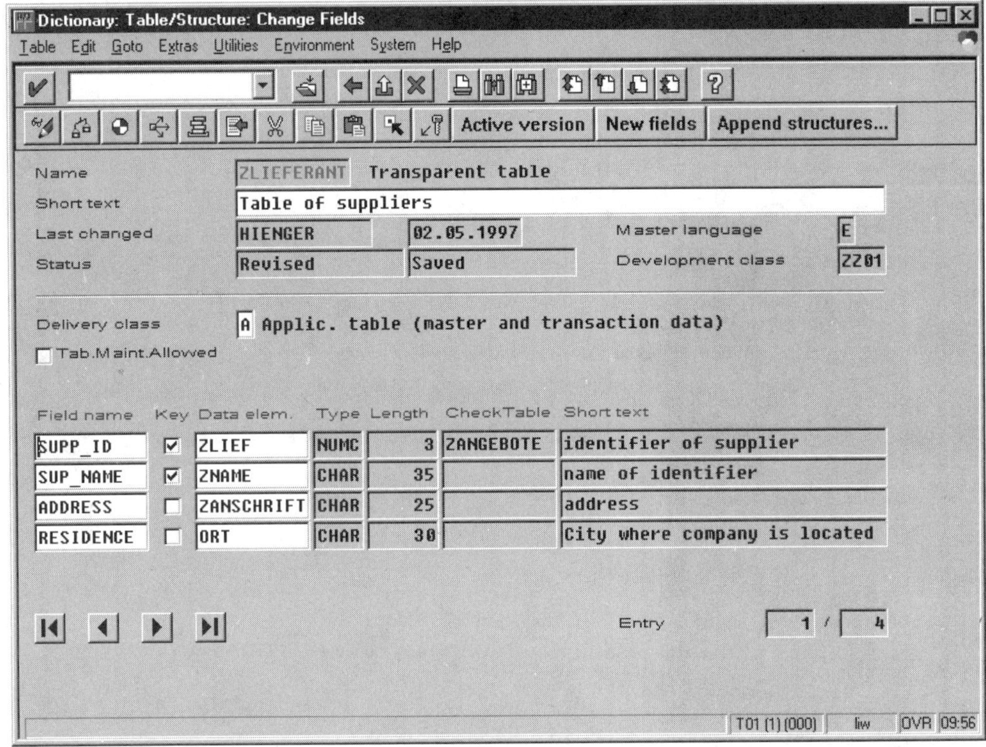

Figure 5.9 Create table

create a new data element. If the data element already exists, the system automatically transfers its properties, and those of the corresponding domain, to the columns *Type*, *Length*, *CheckTable* and *Short text*. To search for an appropriate, existing data element with an unknown name, branch to the **information system** with the menu path *Utilities → Repository Infosys*.

After defining all the fields and field properties, save the table structure with *Fields → Save*.

5.2.6 Technical settings

After specifying the table structure, click on the function *Technical settings*. This setting (see Figure 5.10) uses logical memory parameters to optimize the memory requirements of a table and access behavior.

The *Data type* specifies at a logical level in the R/3 repository which physical area of the database (e.g., a tablespace in Oracle) a table will create.

Choose the **data type** according to the function of the table data.

- APPL0 for master data requiring frequent read access but few changes.
- APPL1 for transaction data being changed permanently.

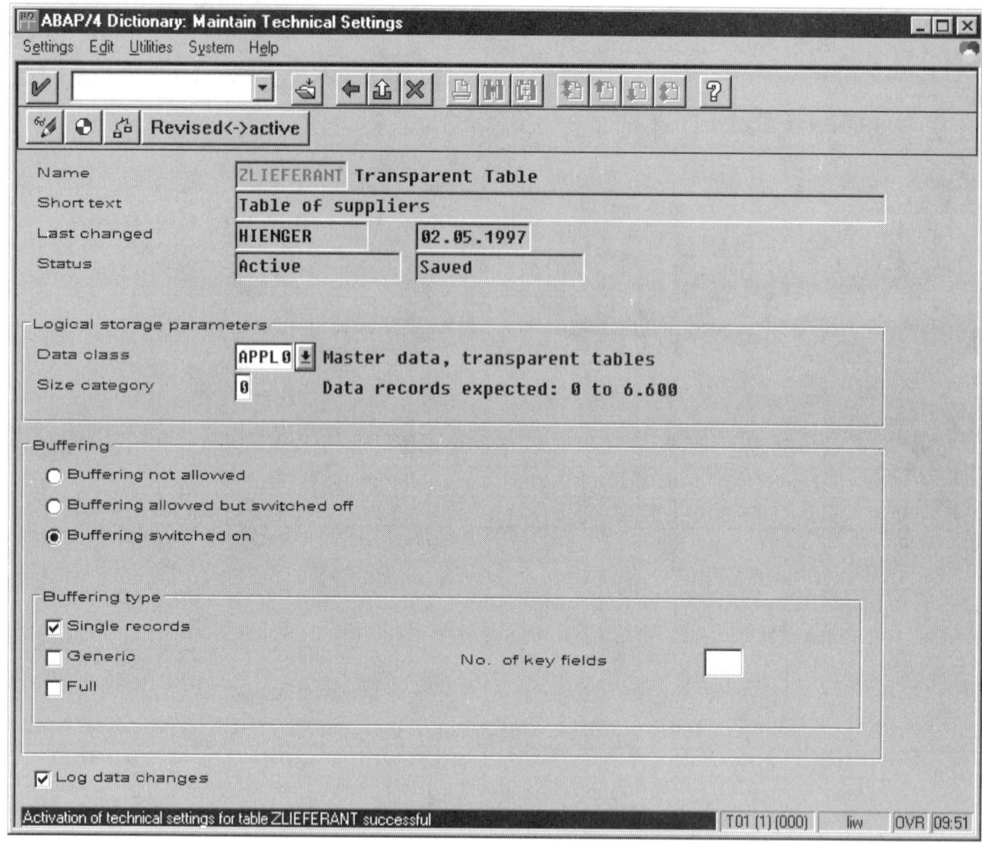

Figure 5.10 Technical settings

- APPL2 identifies organization and customizing data. The values of these tables are entered at installation of the system and rarely change afterward.

The parameter *Size category* helps determine the predicted physical space in the database required by a table. Enter size classes between 0 and 4. A fixed number of data records is allocated to each class value. Display the number of data records with *F4*. If the user sets the category when creating the table, the number of records that can be added without requiring a reorganization of an Oracle or Informix database is already known when the table is described.

Specification of the data type and the **table size category** affects only Oracle and Informix database systems. These parameters do not affect storage of tables under ADABAS D because the RDBMS distributes data in the database on its own, with a view toward better performance. Tables can grow dynamically, but the use of ADABAS D does not require table reorganization, and the filling level of the table has no relevance. Nonetheless, when running an R/3 system with ADABAS D, the system requires entry of a data type and size category.

To increase the effectiveness of table access, define **table buffering**. Buffering means that R/3 holds parts or all of a table's contents in main memory at the local level. Local buffers are located on the application server. This process minimizes time-intensive accesses to the database server. However, only transparent and pool tables can be buffered.

For performance reasons, buffer only those tables with read-only access. If write-access is rarely required, buffering those tables also makes sense. The system implements all changes to buffered tables synchronously in the buffer of the application server. Table `DDLOG` also logs these changes on the database server. Other application servers read `DDLOG` regularly. When they find changes, the database must reread the tables and load them into the buffer after a short wait. This process prevents loading the tables into the buffers permanently. Accordingly, buffered tables that change frequently can affect performance negatively. Buffer only master data tables.

A choice between various types of buffering exists. **Partial buffering** means the buffering of individual records. Accessing one record loads it into the buffer. This procedure reduces the amount of memory that the buffer requires. We recommend this type of buffering for large tables that contain only a few records that require frequent access. Consider, however, the special case of quantity accesses, which partial buffering cannot handle. In such a case, the system must always read from the database, regardless of the selectivity of the WHERE condition. The type of buffering has its own disadvantage: the high level of administration required. Loading the data requires far more accesses to the database as does complete buffering.

Generic buffering loads table areas into the buffer. The key fields determine the area. During access to one record, the system loads that record and all the records that correspond to the **generic key fields** into the buffer. SAP terminology defines generic key fields as the left-justified portion of a primary key. To determine the generic key field, the field *No. of key fields* must contain the number of key fields for the generic key: permissible values lie between 1 and the number of key fields minus 1. The system differentiates generic keys only up to 32 bytes.

To avoid the creation of too many generic areas, do not make the areas too small. Use generic buffering for tables requiring access only to specific areas (language-dependent tables). The system automatically uses generic buffering for completely buffered master data tables.

Marking the parameter *completely buffered* loads the entire table into the buffer (**resident buffering**). Tables no larger than 30K can use resident buffering. Note the following rule for complete buffering: the smaller a table is, the more often it is read and the less often it is changed, the more favorable complete buffering is.

Activation of only the logging of data changes with *Log data changes* has no effect in and of itself. To log the changes, the user must also set the parameter `rec/client` in the SAP profile. This parameter can set logging of tables for all clients or for individual clients. If the menu option and the profile trigger logging, a file stores the changes to the tables. View the file with transaction `scu3`.

The user must click the push button *Activate* to activate the table. Unlike the process in version 2, activation of a table automatically creates it in the database (if it does not already exist there). This procedure does not require explicit use of the database utility (see Section 5.9). If the table already exists in the database, convert it with the database utility. In addition, the repository creates the key specified as the primary key to the table as the `unique index` with an index ID of '0' in the database. Define **secondary indexes** in addition to the primary index, specified with the field *Key* when describing the structure of a table and created in the database. As Figure 5.9, *Table/Structure: Change Fields*, indicates, use the push button *Indexes* to create secondary indexes that will improve access time to this table.

5.3 Types of tables

A table can be created in the database once the repository contains a description of it and all its elements. As Section 5.1 indicates, the data model of the R/3 repository with its table structure overlays the relational model of the underlying database. Tables described in the repository are known as **logical tables**. The relational tables of the database system that arise are called **physical tables**. A logical table does not necessarily correspond directly to a physical table in the database. The logical data model therefore expands the relational model. The following section describes the various types of logical tables.

5.3.1 Transparent tables

A table described in the R/3 repository as transparent receives the object type `Table`, and is created 1:1 in the database under the name described in the repository. The database stores the data records of a transparent table in such a manner that the structure and content of the resulting physical table in the database agree with the logical table in the R/3 repository. Transparent tables are abbreviated as `TRANSP` in the remainder of this book. The R/3 system stores all business and application data in transparent tables. Editing of transparent tables can take place within an ABAP/4 program by using the command `EXEC SQL` or with `SAP-SQL`. Users can build join views and indexes on the foundation of transparent tables. Transparent tables provide the user with access to R/3 data from outside an R/3 system with means provided only by the database, SQL query language (e.g., `SQL-PLUS` from Oracle or `QUERY` from ADABAS D). Users can safely create table calculations, for example, with database tools such as `OFFICE-PLUS` (ADABAS D) or `SQL*Forms` (Oracle). These tools read R/3 table data but do not change it. Nonetheless, if tools outside the control of the R/3 system manipulate R/3 data, the consistency of the R/3 system can no longer be guaranteed. Relationships exist between the individual objects of an R/3 system that only the R/3 repository can recognize. The database cannot decipher the relationships on its own.

5.3.2 Table pool and logical pool tables

The class of tables known as the table pool (hereafter: pool) constitutes another type of logical R/3 table. In this context, a table class describes the common properties of the table of the same type that belong to the class. A **table pool** is a table created in the database. Its name and structure correspond to the description of the table in the R/3

Table 5.3 Data records of the table pool ATAB

TABNAME	*VARKEY*	*DATALN*	*VARDATA*
TZCU2	CLOSE	–32757	000 00 0B1
TZCU2	COPY	–32757	000 00 0F4
TZCU3	PASTE	–32757	000 00 0A6

repository. Unlike transparent tables, a table pool consists of several logical SAP tables. These logical tables are called **pool tables**: despite the similarities in terms, do not confuse pool tables with table pools. Pool tables are not created in the database as independent tables, but are stored together in one single physical database table, the table pool. The repository describes them as a pool table with the table type `POOL` and allocates them to a table pool. Table 5.3 displays the structure of a table pool using the central control table ATAB as an example.

A pool contains the table names of the pool tables that belong to the pool in a field of the first column named TABNAME (TZCU2 and TZCU3). In addition, another field of the type `VARKEY` holds all the key fields (e.g., CLOSE and COPY) of the individual pool tables. Accordingly the number of key entries (CLOSE, COPY) of the pool table, here TZCU2, determines the number of records of a pool table (TZCU2) in the table pool (ATAB). That means that each pool table can contain multiple data records in the table pool. Taken together, the table name (TABNAME) and a second field (VARKEY) of the pool form the key. An additional field of the type `VARDATA` stores the remaining data of the data record as a string in hexadecimal form.

- *Advantages of pool tables*
  Relational database systems usually limit the number of tables that users can create. Pool tables thus have the advantage of creating fewer database tables and avoiding possible bottlenecks. From the viewpoint of ABAP/4 programming, pool tables require fewer different SQL statements, which leads to a discharge of the SAP cursor cache. Compressing the data independently of the database system can lower the need for storage space. Because (de)compression takes place on the application server, network traffic is reduced. Insertion of the pool table in the table pool (INSERT command) create a new pool table; SQL-DDL commands create transparent tables. Use of the INSERT command makes administration of pool tables easier.

- *Disadvantages of pool tables*
  The key of a pool table can be rather long because the key contains the table name of every individual record. If every key in the pool has the same length, the physical key to individual tables can lengthen considerably. Another disadvantage: the database offers fewer functions for processing pool tables. No indexes and no database joins can be added to pool tables, for example. Access to pool tables must result from the primary key because the field `VARDATA` stores the remaining data as a string. No further column classification is present. The data in pool tables is therefore not transparent to external programs and other database tools. SAP often suffers criticism

because these tools cannot evaluate data. Partly for that reason, the use of pool tables has been limited to internal administrative data.

Meeting the following conditions determines if the use of pool table makes sense:

- The table has low volume,
- Access to single records takes place only via the key,
- 100% Buffering in main memory.

In the R/3 system a pool serves internal purposes such as the storage of control data. **Control data** includes screen data, program parameters and other temporary data.

5.3.3 Table clusters and logical cluster tables

Table clusters (see Figure 5.11), abbreviated as cluster in the following, are similar to a pool. As tables stored in the database, their name and structure agree with the logical description of the table in the R/3 repository. A cluster stores several tables of type 'CLUSTER,' or **cluster tables**. Cluster tables do not exist as independent, physical tables in the database. Unlike the pool, however, several logical lines of a cluster table combine to form a physical data record of a cluster. In other words, exactly one data record exists in the cluster for every logical cluster table. Clusters therefore enable object-oriented

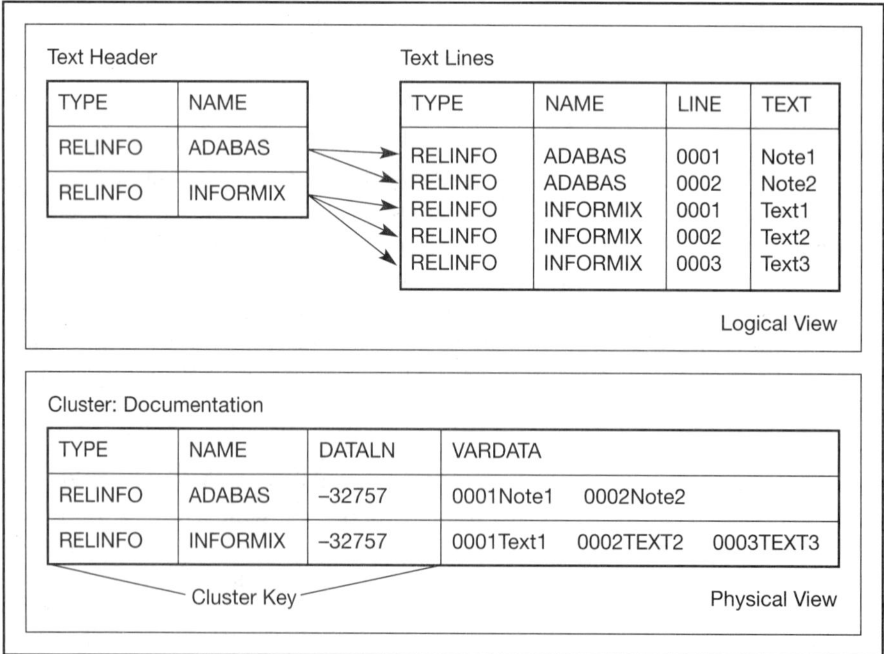

Figure 5.11 Table cluster

storage of data and access to it. Accordingly, use cluster tables to store consecutive texts and for documentation.

The preconditions that permit the combination of several cluster tables into a cluster exist only when at least part of the keys in the various cluster tables agree. A cluster has a transparent cluster key composed of the keys (or parts of keys) of the cluster tables making up the cluster. The columns *TYPE* and *NAME* make up the key in the example. A cluster also receives an additional field, of type `VARDATA`, that contains the remaining data of the logical cluster table. Storage in clusters means that the system stores all records with the same cluster key in combined form and in context. One physical data record can depict several logical records (one logical cluster table).

- *Advantages of clusters*
  A cluster enjoys the same advantages as a pool. In addition, a cluster enables object-oriented buffering via the database interface. This buffers offers yet another advantage: the database system receives fewer queries. Storing logically connected records in a physical context decreases I/O accesses to the disk.
- *Disadvantages of clusters*
  A cluster enjoys the same disadvantages as a pool. Clusters can also lead to significant performance problems if only a few logical records of a physical cluster record require processing. Each process applied to a cluster requires decompressing it, reading or writing it and then compressing it again.

Given the advantages and disadvantages noted above, use clusters not only when access takes place via a cluster key but also if several (logical) records belonging to a cluster key require processing.

5.3.4 Creating a pool or cluster

To create a pool or cluster, enter the name of the pool or cluster in the initial screen of the data dictionary (se11). Then branch via *Utilities → Pool/Cluster* to the menu *Dictionary: Maintain Pool/Cluster*.

As with transparent tables, enter a short description and an activation type (see Figure 5.12).

Go to 'technical settings' and enter the midrange number of expected data records at the table size. Branch to field maintenance with 'new entries.' This option displays all the suggested fields of the pool/cluster. Users can modify only the field *VARKEY*.

When creating a cluster, users can specify the name of the desired key fields. Creation of a pool does not require entry of key fields, only the maximum length of the key of the logical pool table. After completing field maintenance, branch back to the pool/cluster maintenance menu to activate the pool/cluster. The database utility can create the pool/cluster table in the database. Create individual pool and cluster tables in the same manner as transparent tables with transaction se11. The only difference between creating transparent tables and pools/clusters is the specification of `POOL` or `CLUSTER` as the table type and entry of the name of the pool/cluster. Note that the combined key length cannot overstep the value given in the pool/cluster. Also, the key of the logical table must begin

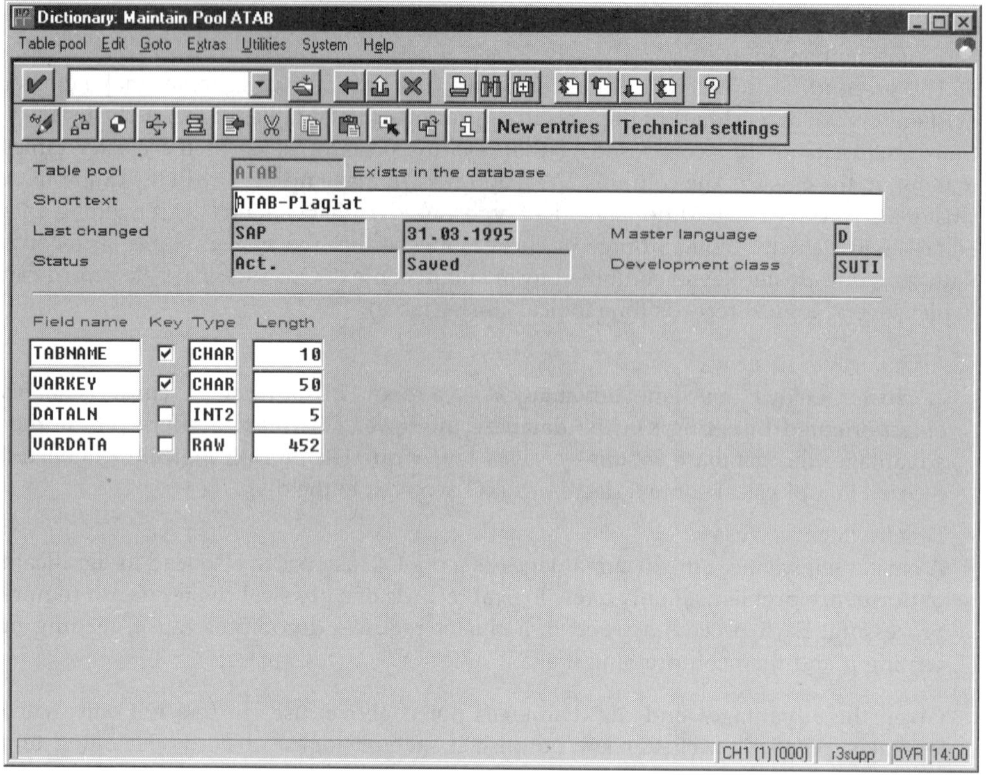

Figure 5.12 Pool/cluster properties

the table description in continuous form. A logical pool/cluster table requires activation; it does not require creation in the database.

5.3.5 Internal structures

So far we have considered the various table types in the R/3 repository and their physical storage in the relational database. Unlike the table types `TRANSP`, `POOL` and `CLUSTER`, internal structures do not depict physical data records in the database. In ABAP/4 programming, internal structures serve to define the interface between programs or between screens and ABAP/4 programs. Consider the transfer of parameters to function modules as an example. The R/3 repository describes internal structures with the type `INTTAB`. Although internal structures exist as logical objects in the repository, no physical data record exists in the database. Examples of internal structures include data type definitions for fields used only in programs or screens but are not a constitutive part of a database table. Temporary tables created within an ABAP/4 program also exemplify internal structures. See Chapter 6 for a more exact description of the use of internal structures in ABAP/4 programming.

5.3.6 Client-dependent and client-independent tables

Business terminology defines a client as a logical, functional unit in an enterprise. A **client** can be, for example, a company within a group of companies or a division of a company. The SAP client concept allows users to distinguish individual areas by function: R/3 test and production clients, for example.

The R/3 repository subdivides all tables into **client-dependent** and **client-independent** tables. Client-independent tables are valid for all the clients of an R/3 system: they apply beyond the limits of one client. The contents of these tables have general validity. Client-independent table store SAP control data (e.g., the table `ATAB`), language keys or transaction codes. Store data that applies to only certain clients in client-dependent tables. The table definition in the R/3 repository determines whether a given table is client-dependent or independent. Client-dependent tables have client as their first field and the first position of the key. Application tables, and therefore transparent tables, overwhelmingly use client-dependence. Tables of type `POOL` or `CLUSTER` are client-independent.

5.3.7 Changing table types

Version 3.x supports later changes to already defined table types. To do so, use the function *Extras → Change table type* in the figure *Table/Structure: Change table type*.

An additional window contains a check mark indicating the current table type. Use this window to choose and confirm the new table type with the function *Choose*. The following conversions between table types are available:

- Transparent into structure,
- Structure into transparent,
- Pool into transparent,
- Cluster into transparent.

Converting a transparent table into a structure or a pool/cluster table deletes the technical settings upon activation of the new table, since these table types have no technical settings. As a consequence, users must maintain the technical settings of any structures or pool/cluster tables changed into transparent tables before activation of those tables. Convert pool tables with the procedure provided above or with the transparent flag. The use of a transparent flag to convert a pool table into a transparent table ensures that the transparent table keeps that property during a release upgrade. If the new SAP release delivers the table as a pool table, it remains a transparent table for the customer. If the table type was changed directly, as described above, the release upgrade would convert it back into a pool table.

Each of these changes to a table type converts the table in the database. Physical reorganization (see Section 5.9) performs the conversion.

5.4 Relationships between tables: foreign keys

Within the relational database model the opportunity exists to describe relationships between the tables at the database level. The R/3 repository defines table relationships with foreign keys. SAP understands a **foreign key** as a column or combination of columns in a table that is also a primary key in another table. A foreign key thus defines the allocation of fields of one **dependent table** to the key fields of another table, called a **referenced table**. Foreign keys can ensure that the fields of a dependent table use only values present as key values in the referenced table.

A relationship between the tables *Order Header* and *Customer Master* can be created by creating the fields *MANDT* and *KDNR* as a foreign key in the R/3 repository. These foreign key fields are allocated to the primary key fields *MANDT* and *KDNR* of the referenced table *Customer Master*. The table *Order Header* thus becomes a dependent **foreign key table** and the table *Customer Master* becomes a referenced **check table** (**value table**). Each record of the foreign key table references exactly one record of the check table. Clearly, several records of the foreign key table can reference the same record of the check table (1:1 relationship). Foreign keys ensure **referential data integrity** within the R/3 system. In the example shown in Figure 5.13, the user cannot enter customer '004712' in the table *Order Header* because client '002' does not exist in the check table. To establish a unique relationship between check tables and foreign key tables, it is sufficient to use the appropriate fields to make the key of the check table available to the foreign key table.

Allocation of a foreign key field of the foreign key table to each key field of the check table establishes a foreign key relationship (see Figure 5.13). The allocation requires that the primary key field and the foreign key field have the same formal attributes. They must belong to the same domain. The concept of value tables for domains in the R/3 repository simplifies the definition of foreign keys.

5.4.1 Check field

If the primary key of the check field combines several key fields, the foreign key table contains exactly as many foreign key fields. To allow a rapid validity check of the foreign key fields, users specify one field (the **check field**) of the foreign key fields with which to begin the referential integrity check. Choose the most selective of the foreign key fields for this purpose. The most selective field contains the most varied values. In Figure 5.13, the most selective field is *KDNR*. Maintain the foreign key relationship only for this check field (KDNR). To function as a check field, a value table must exist behind the domain of the field *KDNR*. Before it allows an entry, the system checks the field value against the check table. If the check table does not contain the value (e.g., KDNR=4713), the system rejects the entry on the basis of this single value. If, however the value is found one or more times in the check table (e.g., KDNR=4711), the system creates a result quantity internally. It then uses the result quantity to check the remaining foreign key fields (MANDT) for validity.

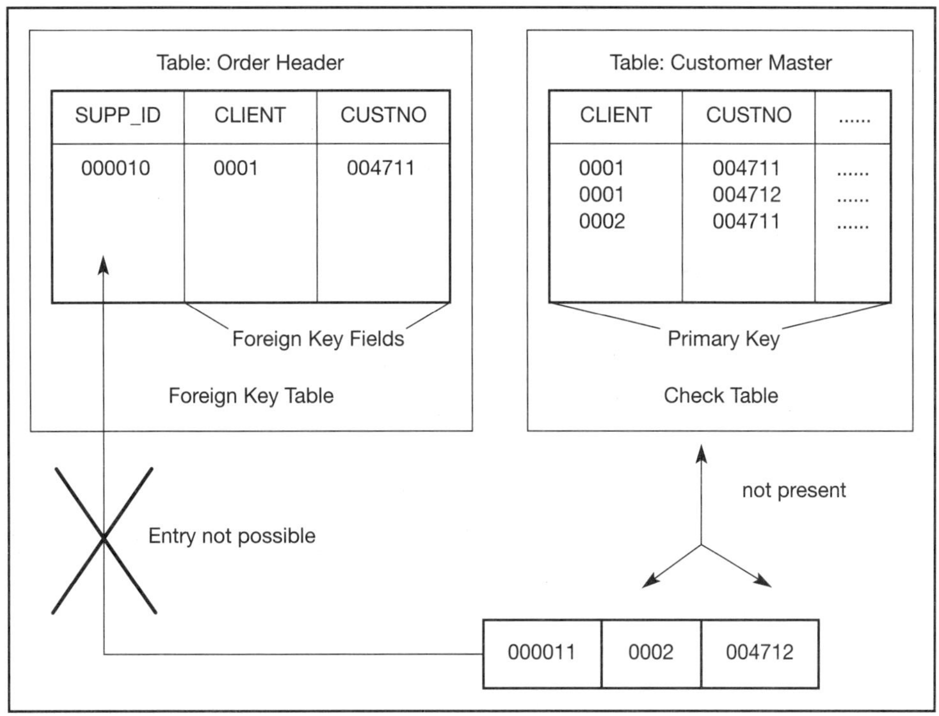

Figure 5.13 Foreign key relationship

5.4.2 Partial (generic) foreign key

For the sake of clarity, please note again that as of version 3.0 a corresponding foreign key field in the foreign key table need not exist for every key field of the check table. Section 5.4.4 discusses this adapted foreign key.

In some R/3 applications, however, a check of all foreign key fields may not make the most sense. Consider as an example those check tables whose primary keys also contain version numbers. As Figure 5.14 indicates, a table might contain all ABAP programs and their version numbers. To create program documentation, the entry field *Program* undergoes a validity check against the table *Programs*. In such a case, the program `RSSQD001` must appear in table *Programs* at least once. For the overall production of documentation, the individual version numbers have no relevance. For such cases, users can apply a **partial foreign key**. Define a partial foreign key as follows. When allocating the individual foreign key fields to primary key fields of the check table, do not allocate the irrelevant, **generic field** at the logical level in the R/3 repository. No check occurs for the remaining fields.

As of version 3.0 users can append key fields to tables that are used in foreign key definitions as check tables. This process automatically redefines all the foreign keys involved as partial foreign keys in relation to the new key fields.

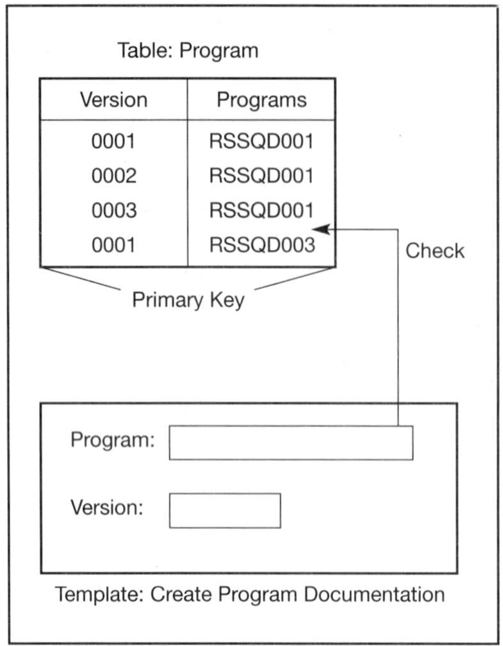

Figure 5.14 Generic foreign key

5.4.3 Constant foreign key values

Use constant values for foreign keys if the entries to be checked have a fixed value in the check table. The foreign key field will then always have a fixed value assigned to it. For this field, a check is performed only against the constant.

5.4.4 Adapted foreign key

Adapted foreign keys allow allocation of a field that is not contained in the foreign key table to a field in the check table. Such an allocation can exist for any field except the check field. These allocations make sense when no field in the check table with the same technical attributes exists in the foreign key table.

5.4.5 Screen foreign key

Screen foreign keys check only values entered on the screen. Use them, therefore, only for special cases such as internal tables that do not belong to the data model and therefore do not possess a semantic foreign key. Screen foreign keys can also serve as subsets of semantic foreign keys to check the entry for a portion of a foreign key.

5.4.6 Semantic foreign key

Semantic foreign keys not only check the values entered on the screen but also analyze the type of relationship between two tables more exactly. The on-line help system, for example, can use a semantic foreign key to recognize the availability of help texts for a given table. Semantic foreign keys also create definitions of views, matchcodes and lock objects (see Section 5.5). A semantic foreign key consists of the following parts:

- foreign key definition,
- cardinality,
- type of foreign key fields.

The **cardinality** (n:m) of a foreign key indicates how many dependent records (n=records of the foreign key table) or how many records of the check table (m) are allocated to a foreign key relationship. Table 5.4 shows the various cardinalities in the R/3 system.

Table 5.4 Cardinalities

Cardinality	*Description*
n=1	Exactly one record in the check table exists for every record in the foreign key table.
n=C	Some records in the foreign key table do not refer to a record in the check table.
m=CN	Any number of dependent records in the foreign key table exist for every record in the check table.
m=C	At most, one record in the foreign key table exists for a record in the check table.
m=N	At least one record in the foreign key table exists for every record in the check table.
m=1	Exactly one record in the foreign key table exists for every record.

5.4.7 Types of foreign key fields

Cardinality shows the characteristics of relationships from the viewpoint of the check table and the viewpoint of the foreign key table. R/3 version 3.x no longer recognizes the term **dependency factor**. Extended specification of cardinality and the type of foreign key fields have replaced the dependency factor. Specification of the **type of foreign key field** (see Table 5.5) indicates whether the foreign key fields for the foreign key table are (partially) identifying for key fields or key candidates.

5.4.8 Specification of a foreign key relationship

Begin at the screen for field maintenance of table to define a foreign key for every field whose domain includes a value table. Mark the field and then use the menu path *Goto →*

Table 5.5 Type of foreign key fields

No key fields/candidates	The foreign key fields are neither primary key fields of the check table nor are they key candidates. They do not identify the record in the check table uniquely.	Not (partially) identifying
Key fields/candidates	The foreign key fields are either primary key fields of the check table or identify every record in the check table uniquely.	(Partially) identifying
Key fields of a text table	The foreign key table is a text table for the check table. The key differentiates itself from the check table only in the language key field.	(Partially) identifying

foreign key or, to maintain several foreign keys, *Goto → Next foreign key*. If a foreign key has not yet been maintained, a dialog box appears with the text, 'Foreign key does not exist. Suggest a default?' Confirm the proposal by selecting the push button *YES* to branch to the screen (see Figure 5.15) *Create foreign key <Table_name-Field_name>*.

First enter a short description for the foreign key relationship. The name of the default value table appears in the field *Check table*. Users can overwrite this value. The name of

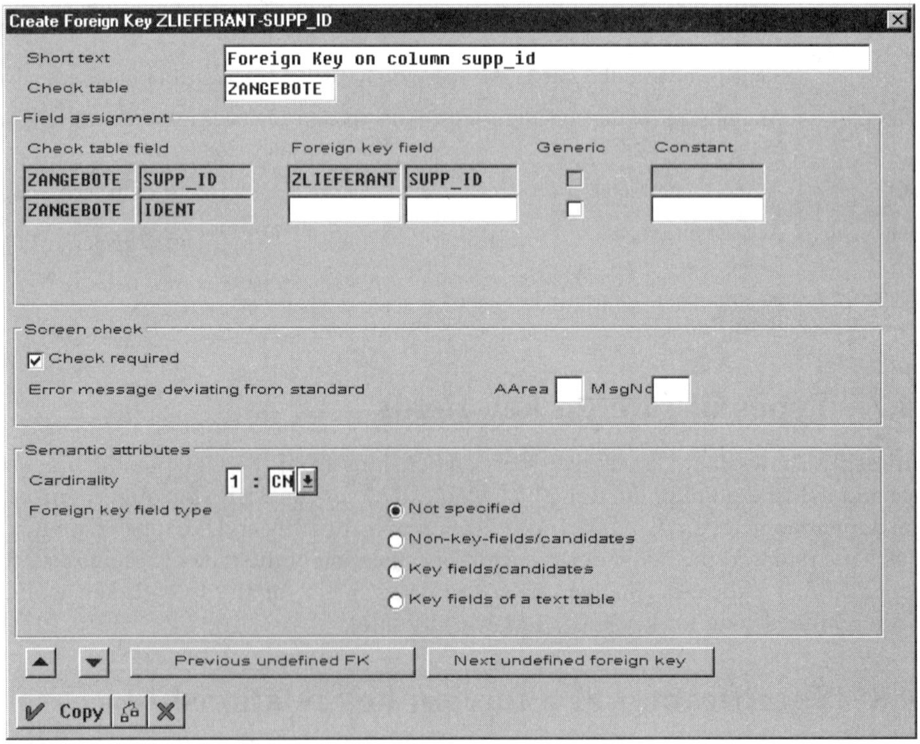

Figure 5.15 Foreign key

any table can be entered here: definition of a foreign key relationship requires only that the check table has at least one transitive relationship to the value table. Specify the *Field allocation* by marking the flag *generic* to perform a generic foreign key check. To perform a check against a constant, enter it within quotation marks in the field *Constants*. In that case, remove the entries for table name and field name in the column *Foreign key field*. When a screen foreign key is involved, mark the flag *Check desired* to activate a check for screen fields. Enter the semantic properties by completing the fields for cardinality (n:m) and the type of foreign key fields. The type of foreign key fields indicates whether a for key is identifying.

5.5 Aggregate objects

Besides the basis objects described in Section 5.1, the R/3 repository uses additional object classes, called **aggregate objects**. Aggregate objects consist of several connected tables. Aggregate objects include:

- View,
- Matchcode objects and
- Lock objects.

A base table, also called a primary table, serves as the starting point for an aggregate object. All additional tables belonging to an aggregate object are called secondary tables. Secondary must have a direct connection to the **primary table** with a foreign key relationship or an indirect, transitive relationship that connects the primary table to the other tables. All the tables of an aggregate object are known as **base tables**. Base tables form a tree structure in which each table may appear only once. The primary table is the root of the tree.

5.5.1 Views

The term **view** comes from the world of relational databases. A view is a **virtual table** that is derived from one or more database tables. It does not exist as a physical table in the database. A view works like a window that is placed over an existing table: it hides some parts of the table and makes others visible. Views hide individual fields of a table from users. In a given application, users see only those fields that interest them.

Hiding the fields of a base table is called **projection**. If a view contains only certain entries in a base table, it is called a **selection**. However, a view can combine elements from several base tables with a **join operation**. The definition of a view at the database level can involve all three of these procedures.

Creation of a delivery note requires data from various base tables: the fields MANDT, KDNR and ANSCHRIFT from the table *Customer master*, the fields MATERIAL and ANZAHL from the table *Order* and the material identifier from the table *Material*. A join condition transfers all the required fields from the base tables into the view structure. The creation of a view takes place at the database level with the command `CREATE VIEW`.

A WHERE condition generates the join condition that creates the connection between the base tables. In principle all three operations can operate at the database level to build a view. Note, however, that R/3 changes (update operations) allow only views that arise from a base table, not those built with a join condition. Figure 5.16 clarifies join operations.

The R/3 repository distinguishes between various view types. The view type determines if a view is created in the database and how it can be accessed. Views in the R/3 environment are specific to an application. As in the case of tables, users must describe a view in the R/3 repository before creating it in the database. To define views SAP uses the three basic operations noted above. Join operations, however, do not connect the individual tables dynamically. As described in Section 5.4, the foreign key concept (semantic foreign keys) performs this task. The R/3 repository thus describes the semantic relationships between tables statically. Because each application tunes all R/3

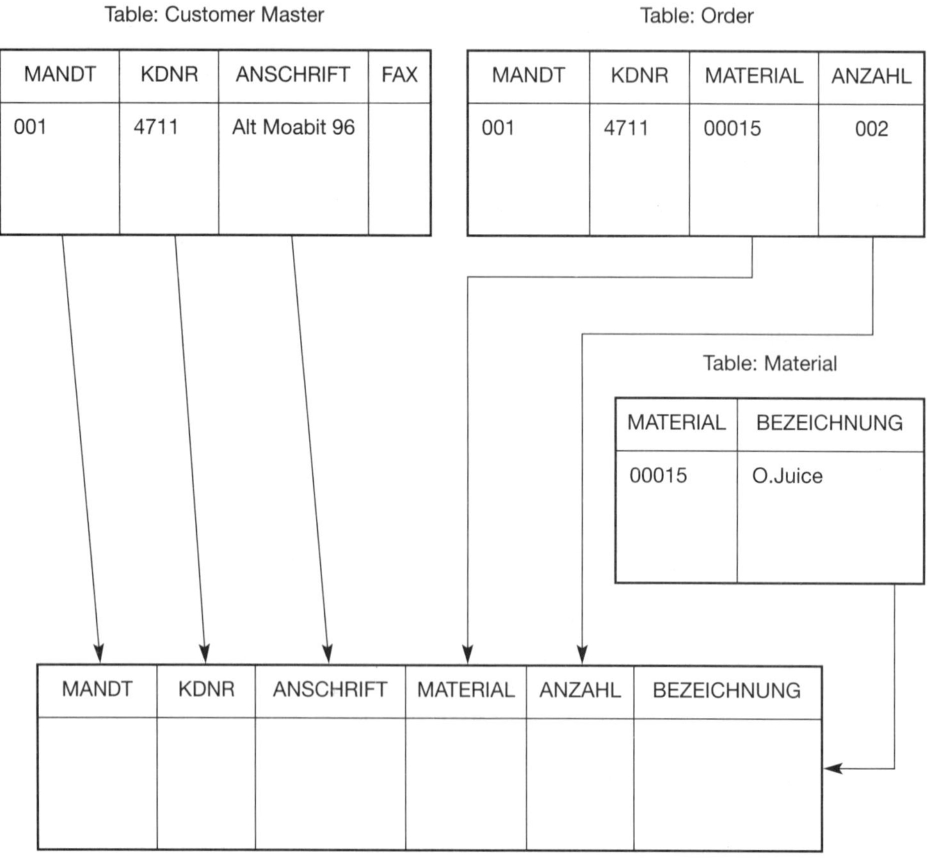

Figure 5.16 View structure

views, view definition must take place in the R/3 repository based on the semantic relationships of the base tables to each other. Therefore, only those views that are connected with the appropriate key relationships in the R/3 repository can be linked in one view.

The R/3 system distinguishes between various view types:

- Database views (view type D)
- Projection views (view type P)
- Help views (view type H)
- Structure views (view type S)
- Maintenance views (view type C)

Database views

An R/3 database view is created 1:1 in the database as described in the R/3 repository. As a precondition, all tables for which the view exists must have the table type `TRANSP`. If more than one table belongs to the view, the system has only read access to the data. As its goal, the view limits the number of accesses to the database with the join built at the database level. Create DB views when users require simultaneous selection of logically connected data from several tables. Access to views generally demands less time than access to the individual base tables. Note, however, that the base tables have indexes to improve performance when accessing a view.

Projection views

A projection, which hides certain fields of the base table, creates projection views. During database access, therefore, only the data actually required is transferred. Projection views can be built from only **one** table, regardless of the type of table: `TRANSP`, `POOL` or `CLUSTER`. No selection conditions may be used when accessing the data. A projection view has no corresponding view in the database: the R/3 system converts access to the proper base table. Projection views can not only select data, but also insert it. The system sets hidden fields to their default values during insertion. This procedure avoids NULL values.

Help views

As mentioned above, *F4* invokes the help system to display the values of value tables. Help views supplement the values with explanatory texts. The texts always appear in the logon language. A foreign key relation joined to a corresponding check table store the texts in a table. Only one help view can be created for each check table.

Structure views

At the view level, structure views share a number of similarities with `INTTAB` tables. They help generate table structures from view fields in SBAP/4 programming. This type of view does not exist as an independent view in the database. `EXEC SQL` or `SAP-SQL` cannot, therefore, process it. The application must program evaluation of such views. Before version 3.0, tables of the type `TRANSP`, `POOL` or `CLUSTER` could build structures. As of version 3.0, the system no longer supports structure views because they do not differentiate themselves from pure structures. Users, however, can still process existing structure views.

Maintenance views

Maintenance views enable a business-oriented look at the data. They permit both read and write access to fields. Access occurs by means of table maintenance (transaction `sm31`), or customizing transactions that make common processing of data from the basis table of view possible. Maintenance views can belong to the types `TRANSP`, `POOL` or `CLUSTER`. Secondary tables, however, must have an n:1 relationship to the primary table.

5.5.2 Matchcodes

In the R/3 system, **matchcodes** function as special views of R/3 tables. A matchcode can serve as a search aid when, for example, the situation requires an object's key in an entry field, but the user knows only certain non-key fields. A matchcode thus offers a secondary access path to key fields. Do not, however, confuse a matchcode with a database index. Note the following differences:

- a matchcode can consist of fields from several tables,
- matchcodes can be built on pool, cluster and transparent tables,
- the R/3 help system can use matchcodes as entry helps, and
- the structure of a matchcode can be linked to certain conditions by specifying selection conditions.

Components of a matchcode

A matchcode consists of a **matchcode object** and **matchcode IDs**. The matchcode object defines an aspect (analogous to a view) of one or more R/3 tables. Define matchcode objects by specifying the relevant tables, their fields and the existing foreign key relationship. Projections (field choices) and selections (specification of restrictions) derive matchcode IDs from matchcode objects. Several (up to 36) matchcode IDS can be created for a single matchcode object. The name of the matchcode ID consists of the name of the corresponding matchcode object and a number. The system allows creation of an individual selection condition for each matchcode ID of a matchcode object. The selection condition then functions as a filter for the matchcode being built. For example, a matchcode might include only those customers who were new in 1995.

The R/3 system differentiates between **temporary** (built at the time of access) and **physical** (physically stored in the R/3 system) matchcodes. In any case, the database does not store the matchcode itself, as in the case of a view, but only its definition.

Update types

At **definition of the matchcode ID**, the user can determine when the system builds or updates the matchcode, when a base table changes, for example. Note, however, the distinction between the update types for physical and temporary matchcodes.

- *Physical matchcodes*
  A pool stores the matchcode IDs for a matchcode object. At the time defined for generation of the matchcode object, the system creates and activates a description of the object in the repository. The table name consists of the prefix *M_* and the name of the matchcode object. Use the matchcode utility (SAPMACO) to create this table in the database.
  At each generation of every matchcode, the system creates a table definition of type `POOL` in the repository. It then stores the pool table thus generated in the pool of the matchcode object.
  The name of the pool table consists of the prefix *M_*, the name of the matchcode object and the matchcode ID. Table 5.6 shows the update types for physical matchcodes.

- *Temporary matchcodes*
  Temporary matchcodes include transparent matchcodes for views and indexes and classification matchcodes.
  Only transparent tables can form the foundation of a **transparent matchcode**. At activation of a transparent matchcode (**update type I**) the system automatically stores a view definition in the R/3 repository. This view definition consists of the fields specified in the matchcode ID definition (in the same order) and any defined matchcode restriction. To improve access to this view, the system stores an index of the first fields (of the same table) of the matchcode ID in the repository. The database utility creates the corresponding database view, it does not occur automatically.
  Classifying matchcodes (**update type K**) are application-related search paths. Query classifying matchcodes with the *F4* key. A function module allocates application-specific search path. Specify the function module at definition of the matchcode ID. Matchcode selection calls the module.

Table 5.6 Update types for physical matchcodes

Update type	*Effect*
Asynchronous (A)	The database utility builds the matchcode data at a particular time.
Synchronous (S)	Any changes to the contents of tables are updated immediately in the matchcode without any explicit request from the application program to do so.
Within an application program (P)	The application program itself triggers the update of the matchcode.

Creating matchcodes

Enter the four-character name of the matchcode to be created in the initial screen of the data dictionary and choose the object class *Matchcode objects*. Execute the following steps to define a matchcode:

- Specify the attributes of the matchcode object,
- Choose the secondary tables,
- Choose the fields of the matchcode object,
- Activate the matchcode object,
- Maintain the matchcode IDs,
- Create the matchcode pool in the database for update types A, S and P,
- Create the database view and the index for update type I,
- Create the function module for update type K.
- *Create matchcode object*
  The screen *Maintain Matchcode Object (Attributes)* (see Figure 5.17) gives the attributes of the matchcode object. When creating a new matchcode, enter the short description and table name, for example *KNA1*, in the field *Primary table*. Note that the system automatically fills the fields *Primary table*, *Secondary tables* and *Matchcode pool* only

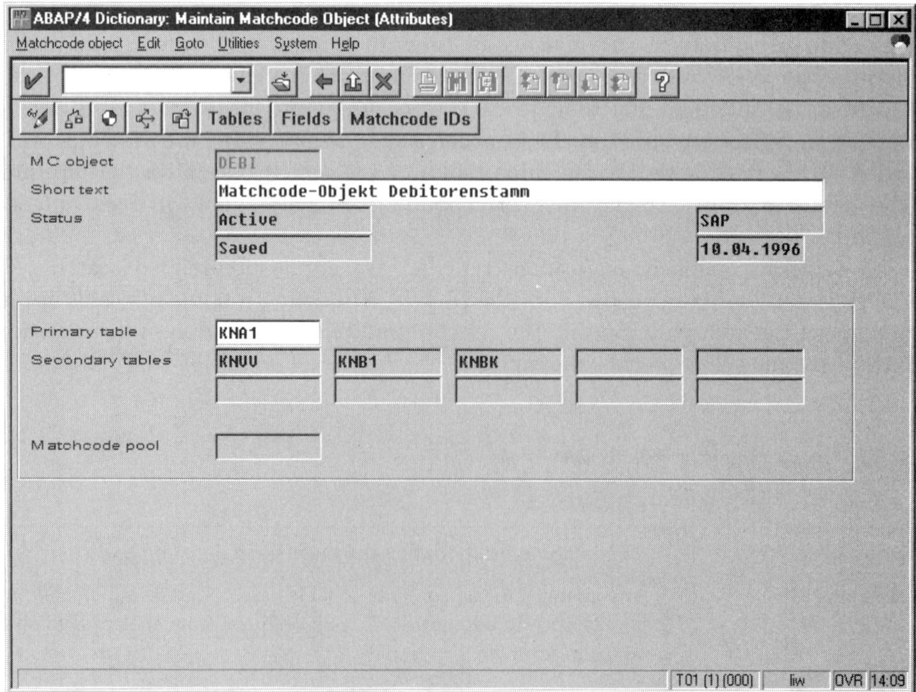

Figure 5.17 Matchcode object

when the matchcode object already exists as active. After saving the attributes, determine the tables belonging to the matchcode with the menu path *Goto → Tables*. The choice of a table begins with one table, the **primary table**. All tables connected with this table by a foreign key can be chosen as **secondary tables**.

The figure *Maintain matchcode object (Tables)* shows how to choose individual tables in order by placing the cursor on the table names and clicking on *Edit → Foreign key fields*. These actions provide the user with a list of all tables linked to the chosen table with foreign keys. A return to the maintenance screen transfers all the chosen tables as secondary tables. After saving the choice of tables, allocate the individual tables of the fields to the matchcode object with the menu path *Goto → Fields*. The figure displays all the key fields of the tables. All the primary key fields that are not also concurrently foreign key fields must be transferred to the matchcode object. Fields that will later be used in the matchcode ID must also be transferred. Choose individual fields analogously to tables. Saving the field choices and activating the matchcode object closes maintenance of matchcode objects.

- *Create matchcode ID*
  Starting at the screen *Maintain Matchcode Object (Properties)* (see Figure 5.17), branch to matchcode maintenance with the menu path *Goto → Matchcode IDs*. Analogously to the matchcode object, maintain matchcode ID properties including the choice of tables. Choose individual tables and, if desired, specify the selection conditions (see Figure 5.18).

  Regarding the properties, note that the system requires an entry in the field *Update type* of the identifiers discussed in Section 5.5.2. The *System matchcode* and *Authorization check* are optional specifications. If a matchcode carries the system matchcode description, the SAP software employs this matchcode and users may not change it.

  Tables and field choice follows matchcode object maintenance analogously, but in field selection users may choose only fields from tables that are linked with foreign keys. The sequence of fields in the matchcode ID has significant influence on how quickly the matchcode is accessed. For this reason, the most frequently accessed field should stand at the beginning of the matchcode. Use selection conditions to limit the output quantity of the matchcode search.

  Start at *Maintain matchcode-ID (Fields)* to branch to *Maintain matchcode ID (Selection conditions)* with the menu path *Goto → Selection conditions* as shown in Figure 5.18. Specify selection conditions for every matchcode field here using the form *<MC-Field><op><Constant>*.

  Make sure that the quotation marks always enclose the constant.

  For *op*, enter any of the operators EQ, NE, LE, LT, GE, GT and LK (Like). These operators have the same meaning as in Standard-SQL. Save the selection conditions and activate the matchcode ID.

  Use the database utility to create the matchcode in the database according to its type (pool, view, function module).

In Figures 5.17 and 5.18, the user works in a customer area. The matchcode available to the user here makes a search for customer names within a sales group much easier. For example, in the initial screen of accounting, the user might search for a customer by using

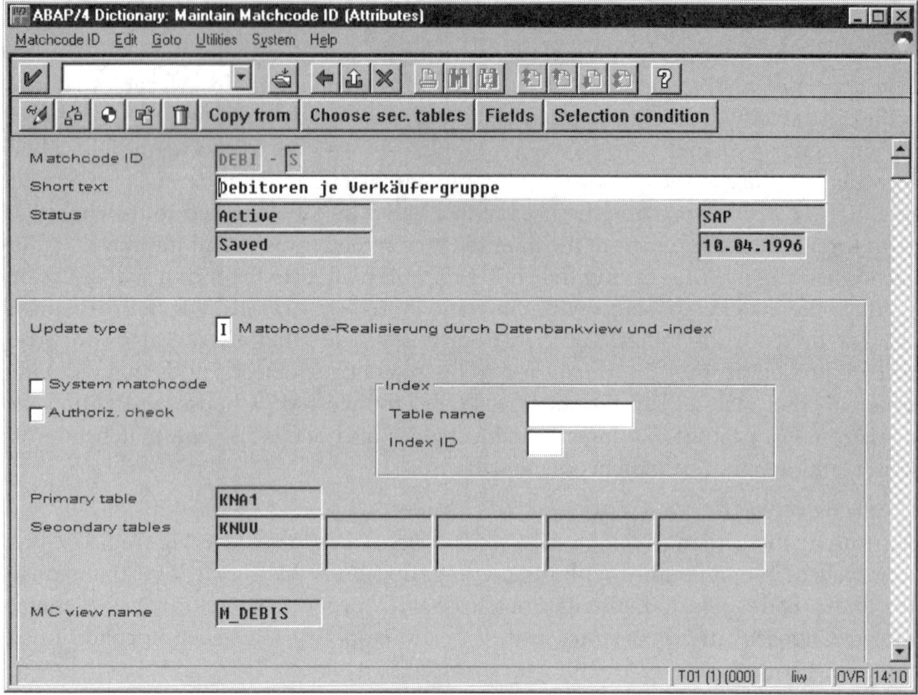

Figure 5.18 Matchcode ID

the matchcode. Place the cursor on the appropriate entry field (customer) and press the *F4* key. When choosing matchcode IDs, choose the ID `S` for customers according to sales group and branch to the mask for search entries. After user specification of the search criteria, the system returns a list of data records (customers) corresponding to the search criteria.

Building matchcode data with the matchcode utility

For update types A, S and P build matchcode data from the screen *Maintain Matchcode Object (Properties)* with the menu path *Utilities* → *Matchcode data* → *Build* for each matchcode. Choose the matchcode IDs to be created from the list provided. As an alternative method, start program `SAPMACO` with transaction `se38`. Table 5.7 shows the parameters to set.

Conversion to transparent matchcodes

The following preconditions must be met to convert a physically stored matchcode ID (update types A, S, or P) into a transparently stored matchcode (update type I):

- All base tables of the matchcode ID must be table type `TRANSP`.
- No subfields can be defined.

Table 5.7 Parameters of SAPMACO

Parameter	*Description*
Matchcode object name	If dealing with only one matchcode, enter its name here. If dealing with several matchcodes, use the typical SAP-SQL 'like' model.
Client	When building a client-specific matchcode, enter the client here (default: logon client). If building a matchcode for all clients, enter an asterisk (*) here.
Function	CRE: Build the MC ID records, delete old records DEL: Delete the MC ID records DMA: Delete the MC IDs with delete flags REC: Restart building MC IDs PRT: Display log GEN: Generate internally required function modules
Batch processing	Enter an X if the program is the program is to run in the background.
Immediate	If the background processing is to start immediately.
Date	Planned execution date of the batch job.
Job repeat period	Starts the job at any regular interval desired.

First delete any existing matchcode data from the database. If converting all the physical matchcode IDs of a matchcode object, use the database utility to delete the pool. If converting only one matchcode ID of an object, use the matchcode utility. After deleting the matchcode data, branch to the screen shown in Figure 5.18. Change the entry for update type to the value `I` here. Then activate the matchcode ID. Activation deletes the matchcode pool in the database and automatically creates a matchcode view. The conversion of the matchcode ID makes the matchcode search case sensitive. In addition, the hit rate of a search with transparent matchcode IDs may be smaller, since inner joins implement the search. Outer joins implement the search for physical matchcodes.

Matchcode index

The lack of a corresponding index to transparent matchcodes can lead to significant performance losses. If no such index exists at activation of the matchcode ID, the system issues a warning. Matchcode views that contain fewer than 1,000 data records do not require an index. Matchcode views with significantly more records should have a matchcode index. Consider the optimizer of the database system in use when choosing the index. Make sure that the secondary index being created is better than the primary index created as the default. In this case, the first entry in the index will contain the fields searched for with an equals condition.

5.5.3 Lock objects

Independently of the database system, the R/3 system offers its own **lock mechanism** to prevent problems that might arise from several users accessing the same data. Specific function modules within ABAP/4 programming control how locks are set and released. **Lock objects** automatically generate these **function modules**. The R/3 repository contains descriptions of lock objects. The descriptions contain specifications of all the tables and fields for which a program will later request locking. A lock mode must be allocated to the individual fields of a lock object. **Lock mode** E (exclusive) means that only one user may access the locked data. **Lock mode** S (shared) indicates that several users have simultaneous access to the same data. As soon as a user changes the data, however, other users can no longer access the data. Combine all the key fields of tables belonging to a lock object into a **lock argument**. If a lock object consists of only one table, the lock argument is identical to the primary key of the table. If a lock object consists of several tables that have a hierarchical relationship to each other, the lock object must contain both keys. If, for example, the key to table 2 depends on the key to table 1, the entire key to table 1 must stand at the head of the lock argument. The lock argument would then require the addition of only the missing key fields of table 2, the dependent table.

5.6 Repository information system

The repository information system, abbreviated as infosystem in the following, provides information about individual repository objects as lists, generally called **reports**. These lists can be produced both on-line and in the background. Table 5.8 indicates what information the infosystem can provide.

5.6.1 Entering the information system

Enter the infosystem from the initial screen of the data dictionary with the menu path *Environment → Repository infosys* or directly from the individual object maintenance

Table 5.8 Information from repository infosystem

Information	*Example*
Information search by object properties	A list of all objects of the type domain with the property CHAR (20)
Where-used list	A list of all objects of the type data element that use the object domain NUM8
Information on relationships	Foreign key
Information on changes to objects	A list of all object of the type table that user SAP* has changed since 01.01.95
Data display of individual objects	A list of all objects contained in table TACOB

screens with *Utilities* → *Repository infosys.* At this point, users can also branch to the information system of the workbench organizer and the infosystem of the ABAP/4 development environment as described in Chapters 6 and 7.

Choose an appropriate object class to enter the infosystem. Symbols appear before some of these object classes, indicating that additional information exists. To access the additional information, use the menu path *Edit* → *Expand subtree.* Under basic objects, for example, all the repository objects described in Section 5.1 appear.

The menu option *Repository infosys.* contains the functions *Find* and *Where-used list.* Use the function *Find* to search for object of an object class that meet certain search criteria. The *Where-used list* specifies the use of an object in other objects.

5.6.2 Information search by domains

Begin the search with the menu path *Environment* → *Repository infosys* and the choice of the repository infosystem. Mark the appropriate object class and branch to the figure *Repository-Infosys: <Object_class>* with the menu path *Repository-infosys.* → *Find.* These choices display the default selections for this object; the user may search according to these selections. The screen also displays the maximum number of hits that the search will display. These **default settings** are user-specific. Change the defaults from the initial screen of the repository infosystem with the menu path *Settings* → *User parameters.* Change the maximum number of hits from the default of 500 by entering a new value in that field.

Table 5.9 Entry conventions

Placeholder	*Meaning of the character string*	*Meaning for numeric fields*
char	All characters (except the following) stand for themselves. Case (upper or lower) plays no role.	None
number	None	Entry of a number
date	None	Enter data in the form: DDMMYYYY
*	Any group of characters	None
+	Exactly one character	None
<>	Negation: occurs when the specified character string does not fit.	Negation: occurs when the number is unequal
$	Test for an empty field	None
>	Greater than or equal	Greater than or equal
<	Less than	Less than
&	Logical AND (intersection)	Logical AND(intersection)
,	Logical OR (union of sets)	Logical OR (union of sets)

Table 5.10 Output control

X	Simple output of the list
S	A blank line is added automatically at a group change (when column values change)
H	At a group change, the value is displayed only once in the header
P	At a group change, the value is displayed only once and a page advance is issued

If the name of the domain being searched for is only partially known, enter part of the name in the field *Domain* and use a generic search. Note, however, the entry conventions given in Table 5.9. If searching for the domain KUNNR, for example, and the complete name is not yet known, enter the value 'KU*' in the field domain.

With output control, the user can determine which additional information (properties) of the domain the list will display.

The value in the field *Output* determines if a particular column is displayed. Use the field *Sort* to determine a sorting sequence.

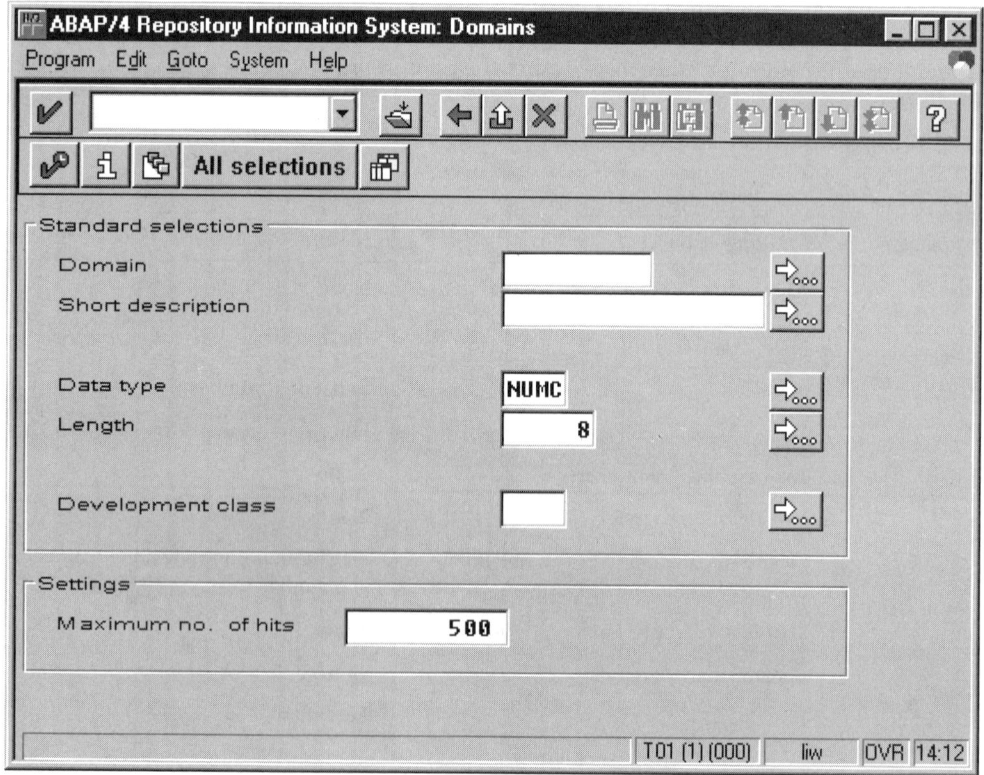

Figure 5.19 Information system

In connection with the sort field, various options (see Table 5.10) set the layout of the list.

If the user does not know the name of the domain, but does know the properties that should fill the domain, search for the domain by these properties.

The screen *Repository Information System: Domains* (see Figure 5.19) specifies the data type and the field length. The entry conventions given in Table 5.9 can also be used here. The command *Program → Execute* generates a list of all domain names and properties that correspond to the specifications entered.

5.7 Activation

As noted, during processing of a program, a generated version of the source code, the **runtime object**, is interpreted rather than the source code itself. Repository objects must also be available to ABAP/4 programs as runtime objects. **Activation** of a saved repository object generates the runtime objects, the **nametabs**. The nametabs are then available to programs and screen masks. Changes to repository objects automatically affect the related objects or programs. At reactivation of a domain or a data element, for example, the system automatically reactivates all the tables involved, but it does not transfer them automatically to the database. When programs start, a check (time stamp) determines if a table has been reactivated since generation of the program. If table reactivation has occurred, the program is automatically regenerated. The activation of a domain, for example, can have effects on numerous other objects. The **where-used list** allows the user to estimate the range of such an activation. Use the maintenance menu options *<Object> → Activate* to activate each object. If activation of a large number of objects is required, use the **mass activation program**.

5.7.1 Mass activation program

A mass activation has a distinct advantage over individual activation. If, for example, a table contains several newly activated domains, the mass activation program must activate the table just once. The program can activate related objects, such as domains and tables, together. Reach the mass activation program from the initial screen of the R/3 system with the menu path *System → Services → Reporting* and enter program `RDDMASG0`. The program activates objects in a two-level procedure.

- *First level*
  The system checks to make sure that the object corresponds to the SAA norms, that it does not use any protected key words and that all its attributes are consistent. In SAP parlance, this type of check is called an **inner check**. After completing the inner check, the system performs an **external check**, which makes sure, for example, that value tables exist if required. If both checks complete their tasks successfully, the system sets the object to the status *active*. If the object fails the external check, the system sets the object to the status *partially active*. Objects intended for activation must pass the first level before the second level begins.

- *Second level*
  The second level of activation checks all objects still marked with the status *partially active* once again for their external contexts. If the check fails again, the object remains as partially active. Nonetheless, it is available for other objects.

In both cases, enter the program name and start the program by choosing *Execute*. Figure 5.20 shows the screen for the mass activation program. Enter any of the following types of mass generation in the field *Function*:

- *ptgen (part generation)*
  The function *ptgen* activates any desired number of objects specified with either a transport request (mask field *transport request*), or with an external table (mask field *external table*) or an internal table (mask field *internal table*).
- *trgen (transport generation)*
  The function *trgen* must activate all objects transported from a development system into a target system. Specification of the objects can occur only with a transport request (see Chapter 3). This function cannot provide a specification with an external or internal table.

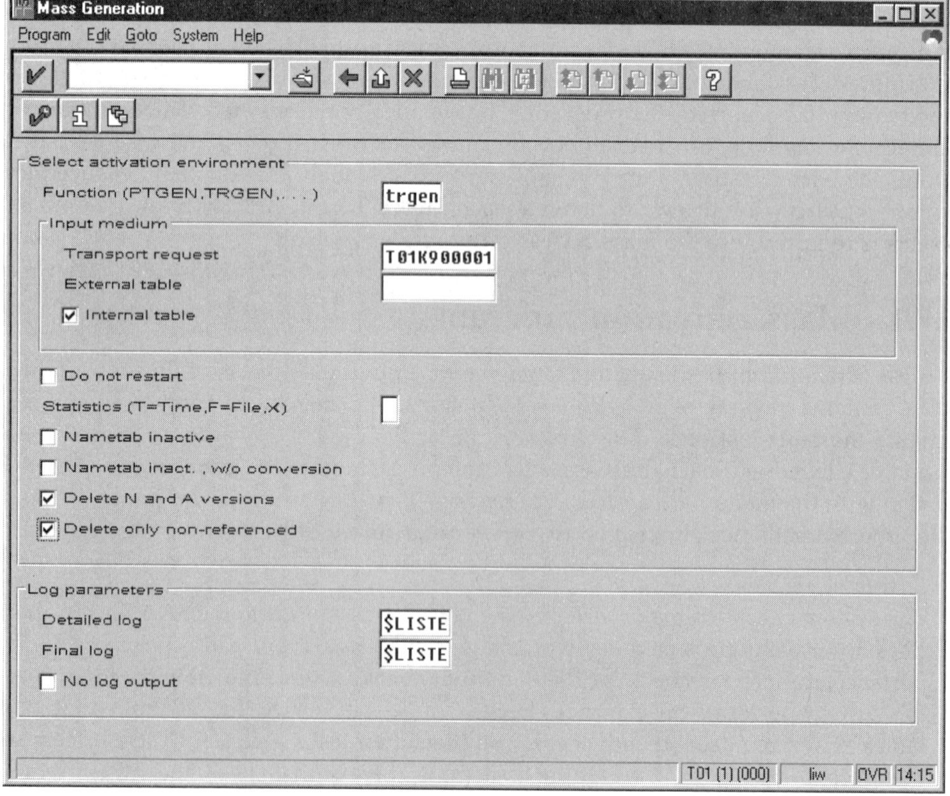

Figure 5.20 Mass activation program

- *mtgen*
  The function *mtgen* works similarly to the function *trgen*, but is used only during an update procedure to activate objects. It ignores external log entries. No final log appears on the screen.
- *mtgea*
  This function works similarly to *trgen* and *mtgen*, but is used only during an upgrade from version 2.1. It ignores lock objects (ENQU).
- *mtgeb*
  The function *mtgeb* works similarly to *trgen*, but is used only during an upgrade from version 2.1. Unlike the function *mtgea*, it applies exclusively to lock objects.

A transport request can be specified in the mask field *Transport request* for all activation functions. All the objects specified in the transport request will be activated. A log will note the objects for which activation took place successfully. In addition, the functions *trgen* and *mtgen* check the orderly importation of the objects before attempting to activate them. Users can also enter the objects intended for activation in an external table, TACOB. Create the table with table maintenance via transaction `sm31` or the menu path *System → Services → Table maintenance*. Enter the table name TACOB and choose *Maintain*; then enter the individual objects and their object types. ATAB tables may be used only when the correspond to the structure of table TACOB.

Should a mass activation run terminate, the mask field *Do not restart* triggers a **restart mechanism** by keeping the default blank character. At a restart, the system will activate only those files that have not yet been activated. Entering an `X` in this field reactivates all objects independently of their status.

The mask field *Statistics* controls the output of a log on how long the object activation takes. Enter a `T` to display the length of activation time for each object at the end of the log. Enter an `F` to have the statistics written to a file. Evaluate the log file with program `RDDTRA01`. Enter an `X` to generate both sets of statistics.

Use the parameters *Nametab inactive* and *Nametab inact., w/o conversion* exclusively during an update procedure. In an operational system, these parameters can cause inconsistencies. Their treatment here is therefore short. *Nametab inactive* means that the individual runtime objects are generated in an inactive version. Only after completion of the entire activation procedure does a C program convert the objects into active nametabs. If the table have undergone structural changes, repeat the changes in the database with a **conversion** before activating them in the repository. *Nametab inact., w/o conversion* means (unlike *Nametab inactive*), that the system changes the objects into active names without a previous conversion.

If a delete flag is set for an object, the system deletes the active version of the object as a default. If an edited version exists, the system deletes it only when this parameter is active. If an object has a delete flag but other objects still use it, the system does not delete it if the parameter *Delete only non-referenced* is marked.

The parameters *Detailed log* (detailed information on the two-level activation) and *Final log* (overview of the activation) control log output. The default value, `$LISTE`, outputs the log only to the screen. One exception is the function *mtgen*, which produces an additional file log. Overwrite the default name with any six-character name desired.

Table 5.11 Mass activation logs

Function	*Transport request*	*External table*	*Internal table*	*Entry for log name*	*Internal log name*	*Storage*	*ABAP for evaluation*
ptgen	x			6-character name	<Name> + time	DB	RDDPROTA
ptgen		tacob		No entry	A <yymmdd>. <SID>	File	
trgen	x			No entry	<Source>A. Transp. <Target>	File	
mtgen	x			No entry	<Source>A. Transp. <Target>	File	

Table 5.11 provides an overview of the logs. If *No log output* is marked, nothing is output to the screen.

5.7.2 Deletion requests

As of R/3 version 3.x, the mass activation program can also delete objects. The following object types can be deleted:

- Domains,
- Data elements,
- Structures,
- Tables,
- Indexes,
- Views,
- Matchcode objects,
- Matchcode IDs.

Enter a `D` in the appropriate column of the internal tables of each transport log to delete these objects. Note that deletion of the technical settings of tables can occur only in the context of the tables themselves.

The ability to transport these deletions of objects into another system also exists. Actual deletion of the object takes place with the data dictionary maintenance in the source system. The system then enters the function `D` in the transport request (see Chapter 7). In any case, however, the system can delete only those objects that no longer refer to another object. The transport request is then released. Deletion of the objects in the transport requests is triggered in the target system during a run of the mass activation program. The mass activation program determines all existing references to an object marked for deletion. The program deletes the objects regardless of any references they may contain. The user must then employ the log to determine and adjust any objects to which the deleted objects refer.

5.7.3 Batch activation

Mass activation often takes a great deal of time: it activates not only the objects marked for activation but also all dependent objects. To alleviate possible difficulties, use program `RDDMASG0` to start **background processing** when the system runs a lighter load. Doing so starts activation with the external table TACOB. Use table maintenance (`sm31`) to fill the table with the objects intended for activation before beginning background processing. Then schedule the appropriate background job for program `RDDMASG0`. See Chapter 3 for a more detailed description of batch job scheduling.

5.7.4 On-line activation

On-line activation occurs either directly, from within object maintenance for each object, or in common by the information system for a group of objects. Unlike batch activation, on-line activation can activate in common only objects that belong to the **same object class**. An active version of these objects must already exist. Choose the object class from the initial screen of the information system. Use the appropriate selection conditions in the subsequent menu to request a list of object. Mark the objects to be activated in the list and activate them with the command *<Object> activate*.

5.8 Version management

As described in Section 5.7, individual objects can possess different types of status depending on the type of processing. The status of an object identifies its version. Table 5.12 shows the different types of status that an object can possess.

Table 5.12 Status of objects

Status	*Function*
new	Identifies, new, not yet activated objects.
active	Identifies the single active version.
partially active	The object itself is active, but errors occurred during activation of dependent objects. For example, if tables are not converted before a domain change, the domain has the status partially active.
revised	An object with an extant active version is being edited. The active version remains as a nametab until reactivation of the revised object.
deactivated	Exists only for matchcode IDs that the F4 key does not offer as possible entries.

Table 5.13 Versions of the version catalog

Version	*Originates*	*Disappears*	*Identifier in catalog*
revised	At creation of a new object or when an existing object is edited	At activation	mod
active	At activation of an object, independent of an active or partially active status	At reactivation (the old version is deleted)	act
temporary	When an active version is temporarily stored in the version database	At correction release	sequential number + U
historical	When a correction is first opened for an object and at every correction release	Does not disappear, remains stored	sequential number + correction number

The repository can store the active and (if performed) revised versions of an object. During a correction release (see Chapter 3) the system stores a **historical version** in a **version database**. The version catalog provides the user with information on versions, as shown in Table 5.13. Call the version catalog in repository maintenance or the display menu of the individual objects with the following functions: *Utilities → Version management*.

- *Display versions*
  Choose only one version for display with the push button *Display*. The system displays the properties of the object.
- *Retrieve versions*
  Maintenance mode can retrieve old (historical) versions with the function *Retrieve*. Checking the appropriate version in the version catalog makes it available in the repository as a revised, saved version. The repository stores a maximum of two versions: active and revised. If the user retrieves a historical version, the active version remains active.

  Should the user attempt to active the retrieved version, the activation will not work if other dependent objects have not changed in the meantime.
- *Compare versions*
  Use the initial screen of the version catalog to compare two versions with each other. Check both versions and then choose the function *Compare*. The system displays the newer of the two versions completely. For the older version, it highlights deviations. If the user marks only one version, the system compares that version with the next highest (active or revised) version.
- *Cancel changes*
  To cancel that changes made to an object marked with the status *revised* and return to the version last active, execute the function *<Object> → Cancel changes* in repository maintenance.

- *Drag versions*
  Drag version means the temporary storage of an active version in the version database. To perform this task use the function *<Object>* → *Drag version* in repository maintenance.

- *Change versions*
  Use the menu path *Edit* → *revised* × *active* to switch between revised and active versions. This function simplifies a comparison of both versions.

Figure 5.21 shows a historical version of the table SDBASQLHIS and its properties.

```
           Version display Table SDBASQLHIS
--------------------------------------------------------------
Name        Version                  Correction
--------------------------------------------------------------
SDBASQLHIS 00001                     K11K056982 11.17.1994   SAP
Page 1                 General attributes
--------------------------------------------------------------
Version    Name       last changed by
00001      SDBASQLHIS SAP          02.08.1994 19:11:15
Short description...... ADABAS DBA: xbackup request history
Table type...... INTTAB
Delivery class....
Activation type... 00
Buffering.........
Tab.maint. allowed
--------------------------------------------------------------
Name        Version                  Correction
--------------------------------------------------------------
SDBASQLHIS 00001                     K11K056982 11.17.1994   SAP
Page 2                 Fields
--------------------------------------------------------------
Field name Key Data elem. Check tab.
SAVID       X   SDBASAVID
SAVTYP          SDBASAVTYP
BEGDAT          SDBADATE
BEGTIM          SDBATIME
ENDDAT          SDBADATE
ENDTIM          SDBATIME
MEDIA           SDBAMEDIA
SAVSTAT         SDBASAVSTA
RETCOD          SDBARETCOD
--------------------------------------------------------------
Name        Version                  Correction
--------------------------------------------------------------
SDBASQLHIS 00001                     K11K056982 11.17.1994   SAP
Page 3                 foreign key fields
--------------------------------------------------------------
       - - - - - - - - - none - - - - - - - - -
```

Figure 5.21 Historical version of table SDBASQLHIS

5.9 Database utility

The **database utility** is the interface between the R/3 repository and the RDBMS beneath it. The database utility allows for creation of repository objects (tables, indexes, views and matchcodes) in the database from within the R/3 system. The utility also frees the user from familiarity with the specific database commands. Reach the database utility directly from object maintenance or from the initial screen of the data dictionary with the menu path *Utilities → Database utility* (`se14`).

Execute the basic functions (create, delete and convert) of the database utility directly, in the background or as mass processing. Use the processing type *Direct* with caution: it can overload the system. It generates, and immediately executes, a program that contains all the changes to the database. A choice of the processing type *Background* has the advantage of not burdening the system too much. *Mass processing* enters all the objects to be created in the database in the table TBATG. The system then processes the table at a later defined time. Check the successful creation, deletion or conversion of objects in the batch log.

Two additional types of processing exist for tables:

- Generate program,
- Force conversion.

For tables, the option exists to choose the processing type *Generate program*. As in the case of the processing type *Direct*, the system generates a program. However, unlike direct processing, the system does not execute the program immediately, but later. Use of this processing type makes sense only when a physical reorganization converts tables. We do not recommend direct processing for other actions, since direct database commands execute the conversion and no report must be produced. This affects performance very positively. Produce the report with the menu path *Extras → Generate conversion program*.

The menu option *Extras → Force conversion* causes a table conversion even if the table has not experienced any structural changes. This function makes sense when the database parameters have changed.

5.9.1 Create

After tables, views or matchcodes have been described in the repository, use the database utility to create them in the database. Defined indexes are also automatically created for transparent tables.

5.9.2 Delete

This function deletes a transparent table and its indexes in the database. All database systems except Oracle also delete all the database views that exist for a table. Oracle simply invalidates such views.

For table pools and clusters the function deletes the physical pool or cluster in the database. To delete a matchcode, the system distinguishes between matchcode objects and matchcode IDs. It deletes a matchcode ID by deleting all the entries of the matchcode ID in the matchcode pool. The deletion of matchcode objects triggers the deletion of the matchcode pool itself. The database utility also offers the ability to delete objects explicitly and then to recreate them.

The function *Delete, create new* has the same effect as the sequential execution of the functions *Delete* and *Create*.

5.9.3 Convert

As noted, before they can be activated in the R/3 repository, the tables must first be converted in the database for structure and format changes to objects. Table 5.14 lists the changes required by table conversion.

If, for example, a domain has changed, use the information system to determine the tables that use the domain in question. These tables may not have the status *revised*, otherwise the revised version would be converted.

Now activation of the domain can take place. It first receives the status *partially active* because the tables have not yet been converted. To convert the tables, branch to the table maintenance menu and convert them individually with the menu path *Utilities → Database-Utility*. After conversion of all the tables, reactivate the domain to bring it to the status *active*.

Conversion of a table can occur in three different ways:

- Deletion and recreation of the table,
- Changing the database catalog (alter table),
- Physical reorganization.

Deletion and recreation delete the table in the database, activate the revised table in the repository and recreate it in the database. Changing the database catalog alters the description of the table in the database. The advantage here is that the data contained in the table remains. However, any indexes existing for the table may require rebuilding.

Table 5.14 Changes required by a conversion

Insertion and deletion of table fields
Changing the order of fields within the table
Renaming fields
Changing the primary key
Changing the table type
Changing the allocation of a table to a table pool or table cluster
Changing field formats by changing the domains

The physical reorganization of a transparent table occurs in five steps:

- *First step*
  Generation of a program that executes the conversion of a table immediately.
- *Second step*
  This renames the database table to be converted (the old table) and deletes all indexes for the table. The name of the temporary table consists of the prefix QCM together with the table name. Note that when a temporary table already exists for a table to be converted, the system deletes the temporary table before a new attempt to rename it. In some cases, data might be lost if the temporary table contains data.
- *Third step*
  This activates the revised version (with the new structure) in the repository. It creates the table with the new structure and primary index in the database. The table does not yet contain any data.
- *Fourth step*
  This reloads the data from the temporary table into the new table. After this step, both the temporary table and the new table contain the data. If the primary key of a table was abbreviated, not all the data records might be reloaded because of duplicate keys.
- *Fifth step*
  The last step creates the indexes already defined in the repository in the database.

After conversion, delete the temporary table only if no restart log exists for the table. Lack of a log indicates a successful conversion. Data will be lost if the table is deleted despite the existence of a restart log.

A transaction handles the entire conversion cycle. Note, therefore, that the log areas of the database are configured large enough. Log requirements for conversion depend on the size of the table. In addition, the conversion locks a number of tables. Converting large tables can cause bottlenecks.

The time required for the conversion depends on the size of the tables and the number of indexes defined for the tables. The larger the table and the more indexes present the longer the conversion will last. The conversion time can increase dramatically if the push button *Initial* was activated during definition of the tables. Activation of that setting means that the system enters a default value in the database for every table field for which an initial value is desired. An entry is made for every data record of the table.

Table 5.15 provides an example of the changes triggered in the R/3 repository by the various database systems. A physical conversion is marked by a `U`, a change to the database catalog is marked by an `A`.

Again, note that as a rule, the physical conversion of a table demands much more time than conversion by changing the database catalog. However, if several indexes are defined for a table, conversion by changing the database catalog (alter table) can overload the performance abilities of the entire system.

Table 5.15 Conversion of repository changes by the various RDBMS

Action	*ADABAS D*	*Informix*	*Oracle*	*SQL-Server*
Insert a field	A	A	A	U
Delete a field	U	A	U	U
Change a DB data type	U	U	U	U
Shorten field	U	U	U	U
Lengthen field	A	A	A	A
Decrease decimal places	U	U	U	U
Increase decimal places	A	A	A	A
Add key field	U	A	A	U
Delete key field	U	U	U	U
Lengthen key field	U	A	A	U
Remove key field from key	U	U	U	U
Add non-key field to the key	U	A	A	A
Change sequence of key fields	U	A	A	A

6 Introduction to ABAP/4

6.1 Introductory remarks

Business usage provided the original impetus for ABAP/4 at the beginning of the 1980s; it has undergone systematic expansion and development since then. The name of this programming language consists of an acronym for 'Advanced Business Application Programming.' As a fourth-generation programming language, ABAP/4 displays the following properties:

- Structurability,
- Rich syntax,
- Functionality.

ABAP/4 makes available a large number of function modules to meet the business demands of an R/3 system. The wide variety of data contained in the repository provides much of the information needed for users' programs.

ABAP/4 processes programs interpretatively, generating intermediate code at the first call of a program. Alternatively, users can request the loading of intermediate code for selected ABAP programs at the time of system installation. Doing so frees the system of any `transience` and makes a high-performance system available from the very start. Internal structures hold the generated or loaded code and hold it available for additional calls. The generation of intermediate code does not include any fixed linkage of programs to external data. If the structure of the data changes, R/3 needs to regenerate only the affected sections. The system does not need to regenerate the complete code.

The use of a powerful on-line debugger to step through ABAP/4 programs interpretatively simplifies the search for errors.

The construction and structure of ABAP/4 employ the top-down principle. Accordingly, it first designs a global framework for the program. Then, using the framework, it expands the program by adding the required functions. Such a procedure is also known as early prototyping.

6.2 Specification of program objects

A program written in ABAP/4 is called an ABAP/4 program, or simply an ABAP. The programs, however, differentiate themselves depending on the information a program produces and how it produces that information.

An ABAP/4 program that produces a list is known as a **report**. Such a program represents the almost classic type of program. Typical for this class of programs is the production of long lists, usually combined with long print runs. The program builds the list from data it selects according to specific criteria and then sorts the data.

Extended forms of reporting also include an interactive dialog with the user. Provision of entries on the screen along with function keys and push buttons allow the user to control the flow of a program. SAP distinguishes between **function keys and push buttons**. Unlike function keys, the system depicts push buttons as actual buttons on the screen. A click of the mouse 'presses' the buttons and makes the function active. Pressing a specific function key provides the only means of starting the functions assigned to that key. The system often allows users the ability to address a given function by function key or push button.

An ABAP/4 report controlled on-line is called an **interactive report**. Various ABAP/4 modules help to control screen programs. All the modules belonging to a given program form a **module pool**. The module pool is, therefore, an ABAP/4 program that contains modules.

An **R/3 transaction** consists of the following objects:

- Description of the CUA,
- Screen programs,
- Module pool,
- Documentation.

A transaction contains properties such as access rights along with transport and correction characteristics. Entries in certain tables permit the system-wide call of a transaction with a transaction code. Transactions differ from reports in their complexity and role in the R/3 system. Reports, however, often form a constitutive part of a transaction. Users can generate multiple reports in one transaction.

As known, menu functions also invoke transactions; transaction codes also address the functions.

The following material first presents the most simple ABAP/4 programs, classic reports. It then broadens the discussion to include the instructions that ABAP/4 uses to prepare reports in steps, including elements of on-line and screen control.

Similar to version management in the repository and the CTS, R/3 also offers version management for ABAP/4 programs. In this case, version management consists of one active version and any desired number of historical development versions. A menu allows the user to determine when to set a particular version as final. In addition, the release of a correction automatically generates a new version.

6.3 Structure of a report

ABAP programs consist of statements. The statement syntax ends with a period. The report statement begins every ABAP/4 report:

```
REPORT <name>.
```

The declaration section for the program's global variables usually follows, but this is not always required. To provide others with a good overview of the program, however, we recommend placing the global variables here if possible, rather than placing them in random locations within the program. The statement section follows the declaration section; the statement section can subdivide into various processing blocks.

Comments can occupy an entire line or a portion of a line. Place an asterisk (*) in the first column to make the entire line a comment line. The quotation character (") marks the remaining part of the line for treatment as a comment. Comments, however, may not appear within `EXEC SQL` blocks.

6.4 Declarative language elements

Define variables and, if necessary, default values, in the declaration section. Variables can represent the following data objects:

- internal fields and their relationships,
- internal tables,
- field groups,
- field symbols,
- selection conditions and parameters.

Use the DATA statement to define variables.

```
DATA <name> TYPE <type>.
```

Table 6.1 presents the possible data types and their default values.

Specify the length of a variable after the variable name. For example:

```
DATA string(5) TYPE C.
```

Table 6.1 Data types

Type	*Meaning*	*Standard length*	*Possible length (bytes)*	*Standard default value*
C	Character string	1	1–65535	Blank
F	Floating decimal number	8	8	0.0
I	Integer	4	4	0
N	Numeric text	1	1–65535	'00...0'
P	Packed number	8	1–16	0
X	Hexadecimal number	1	1–65535	X'00'
D	Date: Format YYYYMMDD	8	8	'00000000'
T	Time: Format HHMMSS	6	6	'000000'

One statement can contain several variable definitions. Simply place a colon (:) after the keyword DATA and separate the definitions by commas (,). For example:

```
DATA:   name1 TYPE I,
        name2 TYPE C.
```

If no specification for the data type exists, the system assumes type C. Since the default length for this type is 1, the statement

```
DATA character.
```

defines the variable character as type C with length 1: one character.

Change the standard default values with a VALUE clause. Consider the following possible definitions:

```
DATA:   floatnumber TYPE F VALUE '3.14',
        textnumber(2) TYPE N VALUE '12',
        today TYPE D VALUE 19960111.
```

Note that an apostrophe begins and closes values for floating numbers. The period (.) indicates the number of places after the decimal point. Enclosing a numeric value within apostrophes is typical of all numeric entries.

The VALUE clause enables the user to assign a value to a variable used as a constant in the report. We recommend placing all the DATA statements in one section of the program. If the program later requires changes involving the value of a constant, then making the changes will take little effort.

A user often wishes to assign variables the same properties as a given table field. In such cases, use the LIKE clause.

Example

```
DATA <name> LIKE <table_fieldname>.
```

According to this declaration, the variable <name> has the same data type as the field <table_fieldname> in table <table>. Flexibility is a significant advantage of this declaration. Consider a case in which the data type of field <table-fieldname> changes by, for example, becoming longer. Using the LIKE clause to declare the variable means that the report needs no adjustments to compensate for the changed field length.

Use the DECIMALS clause for data type P. Make sure to mark *Floating point arithmetic active* while specifying the properties of the report. The declaration

```
DATA field1 TYPE P DECIMALS 2.
```

will calculate intermediate results with the exactitude normal for the computer and the database; display or output will be limited to two decimal places.

Structures combine several variables; the sequence of the declaration also determines the memory sequence. Structures defined in this manner are called **field strings**.

Example

```
DATA:  BEGIN OF fieldstring,
          name LIKE table-name,
          birthdate LIKE table-date,
          salary TYPE F,
       END OF fieldstring.
```

Unless a VALUE clause has determined otherwise, the fields of a structure are initialized as indicated in Table 6.1.

A report addresses the field strings in the following notation: <fieldstring>-<fieldname>. In the above example:

```
fieldstring-name
fieldstring-birthdate
fieldstring-salary
```

An OCCURS clause transforms a field string into an internal table. Internal tables differ from field strings in their internal processing and presentation. The above example would appear as follows:

```
DATA:  BEGIN OF fieldstring OCCURS 5,
          name LIKE table-name,
          birthdate LIKE table-date,
          salary TYPE F,
       END OF fieldstring.
```

In R/3 version 2.2, the number after the OCCURS clause determines the number of table lines retained in main memory. If the table contains additional data records, an internal swapping mechanism comes into play, thus increasing processing time. It is important, therefore, to consider ahead of time how many lines to expect for internal tables. As of release 3.0, the R/3 OCCURS parameter does not have such an important meaning. In this development generation, the system automatically manages virtual memory for internal tables. The fields of internal tables are addressed in the same manner as the fields of field strings.

The declaration of internal tables based on existing definitions of field strings is particularly easy.

```
DATA:  BEGIN OF <Name> [ OCCURS <n>].
          INCLUDE STRUCTURE <Table>.
DATA:  END OF <Name>.
```

PARAMETERS statement

The ability to set parameters contributes to the creation of a flexible report. ABAP/4 offers the PARAMETERS statement to this end. Position the PARAMETERS statement in the declaration section in the same manner as the DATA statement.

Example

```
PARAMETERS:   name(30) TYPE C,
              birthdate TYPE D.
```

Initialize values with the DEFAULT clause as follows:

```
PARAMETERS  name(30) DEFAULT 'Anthony'.
```

If a report uses the PARAMETERS statement, the fields defined with the statement contain a value, depending on the type of processing. In the case of foreground processing, the system asks the user to enter a value for the variable; a screen mask is generated automatically.

If another report calls the report, or if processing takes place in the background, the values must be transferred to the calling report as parameters. The following paragraphs discuss this process in more detail.

To transfer entire value sets, declare selection criteria.

```
SELECT-OPTIONS: <Name> FOR <Field> DEFAULT
                       [NOT] <Value1> [ TO <Value2>].
```

<Name> represents the name of the SELECT option. <Value1> and <Value2> can be replaced by a single value (enclosed in apostrophes) or by the name of a field whose contents are used as a default. Additions to the TO clause select or exclude an area.

Note an additional variant of the SELECT-OPTIONS statement:

```
SELECT-OPTIONS: <Name> for <Field> DEFAULT [ NOT] <Value_1> OPTION
<logical operation> <Value_2>
```

Valid logical operations include EQ, NE, CP, NP, GE, LT, LE and GT.

Example

```
SELECT-OPTIONS: salary FOR table-salary DEFAULT '1000' OPTION GE.
```

A selection criterion is defined for the field salary with the request that the value in the field table-salary is greater than or equal to 1,000. A CHECK statement, described in Section 6.6.1, checks values against the criterion.

The SELECT-OPTIONS statement offers additional variants that cannot be treated here. Interested readers should consult the available literature, particularly Matzke (1996) or the help functions of the ABAP/4 workbench.

Define field groups if an effective sort of tables is involved. Combine several fields under one name and use the combined field as the sort criterion. The section on internal tables treats these options in more detail (see Section 6.7).

6.5 Operative language elements

6.5.1 Value assignment

Several options exist to assign a value to a variable. The following statements have identical effects. The use of one or another statement depends entirely on the taste of the programmer.

```
MOVE <field1> TO <field2>.
```

The value of <field1> is assigned to <field2>. The following does the same:

```
COMPUTE <field2> = <field1>.
```

or, even more briefly

```
<field2> = <field1>.
```

Several statements can be combined. Consider

```
<field1> = <field2> = <field3>.
```

instead of

```
<field2> = <field3>.
<field1> = <field2>.
```

Please note the type conversions between fields with differing types possible during value assignment. As a rule, an automatic conversion pattern exists between all fields. However, the rules governing conversion between character types and numeric fields are not at all obvious, and demand specialized knowledge in individual cases. Please refer to the manuals and use the on-line help available on the system regularly.

The MOVE statement permits the assignment of a portion of the value of one field to a particular position within another field. The statement functions only for character strings. The first character in the string is fixed as position zero.

Example

```
field1 = 'Isabella'.
field2 = 'Annastasia'.
MOVE field1+3(4) TO field2+4(4).
```

field2 thus has the value 'Annabellia'

Isa[bell]a Anna[stas]ia → Annabellia

If position and length specifications for the assignment are variable, the WRITE statement is required.

Example

```
DATA:   name(25) value 'Annafried',
        name2(25) value 'bella',
        position TYPE P,
        length TYPE P.
position = '4'.
length = '5'.
WRITE name2 TO name+position(length).
```

The field *name* thus contain the value 'Annabella.' The MOVE-CORRESPONDING statement assigns values between two field strings.

```
MOVE-CORRESPONDING <fieldstring1> TO <fieldstring2>.
```

This statement assigns the fields of the field string <fieldstring1> to the fields with identical names in the other field string <fieldstring2>. The assignment is performed similarly for internal tables.

6.5.2 Arithmetical operations

Different options exist to perform the four basic arithmetical operations. The first appears most frequently in programming languages:

```
a = b + c.    a = b - c.
a = b * c.    a = b / c.
```

as does the second, which uses a COMPUTE statement:

```
COMPUTE a = b + c.
```

Key words (ADD TO, SUBTRACT FROM, MULTIPLY BY and DIVIDE BY) can also be used.

```
a = a + b.
```

could also be written as

```
ADD b TO a.
```

Implementation of other operations is similar. The following mathematical functions are also supported:

EXP(<variable>)	Exponential, e***x*
LOG(<variable>)	Natural log
SIN(<variable>)	Sine
COS(<variable>)	Cosine
SQRT(<variable>)	Square root
<variable1> DIV <variable2>	Integer quotient
<variable1> MOD <variable2>	Remainder for integer division
STRLEN(<character_string>)	Length of a character string
<variable1> ** <variable2>	power function, computes *x****y*

These functions also permit the formulation of statistical evaluations, even if business needs do not require such calculations on a regular basis.

Arithmetical functions are limited to the four basic operations for field strings. Their syntax is similar to that of the MOVE-CORRESPONDING statement:

```
ADD-CORRESPONDING
SUBTRACT-CORRESPONDING
MULTIPLY-CORRESPONDING
DIVIDE-CORRESPONDING
```

Use these operations between internal tables and structures that have fields of the same name; they take effect in the corresponding fields. ADD-CORRESPONDING offers possibilities beyond the scope of this book but contained in the documentation for a running R/3 system.

6.5.3 Character string operations

Numerous functions simplify the processing of character strings.

```
SHIFT <field> BY <n> PLACES [RIGHT | CIRCULAR |
                             CIRCULAR RIGHT ].
```

moves the character string by <n> places to the left, right, circularly or circularly to the right.

Example

```
DATA:  string(20).
string = 'Annabella'.
SHIFT string BY 4 PLACES.                  "-->'bella    '
SHIFT string BY 4 PLACES RIGHT.            "-->'    Annab'
SHIFT string BY 4 PLACES CIRCULAR.         "-->'bellaAnna'
SHIFT string BY 4 PLACES CIRCULAR RIGHT.   "-->'ellaAnnab'
SHIFT <field1> UP TO <field2>.
```

moves the characters of the character string <field1> to the left, up to the first appearance of the character string <field2> in the character string <field1>.

The REPLACE statement can replace the entire contents of a field.

```
REPLACE <field1> [ LENGTH <value> ] WITH <field2> INTO <field3>.
```

<field2> replaces the first appearance of the character string <field1> in <field3>. Abbreviation of the length is possible.

```
TRANSLATE <field> TO UPPER CASE.
```

converts all characters to upper case (capital) letters.

Similarly, the LOWER CASE clause converts all characters to lower case (small) letters.

The OVERLAY statement

OVERLAY <field1> with <field2> overlays all the blank spaces in <field1> with the characters in <field2>, in the corresponding positions. For example:

```
DATA:  first(12),
       second(12).
       first  = 'H ll  W rld'.
       second = 'Hello Johann'.
OVERLAY first WITH second.
```

These statements alter the character string of the variable 'first' into 'Hello World.' Adding ONLY <field3> to the OVERLAY statement would overlay only those characters in <field1> that <field3> contains.

Search for a character string within another character string or a table.

```
SEARCH [ <table> | <field1> ] FOR <field2>
[STARTING AT  [ <target1> | <position1> ] ]
[ENDING AT [ <target2> | <position2> ] ].
```

The search can be limited to a starting or ending line or position. Adding AND MARK converts the character string found into upper case letters. Use the CONDENSE statement to reduce the blank spaces in a character string.

```
CONDENSE <field>.
```

This statement removes all leading spaces from the character string <field> and replaces all other sequences of spaces with exactly one blank space.

6.5.4 Simple output statements

The creation of list output fulfills the central purpose of report programming. Accordingly, the functions that control the formatting and output of data are rather complex. In this section, we simply wish to discuss the most important output statements and refer the reader to R/3 documentation for further information.

The basic form of an output statement to the printer or screen is the following:

```
WRITE <variable>.
```

One statement can combine the output of several fields:

```
WRITE:  <variable1>, <variable2>.
```

Output remains in the same output line until it becomes full. Output then continues on automatically on the next line. Trigger a line advance with the forward slash (/) character:

```
WRITE: / <variable1>.
```

Add column and length specifications in the form <column>(<length>). An offset specification also exists, so that the values for <column> and <length> may not be variable (determined dynamically at runtime).

```
WRITE: 5(10) name.
```

This command outputs ten characters of the field name, beginning in column 5. If the name contains less than ten characters, the output will be padded with blank spaces.

The statement

```
SKIP <n>.
```

produces <n> blank lines.

```
ULINE.
```

produces an underline. Line advances, position and length specifications can be added to the ULINE statement. For example:

```
ULINE at /5(60).
```

Produce vertical lines by using the system variable sy-vline. For example:

```
Write /1(80) sy-vline.
```

The FORMAT command produces color effects.

```
format [color <1,..>] [intensified [ON|OFF]].
```

Note that as of version 3.0, R/3 can use symbols and icons. Add the following lines to a report:

```
include <symbol>.
include <icon>.
```

The contents of the libraries are self-explanatory and provide numerous patterns.

The statements discussed above suffice to produce an ABAP/4 program:

```
REPORT REP01.
DATA HELP TYPE I.
PARAMETERS: A TYPE I,
            B TYPE I.

HELP = A + B.
WRITE: /5 'Total A+B:', 20 HELP.
HELP = A - B.
WRITE: /5 'Difference A-B:', 20 HELP.
HELP = A * B.
WRITE: /5 'Product A*B:', 20 HELP.
HELP = A / B.
WRITE: /5 'Quotient A/B:', 20 HELP.
ULINE.
```

This report determines the results of four types of basic operations. It declares the variables A and B as parameters; every call of the report issues a request to input entries for A and B. The result calculated by the program is assigned to the variable HELP. The WRITE statement begins output of the result at column 5 and of the variable HELP at column 20. If a user enters 12 for field A and 3 for field B, the list produces the following results:

```
28.07.1994                    rep01- Basic operations             1
-----------------------------------------------------------------
     Total a+b:                15
     Difference a-b:            9
     Product a*b:              36
     Quotient a/b:              4
-----------------------------------------------------------------
```

The variable *help* in the above example is of the type integer. Division of a and b might, however, produce a remainder. In this case, it would be advantageous to choose type F for the variable *help*. Use formatting masks to produce proper output: the USING EDIT MASK clause with specification of a formatting template.

The template can contain the following characters:

- `_` for any character in this position,
- `:` separator; other separator characters can be used than an underscore (_),
- `LL` left-justified output; must be at the beginning of the template,
- `RR` right-justified output; must be at the beginning of the template.

Editing masks can modify the output of the report *rep01* so that the quotient appears with decimal places. To do so, define the field HELP as type P and make sure that the report also has the property *Fixed point arithmetic*.

```
REPORT REP01.
DATA HELP TYPE P DECIMALS 3.
PARAMETERS:  A TYPE I,
             B TYPE I.

HELP = A + B.
WRITE: /5 'Total A+B:', 20 HELP USING EDIT MASK 'RR___.___'.
HELP = A - B.
WRITE:/5 'Difference A-B:',20 HELP USING EDIT MASK 'RR___.___'.
HELP = A * B.
WRITE: /5 'Product A*B:',20 HELP USING EDIT MASK 'RR___.___'.
HELP = A / B.
WRITE: /5 'Quotient A/B:', 20 HELP USING EDIT MASK 'RR___.___'.
ULINE.
```

Entering the value 4 for field A and the value 3 for field B would then produce the following output:

```
Quotient a/b: 1.333
```

Create and maintain list headings, text elements and titles apart from the source text of each report. Doing so allows greater flexibility and language-independent headings.

Creation of texts occurs with transaction 'se38' → *Text elements*.

This feature automatically assigns list and column headers to the results of a report. The report can address the text elements by number: TEXT-<nnn>. The program then uses the numbered text element in the language determined by the user.

The report in the above example can become even more flexible with the use of numbered text elements. For example:

```
No  Text                    Language E
001     Total a+b:
002     Difference a-b:
003     Product a*b:
004     Quotient a/b:
```

The report could then use the appropriate text elements instead of literal quotations that are difficult to maintain. The WRITE statement for the sum of a and b could thus be formulated as:

```
WRITE: /5 TEXT-001, 20 help.
```

6.5.5 Logical expressions

Users can employ control and loop structures to direct the processing sequence. Use word symbols such as IF and ENDIF or CASE and ENDCASE to combine processing sequences into blocks. Depending on the results generated by the logical expressions, processing may take place within the blocks. Conditions also assist in the control of various program branches.

Build logical expressions on the bases of operators. The available logical operators include OR, AND and NOT. Table 6.2 provides an overview of the available relational operators. In some cases ABAP/4 allows several ways of writing the same relational operator. In all cases, the operands include database fields, fields (variables) or constants. Automatic type conversion takes place for relational operations between different data types. The most important conversion rules include:

1. One operand of type F → Conversion to type F.
2. One operand of type P, the other is not of type F → Conversion to type P.

Table 6.2 Operators

Relational operator			
Equal	EQ	=	
Not equal	NE	<>	><
Greater than	GT	>	
Less than	LT	<	
Greater than or equal	GE	>=	=>
Less than or equal	LE	<=	=<

3. The operands are neither of type P nor type F; one operand is of type D or T → The other operand is converted to type D or T.
4. A comparison between a date field (D) and a time field (T) is not supported.
5. One operand of type C, the other of type X → The operand of type X is converted to type C.
6. In a comparison between an operand of type C and one of type N, both are converted to type P and then compared. Conversion of an operand of type C into a numeric data type can take place only if the character string can be interpreted numerically, i.e., it contains a number.

Other operators compare character strings. After evaluation of expressions with the operators, consider the system variable SY-FDPOS. It contains a value dependent on the result of the evaluation of the logical expression (see Table 6.3).

Table 6.3 Character string operators

		SY-FDPOS	
Operator	*Meaning of <a> operator <b>*	*True at result*	*False at result*
CO	Character string <b> contains only characters from <a> Contains only	Length of <a>	Position of the first character in <a> that is not contained in <b>
CN	Character string <b> contains not only characters from <a> Contains not only	Length of <a>	Position of the first character in <a> that is not contained in <b>
CA	<a> contains at least one character from <b> Contains any	Position of the first character in <a> that is not contained in <b>	Length of <a>
NA	<a> contains no characters from <b>; trailing blank spaces are ignored Contains not any	Position of the first character in <a> that is not contained in <b>	Length of <a>
CS	<a> contains <b>; trailing blank spaces are ignored; upper and lower case are ignored Contains string	Starting position of <b> in <a>	Length of <a>
NS	<a> does not contain <b> Contains not string	Starting position of <b> in <a>	Length of <a>
CP	Comparison with 'wildcards.' '*' stands for any character string '+' stands for a particular character Independent of upper and lower case Contains pattern	Position of <b> in <a>; any '*' at the beginning is ignored	Length of <a>
NP	<a> does not contain the pattern <b> contains not pattern	Position of <b> in <a>; any '*' at the beginning is ignored	Length of <a>

Some examples will help clarify the operators and their effects. The character position is set to begin with 0.

1. 'Bella' CO 'Annabella' ==> FALSE; SY-FDPOS = 0
2. 'bella' CO 'Annabella' ==> TRUE ; SY-FDPOS = 5
3. 'bella' CN 'Annabella' ==> FALSE; SY-FDPOS = 5
4. 'Isabell' CA 'Annabella' ==> TRUE ; SY-FDPOS = 2
5. 'Anna' CA' bella' ==> TRUE ; SY-FDPOS = 3
6. 'Anna' NA' bella' ==> FALSE; SY-FDPOS = 3
7. 'Annabella' CS 'Bella' ==> TRUE ; SY-FDPOS = 4
8. 'Annabella' CS 'Bello' ==> FALSE; SY-FDPOS = 9
9. 'Annabella' NS 'Bello' ==> TRUE ; SY-FDPOS = 9
10. 'Annabella' CP 'Anna*' ==> TRUE ; SY-FDPOS = 0
11. 'Annabella' CP '*Bella' ==> TRUE ; SY-FDPOS = 4
12. 'Annabella' CP 'Anna+' ==> FALSE; SY-FDPOS = 9

Release 3.x makes available two other useful functions.

```
SPLIT <a> AT <b> INTO [<c1> ... <cn>|TABLE <internal_table>].
```

This function splits character string <a> wherever character string <b> appears within <a>. If <b> appears in <a> several times, <a> is split into the corresponding number of parts, <c1> ... <cn>. The sequence of dividing characters is removed in each case. The user must provide sufficient target variables. If variables (<c1> to <cn>) are available, the value 0 is assigned to the system variable SY-SUBRC. If, however, not enough variables are available, SY-SUBRC is given the value 4.

If the number of parts into which <a> will be split cannot be predicted, we recommend the use of an internal table. Doing so will add a line to the table for each section of <a>.

```
CONCATENATE <a1> ... <an> INTO <b> { SEPARATED BY <c> }.
```

This function performs the opposite function, joining the character strings <a1> through <an> to the character string <b>. In the process, users can add a separating string <c> between each occurrence of <a>. If character string <b> is long enough to accept the resulting character string, SY-SUBRC is given the value of 0. If it is not long enough, SY-SUBRC is given the value of 4.

6.5.6 IF statement

The IF statement determines, based on the evaluation of the logical expression, which processing block to branch to.

```
IF <logical expression 1>.
  <processing block 1>.
{ ELSEIF <logical expression n>.
  <processing block n>.}
```

```
[ ELSE.
  <processing block n+1>].
ENDIF.
```

If <logical expression 1> delivers a negative result, the program branches to the ELSEIF branch whose logical expression delivers the value TRUE. The ELSE branch of the IF statement is processed if all the previous logical expressions deliver a negative result. The following example imitates a small calculator to show the useage of the IF statement.

```
DATA: HELP TYPE F.
PARAMETERS: OP TYPE C,
A TYPE I,
B TYPE I.
IF OP = '+'.
  HELP = A + B.
  WRITE: /5 'Total a+b:', 20 HELP.
ELSEIF OP = '-'.
  HELP = A - B.
  WRITE: /5 'Difference a-b:', 20 HELP.
ELSEIF OP = '*'.
  HELP = A * B.
  WRITE: /5 'Product a*b:', 20 HELP.
ELSE.
  HELP = A / B.
  WRITE: /5 'Quotient a/b:', 20 HELP.
ENDIF.
ULINE.
```

Depending on the operators specified by the user, the program branches to the appropriate IF branch.

6.5.7 CASE statement

Simplify a complex and multi-faceted IF statement by using a CASE statement.

```
CASE <field>.
WHEN  value_1.
    <processing block 1>.
...
{WHEN value_n.
    <processing block n>.}
[WHEN OTHERS.
    <processing block n+1>.]
ENDCASE.
```

A WHEN clause exists for every case that requires a decision. The program tests the value of the field <field> for equality against one of the values between value_1 and value_n. If none of the cases apply, the program executes the processing block allocated to the WHEN-OTHER clause. If no WHEN-OTHERS branch exists, the program goes to the CASE statement.

The above example of the IF statement will now show the implementation of the CASE statement.

```
DATA: HELP TYPE F.
PARAMETERS: OP TYPE C,
A TYPE I,
B TYPE I.
CASE OP.
  WHEN '+'.
    HELP = A + B.
    WRITE: /5 'Total a+b:', 20 HELP.
  WHEN '-'.
    HELP = A - B.
    WRITE: /5 'Difference a-b:', 20 HELP.
  WHEN '*'.
    HELP = A * B.
    WRITE: /5 'Product a*b:', 20 HELP.
  WHEN '/'.
    HELP = A / B.
    WRITE: /5 'Quotient a/b:', 20 HELP.
     WHEN OTHERS.
          WRITE: / 'Operator not allowed.'.
ENDCASE.
ULINE.
```

6.5.8 Loop statements

DO loop

```
DO <n> TIMES.
  <Processing block>.
ENDDO.
```

The positive integer value <n> determines how often to process the given processing block. The loop does not execute if the value is less than or equal to zero. Either a constant or a calculated variable value can determine the number of times a loop executes. At runtime, the system field SY-INDEX contains the DO loop and the current number of executions within the processing block. After the DO loop executes, SY-INDEX contains the total number of executions. DO loops can be nested without limitation. Users can also define their own increments for DO loops. The program will repeat this procedure exactly <n> times.

```
DO <n> TIMES VARYING <variable> FROM <field1> NEXT <field2>.
  <processing block>.
ENDDO.
```

Column spacing between <field1> and <field2> determines the increment to the next field. Definitions of table spacing between <field1> and <field2> therefore form the basis of the following fields. The program adds the contents of the fields, beginning with <field1> to the field <variable>.

Consider, for example, the table KNC1 from financial accounting. As noted earlier, users can see the structure of the table from within the editor by using the editor command SHOW KNC1. For each month, the table contains a credit field, from UM01H to UM12H. The following excerpt from the definition of table KNC1 shows that 24 positions separate the fields UMxxH.

```
...
UM01S     P 8    Total of the debit postings for the month of January
UM01H     P 8    Total of the credit postings for the month of January
UM01U     P 8    Sales in the posting period
UM02S     P 8    Total of the debit postings for the month of February
UM02H     P 8    Total of the credit postings for the month of February
UM02U     P 8    Sales in the posting period
UM03S     P 8    Total of the debit postings for the month of March
UM03H     P 8    Total of the credit postings for the month of March
UM03U     P 8    Sales in the posting period
```

To calculate the annual total, use the DO statement. Because of the definition of table KNC1, all the necessary fields have the same distance from each other. In other words, beginning with field UM01H, the value of each fourth field is added to the field CREDIT.

```
TABLES: KNC1.
DATA: CREDIT TYPE P.
DO 12 TIMES VARYING CREDIT FROM KNC1-UM01H NEXT KNC1-UM02H.
ENDDO.
WRITE: / 'Total for the Year: ', CREDIT.
```

WHILE loops

A WHILE statement can also program a loop.

```
WHILE <logical expression>.
  <Processing block>.
ENDWHILE.
```

The logical expression is evaluated before each loop run. If the run returns the value TRUE, it processes the processing block. Otherwise the WHILE loop ends and the program continues with the next statement.

LOOP loops

Loops within a LOOP execute until explicitly terminated by an EXIT statement. EXIT can be used for all loops and for the IF statement.

```
LOOP.
  <Processing block>.
ENDLOOP.
```

If the programmer has nested loops in a hierarchy and the program encounters an, EXIT, processing continues at the next highest level of the hierarchy.

```
LOOP.
  ...
  LOOP.
    ...
    DO <n> TIMES.
      ...
      IF <condition>.
  ...
        EXIT.
      ENDIF.
      ...
    ENDDO.
    ...
  ENDLOOP.
  ...
ENDLOOP.
```

6.6 SQL subset

A subset of the query language SQL can create data in R/3. This feature allows R/3 SQL commands to access not only tables in the sense of the RDBMS (transparent tables) but also pool and cluster tables. In a certain sense, the SQL commands are embedded in the ABAP/4 business language. The ABAP/4 processor converts the commands in a corresponding manner. From the point of view of an ABAP programmer all tables are relational.

SAP's SQL subset includes only rather simple and basic SQL commands, as known in the SQL/2 standard.

The subset considers only the data allocated to a particular client. It generates a limitation to the given client for each statement before any queries to the database.

The commands SELECT, UPDATE and DELETE support the usual quantity operations. Only an asterisk (*) is available for field choice. Nested statements are not currently permitted. Formulate WHERE conditions with the logical operators AND, OR or NOT. The operations shown in Table 6.4 are also available.

Unlike the SQL standard, tables can also contribute to the formulation of the WHERE condition. For example:

```
<field> NOT IN <relational_table>
```

Use INSERT, UPDATE and DELETE for individual operations. MODIFY serves as a combination of INSERT and UPDATE at the level of the individual record. Depending on

Table 6.4 Logical operators

Operator variant 1	*Operator variant 2*	*Explanation*
EQ	=	
NE	<> or ><	
LT	<	
LE	<=	
GT	>	
GE	>=	
BETWEEN <field1> AND <field2>		The values in <field1> and <field2> form an interval in which to search for the desired value.
NOT IN (<value_1>, <value_n>)		Listing the values from <value_1> to <value_n> creates a quantity in which to search for the desired value.
LIKE <Mask>		To build a mask, use: '_' any single character '%' any series of characters, including blanks
NOT LIKE <Mask>		The usual rules for building a mask apply, as for the operator LIKE.

the existence of a record in the table, MODIFY creates an UPDATE or INSERT. To read one particular record, use the statement

```
SELECT SINGLE * FROM <Table> [WHERE <condition>].
```

The most advantageous aspect of this statement is that it demands only the memory required. The statement

```
SELECT * FROM ...
```

does not allow the processor to estimate accurately how many records the statement will return. If users know that a WHERE condition will reduce the number of records to one (because it is a primary key field), they should always employ SELECT SINGLE. Another advantage lies in the access strategy developed by various RDBMS for the SELECT SINGLE-statement. ADABAS D, for example, can use such an access to read the system's own key strategy. The SELECT SINGLE therefore provides better performance.

INSERT, UPDATE, MODIFY and DELETE can also be used for the special SQL subset, array variants (quantity variants).

```
[INSERT | UPDATE | MODIFY | DELETE ] <table> FROM
                                     <internal table>.
```

The internal table thus delivers the quantity of records to be processed. As discussed in Section 6.5.2, filling and editing the internal tables must have taken place already. The array variants of commands can change, insert, modify or delete entire groups of records without having read them previously. A sequence of individual and quantity commands of the SQL query language convert the array commands internally. The values of the key fields of the table serve as the key between the tables to be changed and the internal table.

The SELECT statement can also be used as a loop statement.

```
SELECT * FROM <table> [INTO :<field>]
[WHERE <condition> ][ORDER BY <Field_1 ... FIELD_n>].
  <Processing block>.
ENDSELECT.
```

Each record found triggers the execution of the processing block. For example:

```
SELECT * FROM KNB1.
  WRITE:/ 'Company Code: '; KNB1-BUKRS.
ENDSELECT.
```

The addition of INTO :<field> causes the temporary storage of data in a work area. The field represented by the work area must have a structure that corresponds to the structure of the table. In other words, all fields that appear in the table must have exactly the same definitions in the work area. An INCLUDE STRUCTURE clause provides the easiest means to define an existing work area.

The ORDER BY clause determines the sequence of records as in SQL. Unlike SQL, however, the ORDER BY clause can also be used as ORDER BY PRIMARY KEY, which produces an increasing sort according to the primary key.

When working with the SQL subset from SAP, the system fields SY-SUBRC and SY-DBCNT have particular importance. After processing an SQL command, SY-SUBRC delivers a return code that allows the user to determine if the processing concluded successfully or terminated. If SY-SUBRC is equal to zero, the search found the records matching the condition in the table and processed them successfully. If SY-SUBRC does not equal zero, an error occurred. The search may not have found any records matching the condition. Errors terminate the INSERT statement, but DELETE, UPDATE and MODIFY statements continue with the next record.

During array operations SY-DBCNT receives the number of successfully processed records. The number of records in the internal table, less the value of SY-DBCNT, provides the number of records that could not be processed. If the difference does not equal zero, SY-SUBRC is set to the value 4.

When creating transactions, it is particularly important to make sure that processing steps or transactions (as used in the database) close in an orderly manner.

The statement COMMIT WORK confirms and writes all previous changes. The statement ROLLBACK WORK does the opposite for all previous transactions, just as it does in SQL. Transactions should become only as long as their smallest logical unit. Lengthy transactions can lead to unpleasant side effects within the RDBMS. A delay in writing checkpoints is only one example. The literature on databases discusses the problem in more detail. See, for example, Weikum (1988).

6.6.1 Authorization check

The system executes the SELECT statement on the objects without checking the user's authorizations. Accordingly, user authorization can be checked before executing the R/3 SQL request. As described in Chapter 2, the authorization concept contains special objects that grant or remove authorizations or special values, such as company codes.

The AUTHORITY-CHECK statement is closely related to the SELECT statement. To run an authority check, the object containing the authorization for a particular table must be known. Use the menu path *Tools → Administration → Maintain users → Authorization* to receive a list of all authorization objects. Mark the appropriate application area and switch to *Technical names*. The system will display the internal name of the authorization object. Use the appropriate menu option to view documentation for the authorization object. The transfer parameters (and their values, if necessary) described in the documentation must agree exactly with those of the AUTHORITY-CHECK statement.

From the editor, use the editor command *SHOW AUTHORITY <object>* to display information on an object. The AUTHORITY-CHECK statement has the following syntax:

```
AUTHORITY-CHECK OBJECT '<Object_name>'
  ID <name> FIELD <field>
  ...
```

If not all the parameters, i.e., fields require an authorization check, enter the keyword DUMMY instead of the field name, as follows:

```
ID <name> DUMMY.
```

After the AUTHORITY-CHECK statement, the system field SY-SUBRC shows whether access and the tested type of access are permitted. A value other than zero indicates that access is not allowed.

When working with table KNB1, the AUTHORITY-CHECK would work as follows. An authorization object exists for the table under the technical name 'F_KNA1_BUK'. Short text: Customers: Authorization for company code. The documentation provides the following help for the object:

Definition

With this authorization object you set the activities allowed in a company code-dependent area of the customer master data.

Defined fields

The object consists of the fields 'Activity' and 'Company code'.

- *Activity*
  Here you determine the permissible activities. Possible values:

01 = Create
02 = Change
03 = Display
05 = Lock/Unlock
06 = Set delete flag
08 = Display change document
* = All activities

- *Company code*
  Here you determine the company code in which the activities set above are permitted.

This description, and the knowledge that the company code ID is 'BUKRS' and the activity ID is 'ACTVT', can be used as follows:

```
DATA: BUKREIS LIKE KNB1--BUKRS.
..
BUKREIS  =  '0001'.
...
AUTHORITY-CHECK OBJECT 'F_KNA1_BUK'
   ID BUKRS FIELD BUKREIS
   ID 'ACTVT' DUMMY.
IF SY-SUBRC = 0.
  SELECT * FROM KNB1 FROM KNB1
WHERE KNB1-BUKRS = BUKREIS.
  ...
  ENDSELECT.
ELSE.
  WRITE:/ 'Access to the company code', BUKREIS.
  WRITE : ' is not allowed.'.
ENDIF.
...
```

If the authorization check returns a positive value (SY-SUBRC=0), the data belonging to the company code can be processed. In the contradictory case, the system returns a message.

6.6.2 Embedded SQL commands

Transparent tables in R/3 are converted one-to-one into tables of the RDBMS. The tools provided by each RDBMS can therefore access such tables. However, we strongly discourage changing these tables outside of R/3. As discussed in Chapter 5, R/3 has its own repository. Work performed outside of R/3 may produce changes that damage or destroy relationships to other tables and objects.

For work with transparent tables, R/3 offers another method. The EXEC SQL statement initiates any, even RDBMS-specific, query commands that are then passed on directly to the RDBMS. The disadvantage of such commands, of course, is their poor portability.

```
EXEC SQL.
  <Statement> [;]
ENDEXEC.
```

If the statement intended for execution is a SELECT statement, the report must already contain a table or field string to accommodate the result. Such a table or field string can be declared as easily as possible with an INCLUDE-STRUCTURE clause (see p. 256).

In any case, note that EXEC SQL statements do not execute automatic processing of clients, as is the case for an SQL subset.

The data for customer number '0000000007' from table KNA1 can thus be selected and processed in the internal field string INT_KNA1.

```
DATA: BEGIN OF INT_KNA1.
      INCLUDE STRUCTURE KNA1.
DATA: END OF INT_KNA1.
...
EXEC SQL.
  SELECT * FROM KNA1
     WHERE KUNNR = '0000000001'
     INTO :INT_KNA1
ENDEXEC.
...
```

6.7 Field strings and internal tables

Section 6.4 described how to declare internal tables and field strings. Other sections also touched on this topic.

Internal tables represent a structure with a number of records. In a certain sense, internal tables depict a matrix of field strings. Such tables come into play for the intermediate storage of results or to combine data for later processing. The following provides an example of how to define an internal table:

```
DATA: BEGIN OF ITAB OCCURS 15,
         NAME(25),
         VORNAME(25),
         SALARY TYPE F,
      END OF ITAB.
```

An internal table consists of a header and the table lines. The structure of the header corresponds to exactly one table line. It represents the work area of an internal table. Reading from and writing to internal tables takes place via the intermediate filling of the header. The selected record is first stored in the header and then directed to the internal table or vice versa.

The OCCURS parameter makes a field string into an internal table. It sets the maximum number of records that should be held in the main memory available to R/3 (roll area). If a table contains more records than fit in the roll area, the system writes them to disk. This procedure, however, can affect performance negatively. Therefore, make sure that requirements do not exceed the capacity of the available main memory. Use the OCCURS parameter with caution and deliberation.

The name of the table or the field addresses the fields of a field string. For example: ITAB-NAME or ITAB-VORNAME. The MOVE statement can transport values between two field strings or to a particular field assignment.

```
MOVE-CORRESPONDING  <f1> TO <f2>.
```

The system assigns the proper values to all fields of field list <f2> that are identical (in name) in field strings <f1> and <f2>.

```
MOVE <field1> TO <field2>.
```

assigns the value of <field1> specifically to <field2>.

When applied to internal tables, the MOVE statement places the values to be assigned in the header. To enable a transfer of the values into the internal table, use the APPEND statement.

```
APPEND <internal table>.
```

The statement stores the value at the end of the internal table.

```
APPEND <internal table> SORTED BY <field_1> {<field_n>}.
```

sorts the record from the header, depending on the sort criterion, into the internal table in descending order.

Example

The following program places all the birth dates (BIRTHDATE) before 1934 contained in the table ADDRESS into an internal table for later processing. Let the structure of table ITAB correspond to the structure of the transparent table ADDRESS.

```
REPORT PENSIONERS.
TABLES: ADDRESS.
DATA:  BEGIN OF ITAB OCCURS 15,
          INCLUDE STRUCTURE ADDRESS,
       END OF ITAB.
...
SELECT * FROM ADDRESS WHERE BIRTHDATE < '00001934'.
  MOVE-CORRESPONDING ADDRESS TO ITAB.
  APPEND ITAB SORTED BY BIRTHDATE.
ENDSELECT.
...
```

The program inserts table entries into the table ITAB and simultaneously sorts the birth dates (BIRTHDATE) in descending order.

The COLLECT statement takes values from the header and enters them in the internal table as new entries. The process takes those values that differ from the previous values and are not of type P, I or F. For all purposes, the system uses the non-numeric fields as keys.

Example

```
REPORT INCOME.
TABLES: INCOME.
DATA:   BEGIN OF ITAB OCCURS 15.
          DEPARTMENT(25),
          SALARY TYPE F.
        END OF ITAB.
...
SELECT * FROM INCOME.
  MOVE-CORRESPONDING INCOME TO ITAB.
  COLLECT ITAB.
ENDSELECT.
...
```

The internal table ITAB consists only of the fields DEPARTMENT and SALARY. The MOVE-CORRESPONDING statement transfers the values of the corresponding fields from the table INCOME into the internal table ITAB. Result: the salaries are added to each other by department.

Various means exist to process the data once the internal table contains it. Sort internal tables with the SORT statement. Sorting requires a large roll area in the R/3 system; use the SORT statement only after considering its demands. Sorting might also occur when filling the table.

```
SORT <internal table> [BY <field>
       [ASCENDING | DESCENDING ]
       { <field> [ASCENDING | DESCENDING ]} ].
```

Without additional commands, the program will sort the internal table by all fields, in the sequence of their definition, in ascending order. It will not consider fields of type P, I or F. Efficiency considerations make it much more advantageous to specify sort criteria.

Example

```
SORT ITAB BY LAND ASCENDING DEPARTMENT DESCENDING.
```

In the example, the program sorts ITAB in increasing order according to the field LAND and sorts that field in decreasing order according to the field DEPARTMENT.

A special loop statement is available for processing internal tables.

```
LOOP AT <internal table> [WHERE <condition>].
  <processing block>.
ENDLOOP.
```

The LOOP statement returns one record for each execution of the loop. The program then places the record in the header of the internal table, making it available for processing. A WHERE condition can limit the number of records returned. Nonetheless, the program reads the table completely record by record. This procedure is known as **scanning**. If the table entry meets the WHERE condition, the system field SY-SUBRC returns a value other than zero. At each execution of the loop, the system field SY-TABIX contains the internal number of the record from the internal table that the program places in the header.

Entering the line numbers of table entries to be searched can also limit the amount of data processed by the loop statement.

```
LOOP AT <internal table> FROM <linenumber1> TO
   <linenumber2>.
   <processing block>.
ENDLOOP.
```

In this case the program reads only the lines with the corresponding numbers. A complete scan of the table does not take place.

Use specific event key words within the LOOP statement to control the process. It is important to sort the table appropriately beforehand. The following statements enable processing according to sorted groups:

```
AT FIRST
  <processing block>.
ENDAT.
```

first record

```
AT NEW <field>.
  <processing block>.
ENDAT.
```

Up to the contents of field <field> exchange → exchange groups

```
AT END OF <field>.
  <Processing block>.
ENDAT.
```

at the end of a group consisting of all field contents before the specified including the specified field

```
AT LAST.
  <processing block>.
ENDAT.
```

last record

The following example contains a report that produces a sorted list of all customers according to customer number It outputs the credit in month 01 (UM01H) and the total.

```
REPORT REPOITAB.
 TABLES: KNC1.
 DATA: BEGIN OF ITAB OCCURS 50,
       BUKRS LIKE KNC1-BUKRS,
       GJAHR LIKE KNC1-KUNNR,
       KUNNR LIKE KNC1-KUNNR,
       UM01H LIKE KNC1-UM01H,
 END OF ITAB.
 SELECT * FROM KNC1 ORDER BY BUKRS.
   MOVE-CORRESPONDING KNC1 TO ITAB.
   APPEND ITAB.
 ENDSELECT.
```

```
 LOOP AT ITAB.
   AT FIRST.
     WRITE : ' List of sales in January for each customer and '.
     WRITE : 'Company Code:'.
   ENDAT.
   AT NEW BUKRS.
     SKIP.
     WRITE: / 'Company Code:', ITAB-BUKRS.
     ULINE /.
   ENDAT.
   WRITE:/ 'Kunnr:',ITAB-KUNNR, ITAB-GJAHR,ITAB-UM01H.
   AT END OF BUKRS.
     SUM.
     WRITE: / 'Total Credit', ITAB-UM01H UNDER ITAB-UM01H.
     ULINE /.
     SKIP.
   ENDAT.
ENDLOOP.
```

The list would then appear as follows:

```
17.05.1995   Internal Table Processing - LOOP                1
------------------------------------------------------------
List of sales in January for each customer and company code:

Company Code: 0001
------------------------------------------------------------
Kunnr: FID0000000 1994                    1,234.00
Kunnr: FID0000000 1995                    7,834.00
Kunnr: FID0000001 1994                       12.00
Total Credit                              9,080.00
------------------------------------------------------------

Company Code: 0002
------------------------------------------------------------
Kunnr: FID0000000 1995                    9,888.15
Kunnr: FID0000001 1994                      778.00
Kunnr: FID0000001 1995                   13,421.56
Total Sales                              24,087.71
------------------------------------------------------------
...
```

The SUM statement builds the total of all the numeric fields of a group consisting of the contents of a line up to and including the specified field. The totaled values are placed in the header so that <internal table>-<field>, e.g., ITAB-UM01H, contains the total of the field contents. In the example, the total reflects the combined credit of each group in the company code. It is important to consider the order of statements. When several events occur simultaneously, the order of the statements determines the order of their execution. Use the READ statement to target reading of specific records.

```
READ TABLE <internal table>
[WITH KEY <condition> {<condition>}
|INDEX <index>].
```

Using the READ statement without the addition of a WITH KEY or INDEX clause requires that the header of the internal table be filled previously. In this case, the values of the non-numeric fields in the header serve as a key for the read.

Example

```
TABLES: KNA1.
DATA: BEGIN OF ITAB OCCURS 10,
  LAND1 LIKE KNA1-LAND1,
  KUNNR LIKE KNA1-KUNNR,
  ORT01 LIKE KNA1-ORT01,
END OF ITAB.
MOVE 'DE' TO ITAB-LAND1.         "Filling the header
MOVE '0000000007' TO ITAB-KUNNR.
READ TABLE ITAB.                 "Reading records with LAND1='DE',
                                 "KUNNR='0000000007'
```

Reading the record specified by the header places the first line of the table that satisfies the conditions in the header of the internal table. Use of the WITH KEY omits the need to fill the table's header. Conditions can be specified directly. Patterning the table occurs sequentially; in most cases the table should already have been sorted.

```
READ TABLE ITAB WITH KEY LAND1 = 'DE'.
```

In R/3 versions from 2.x onward, the WITH KEY clause works from the beginning of each table line. The clause compares the beginning of each table line to the search argument. In the example, the search might look for LAND1:

```
READ TABLE ITAB WITH KEY 'DE'.
```

In version 3.x the condition consists of the specification of the key field and the desired value. Several conditions can be specified.

Adding the key word BINARY SEARCH to the WITH KEY clause instructs the program not to execute sequential patterning of the table. It assumes that the table is sorted in ascending order according to the specified key. Starting from the table, each access cuts the number of records read in half. Of the total number of records <n>, the program compares <n/2> to the key. The results of the comparison determine if the search continues in the same way in the upper or lower half of the records. This process greatly reduces the number of required read accesses. The INDEX clause reads the record with the specified record number. For example:

```
READ TABLE ITAB INDEX 10.
```

This instruction reads the tenth line of table ITAB. When reading with READ, the system field SY-TABIX contains the record number of the current record.

Changes to values in internal tables also occur via the header. The record to be changed must be transferred to the header by, for example, the READ statement. Only then can the values be changed by the MOVE statement or by a direct value assignment.

```
DELETE <internal table>.
```

deletes the record inseted in the header of the internal table. If the number of the record intended for deletion is known, specify the record with the index:

```
DELETE <internal table> INDEX <number>.
```

Modifications to records in internal tables occur in a similar manner. After the record to be changed has been placed in the header, the value assingments can be adjusted. The MODIFY statement performs changes within internal tables.

```
MODIFY <internal table> [INDEX <number>].
```

Use of the INDEX clause overwrites the record with the specified number with the values contained in the header.

```
INSERT <internal table> [ INDEX <number>].
```

The statement inserts the value contained in the header into the table as a new record. If an index was used, the new record is inserted ahead of the record with the specified number.

For work with internal tables, other statements, besides those related to loading and processing, have particular importance.

```
FREE <internal table>.
```

If the later portion of a program run no longer requires an internal table, the memory it occupied should be released explicitly. Otherwise the memory becomes available to other users only after the program has ended.

```
REFRESH <internal table> [ FROM TABLE <table>].
```

The REFRESH statement deletes the contents of the occupied memory and the header once it has received the memory. It can also transfer the entire contents of an existing table into an internal table. R/3 can handle only tables beginning with a 'T' in this manner. See Chapter 5 on the repository.

```
CLEAR [<internal table> | < field string> ].
```

initializes all fields of the internal table or the field string.

```
DESCRIBE TABLE <internal table>
[LINES <field>|OCCURS <field>].
```

The DESCRIBE statement provides users with information related to the number of records contained in an internal table or the size of the OCCURS parameters at runtime. The corresponding value is placed in the specified field at runtime.

6.8 Event control with logical databases

Most programming languages contain types of flow statements as discussed in Section 6.5. ABAP/4 distinguishes itself from `normal` programming languages in the manner in which it processes the logical database (see Figure 6.1).

The methods used and possibilities offered by ABAP/4 mirror this distinction. The structure of the R/3 database is closely joined to the logical database.

A logical database is essentially a logical view of a physical database table. It mirrors the links between the individual tables. As the following example, a customer database DDF from financial accounting, shows, a logical database displays the hierarchy within the customer tables. The transaction 'SLDB' provides information on an existing logical database. The same transaction permits creation of new logical databases (see Figure 6.2). Figure 6.4 depicts the tree structure for the logical database DDF. DDF stands for unit DD from application F, financial accounting. Table KNA1 builds the entry point, the root of the database DDF.

Logical databases can control the read processes of the ABAP/4 processor. To take full advantage of this capability, the appropriate logical database must be referenced with the report program. The declaration portion of the report identifies the tables of the logical database that will come into play later. For example:

```
TABLES: KNA1, KNB1, KNC1.
```

The ABAP/4 processor handles reading interrelated data from these tables in the logically correct and contextual order. Event key words control processing within the program.

```
KNA1

 KNA1          Customer master (General portion)
 |
 |---KNAS      Customer master (general portion EC Tax numbers)
 |---KNKA      Customer master Credit management: Central data
 |---KNKK      Customer master Credit management: Control area date
 |---KNBK      Customer master (Bank accounts)
 |---KNB1      Customer master (Company code)
     |
     |---KNB4  Customer payment history
     |---KNB5  Customer master (Dunning data)
     |---KNC1  Customer master Transaction figures
     |---KNC3  Customer master Transaction figures Special G/L transaction
     |---BSID  Financial accounting: Seconary index for customers
         |
         |---BKPF          Document header for financial accounting
             |
             |---BSEG      Document segment Financial accounting
                 |
                 |---GSEG  Offsetting item to BSEG in Reporting
```

Figure 6.1 Structure of the logical database DDF

```
REPORT REP02.
TABLES: KNA1, KNB1, KNC1.
DATA: UMSATZ LIKE KNC1-UM01H.
START-OF-SELECTION.
  WRITE: 'List of all Customers ...'.
  ULINE /.
  SKIP 2.
GET KNA1.
  UMSATZ = 0.
  WRITE: / 'Customer number: ', KNA1-KUNNR.
  WRITE: / 'Country         : ', KNA1-LAND1.
  WRITE: / KNA1-PSTLZ,KNA1-ORT01.
GET KNB1.
  WRITE: / 'Company Code: ',KNB1-BUKRS.
GET KNC1.
  WRITE: / 'Sales in January for FY '.
  WRITE: KNC1-GJAHR, KNC1-UM01H.
  UMSATZ = UMSATZ + KNC1-UM01H.
GET KNB1 LATE.
  ULINE.
  WRITE: / 'Sales in Company Code ', KNB1-BUKRS.
  WRITE: 'in January '.
  WRITE:    UMSATZ UNDER KNC1-UM01H.
  UMSATZ = 0.
  ULINE /.
  SKIP 2.
```

Figure 6.2 Example – Use of a logical database

```
GET <table>.
```

is always triggered when the program reads a new record in <table>. The program processes the processing block that follows this statement.

An example will present the mechanism and usage area of logical databases most easily. The logical database DDF is a customer database. Assume that a program should create a list of all customers. It should output the customer number, the country, the address and the sales for the month of January for each company code. It should list the total sales for January each time the list changes from one customer to another.

Report rep02 performs these tasks.

When working with logical databases, the system presents a selection screen before actually processing the report. Logical databases usually contain tables that, in their turn, contain a huge number of data records. DDF contains all the data for a company's customers. The first selection screen enables users to limit processing to a specifically targeted group. The complete primary key of the root table serves as the selection criterion. Figure 6.3 shows the selection screen for the logical database DDF. No selections have been made in the example.

This report has already used additional event key words. Before the actual selection begins, the event START-OF-SELECTION occurs. This mechanism is also called fire. In this case, the event START-OF-SELECTION triggers execution of the WRITE statement.

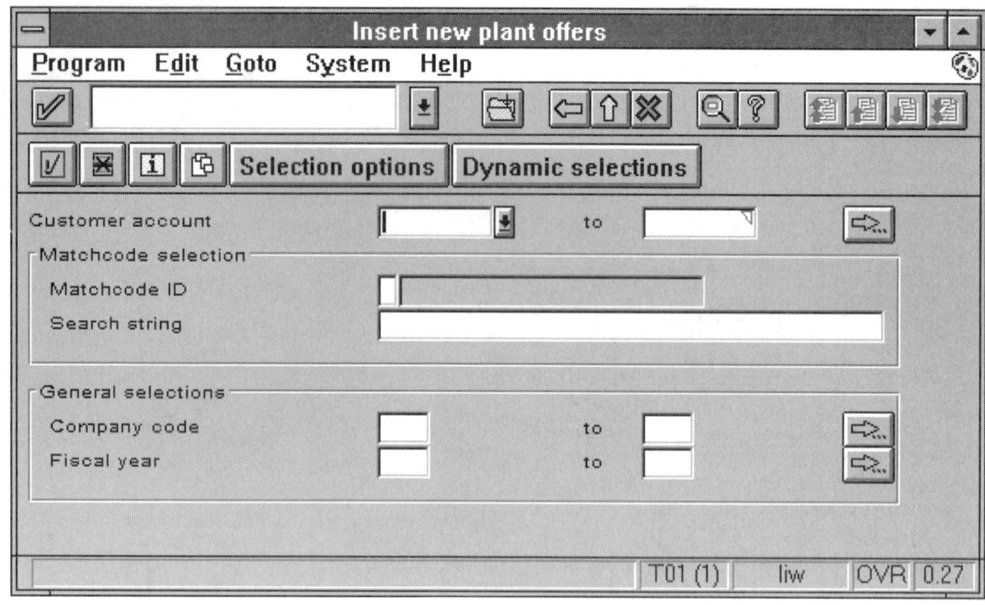

Figure 6.3 Selection menu for a logical database

The processor now begins to read the table ordered highest in the hierarchy, KNA1 in this case.

The program reads the first record with customer number 0000000001 and uses the primary key KNA1-KUNNR to determine all the corresponding records in KNB1. The example finds all the data for the customer with number 0000000001 in company code 001. GET KNB1 occurs when the first corresponding record in KNB1 is read. When all related records from KNC1 have been processed, GET KNB1 LATE occurs. The processing block allocated to GET <table> LATE is executed whenever all the records in a table under the root table have been read but before reading a new record in the root table. This procedure enables, for example, a determination of the total sales to a customer in a particular company code (see Figure 6.1). The UNDER clause produces the output of the totaled sales exactly, under field KNC1-UM01H. Once all the records indicated in the selection screen have been processed, the END-OF-SELECTION occurs. The program processes the last processing block: WRITE 'End of Processing'.

The list with the appropriate data might appear as follows:

```
02.03.1995          Logical Database DDF - Customers          1
-----------------------------------------------------------
List of all Customers ...
-----------------------------------------------------------

Customer number:   6
Country         :  DE
69120       Heidelberg
Company Code:  0001
```

```
Sales in January for FY 1995                         345.00
-----------------------------------------------------------
Sales in Company Code  0001 in January               345.00
-----------------------------------------------------------

Customer number:   7
Country          : DE
69120       Heidelberg
Company Code:  0001
Sales in January for FY 1993                       9,110.00
Sales in January for FY 1994                       2,310.00
Sales in January for FY 1995                       2,035.00
-----------------------------------------------------------
Sales in Company Code  0001 in January            13,455.00
-----------------------------------------------------------

Company Code:  0002
Sales in January for FY 1993                       9,110.00
Sales in January for FY 1995                       1,300.00
-----------------------------------------------------------
Sales in Company Code  0002 in January            10,410.00
-----------------------------------------------------------
```

See the tree depicted in Figure 6.4 to clarify the processes.

Every connection of a branch to the root represents a logically connected record, a unit in the list being produced.

How does processing with logical databases function internally? The creation of a logical database automatically generates a program that contains the processing rules. This procedure links the appropriate tables by their primary keys.

Imagine performing the tasks demanded in the example illustrated in Figure 6.5 without a logical database. The access program (simplified) would appear as shown in the figure.

DDF exists in R/3 as a pre-defined logical database. Use the transaction code 'SDBE' to create a logical database at any time. Here, too, the system generates an access or control program. From this transaction, use the menu options *Goto → Program* to view or change the access program. It may, for example, make sense to provide the access program with default values or checks.

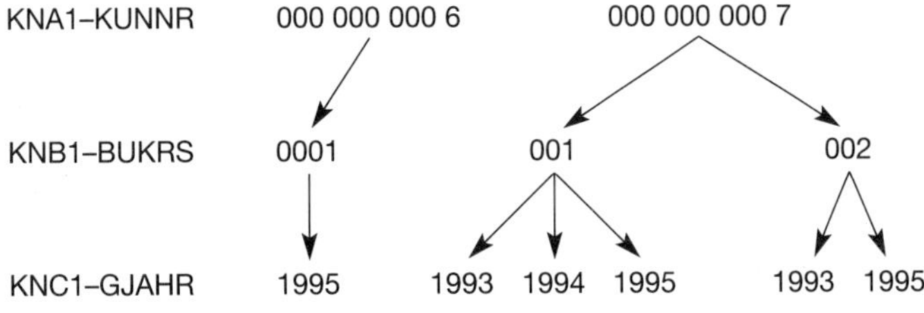

Figure 6.4 Hierarchy tree

```
REPORT REP02.
TABLES: KNA1, KNB1, KNC1.
WRITE: /' List of all Customers..'.
SELECT * FROM KNA1.
  <processing block1>
  SELECT * FROM KNB1 WHERE KNB1-KUNNR = KNA1-KUNNR.
     <processing block2>
     SELECT * FROM KNC1 WHERE KNC1-KUNNR=KNA1-KUNNR
AND KNC1-BUKRS = KNB1-BUKRS.
      <processing block3>
    ENDSELECT.
  ENDSELECT.
ENDSELECT.
```

Figure 6.5 Example – Processing without a logical database

Along with the event key words already noted, the following are available:

- `INITIALIZATION`
  Event changeable before output of selection screen parameters and selection criteria.
- `AT SELECTION-SCREEN`
  The assigned statements are processed directly after entry in the selection screen.

Use the following event key words independently of a logical database:

- `TOP-OF-PAGE`
  Beginning of a new page of output in the list. Use, for example, to insert a page title.
- `END-OF-PAGE`
  End of an output page in the list. Use, for example, to provide page totals.

The following events are triggered by the keyboard:

- `AT LINE-SELECTION`
  Choice of a line.
- `AT PFxx`
  Processing dependent on a function key code.
- `AT USER-COMMAND`
  Any function key triggers the event. The contents of the system field SY-UCOMM depend on the function key pressed.

Additional statements can make process flow under the control of logical databases more controllable.

```
ON CHANGE OF <field>.
  <processing block>.
ENDON.
```

The preceding statements are triggered whenever the value of the field changes. Use this method to cause actions after a group change. In REP02, for example, a line such as

'Company Code:..' should be inserted at each change of the company code. The ON CHANGE statement performs the task easily.

```
ON CHANGE OF BUKRS.
  WRITE:/ 'New Company Code: ', KNB1-BUKRS.
ENDON.
```

Use the CHECK statement to skip processing statements within a loop, depending on the value of a logical expression.

```
CHECK <logical expression>.
   <processing block>.
```

Use the statement whenever special actions require execution when a field contains a particular value. Report REP02 could be changed, for example, to highlight customers with annual sales of more than 100,000.

```
GET KNC1.
  DO 12 TIMES VARYING HABEN FROM KNC1-UM01H NEXT KNC1-UM02H.
    CHECK HABEN GE '100000'.
      WRITE: / 'In the month of:, SY-INDEX.
      WRITE: 'sales of ', HABEN.
      WRITE: 'were reached'.
  ENDDO.
```

Each of the fields KNC1-UM01H, ... KNC1-UM12H contain the sales figures for the corresponding month. All fields have the same definition. The DO <n> TIMES VARYING statement determines the annual sales. Starting from UM01H with the increment UM02H, the program adds the contents of UM<n>H fields one by one. As long as HABEN remains less than '100000', the program skips the processing block indicated in the CHECK statement. When HABEN reaches or exceeds '100000', the CHECK statement occurs and writes output.

In such a case, view the CHECK statement as a conditional termination statement. If the logical expression returns a negative value, processing of the current loop is terminated.

- `EXIT`
  terminates processing of the entire loop. Program a conditional termination with an IF statement.
- `REJECT`
  terminates processing of the current record completely.
- `STOP`
  skips all statements up to the END-OF-SELECTION.
- `LEAVE`
  terminates report processing. Depending on the previous call of the report, branching to a superordinated instance, e.g., a tranasction, is possible.

- SELECT-OPTIONS
  The SELECT-OPTIONS statement permits creation of variable fields for the storage of selection criteria. Section 6.4 on declarative language elements already described the definition of such fields. A declaration might look like this:

```
SELECT-OPTIONS BUKREIS FOR KNB1-BUKRS DEFAULT '0001'.
```

With this processing, the user must first enter values for the variable BUKREIS. An internal table stores the values that can be used as selection criteria for the CHECK statement, for example.

Example

```
...
GET KNB1.
   CHECK BUKREIS
...
```

The example compares the values entered for BUKREIS with those of KNB1-BUKRS. The name of the variable displayed in the selection screen may contain a maximum of eight characters. To create a more comprehensive display, specify special selection texts with transaction 'se38' and the menu *Text elements*.

6.9 System fields

System fields played a role in earlier sections. System fields are **system variables**. The R/3 system provides the variable with certain values during the processing of statements written for the widest variety of reasons. An evaluation of these variables provides the user with information on conditions or flows. R/3 makes a large number of system variables available for ABAP/4 programming. These system fields can be used for evaluations or to treat errors in ABAP/4 programs. Earlier sections have described the system fields applicable to each statement.

Use the editor command SHOW SY to display all system fields. The table SYST contains the fields displayed with the editor command. Unlike the usual convention of <table_name>-<field_name>, address system fields with SY-<field>. Obtain more detailed information on the table SYST and its fields with the menu path *Tools → ABAP/4 Workbench → Development → ABAP/4 Dictionary*. Appendix E lists the most important system fields and provides a short description of each.

The system field SY-SUBRC has particular importance. After each statement, the field receives a return code that determines if an error occurred and if so, which. If there is an error, the field SY-SUBRC has a value of 0 after the statement. A value of 4 indicates a minor error; 8 indicates a serious error.

Use SY-SUBRC, for example, to test whether a SELECT statement found any data records at all.

```
SELECT * FROM KNC1 WHERE BUKRS = '008'.
   WRITE: / 'Credit in January: ', KNC1-UM01H.
ENDSELECT.
IF SY-SUBRC <> 0.
  FORMAT INTENSIFIED ON.
*  the following outputs are displayed
*  intensified
  WRITE: / 'No records found.'.
   FORMAT INTENSIFIED OFF.
" switch intensified output off
ENDIF.
```

The integrated message system in R/3 can provide error messages and informational messages in the status bar. Texts intended for output are stored and maintained in table T100. Work with these texts with the menu path *Tools* → *Development* → *Maintain program* → *Messages*. A message identifier or class can be allocated to every report.

```
REPORT repo02 MESSAGE-ID <identification>.
```

The message class consists of two characters. It limits and allocates error messages. Programmers can set up an individual ID for their work areas. Once a message class has been created or chosen, new message numbers can be written or existing once changed.

Table T100 has the following structure:

Field	Short description
SPRSL	Language
ARBGB	Work area
MSGNR	Message number
TEXT	Message text

The message identification (work area) builds a subset within the message table T100. Only one message identification can be assigned to a report.

Assume the creation of a work area named ZZ in table T100 with the text: 'Division by zero not permitted.' Report rep01 could then be expanded with the MESSAGE clause as follows:

```
REPORT REP01 MESSAGE-ID ZZ.
 ...
 IF B = 0.
    message A001.
* Terminate and display the message
 ENDIF.
...
```

A letter indicating the message type preceeds the three-character message number. The example uses an 'A.' The message type determines the later flow of the report. Note the following possibilities:

A Termination – Abnormal end
The program terminates.

E Error – Error
The program can continue with the entry of new, correct data.

I Information – Information
The enter key continues processing.

S Confirmation – Success
Message output is delayed until the system changes to the next screen.

W Warning – Warning
The entry of new data and pressing the enter key continues the processing.
Includes both E and I qualification.

The message system also offers a means of assigning parameters to messages. Use the ampersand (&) to add place parameters to messages.

Example

Language	ID	Number	Text
E	ZZ	001	Division by & is not desired.

Call and fill the parameter with a WITH clause.

Example

```
MESSAGE A001 WITH B.
```

At output, the value of B replaces the ampersand character (&). Transfer of constants is also possible. A message text can include several parameters. For example:

```
MESSAGE A002 WITH A B C.
```

A blank space separates individual parameters.

At the call, the ampersand is replaced in the order of the transfer. If the number of parameters and parameter symbols do not agree, extra parameters are ignored and missing parameters replaced with a blank space.

6.10 Subroutines

ABAP/4 subroutine techniques enable users to structure programs and combine repeating, logically connected sections. The event control in ABAP/4 requires definition of subroutines before defining the main program of a report. The call of the subroutine represents an event. When using debugging mode, the upper information line clearly shows the event nature of calls to subroutines.

6.10.1 FORM statement

The FORM statement permits the definition of procedures within a report. In its simplest form it combines a processing block without parameter transfer into a procedure.

```
FORM <Name>.
  [<declaration section>.]
  [<processing section>.]
ENDFORM.
```

The procedure can use and, if necessary, change global fields in the report. Local fields in the procedure are those declared within the procedure. No new procedures may be defined within the definition of a procedure. Recursive calls, those that call themselves within a processing block, however, are permitted.

Example for a FORM declaration

```
FORM GET_CUSTOMERS.
  SELECT * FROM KNA1 ORDER BY KUNNR.
    WRITE: / 'Customer Number:', KNA1-KUNNR,
    WRITE:'Country:', KNA1-LAND1.
  ENDSELECT.
ENDFORM.
```

A PERFORM statement calls the procedure. For example:

```
PERFORM GET_CUSTOMERS.
```

The direct linkage of the call with the processing of an external SELECT statement forms a special type of call. The form is called for every record returned by the SELECT statement.

Example

```
...
FORM MAKE_ITAB.
  CLEAR REGION_TAB.
  EXEC SQL PERFORMING MAKE_REGION_TAB.
    SELECT * FROM SYSMON$REGIONS
      ORDER BY REGID
      INTO :REGION_TAB
  ENDEXEC.
ENDFORM.

FORM MAKE_REGION_TAB.
  APPEND REGION_TAB.
ENDFORM.
...
```

Some preconditions must be fulfilled for these statements to function properly. A transparent table, SYSMON$REGION, must exist along with an internal table

REGION_TAB. The internal table must be declared in a manner that permits it to receive data from the transparent table, SYSMON$REGION. The procedure MAKE_ITAB reads the table SYSMON$REGION with the EXEC SQL statement. The INTO clause places every record read from the table SYSMON$REGION in the header of the internal table REGION_TAB. Following those actions, the PERFORMING clause becomes active. Then the form MAKE_REGION_TAB, which adds the data into the internal table, APPEND REGION_TAB, is executed.

6.10.2 Parameter transfer

To make the arrangement of ABAP programs more clear, it makes sense to transfer the variables explicitly to the procedures that use or change them. In this manner, the procedure header tells users which objects the procedure processes. The USING or CHANGING clause transfers fields, field string and field symbols.

USING VALUE (<field>) identifies parameters called by value. Because it transfers only the field contents and processes a copy of the field, changes to field contents outside of the FORM routine are ineffective.

Other parameters, transferred only with the USING clause, behave differently. In this case, the address of the field is transferred (call by reference). This clause processes the field itself; changes to the value become effective externally.

Joined with the VALUE clause, the CHANGING clause functions somewhat like a variation between value transfer and address transfer at declaration of the FORM routine. The field contents of parameters transferred in this manner first remain invisible externally despite changes. Only when leaving the procedure with the ENDFORM statement are changes transferred externally. If leaving the procedure in another manner, such as an EXIT, the field contents remain unchanged.

If internal tables are to be transferred to a procedure, identify them with the TABLES clause.

```
FORM <Name> [TABLES <internal table> {<internal table}]
     [USING <field> {<field>}][VALUE <field> {<field>}
     [CHANGING VALUE <field> {<field>}]].
..
ENDFORM.
```

The TABLES clause must always occupy the first position of the declaration and the call of a procedure. Note that when processing internal tables in procedures, no COLLECT statement is permitted within the procedure.

Identify structures that are to be allowed as transfer parameters with the keyword STRUCTURE only during declaration, not during a call (PERFORM).

Procedures from another report can be called within a report. The call functions as it does for local procedures, but the name of the external report must qualify the name of the procedure. For example:

```
PERFORM <procedure_name>(<report_name>) <parameter_transfer>.
```

Note that event control is thus transferred to the other report. An END-OF-PAGE statement in the called report, for example, might come into effect. In addition, the possibility exists to generate the name of the procedure to be called dynamically, i.e., during runtime.

Example

```
DATA: UPROGNAME(20), REPNAME(8).
...
IF SY-SUBRC = 0.
  UPROGNAME = 'OK_CALL'.
ELSE.
  UPROGNAME = 'ERROR_HANDLING'.
ENDIF.
PERFORM (UPROGNAME) IN PROGRAM (PROGNAME).
...
```

The USING clause also exchanges parameters between reports. The called report passes the transferred arguments to its own parameters that have been defined with the PARAMETERS clause. In the process, the order given in the declaration must be maintained.

The creation and processing of report variants is closely connected to parameter transfer. Create variants for reports regularly called with the same values for their parameters. Variant creation stores the values to be transferred to a report in a list. To create or change a report, start at the ABAP/4 development environment and choose *Goto → Variants*.

Along with selection values, a name and a short description are also allocated to a variant. Users can also make a variant available only for on-line or batch processing. Users can also explicitly protect fields and selection criteria from modifications.

The possible links between ABAP/4 programs are quite complex and extend far beyond what has been presented here. Since most programs created by users perform limited, specialized functions, a more detailed discussion of subroutines is not necessary.

6.10.3 Function modules

Function modules are a special form of subroutines. A library stores function modules centrally. Unlike the subroutines discussed so far, whose properties are defined by a program, function modules are not limited by applications. A clearly defined data interface handles the exchange of data (export and import), tables (TABLES) and exception handling in the case of errors.

The basic version of R/3 contains a large number of function module libraries. Users can display function modules with

```
SHOW FUNCTION <Name>
```

Create and define function modules, however, only with transaction se37 *ABAP/4 Workbench → Development → Function library*. Call functions with the CALL statement, but make sure to keep the interface defined for parameter transfer.

```
CALL FUNCTION '<Name>'
   [ DESTINATION '<Host_name>']
   [EXPORTING <Export-Parameter1> = <Parameter1>
         { <Export-Parameter n> = <Parameter n>}]
   [IMPORTING <Import-Parameter1> = <Parameter1>
         { <Import-Parameter n> = <Paramter n>}]
   [ TABLES <Table_name1> {<Table_nname n>}]
   [EXCEPTIONS   <Exception1> = <Value1>
         [MESSAGE <Message>]
         {<Exceptions> = <Value n>
         [MESSAGE <Message>]}].
```

The function BP_EVENT_RAISE exemplifies the use of function modules. Section 3.6.2 already discussed event control in the R/3 system. The program 'SAPEVT' can initiate an event externally. To trigger an event from within an ABAP/4 program, use the function BP_EVENT_RAISE. The export parameters to be transferred are the event name defined with transaction sm62 and other possible parameters.

```
DATA: EVENTID LIKE TBTCJOB-EVENTID,
*                  TBTCJOB-Job_table
      EVENTPARAM LIKE TBTCJOB-EVENTPARM.

EVENTID    = 'TEST_EXAMPLE'
EVENTPARAM = 'FI'

CALL FUNCTION 'BP_EVENT_RAISE'
"Trigger event
    EXPORTING   EVENTID   = EVENTID
"Event name
                EVENTPARM = EVENTPARAM
"Parameter
    EXCEPTIONS  OTHERS    = 4.
"Exception handling
```

The EXCEPTION clause can execute error handling in a calling program. Allocate a numerical value to every desired event that the calling program assigns to the variable SY-SUBRC. MESSAGE statements, for example, can react to the values of SY-SUBRC. The example assigns the value 4 to SY_SUBRC for all types of exceptions (OTHERS).

The ability to use the DESTINATION clause to set a target computer for program execution is particularly noteworthy. RFC (Remote Function Calls) implement the setting internally. The principles of client/server technology come into play here. Function modules support distributed processing and remote debugging, beyond the confines of one system. The RFC interface can also include external programs. SAP makes a software development kit for that purpose. The principles behind RFC significantly expand usage possibilities. The programmer can exercise explicit influence on the load distribution in a distributed system. The choice of a specific computer makes it possible to perform evaluations independently of the application server the user currently operates from. Special functions, for example, might be available only on the database server.

Taking full advantage of these possibilites demands a great deal of special knowledge, and is best left to experienced ABAP programmers.

6.11 Creating transactions

The previous sections have primarily dealt with the creation of lists with ABAP/4. A user has limited options to influence the flow of a report. The development environment in R/3, however, is much more complex. Based on the techniques of `simple` list programming, a user can develop broadly based on-line transactions. The design of menus and screen masks demands not only a command of the syntax of statements, but also some experience and familiarity with the system itself.

As used in R/3, transactions are created with an entry in table TSTC. Use general table maintenance, `sm31`, to make the entry.

A module pool and starting screen are also allocated to the transaction code. The transaction type determines the kind of transaction involved:

- a dialog transaction,
- a report,
- variants,
- a report menu,
- a parameter transaction.

Include a transaction text for each case to complete the documentation.

The report ZPFLNEUE from the example in Appendix G can be started with transaction code `z000`.

7 Correction and transport system (CTS)

7.1 Preliminary remarks

Section 4.2 discussed the basics of the workbench organizer. With that foundation, this chapter will describe the organization and installation of the correction and transport system as well as the use of the workbench organizer. In some cases, we will also provide background descriptions to partially transparent activities in the CTS.

In the long term, the workbench organizer will replace the correction and transport system (transaction `se01`) of version 2.x for coordinating development. As of version 3.x, the workbench organizer already comfortably handles the greater portion of functions available in the CTS. Nonetheless, situations may arise that require the use of transaction `se01`. The workbench organizer aims at simplifying normal development work. Tasks beyond that scope still require the use of transaction `se01`. This section will indicate such cases explicitly.

Version 3.x introduced new terms that, for the most part, replace those in version 2.x. Table 7.1 shows terms with the same meaning.

Table 7.1 New terms in version 3.x

Term in version 2.x	*Term in version 3.x*
Correction and repair	Task
Transport request (K transport)	Transportable change request

This chapter aims to provide the reader with an overview of the features and purposes of the correction and transport system. The following examples apply to R/3 version 3.x.

7.2 Components

The R/3 system contains an integrated system to coordinate development and to transport software modules. R/3 meets current demands for a modern development environment with the **correction and transport system** (CTS).

The CTS consists of three system components:

- the workbench organizer (request category: SYST),
- the customizing organizer (request category: CUST),
- the transport system.

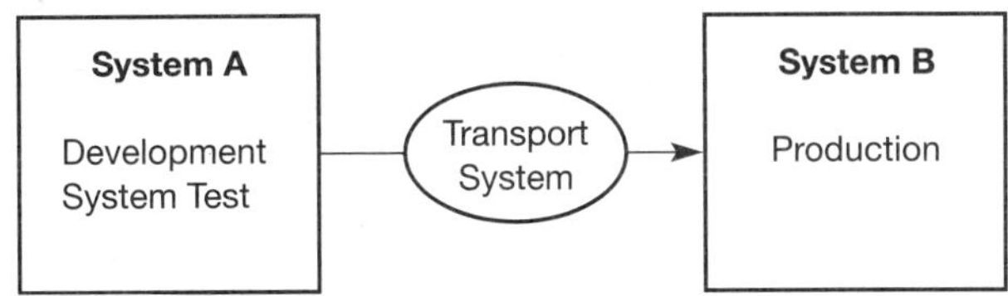

Figure 7.1 Transport system of the CTS

The **workbench organizer** controls, identifies and documents developments and changes in the system (see Section 4.2). The **customizing organizer** records customizing activities and prepares them for transfer into another system. The labor-intensive and error-prone need to copy customizing details manually no longer exists as of version 3.x. Since both tools function almost identically, the following comments refer primarily to the workbench organizer.

A company decides to implement R/3 because of its many advantages. However, the concentration of data in R/3 can also lead to danger if the introduction of the system involved conceptual errors. To avoid system failures caused by users themselves, development and changes to system objects should first undergo a quality check in a test system. The danger of multiple efforts caused by manually copying modifications and new developments does not exist. The **transport system** of the correction and transport system allows users to transport an object from one system into another with great ease (see Figure 7.1).

Both the workbench organizer and the customizing organizer work closely with the transport system.

Transports can serve various purposes. They enable, for example, insertion of objects in a system. However, they also allow a user to target objects for replacement or deletion in another system. R/3 logs all transports, and these logs allow an analysis of transports at any time.

The correction and transport components of the system are finely tuned to each other. SAP itself uses the CTS for developing business applications, which speaks well of the system's high level of features and performance. Changing the versions of the ABAPs in a customer's system involves no more than a transport from an internal SAP system into the customer system.

7.3 Authorizations

The correction and transport system in version 2.x contained no authorization concept: a clear deficiency. The system, as it then existed, could not permit or forbid certain users to create tasks (in 2.x corrections). Within the CTS, the authorization concept divides users into five categories. Table 7.2 displays these user groups and the authorizations allocated to each.

Table 7.2 Usage authorizations for the workbench organizer

Group	*Authorization*
S_A.SYSTEM	S_CTS_ALL
S_A.ADMIN	S_CTS_ADMIN
S_A.CUSTOMIZ	S_CTS_PROJEC
S_A.DEVELOP	S_CTS_DEVELO
S_A.USER	S_CTS_APPLIC

Administrators and operators work with authorizations S_CTS_ALL and S_CTS_ADMIN, while groups of application developers work with authorizations S_CTS_PROJEC, S_CTS_DEVELO, and S_CTS_APPLIC:

- *S_CTS_ALL*
  This authorization opens the full spectrum of functions in the workbench organizer and the transport system to users. This authorization allows execution of functions in the CTS previously reserved to user DDIC. Such users can configure the workbench organizer (see Section 7.5) or work with extended transport tools (transaction `se03`). Beyond the capacities even of user DDIC, holders of this authorization can even modify objects belonging to the ABAP/4 workbench.
- *S_CTS_ADMIN*
  Users with this authorization may access only information on tasks and requests. In actual practice, such users might hold responsibility for analyzing the logs of transports performed at night. These users determine if problems or even errors occurred and provide appropriate solutions.
- *S_CTS_PROJEC*
  This authorization allows a user to set up a development environment for a development project. This user may process both tasks and requests completely. A user functioning as project leader might first establish the framework for a project by creating a new development class as a subject area. This user would then create change requests and tasks that clearly indicate who is responsible for what and who works with whom. Developers then perform their assignments by processing objects.
- *S_CTS_DEVELO*
  Project team members who develop applications usually receive this authorization. It permits work on the project only at the task level. Such a user cannot create tasks or requests independently. The authorization limits the user to the tasks assigned by the project leader. This user signals the end completion of a task by releasing it to the superordinated change request.
- *S_CTS_APPLIC*
  This authorization permits a user to look at tasks, requests and object lists. Accordingly, it mirrors the authorization S_CTS_ADMIN.

Balance: The authorization concept contained in version 3.x permits an excellent overview of the responsibilities present in an enterprise's working organization.

7.4 Customizing the CTS

7.4.1 Types of R/3 systems

Experience has taught that when using complex software solutions, the maintenance of separate systems for testing, development and production avoids disruption of the production system. Such a division provides a definite advantage when poor performance requires analysis by SAP or the database manufacturer. In addition, according to this strategy the money saved by preventing the complete loss of system resources rapidly pays for the investment made in the extra hardware required. Often, for example, searching for errors with debugging in the ABAP/4 development environment can affect performance negatively. Most software products leave the division of production and development up to the discipline of users. R/3 not only supports this conceptual division of tasks but also provides mechanisms in the correction and transport system to ensure its practice. R/3 has adopted and expanded the classic division of production and test systems.

Up to four types of systems can cooperate with each other in a distributed environment. According to their use within the system group, the following four types of system can exist:

- *Development system*
  As its name indicates, this system serves to develop objects. However, use this system to develop particularly critical programs that demand a division from the normal development environment. Using the development system in this manner will avoid disrupting development work performed by others.
- *Integration system*
  This system is intended for actual development work. It is the work area for all developers, except those working on critical project components. This system handles development and system tests.
- *Consolidation system*
  The consolidation system safely stores mature and carefully tested software components. It can also serve as the delivery center for delivery systems.
- *Delivery system*
  A delivery system can also be a production system, an integration system or a development system. Delivery systems reference their objects by subscribing to consolidation system: a delivery system receives copies of transports at regular intervals. Table `TASYS` manages the subscriptions (see Section 7.5.5).

A large number of mechanisms in the correction and transport system build the following hierarchy:

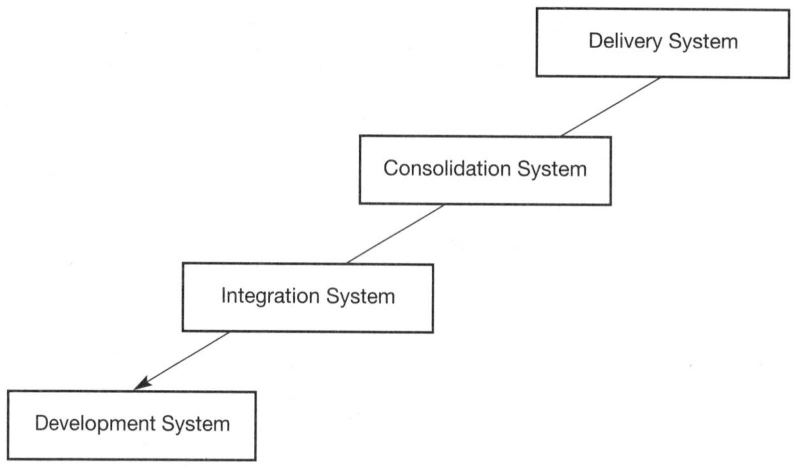

Figure 7.2 Types of R/3 systems

In Figure 7.2, arrows indicate valid transport directions. The arrows show that limitations on transports between various systems exist. For example, the transfer of development environment objects from a development system directly into a consolidation system is not possible. Transports from the development system must first go to the integration system.

7.4.2 System configurations

In most cases, actual practice may not require the implementation of all four system types. Nonetheless, SAP recommends installation of at least an integration system and a consolidation system. To a large extent, local conditions as well as the performance and availability requirements of the R/3 system determine the actual combination of systems in use within a given enterprise.

Companies that wish to drive R/3 with a test system and a production system configure (in SAP terms) an integration system and a consolidation system. The integration system handles development, tests and preliminary use of new versions. The last task, particularly, has taken on increasing importance in practical situations. Preliminary use allows users to gain personal experience at executing an upgrade and thus allows them to limit or avoid previously experienced errors when switching the production system. The integration system regularly provides the consolidation system with tested software. This configuration is preferred at the first installation of an R/3 system. Experience will then indicate if the integration system requires the addition of a development system. The latter would then handle the separate development of critical project components. Users must weigh the advantages and disadvantages of adding a delivery system to the system hierarchy later.

Example of building a system group (example B1)

An enterprise running R/3 first decides on a system group consisting of two systems, T01 and P01. T01 functions as the test system; P01 drives production. The enterprise plans to implement its own applications in ABAP/4.

From the viewpoint of the CTS, T01 is defined as the integration system. The production system, P01, thus becomes the consolidation system. Such a configuration clearly defines the (transport) route of objects developed by the company itself.

The enterprise has a positive experience in introducing R/3 and wants to share both its experience and additional developments with others. To do so, it requires a training system, S01. A copy of the production system would, of course, offer trainees the most realistic work flow with real data volume. To avoid extra work and maintenance, the training system is defined as a delivery system. The transport system now also addresses transports to P01 to S01 automatically.

Application development often suffers during version upgrades because system T01 remains unavailable for long periods. As a solution, however, large portions of individual development efforts can be stored in an additional test system, E01, that will function from now on as a (special) development system. Using the functions `Check In/Check Out` to their full advantage, developers can decide for themselves if system T01 or E01 will process their work.

The system group now consists of four R/3 systems and could be further expanded without any difficulties. Note that each system has its own unique name (SAPSYSTEMNAME). One system group cannot handle systems with identical names.

The examples in the following section refer to the system configuration given above.

7.5 Configuration of the workbench organizer

7.5.1 Setting the system configuration

After the new installation of an R/3 system, one of the system administrator's first tasks involves setting up the workbench organizer and the transport system. Use transaction `se06` as user DDIC or as a user with authorization S_CTS_ALL to initialize the CTS. Figure 7.3 shows the main menu for initializing the correction and transport systems (*Setting up the Workbench Organizer* in transaction `se06`). Compared to version 2.x, the transaction is easier to work with and contains additional functions.

Transaction `se06` handles both the initialization of and modifications to the setup of the workbench organizer. After initialization, only the creation of new systems or a new division of tasks within the system group requires calling this transaction. To avoid unpleasant side effects, make sure that all change requests are closed (`released`) when reassigning tasks.

Transaction `se06` offers the administrator the following functions for setting up the workbench organizers:

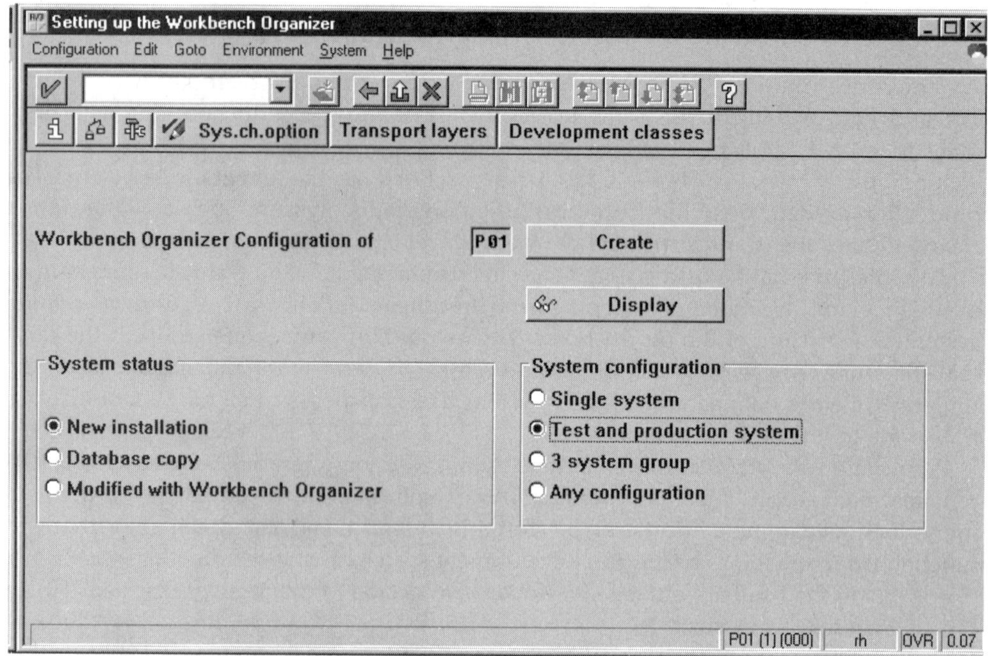

Figure 7.3 Setting up the workbench organizer

- Generation of the basic setup,
- Generation of the standard configuration,
- Maintenance of the configuration of the workbench organizers,
- Configuration check.

During configuration of the workbench organizer (see Figure 7.3), first provide information on what kind of system already exists and what kind will be written. The workbench organizer differentiates between the following types of systems. The information provided here affects further configuration steps in transaction `se06`.

- *New installation*
  Indicates that the workbench organizer is undertaking generation of a new system, installed with R3INST (the R/3 installation program).
- *Database copy*
  Signals the existence of a copy of an already set-up SAP system. R3INST or tools provided by the database manufacturer can provide a system copy.
- *Modified with workbench organizer*
  Choose this system status to perform modification to existing configurations. As an example, consider the addition of another system to the system group. Specification of this system status does not change the basic settings of the workbench organizer.

As of version 3.x, transaction `se06` offers a choice of predefined system configurations. In version 3.0, however, only three possible choices exist. Certainly later updates will make this comfortable feature available to a wider circle of customers. The workbench organizer derives the entries to be generated for the control table (see Section 7.5.5) from the choice of a system configuration made by the system administrator. Version 3.0 supports the following configurations:

- Single system,
- Test and production system,
- 3 system group.

Note that the 3 system group writes an integration system, a consolidation system and a delivery system. To create other system relations, even for three systems, choose the option *Any configuration*.

Example B1 shows how a system group comes into being and expands over time. The example begins with two systems. Setting up the workbench organizer can thus start with the predefined system configuration for a *Test and production system*. After entry of this choice, the workbench organizer displays a screen describing both systems (see Figure 7.4).

Confirm the entries with the function *Continue*; the workbench organizer will mark the test system as an integration system and the production system as a consolidation system in its control table. It will also generate a transport layer, `ZT01`, used to define the standard transport route in the system group. The objects in test system T01 that are intended for transport automatically receive the production system, P01, as their transport target. The workbench organizer then offers the configuration for confirmation (see Figure 7.5). If all the settings are correct, use the function *Continue* to write the configuration.

To set a value other than the default system change option (see Section 7.5.2), use the function *System change option*. This closes the configuration.

The workbench organizer behaves differently during the definition of more complex system groups. The last expansion in example B1 would be such a case. There, four

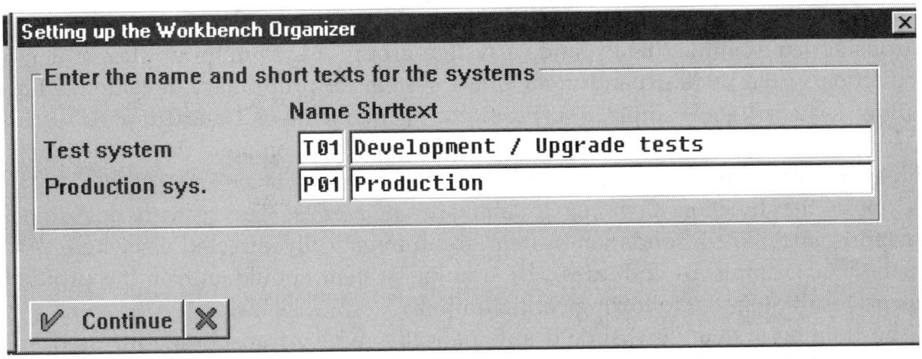

Setting up the Workbench Organizer

Enter the name and short texts for the systems

	Name	Shrttext
Test system	T01	Development / Upgrade tests
Production sys.	P01	Production

Continue

Figure 7.4 Maintaining the system list

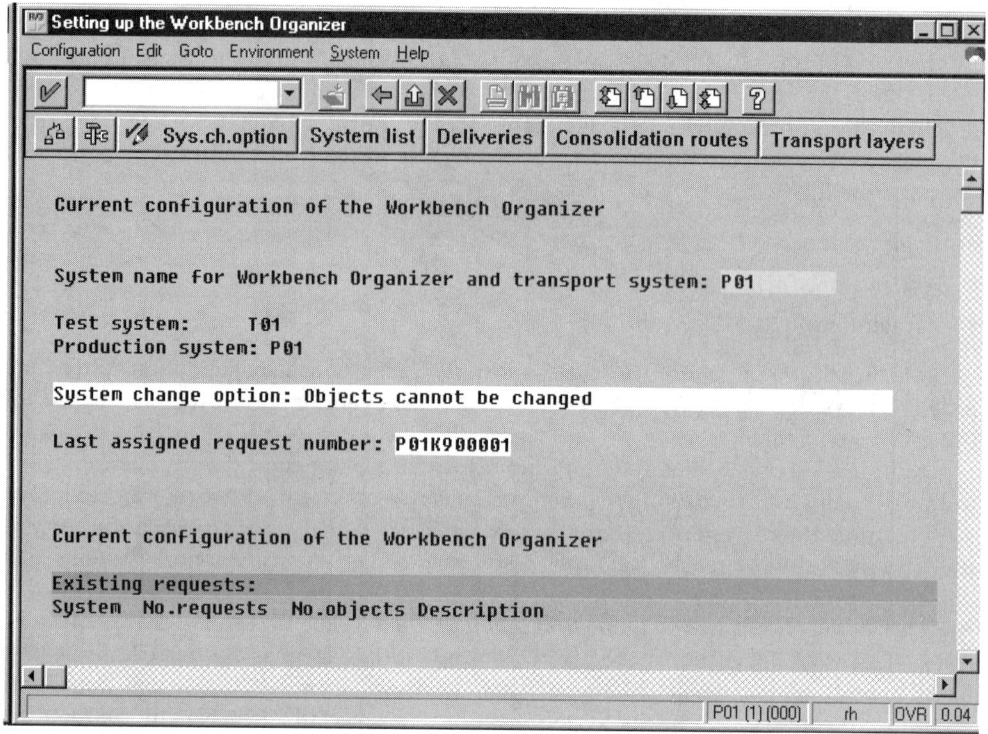

Figure 7.5 Current configuration of the workbench organizer

systems (development system, test system, production system, training system) form one system group. If none of the predefined system configurations apply to the desired configuration, choose *Any configuration* in the initial screen of transaction `se06`. The following screen permits the administrator to specify relationships among the various system components. The workbench organizer uses these specifications to make the appropriate entries in its control table.

Consider an example that expands a system group. A system group (test system and production system) will expand to include a system for proprietary development and a training system (see example B1). From the main menu of transaction `se06` choose *Modified with Workbench Organizer* and *Any Configuration*. Complete the following screen with specifications of the names of both new systems (see Figure 7.6).

Choose the function *Continue* to maintain deliveries. This screen determines if transports into the consolidation system are automatically directed elsewhere. As the situation in example B1 indicates, the training system should mirror the production system, resulting in the following configuration:

The training system, S01, should automatically receive transports addressed to P01 (see Figure 7.7). No other transports to the training system are allows (the column `Cross transports allowed?` remains empty).

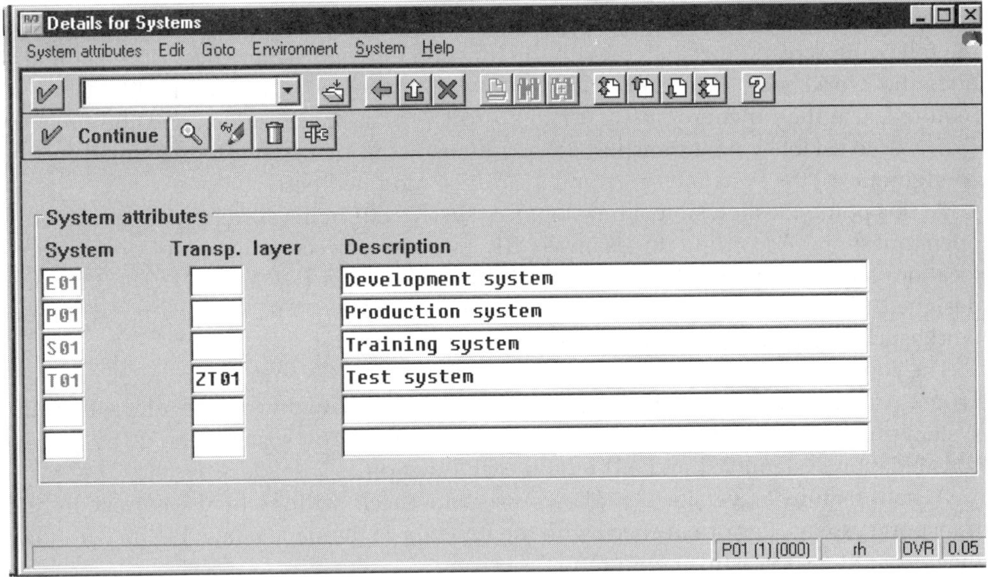

Figure 7.6 Expanding the system list

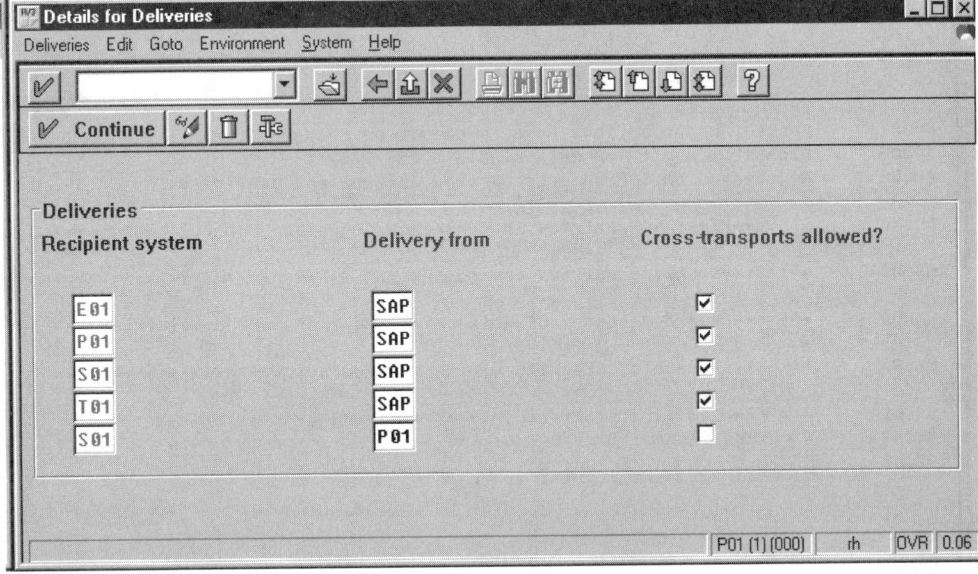

Figure 7.7 Definition of deliveries

Since nothing in the consolidation transport targets (T01 → P01) should change, skip the following screen, unchanged, with the function *Continue*. After successful configuration, the workbench organizer will display an overview of the current settings. If required, use the function *System list* to correct system specifications and the function *Deliveries* to establish new transport subscriptions. As is the case with predefined system configurations, the system change options can be modified here.

At this point, the inclusion of development system E01 in the system group remains an open question. According to example B1, moving objects (transfer of the original location) should implement an exchange between systems E01 and T01. The transport designed for this purpose handles the transfer (see Section 7.9.2); configuration of the workbench organizer need not take system E01 into account.

The configuration described here reflects only one possible organization of a system group. An administrator might, for example, consider a new division of roles within the system group. E01 would then function as a new integration system, and T01 as a new consolidation system; P01 and S01 would each function as a delivery system.

A new feature in version 3.x allows users to check settings in the correction and transport systems. Perform a check with the function of the same name. Figure 7.8 shows the output of a successful configuration check.

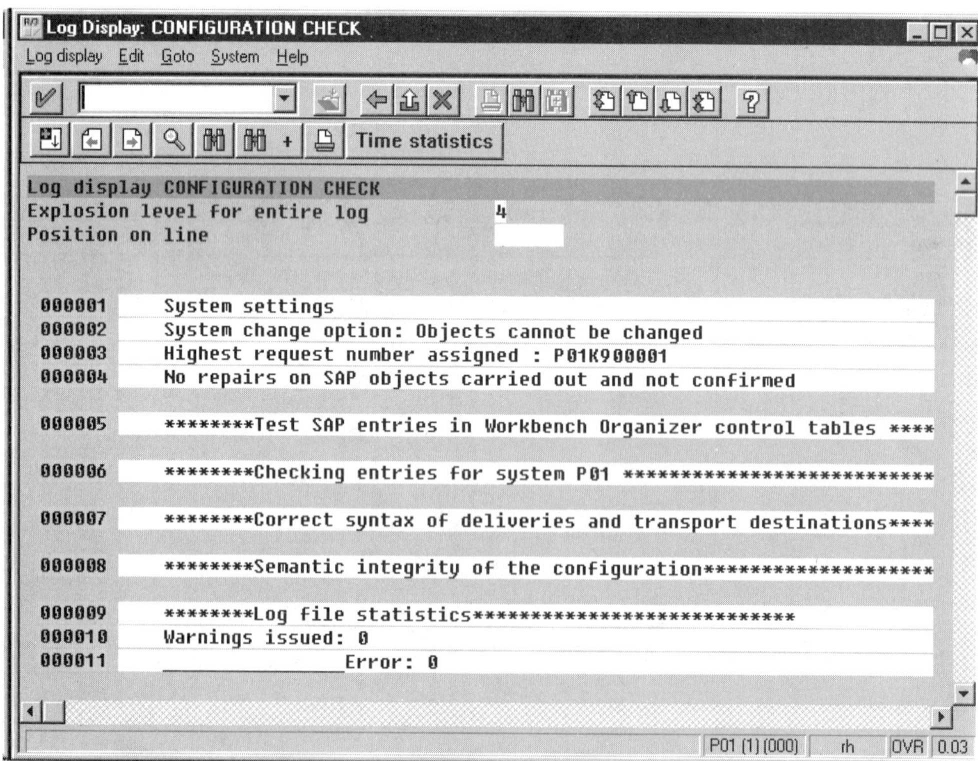

Figure 7.8 Checking settings of the workbench organizer

7.5.2 System change options

Set the **system change options** during configuration of the workbench organizer (transaction `se06` function *System change options*) or at any other time with the menu path *Overview* → *Workbench Organizer* → *Tools*. Only users with authorizations for all components of the workbench organizer may modify the system change options. The system allows the following settings:

- Objects cannot be changed,
- Only original objects can be changed (with the workbench organizer),
- All customer objects can be changed (with the workbench organizer),
- All objects can be changed (with the workbench organizer).

If the system change option is set to *Objects cannot be changed*, no modifications can be performed on development objects in this system. The creation of new objects is also prohibited. The option *All customer objects* permits changes to original objects and to objects in non-original systems. The setting *All objects can be changed* means that all objects in the development environment can be processed. This option also permits changes to copies. The correction and transport system provides a repair mechanism to perform changes to copies.

Initialization of the workbench organizer sets the system change options to the default, *All customer objects can be changed*.

7.5.3 Maintaining transport layers

The term **transport layer** came into use in version 3.x and has the following meaning: a transport layer defines a transport route. The name of the integration system and the name of the consolidation system describe the transport route. Since the transport layer represents a property of development classes, the workbench organizer uses it to determine how to distribute objects of a development class in the system group.

At delivery, a system contains two predefined transport layers. The first, transport layer `SAP`, uses the fictional system `SAP` as an integration system or consolidation system. It is allocated to the development class of the SAP standard. Use the second transport layer, ' ' (blank) as the local transport layer for local, non-transportable objects.

According to the SAP naming conventions, the name of a transport layer must begin with `Y` or `Z`. To complete the name, concatenate the name of the integration system (e.g., ZT01). In simple system configurations the workbench organizer generates a transport layer automatically and assigns it to the integration system (see Figure 7.9).

Table `DEVL` maintains transport layers. Perform maintenance with transaction `sm31` (*System* → *Services* → *Table maintenance*).

7.5.4 Maintaining development classes

Section 4.2.5 discussed development classes as a means to structure or combine objects of the development environment into functional areas. Maintain development classes

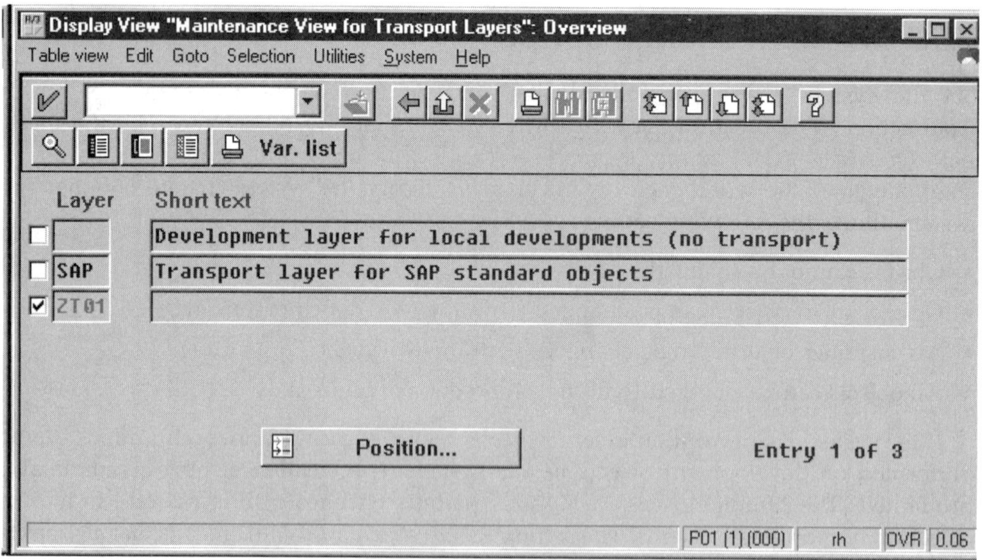

Figure 7.9 Overview of transport layers

during configuration of the workbench organizer (transaction `se06` function *Development classes*) or at any time with transaction `sm31` (*System → Services → Table maintenance*). Simply edit table `TDEVC` or use the object browser (transaction `se80`). Choose the development class for processing in the overview presented and enter the changes in the detail screen of the development class.

To create a new development class, choose the function *New entries* from the overview screen. The following description of the creation of a development class uses the example of class `ZZ01`:

After choosing *New entries*, name the development class and assign its attributes. Note that the SAP-defined name range (see Table 4.3) applies to the name of the development class. Development class `ZZ01`, an example from Appendix G, meets the requirements of the name range.

The attributes of a development class include a short description, the transport layer, the name of a person responsible for the class and a flag switching the workbench organizer on or off. The short description should provide enough information to identify the development area. Recall that the classifications assigned to development classes provide important navigation criteria in the object browser (transaction `se80`). See Figure 7.10.

The transport layer controls whether changes to objects of this class are local or if transport into another SAP system is desired. Figure 7.11 shows the declaration of the development class `ZZ01` with transportable objects.

The declaration sets the default transport route via transport layer `ZT01` (T01 → P01).

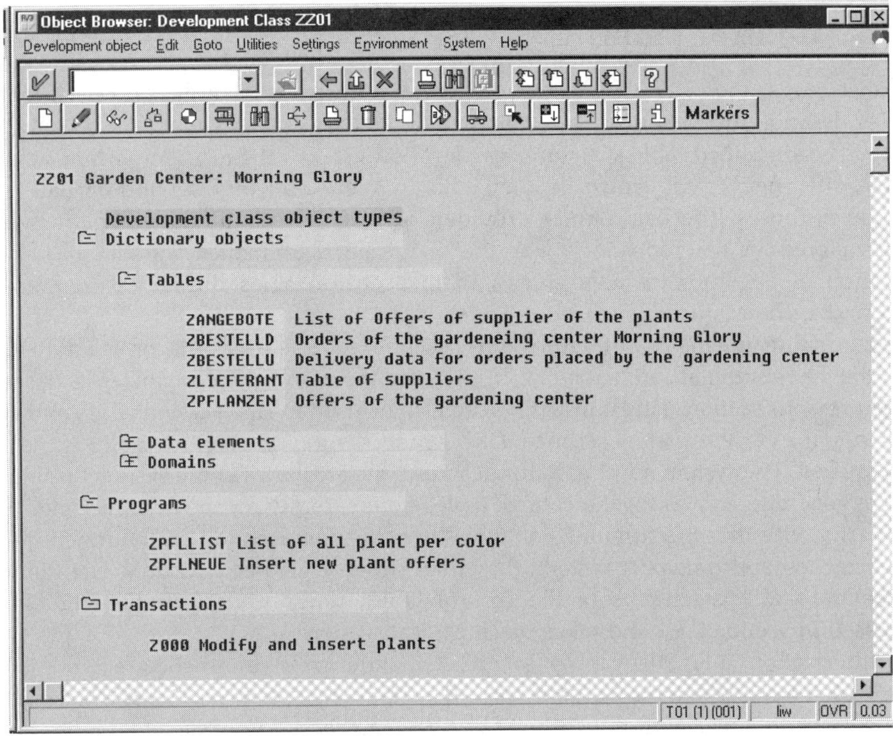

Figure 7.10 Object browser: initial screen with development class 'ZZ01'

Change View "Development Classes": Details
Table view Edit Goto Choose Utilities System Help
Var. list

Development class ZZ01
Short text Garden Center: Morning Glory

Transport layer ZT01

Integration system T01
Consolidation system P01

Person responsible ROCCO

Link to Workbench Organizer

T01 (1) (000) liw OVR 0.05

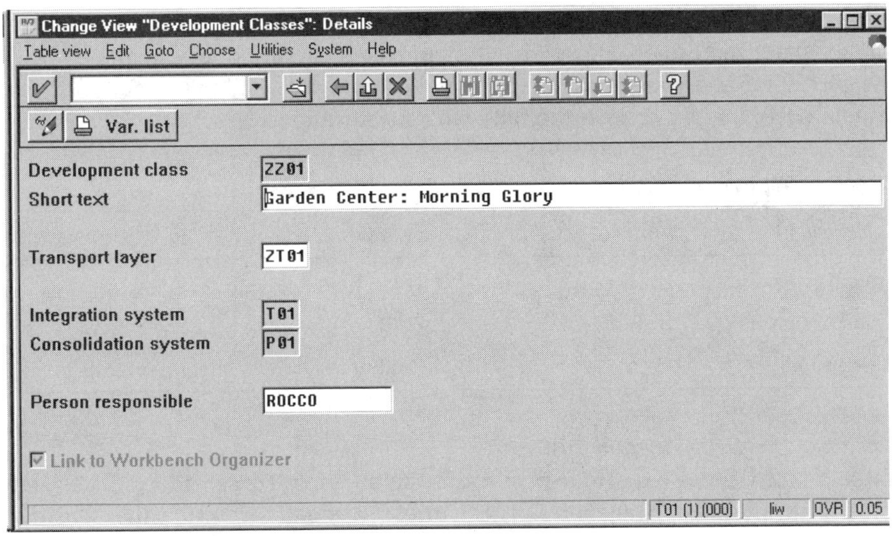

Figure 7.11 Declaration of a new development class

7.5.5 Control tables

In exact terms, the CTS works through entries written to several control tables. The entries describe the system. The tables include TSYST, TASYS, TWSYS, DEVL, TDEVC and TADIR. The simplified table structure which follows shows the most important fields. Of course, other fields exist. However, they hold no interest for the user and partially serve internal purposes. The field names provided represent symbolic identifiers of the field names stored in the repository. For the user, the field names should simplify the allocation of activities to table entries in the control tables during configuration of the workbench organizer (transaction se06).

For initial maintenance of tables use transaction se06 as user DDIC or as another user with the maximum authorization S_CTS_ALL for the workbench organizer as described in the previous section. This transaction can also be used in R/3 versions 2.1G and above to change the current system settings. Direct processing of the control tables is therefore not required. The system administrator describes the attributes of the system on-line. The system generates entries for the control tables transparently for the administrator. Since familiarity with the structure of these tables provides information on the functioning of the correction and transport system, the tables deserve greater attention. The following presentation of the contents of the control tables refers to the sample initialization discussed in Section 7.5.1 and takes place via transaction se06.

Authorization rules also apply to direct maintenance (transaction sm31: *Maintain tables*) of the control tables of the CTS. The table TADIR (object catalog) is always implicitly maintained with transactions during the processing of development environment objects. More specifically, maintenance of that table involves maintaining the transport attributes of a development environment object (e.g., during the creation of a new report with transaction se38).

- *Table* TSYST *– List of R/3 systems available*
  Table TSYST (see Table 7.3) contains system characteristics of essential significance to the correction and transport system. A valid entry for an R/3 system with the SAP system ID T01 might contain the following specifications:

Table 7.3 Table entry for table TSYST *for system T01*

Table field	*Contents*
System name	T01
Transport layer	ZT01
Description	Quality assurance/Integration tests

- *Table* TASYS *– Deliveries from systems*
  Table TASYS defines fixed transport routes. In a certain sense, it formulates standing orders for automatic transports. The entries essentially describe the consolidation system that provides a delivery system with transports. They declare subscriptions for consolidation transports. Table TASYS (see Table 7.4) has a very simple structure. For a

system relationship between consolidation system P01 and delivery system S01, the resulting table entry in table TASYS would appear as follows:

Table 7.4 Table entry for table TASYS *with system ID P01 → S01*

Delivery system	*Consolidation system*	*Cross-transports (O flag)*
S01	P01	

An x in the column *Cross transports* permits the transport from any system into the delivery system. A more exact look at the table contents with transaction sm31 would display yet another line, containing the consolidation system SAP, for every system. This line ensures that the system can be upgraded.

- *Table* TWSYS *– Consolidation route for transport requests*
  In table TWSYS, SAP has left open, for exceptional cases, a means of bypassing the restrictive rules of the correction and transport system that apply to fixed transport routes. SAP did so to enable the transport of modified standard SAP objects into a system group, after error correction for example. Recall that SAP standard objects have the fictitious system SAP as their integration and consolidation system.

  Entries in table TWSYS can reroute default transport routes (*Integration system → Consolidation system*). The rerouting allows changes in both the source system and the target system. If a transport of corrected SAP objects between T01 and P01 is to be permitted (default), the table must contain the following entry (see Table 7.5):

Table 7.5 Table entry: table TWSYS

Field name	*Contents*
Source system	T01
Consolidation system	SAP
Target system	P01

- *Table* TDEVC *– Directory of all development classes*
  Table TDEVC defines development classes. The attributes assigned to a development class apply to all the development objects of that class.

Table 7.6 Table entry in table TDEVC *for development class 'ZZ01'*

Field name	*Contents*
Development class	ZZ01
Transport layer	ZT01
Short description	Morning Glory Gardening Center
Correction	x
Person responsible	Sam Sample

Table 7.6 shows the contents of table TDEVC for development class ZZ01. An x in the field *Correction* activates the workbench organizer connection for the objects in development class ZZ01. That means that changes to objects in this development class will be recorded. The other columns serve internal purposes.

- *Table* TADIR *– Directory of all development environment objects of a system*
  Table TADIR lists all the development environment objects of the R/3 development environment. It displays the object catalog of the R/3 system. Each entry in TADIR describes a development environment object. It also holds the following information for each development environment object:
  - Object name,
  - Development class,
  - Original system,
  - Author,
  - Last correction,
  - Last transport,
  - Object in repair?

  Accordingly, table TADIR contains the transport attributes of a development environment object. Perform modifications only with transactions that allow maintenance of transport attributes (e.g., se09, se38). Maintenance usually takes place with the function *Maintain transport attributes*. Never perform manual changes to entries in this table.

7.6 Editing development environment objects

7.6.1 Generating objects

Before users can work with the tool that generates objects, they must describe the object to the system and allocate it to a development class. Creation of a report, for example, requires prior maintenance of the program attributes. Maintain these attributes at any time with transaction se38 and the function *Attributes* → *Change* (see Figure 7.12).

Only after provision of all the necessary information here can users go to the next screen to allocate a development class (see Figure 7.13). The specification of a development class determines if the workbench organizer will register edits on the objects and if a local or transportable change request should contain the objects (see Figure 7.14).

Assignment to the development class $TMP, for example, is a function of object processing, not the workbench organizer. If, however, users wish to generate the processing and to transport an object further after object development, they must specify a customer development class (e.g., ZZ01) here. The development class determines the administrative unit in which the workbench organizer captures the object processing. If a development class with connections to the workbench organizer is selected, make sure that the subsequent screen indicates the name of the change request used to administer development activities.

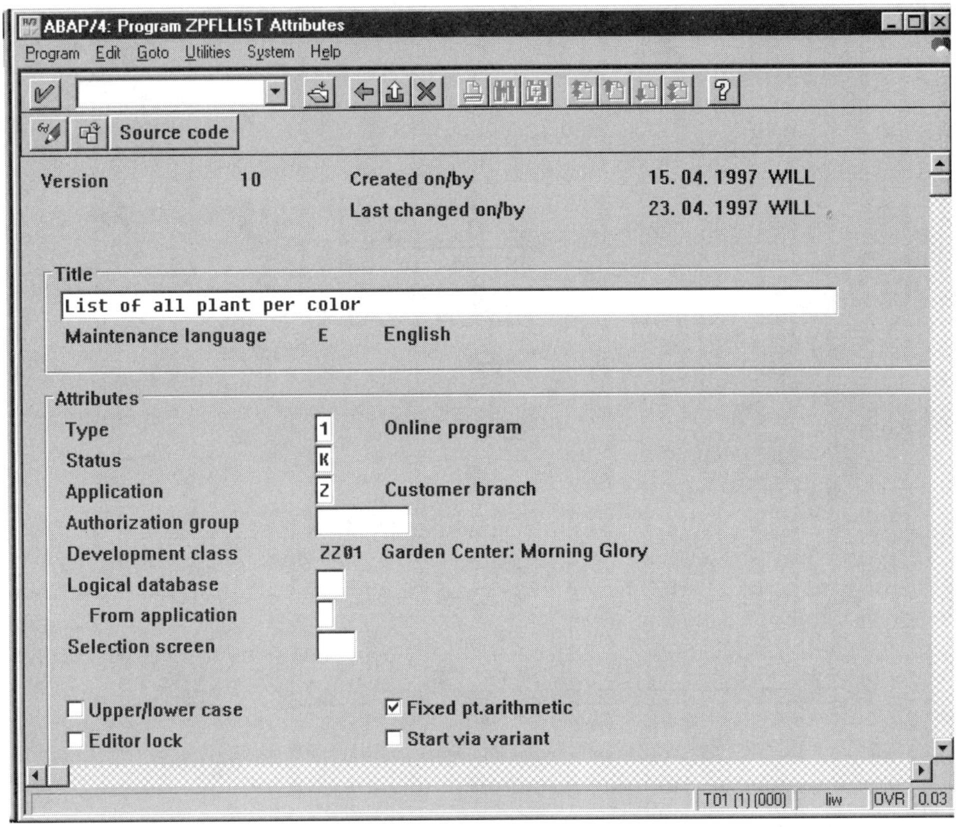

Figure 7.12 Maintaining program attributes

The correction system suggests an appropriate request. The request may be either a new request or a standard request as declared in the workbench organizer. Accept the suggestion or correct it with the function *Own request*. After making this choice, users must mark the desired request in the list of requests displayed.

Note that although the user selects a change request, the processing of the object is first registered in a task of the change request. The task is always of the type **development/correction**.

Editing of the object can begin only after the change request being used becomes clear. Later editing of the object will take place directly in object maintenance (e.g., the ABAP/4 editor). At the end of this development process users signal it to the workbench organizer by releasing the task to the superordinated change request (see Section 7.8.6). The release copies the task's object list to the change request. The object locks remain in effect so that only the users involved in the change request can later change the object.

Once all the tasks of the change request have been released and no superordinated tasks are to be allocated to the request, users can end the 'project' by releasing the change request. The release of a change request fixes the status of objects held in the object list.

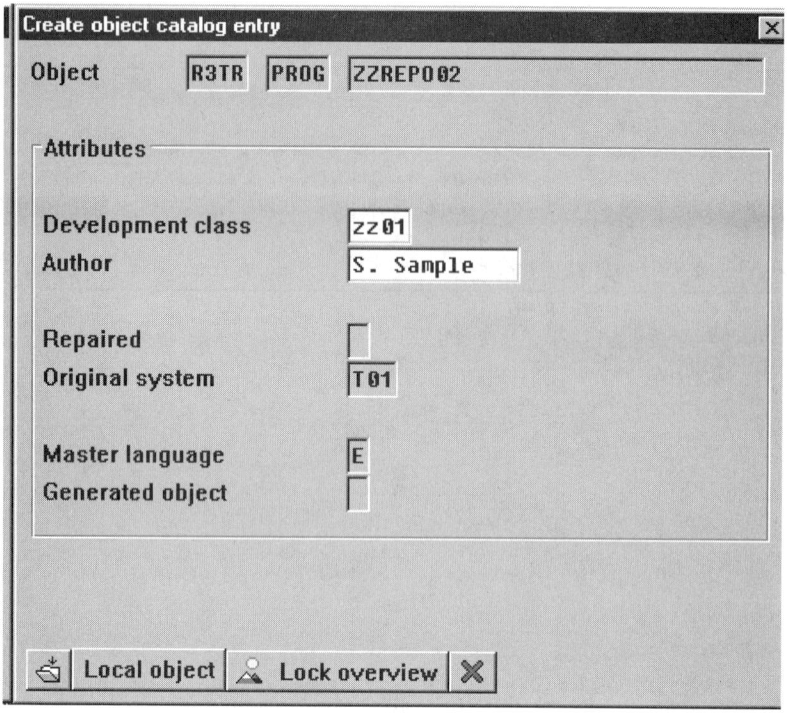

Create object catalog entry

Object	R3TR	PROG	ZZREP002

Attributes

Development class	zz01
Author	S. Sample
Repaired	
Original system	T01
Master language	E
Generated object	

Local object | Lock overview

Figure 7.13 Allocation of a development class during object generation

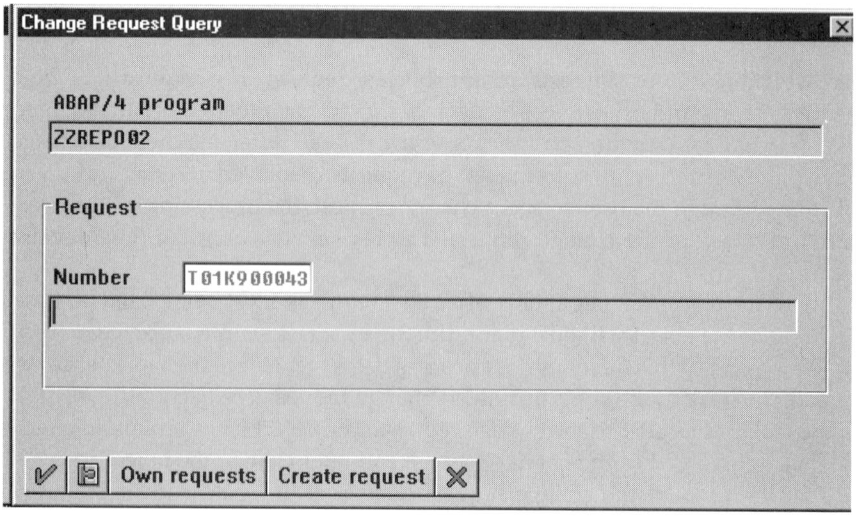

Change Request Query

ABAP/4 program

ZZREP002

Request

Number T01K900043

Own requests | Create request

Figure 7.14 Allocation of a change request

The version database contains a version of each change request in which an object participated. The objects of a transportable change request are then exported; their import into the target system is recorded at the operating system level. Operating system files store the exported objects temporarily. The system releases object locks automatically after a successful release. The objects are then available for editing in later change requests.

7.6.2 Modifying objects

When changing an object, users must differentiate between changes made to an original and those made to a copy. That distinction results in the task type used by the workbench organizer to administer object processing A **development/correction** handles object modifications made to originals, while a **repair** contains changes made to a copy.

The workbench organizer handles changes to originals according to the same principles involved in creating objects. In this case, however, users do not need to provide object attributes or allocate development classes. Contrary to the case when generating objects, the request query window appears only after saving the objects when they have been changed.

A different behavior occurs when modifying copies. As a rule, perform changes of this type only in cases of evident necessity. In any case, note that only maintenance of originals provides objects with permanent adjustments. When processing a copy, first identify it as an object for repair. Doing so prevents an import from overwriting the changes made to the object. Once the changes have become final, the workbench organizer offers a means of canceling the identifying marker. Choose between an already-existing and a new request in the request query screen. If creation of an object generated a request with a task type of development/correction, the workbench organizer, when processing a copy, generates a request and a task identified as a repair. Only a project team member can modify an object undergoing repair. This restriction does not apply to the processing of originals. The workbench organizer does not permit automatic transfer of object processing by other members of the change request (cannot be networked). If another user wishes to continue the repair, she must declare herself as its new owner (person responsible). Once the copies contains all the required changes, release it to the superordinated change request.

At the time of release, users can determine if the release also requires a confirmation. Confirm the repair only after execution of the corresponding changes to the original. If that is not yet the case, the confirmation can be performed later. Confirmation of the repair resets the repair marker. In other words: confirmation of the repair allows importation of the object.

After performing all the object modifications contained in a change request, close the 'project' by releasing the change request.

7.7 Lock mechanisms in the CTS

Before presenting a detailed description of operating the workbench organizer, an introduction to the lock mechanisms used by the correction and transport system seems in order. Doing so allows a better classification of the individual functions in working with this tool.

An object is locked when the task to which it belongs is saved. That means that the CTS immediately refuses any access to the object by other developers, even if the object is not being processed at the moment. All productive development environments should have this function, especially those that claim to support operations involving several users. Two considerations take on particular importance. First, one user session rarely suffices to complete changes. Second, responsibility for the changes should always be transferred to other developers consciously. The expansion of this one-level lock concept to tasks and requests constitutes a particularly noteworthy characteristic of the R/3 development environment.

Locking DE objects represents the first lock level. It takes effect as soon as a task opened or modified by object processing is saved. The lock not only blocks the DE objects from access by other users, but also locks the system components dependent on those objects. If objects were entered manually into the object list of a task, they can be locked with the function *Request/Task → Object list → Lock objects*.

Technically, however, nothing prevents another user from modifying the object while it is not being processed. A second lock level exists to regulate precisely this type of access. Lock operations performed on a change request allow a developer to decide if he wishes to complete his changes independently, before others process it, or to allow parallel processing of the object. If other users should not have access to the object, the workbench organizer offers the function *Protect*. The developer thus excludes parallel processing of the objects by other users conclusively. Without request protection, the developer agrees to parallel development activities for the objects.

A developer grants another user access to a locked object by adding his own task to the superordinated request of the other user. The function *Add user* permits such cooperative ventures. The workbench organizer also allows developers to link requests with *Include*. For successful networking, however, the request under consideration cannot be protected.

Although the first lock level takes effect automatically, the developer must initiate the second lock level explicitly. This mechanism allows the developer to specify the organization of development work.

Because the lock concept also applies to change requests and can operate in conjunction with them, change requests carry a status that aids in their administration. The workbench organizer differentiates only between *Protected* and *Unprotected*; the transport system, however, provides a detailed differentiation of request statuses with transaction `se01` (see Figure 7.15). At any given time, the status indicates the operation performed last. Figure 7.15 shows the most important statuses of tasks/requests and what action will initiate a change in status. Transportable change requests can also have the status *Open*. This status signals either a currently running export or the inability to complete an export successfully because of errors.

The status *Document* contains a change request that has been saved the first time. If a user locks other users out of the request, a change of status occurs. If the system can lock all the development objects of an object list, the CTS sets the status to *LOCKEDALL*. The status *LOCKED* indicates that the system could not successfully set locks for all objects.

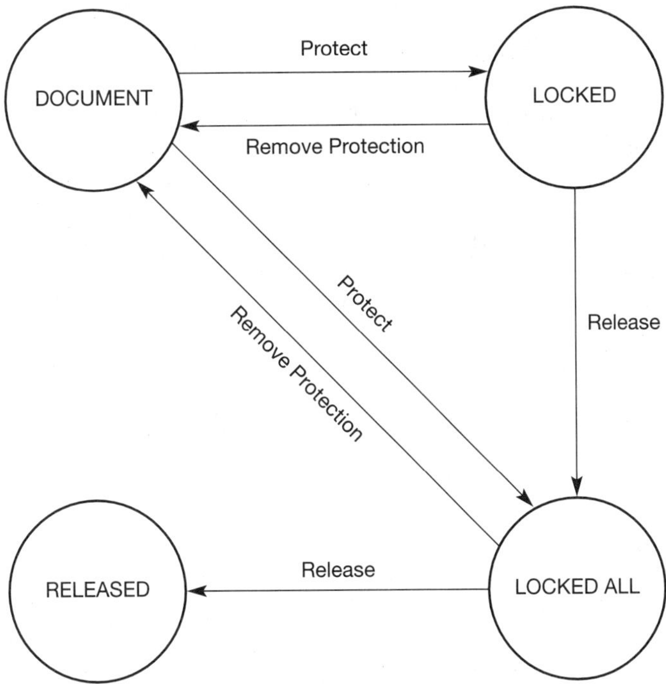

Figure 7.15 Status of a change request

The status *LOCKEDALL* is a prerequisite for a successful release of a request. R/3 defines a release as the closure of a process (task or project (change request)). After release, a request can no longer be changed. Once it has been released, the request serves only to document or verify activities already performed. Users can cancel the locks for a request with the function *Remove protection*. Note, however, that the object locks themselves remain in effect.

The CTS also provides an additional regulating agent for common processing of objects. It splits complex object types into sub-objects. This feature enables very efficient lock behavior, which, in turn, allows the maximum amount of parallel development work.

The following example should clarify this feature. Two users have opened change requests for the processing of development environment objects. User number one edits program `ZZPROG00`. This user modifies the ABAP/4 source code and has already designed some screen definitions. The object list for this project contains the following:

PgmId	ObjType	ObjName	Function	ObjStatus
R3TR	PROG	ZZPROG00		LOCKED

User number two now wants to change a screen definition for the development environment object. For user number two, the CTS generates the following entry in the object list of the request:

PgmId	ObjType	ObjName	Function	ObjStatus
LIMU	DYNP	ZZPROG00	100	LOCKED

This subdivision of objects reduces the number of locks to a minimum. It also, however, clearly indicates who performed what changes.

At this point we again remind readers that networking tasks becomes necessary only when several users wish to work on one particular sub-object of a development environment object. If a clear division of labor exists among developers, each working on a specific set of development environment objects, the tasks do not require networking. In such a situation, no clashes can occur (see Section 7.3).

7.8 Development coordination with the workbench organizer

7.8.1 Getting started

Previous sections have treated the setup of the workbench organizer and its use during day-to-day development work. This section presents a more detailed description of the features and functions of this tool. The following discussion covers both the basic elements of using the workbench organizer and how users might apply its diverse functions.

Reach the workbench organizer by choosing *Environment → Workbench Organizer* from the ABAP/4 development workbench. Both transaction `se09` and other ABAP/4 workbench functions also provide direct access to the workbench organizer.

The initial screen of the workbench organizer (see Figure 7.16) vertically divides tasks/requests on one side and transports/repairs on the other side. Push buttons allow selection of the desired administrative units. The function *Detail selection* permits the choice of additional selection criteria. Default selection criteria for tasks/requests include the status and attributes. The criteria allow the user to list all the modifiable, local requests of a given user.

The check boxes *Transport of copies* and *Tasks without requests* perform a special function. They provide administration of objects created with transaction `se01` by the transport system. The workbench organizer always links non-empty tasks to a change request. However, as it originated in version 2.x, transaction `se01` permits the editing of objects in corrections or repairs (tasks) even when a superordinated change request (transport request) does not exist. *Transport of copies* (Transport type `T`) is a new term, used as of version 3.x, for transport requests without a change authorization (see Section 7.9.2).

The function *Display* provides an overview of each area. It presents a hierarchical list, grouped according to the marked selection criteria. When working with hierarchical lists, the request overview, for example, please note the following:

A double click on a folder in the hierarchy expands or conceals a hierarchy level. Similarly, a double click on the folder symbol for a request will list or conceal the

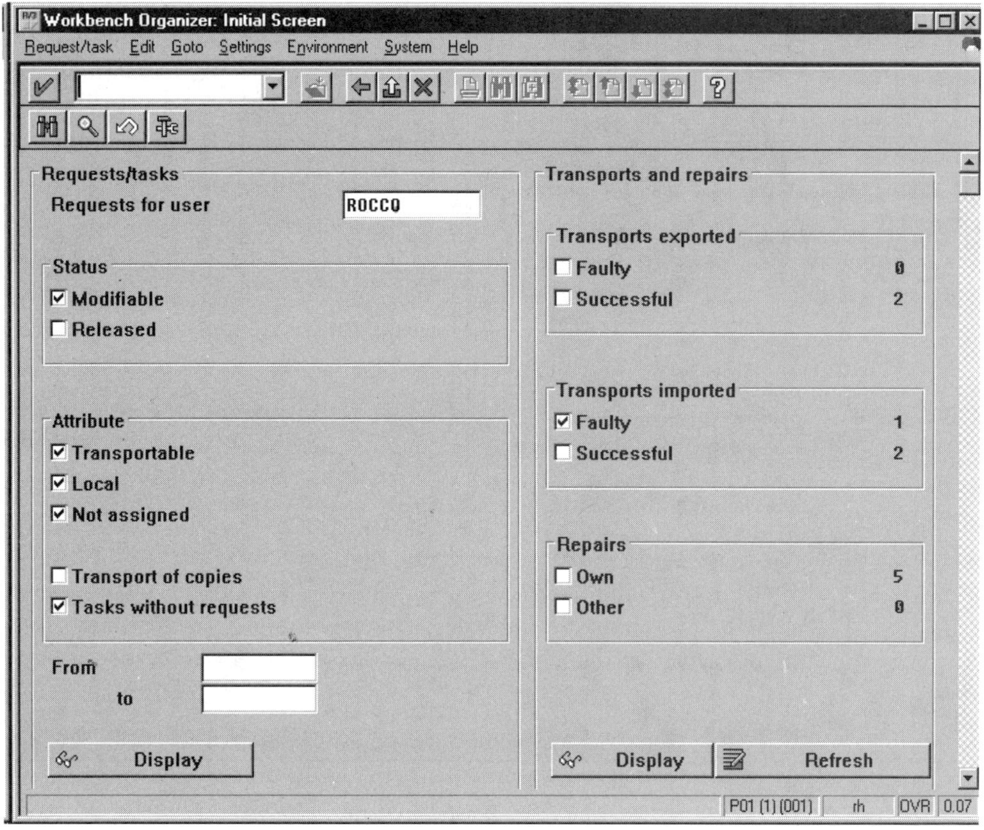

Figure 7.16 Initial screen of the workbench organizer (transaction `se09`*)*

subordinate tasks. A double click on a task or a request branches to the object list of that administrative unit. A double click on the object itself, however, calls the object editor.

The description of editing functions for tasks/requests in this sections is based on the screen overview given in Figure 7.17.

Reach the screen by calling the workbench organizer from the ABAP/4 development workbench or directly with transaction `se09`. Exit the initial screen of the transaction with the function *Tasks/Requests → Display*.

7.8.2 Creating tasks/requests

Section 7.5 described how the workbench organizer normally handles the editing of an object. The correction system forces developers to register their work in a change request.

The workbench organizer supports preparation for a project by advance creation of the administrative units to be used. This procedure prevents the random choice of change requests that would cause users to lose an overview of the overall project. Planned

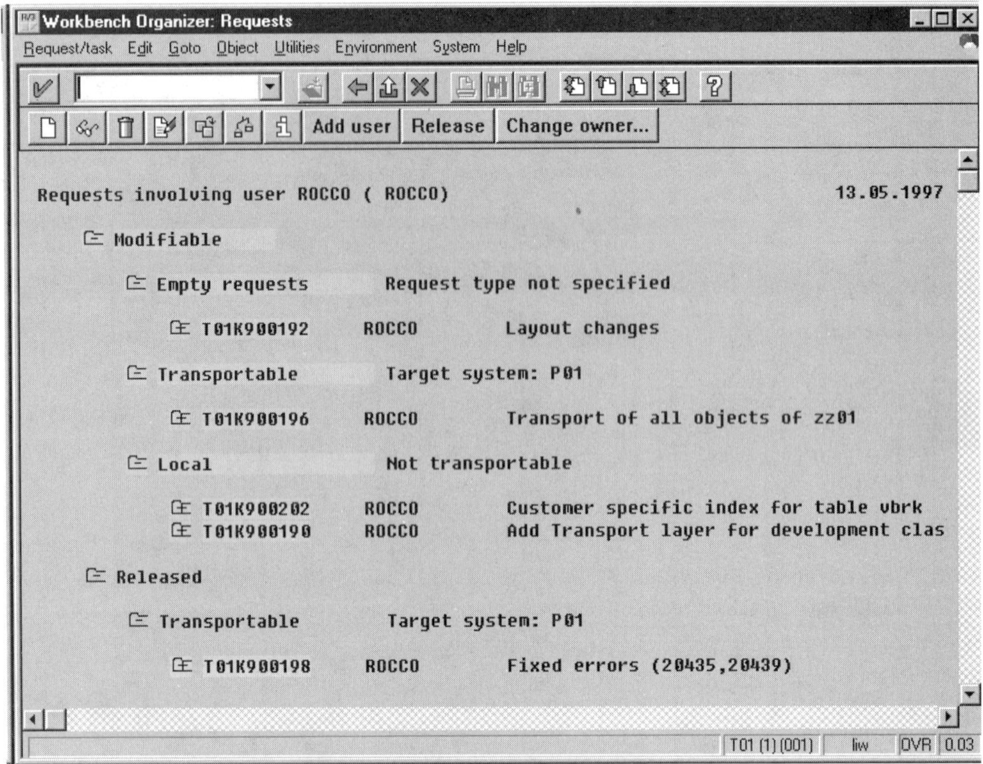

Figure 7.17 Request overview

development work should take advantage of this feature. The project leader can proceed as follows:

All required change requests are created with the function *Request/Task → Create*. The leader can determine at the time or creation, or later with the function *Request/Task → Add user*, which users may participate in a development project (change request). The workbench organizer generates a task for each user. When working on a object, users specify the change request allocated to them. From then on, the object is entered in the task assigned to a particular user within the request. To avoid having to use the registration procedure each time an object is first edited, declare this request as the default in the workbench organizer.

After the creation of a request, the workbench organizer also allows manual recording of DE objects in each administrative unit. However, make sure to set the request and task type ahead of time with the function *Request/Task → Assign attribute*. The workbench organizer distinguishes between the following attributes for requests:

- not allocated,
- transportable,
- local.

Tasks can display the following attributes:

- not allocated,
- development/correction,
- repair.

Assume, for example, that a user wants to edit programs `ZPFLLIST` and `ZPFLNEUE` (see Appendix G) of development class `ZZ01` and then transport them from the integration system T01 into the consolidation system P01. Here the user would choose the request attribute *transportable* and the task attribute *Development/Correction*.

For example, to edit several programs concurrently and to secure exclusive editing rights for these objects in advance, enter the objects in the object list of the task. Then lock them against unauthorized editing by third parties with the function *Request/Task* → *Protect* → *Lock objects*. If only a transport of objects is planned, delete the subordinate tasks and include the DE objects in the object list of the request immediately.

A double click on the task or the request takes the user to the editor in the workbench organizer to create the object list. Entries in the editor use the form of a table. Each DE object occupies one line. Comment lines begin with an asterisk (*) in the column PgmId. The object list could then appear as follows:

PgmId	ObjType	Text	Function	ObjStatus
R3TR	PROG	ZPFLLIST		
R3TR	PROG	ZPFLNEUE		

Table 7.7 contains a summary of the mostly commonly used DE objects.

The field *Function* is meaningful only for a transport. The field *ObjStatus* provides information on the status of an object. It can contain the following values:

- no value → Object not locked
- LOCKED → Object locked
- NOT_IMP → Object not imported
- ERR_IMP → Error during importation of the object
- OK_IMP → Object successfully imported
- OK_GEN → Object successfully imported and generated

Section 7.7 (lock mechanisms) describes when and how the status changes.

Object type `R3TR PROG` allows the specification of generic object names. If a user owns only two programs with the name `ZPFL...`, simplify the object list by making the following notation:

PgmId	ObjType	Text	Function	ObjStatus
R3TR	PROG	ZPFL*		

In addition to creating new objects lists in the editor, users can also reuse existing object lists from earlier correction or transport requests or from lists. To do so, use transaction `se01` (called transport system as of version 3.x) and the function *Transport*

Table 7.7 Frequently used DE objects

DE object	*Meaning*
R3TR CNTD	Control table
R3TR CSRC	C source text
R3TR DIAL	Dialog module
R3TR DOCT	Texts documentation class TX
R3TR DOCV	Documentation
R3TR DOMA	Domains and documentation
R3TR DTEL	Data element with values, documentation and data element supplements
R3TR ENQU	Definition of a lock objects
R3TR FUGR	Function group with screens and CUA . . .
R3TR FUNC	Function module
R3TR LDBA	Logical database
R3TR MACO	Matchcode object
R3TR MCOB	Matchcode object and documentation
R3TR PROG	ABAP/4 program including CUA definition, screens, texts and documentation
R3TR SQLT	Pool/cluster definition
R3TR TABL	Table definition and foreign key, table documentation and maintenance screens
R3TR TABU	Table contents
R3TR TRAN	Transaction identifier and documentation
R3TR XPRA	Report to be executed in the target system after DDIC activation
LIMU DOCU	Document module
LIMU DOMD	Domain definition
LIMU DTED	Data element definition
LIMU DYNP	Screen image
LIMU MACD	Matchcode definition
LIMU REPO	Report
LIMU MESS	Single message
LIMU TABD	Table definition
LIMU TABL	NAMETAB transport
LIMU TABT	Technical properties of a table
LIMU VIED	View definition
LIMU VARI	Report variants

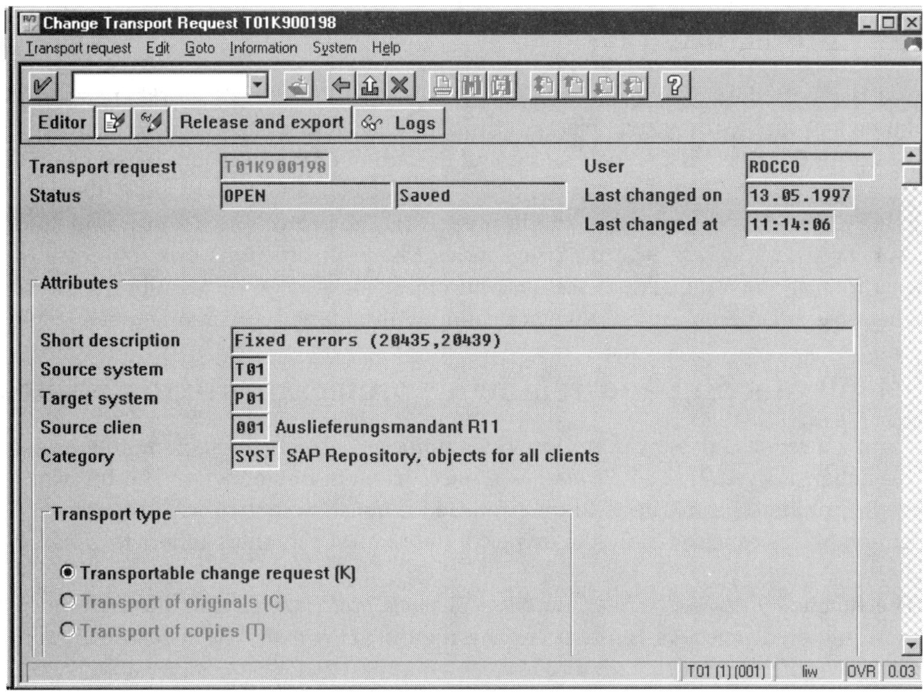

Figure 7.18 Transferring object lists with transaction se01

request → *Include template* (see Figure 7.18). In other words, this function transfers object lists from existing transport requests into the new request.

If users wish to work on an object immediately, they need not enter the objects intended for processing in the change request or the task themselves. When users choose an object for processing, the correction and transport system requires that users assign the planned processing to a request. The CTS suggests either the last request opened by a given user or the default request (if defined). Acceptance of a suggested request number causes the system to add the object to the object list of the tasks assigned to that user. Use of another request number expands the task of that request or, if necessary, creates a new task within the request.

Please note the following when assigning objects to existing change requests. If using a request to transport a group of linked objects, the object should, if at all possible, be related (i.e., belong to the same development class or have similar transport attributes). Otherwise the system may uncover irregularities during the transport that prevent the transport of the entire group of objects.

Use the function *Request* → *Create* to inform the workbench organizer that it should create a new change request. The function automatically places the object intended for processing in the object list of the subordinate request.

After successful creation or assignment of a request for the processing of a DE object, the user can make changes to the object as often as desired. Release of the task signals the end of development work on the object to the workbench organizer.

7.8.3 Protecting a task

Lock a task with the function *Request/Task → Request → Protect*. The workbench organizer will then lock all the unlocked objects in the object list. The status *LOCKED* in the column ObjStatus of the object list signals successful execution of the function. In the event of an error, a log appears that contains the unlockable objects and the reason(s) the function failed (e.g., the object is locked in another request). The protection of a task is identical to the function *Request/Task → Protect → Lock objects*. Both functions prohibit entry of the objects into another request. Processing an object locks it automatically. Accordingly, locking objects is necessary only when dealing with manually maintained object lists.

7.8.4 Protecting and removing protection from a request

Protecting a request also locks any previous unlocked objects that belong to the request. The function *Request/Task → Request → Protect* triggers this activity. The function also prevents linking other requests to the protected request; no networking can occur. After execution of this function, only the owner of the request can allow others to work on the request.

The function *Request/Task → Request → Remove protection* cancels the locking of the request. Other developers can process the request. However, the locks on the objects contained in the request remain in place.

7.8.5 Deleting objects in requests/tasks

To delete an object from the object list or a request or task, position the cursor on the object in the hierarchical list of the request overview and choose the function *Object → Delete* or delete the appropriate line from the object list in the editor. If the object is locked, a dialog box requests confirmation of the deletion command. Deletion of an object fails if the active version of an object (intermediate version) is not the final version (version after the last request release, see Section 7.8.10). In such a case, reset the object to the status of the last version before re-attempting to delete it. Remove redundant entries in an object list with the function *Sort/Compress*. These comments should make clear that users should work rarely and carefully with the function *Object → Delete*.

7.8.6 Releasing a task

After performing all the changes to objects within a task, users inform the workbench organizer that processing has ended with the function *Task → Release*.

Tasks are always released to change requests, thus transferring the object list of the task to the object list of the request. Locks on objects remain in force. If the task being released is a repair, the user must decide if the release also confirms the repair. If the changes contained in the repair already exist in the original system, agree to the automatic confirmation. If the changes have not yet been transferred to the original system, cancel the confirmation. Perform the confirmation at an appropriate time with the function *Task/Request → Task → Confirm repair*. Objects of a released repair then become available to others assigned to the change request. After removal of the repair flag, the system once again allows importation of objects contained in the repair.

7.8.7 Releasing a request

The function *Request → Release* releases a request. To release a change request successfully, all the subordinate tasks it contains must have been released previously. In other words, a project cannot be closed until all participants have completed (released) their tasks. At this point the object list contains all the objects that constitute the task. The comment entry CORR references the tasks.

PgmId	ObjType	ObjName	Function		ObjStatus
CORR	RELE	T01K900037	19960426	164604	S.Sample
R3TR	PROG	ZPFLLIST			LOCKED
R3TR	PROG	ZPFLNEUE			LOCKED

Release of the request indicates closure of the project to the workbench organizer, which then initiates the following activities. Definition of a version preserves the current status of all objects.

If the request intended for release is transportable, the system exports the objects and notes their import into the target system at the operating system level. To avoid difficulties during export from the very beginning, schedule program RDDIMPDP in client `000` and in every other client in use. Use program RDDNEWPP to establish the schedule (see also Section 7.9.7).

A release of a request also cancels the locks on the objects. The objects then become available to other projects (requests). Accordingly, do not allow requests to remain open too long; each non-released request can impede work by other developers.

A released change request cannot be modified. The workbench organizer considers it evidence of a completed modification. Users can employ a released request only as a template for new requests.

7.8.8 Participation in a request

The procedure to add several developers to a development project team is rather simple; the workbench organizer offers the function *Request → Add user* for this purpose. Execution of the function creates a task for the user within the request. If the request referenced here is unprotected, each authorized developer can define his or her own work on the project by executing this function. Only the request owner can allow other developers to work on a locked project (request). The function can be applied to a project at its creation or at a later time.

7.8.9 Including requests

In addition to the function *Request → Add user*, the workbench organizer also offers the function *Request → Include* to permit linking requests or networking them at a later time. After triggering the function, the system requests entry of the request for inclusion. The workbench organizer then transfers the task to the target request. A successfully included request disappears from the request overview.

Participation in or networking of tasks/requests allows developers to access locked objects belonging to other developers, as long as the objects are not being worked on at the same time.

7.8.10 Versions

The development of a software product is generally a lengthy process accompanied by highs and lows. Full functional implementation of a program occurs only in stages. Developers often discover that the routes to some solutions are not passable, which requires locating the starting point for a new and different solution. For this reason general practice freezes the status of a program at a given time. These frozen development levels are considered versions of an object.

R/3 supports this procedure with version management, available for all objects of the ABAP/4 workbench as of version 3.x. Versions provide a quick overview of an object's modification history. Developers can use versions to determine the modifications last made to an object or return to an earlier version. Version management also gives administrators extraordinary oversight options.

Versions are automatically generated within the context of request release. Maintenance transactions of repository objects also give the developer the option of creating intermediate versions. Use the function *Retrieve version* to create intermediate versions. At release of a request, the system combines all the intermediate versions of an object into one (complete) version.

Versions exist only for the changed objects within a system. An import updates the version database for these objects. However, at importation of an unchanged object no entry exists in the version database. The version database stores a complete version and n delta sets (variants from the complete version). 'N delta sets' stands for n number of changes to the object. Storage of delta sets reduces the required disk space to a minimum.

Reach version management for a given object with the function *Utilities → Version management*. Choose the function *Display versions* from within the workbench organizer.

7.9 Transports

7.9.1 General remarks

The previous sections demonstrated how to use the workbench organizer to control development flow and showed the options available in the workbench organizer to organize a system group.

The transport system coordinates and implements the exchange of DE objects in a networked development environment. Its tasks are hardly limited to data transfer; tasks performed by the transport system are quite complex. The system must provide up-to-date information on who performed which transports. The system therefore keeps extensive logs.

In heterogeneous configurations, the transport system also enjoys responsibility for equalizing differences between the operating systems. Any necessary conversions (e.g., character sets) occur automatically and transparently for the user. The transport system permits the transport of any DE objects. It supports the insertion, overwriting, replacement and deletion of objects. Limitations placed on transports regulate the maintenance of system hierarchies (see Sections 7.4.1 and 7.9.2).

A transport consists of two principal stages:

- export from the source system and
- import into the target system.

The R/3 system considers each phase as assigned to different groups. Developers perform exports themselves; administrators normally perform imports.

The transport system administers all transports by delivery notes, called **transport requests**. The system distinguishes between the following types of transport requests (based on their purpose):

- transportable change requests (`K` transport),
- transport request for the transport of copies (`T` transport),
- transport request for the transport of originals (`C` transport).

Section 7.9.2 treats the terms in parentheses.

A request always shows the request owner what DE objects are involved and the intended target system for the objects. It also notes how far execution of the request has proceeded and where, for example, difficulties arose during the transport.

The workbench organizer and the transport system are finely tuned to each other. Transfer from one to the other occurs transparently to the developer. The release of a transportable change request automatically causes the workbench organizer to trigger an export.

Reach the initial screen of the workbench organizer with the function *Transport/Repair → Display* in much the same way as the function *Request/Task → Display* in an overview screen. Here transports and repairs are classified in the form of a hierarchical list, presented according to exports, imports and repairs (see Figure 7.19).

Navigate within the list up to the transport step level (see also Section 7.9.5).

7.9.2 Transport types

The correction and transport system distinguishes four various system types (see Section 7.4.1), among which pre-defined transport rules exist. Three types of transports implement these rules, also called **transport limitations**.

Note the transport types shown in Table 7.8.

Transport type `K` implements transports of DE objects from the integration system into the consolidation system. The workbench organizer always chooses this transport type. That means that all the transportable change requests stored in the workbench organizer are allocated to this transport type.

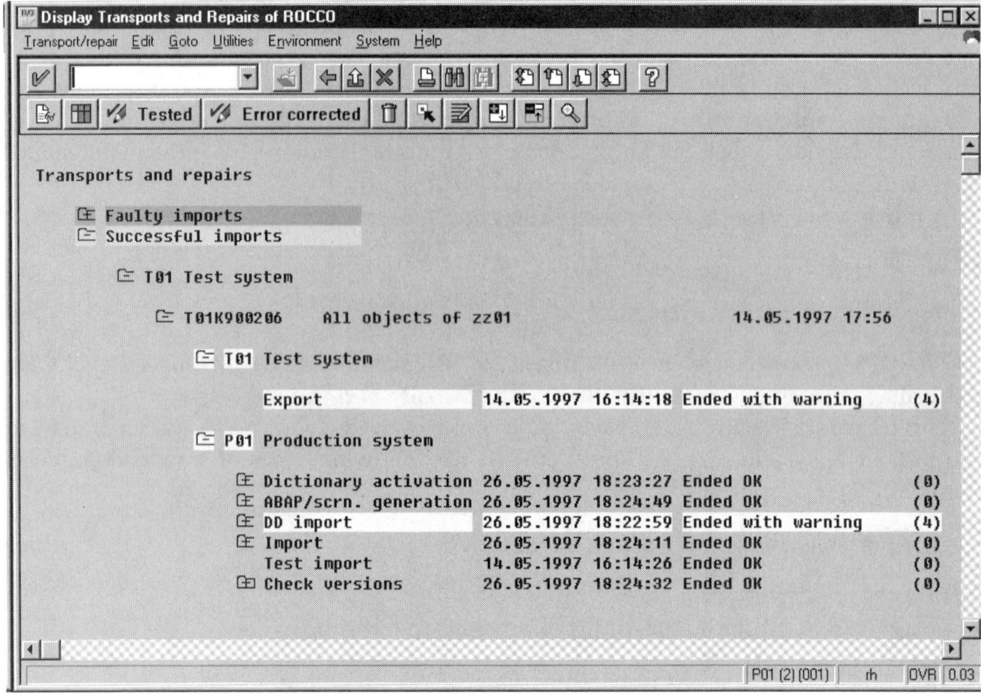

Figure 7.19 Overview of transports and repairs

Use transaction `se01` to exchange objects in the system group with another transport type (see Figure 7.18). Reach transaction `se01` from the workbench organizer with the function *Utilities → Transport system.*

Use transport type `C` to transport the original from one system to another. In the process, the source system loses its status as the original system for the object. The target system becomes the new original system. That means that change authorizations are also transported. R/3 literature refers to this type of transfer as `Check in/Check out`.

When a system (other than the consolidation system) receives a copy of a DE object, the corresponding transport takes place with transport type `T`. The target system does not contain a change authorization for the transported object. Use repairs to make any

Table 7.8 Transport types of the transport system

Transport type	*Meaning*
K	Transports a copy of a DE object from the integration system into the consolidation system
T	Transports a copy of a DE object
C	Transports the original DE object

temporary changes (if necessary). This transport type is used, for example, to supply delivery systems.

Use of the individual transport types will be demonstrated based on the configuration presented in example B1.

Use transport type `C` if object moving (change of original location) transfers DE objects from test system T01 into development system E01 during development. This transport type ensures continuation of development in the system E01 with the original. To transfer objects from the system E01 back to the system T01, two scenarios come into play:

E01 should remain as the original location because the current development phase is still regarded as critical. Accordingly, T01 receives only a stable intermediate version of the object, used to test the interplay with other components. In this case, use transport type `T` to transport a copy. If integration in system T01 runs successfully, transport the object further into production system P01 as follows:

- First, create a transportable change request in system T01 in the workbench organizer or a transport request for a consolidation transport in the transport system (transaction `se01`). Then include the object list of the transport request (E01 → T01) as a template. Releasing this request supplies the production system.
- The critical development sections are now closed. Additional work in system T01 does not prevent other developments. In this case, use object moving to leave the special development system E01 (until the next time). Link the object list (transport request) used to move the objects from T01 to E01 in a transport request of type `C` with transaction `se01`. Add new objects to the list (if required) and then release it.

Use transport type `T` to supply the training system S01 from the production system. This transport type is always used to copy objects into any system other than the consolidation system.

Figure 7.20 displays a summary of the various uses of the different transport types. Note that copies of objects (transports without change authorization) can be transported from any type of system into other systems. Use the proper transport type when transporting an object into a different type of system.

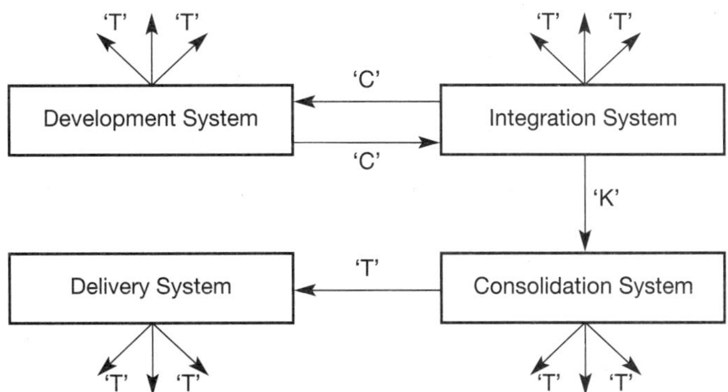

Figure 7.20 The use of transport types between various system types

7.9.3 Creating development environment object lists

Previous sections showed that users create object lists for tasks and change requests manually or that the workbench organizer places DE objects in object lists automatically during object processing. Occasionally SAP uses the term `Commandfile`, which originated in the R/2 environment. When using transports repetitively (for example, collective transports at fixed delivery times), object lists can be stored separately and used as a template for transport requests. R/3 uses development environment object lists for this purpose.

Development environment object lists are closely related to object lists. They, too, represent a list of DE objects. They differ from object lists only in that they have no set allocation to a task or change request and, accordingly, are not subject to the lock concept of the CTS. That means that saving objects in development environment object lists does not lock them, as is possible with change requests.

Development environment object lists have a purely generative function. They automate frequently repeated, complex transports within a system group by serving as templates. Use the environment analyzer (transaction `se02`) in the CTS to generate such lists (see Figure 7.21).

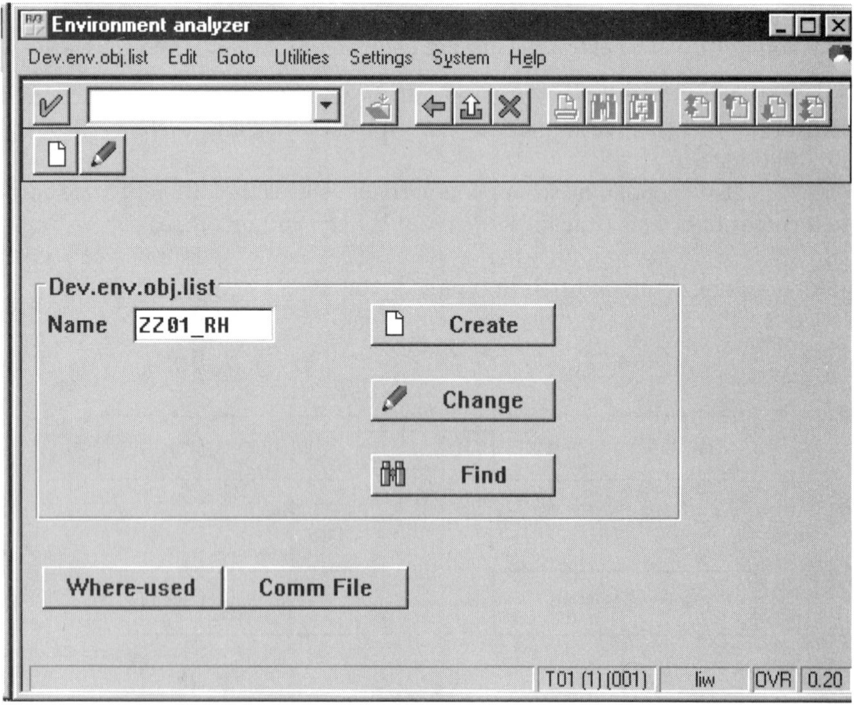

Figure 7.21 Generating development environment object lists

The environment analyzer offers a number of choices to generate development environment object lists an. Users may, for example, establish a development class as a criterion for inclusion in the list.

If, for example, the development environment object list `ZZ01_RH` should contain all the objects of development class `ZZ01`, first choose the function *Comm File* (see Figure 7.21). Then enter `ZZ01` in the entry field of the following screen.

7.9.4 Tracing transports

After triggering a transport by releasing it, users can follow the transport with the workbench organizer from the source system or the target system. As mentioned in Section 7.9.1., use the function *Transport/Repair → Display* from the initial screen of the workbench organizer to trace the transport. Place the cursor on the transport step of a request intended for tracing in the hierarchical list.

Even here a user can get a first impression of how the step has run by examining the return code. The return code indicates if the step ran successfully or encountered problems. Table 7.9 displays the return codes generated during a transport and the error conditions the codes represent.

Table 7.9 Return codes during transports

Return code	*Meaning*
0	Transport successful, no problems
4	Warnings, no serious problems
8	Errors. Transport completely stopped. Correct the causes of the errors and repeat the transport.
12 | 16	Fatal error. The causes most likely lie outside of the transport system.

A double click branches to the log display for the transport step. Users can also set the level of detail the log provides. Table 7.10 shows the detail levels provided by the system and their meaning.

Table 7.10 Detail levels for transport logs

Log detail level	*Meaning*
1	Overview of the step run
2	Error messages
3	Warnings and detailed comments on the step run
4	Information for experts

The following somewhat compressed list comes from an export log of detail level 4.

```
1 ETP199X######################################
1 ETP150 MAIN EXPORT
1 ETP101 transport order     : "T01K900118"
1 ETP102 system              : "T01"
1 ETP198
4 ETW000 R3trans version 5.26.10 (release 30B - 05.10.95 - 16:59:08).
4 ETW000 ===============================================
4 ETW000
4 ETW000 control file: /usr/sap/trans/tmp/T01K0118.T01
4 ETW000 date&time    : 02.07.1996 - 15:56:14
4 ETW000 Connected to DBMS = ADABAS --- DBNAME = 'T01' --- SYSTEM =
'T01'.
4 ETW000
4 ETW000 ================== STEP 1 =====================
4 ETW000 date&time    : 02.07.1996 - 15:56:16
4 ETW000 function     : EXPORT
4 ETW000 data file    : /usr/sap/trans/data/R900118.T01
4 ETW000 client       : 001
4 ETW000 Replace      : YES
4 ETW000 Language     : ABCDEFGHIJKLMNOPQRSTUVWXYZ0123456789
4 ETW000 foreign lang: COMPLETE
4 ETW000
3 ETW673XUse Commandfile "T01K900118"
4 ETW000       /* Transfer zzpfllist and zzpflneue */
4 ETW000       trfunction: 'K' (transport to consolidation system)
4 ETW000       trstatus  : 'O'
4 ETW000       tarsystem : P01
4 ETW000       user      : ROCCO
4 ETW000       date      : 02.07.1996 - 15:56:07
4 ETW000
4 ETW000   1 entry from E070 exported (T01K900118).
4 ETW000   2 entries from E071 exported (T01K900118).
4 ETW000   0 entries from E071K exported (T01K900118).
4 ETW000   1 entry from E070C exported (T01K900118).
4 ETW000   1 entry from E07T exported (T01K900118*).
4 ETW678Xstart export of "R3TRPROGZPFLLIST                     " ...
4 ETW000   1 entry from TADIR exported (R3TRPROGZPFLLIST).
4 ETW000 REPOS ZPFLLIST AM exported
4 ETW000 REPOTDZPFLLIST AM exported
3 ETW679 end export of "R3TRPROGZPFLLIST                     ".
4 ETW678Xstart export of "R3TRPROGZPFLNEUE                     " ...
4 ETW000   1 entry from TADIR exported (R3TRPROGZPFLNEUE).
4 ETW000 REPOS ZPFLNEUE AM exported
4 ETW000 REPOTDZPFLNEUE AM exported
4 ETW000 DYNPS ZPFLNEUE0100 exported
4 ETW000 DYNPS ZPFLNEUE0200 exported
4 ETW000 DYNPS ZPFLNEUE0300 exported
```

```
4 ETW000 DYNPS ZPFLNEUE0400 exported
4 ETW000   4 entries from D020T exported (ZPFLNEUE*).
4 ETW000  23 entries from D021T exported (ZPFLNEUE*).
4 ETW000   1 entry from EUDB exported (CUZPFLNEUE                    *).
4 ETW000   1 entry from D344L exported (ZPFLNEUE*).
4 ETW000 CUAL ZPFLNEUE0100     exported
4 ETW000 CUAL ZPFLNEUE0200     exported
4 ETW000 CUAL ZPFLNEUE0300     exported
4 ETW000 CUAL ZPFLNEUE400      exported
4 ETW000 CUAT ZPFLNEUED exported
3 ETW679 end export of "R3TRPROGZPFLNEUE                          ".
4 ETW000 T01K900118 released.
4 ETW000 18497 bytes written.
4 ETW000 Transport overhead 17.4 %.
4 ETW000 Data compressed to 35.2 %.
4 ETW000 Duration: 5 sec (3699 bytes/sec).
4 ETW000 COMMIT (18497).
4 ETW000
4 ETW000 Summary:
4 ETW000
4 ETW000   1 COMML exported
4 ETW000   1 COMMT exported
4 ETW000   4 DYNPS exported
4 ETW000   4 DYNPT exported
4 ETW000   2 REPOS exported
4 ETW000   2 REPOT exported
4 ETW000   4 CUAL exported
4 ETW000   1 CUAT exported
4 ETW000 Totally 20 Objects exported
4 ETW000 Totally 3 tabentries exported
4 ETW000
4 ETW000 Disconnected from Database.
4 ETW000 End of Transport.
4 ETW000 date&time: 02.07.1996 - 15:56:21
1 ETP150 MAIN EXPORT
1 ETP110 end date and time    : "19960702155622"
1 ETP111 exit code            : "0"
1 ETP199 ######################################
```

The log describes the export of objects `R3TR PROG ZPFLLIST` and `R3TR PROG ZPFLNEUE`. Note that choosing the complex object type `R3TR PROG` causes the transport system to transport the corresponding screens automatically.

After a successful export, the transport system normally executes a test import. The test serves to uncover any irregularities during transport as early as possible and to give the user an opportunity to correct any error conditions. During a transport, the system checks, for example, if the object intended for import exists under repair or even as an original in the target system. If the test import has not yet taken place, execute it manually with the function *Trigger test import*.

Working with transport tracing and evaluating individual transport logs is quite comfortable in R/3. What happens, however, when the system is unavailable (during an update, for example) or the user interface (SAPGUI) cannot be used because of terminal problems? Users should have access to transport tracing even in these situations. Accordingly, users should know how to find transport logs at the operating system level and which files contain the individual logs.

Transport logs are stored in the subdirectory `log` of the central transport directory (see Section 7.9.5). Despite the wide variety of hardware and operating systems used with R/3, the system features both standard logging of transport steps and systematic naming of log files. The following description of the syntax used to name log files in the subdirectory `log` should help users in the case of emergency:

Log file name:= <Source system><Action><6 places>.<Target system>

The field action determines the transport step and can record the following values:

- A → Activation of the repository
- C → C source transport
- D → Import of application-defined objects (e.g., : forms)
- E → `R3trans` export
- G → Generation of programs and screen images
- H → `R3trans` repository import
- I → `R3trans` main import
- L → `R3trans` import of the command files
- M → Activation of the enqueue modules
- P → Test import
- R → Execution of the XPRA programs after an update
- T → `R3trans` import of table entries
- V → Setting the version ID
- X → Export of application-defined objects

The workbench organizer permits the assignment of attributes to transport requests after importation. If errors appeared during a given transport step and have been subsequently corrected by error analysis and a repeated transport, users can assign the attribute *Error corrected* to the request. The attribute *Subsequently tested* signals the workbench organizer that the user is convinced that the object intended for import functions correctly. After marking the requests with attributes, the workbench organizer permits deleting them from the display. To keep an overview, users should take advantage of this feature from time to time.

7.9.5 Transport directories

Initialization of the correction and transport system includes several steps: configuration of the workbench organizers, maintenance of the control table with transaction se06 and setting up the transport directories at the operating system level.

The actual transport of DE objects between R/3 systems takes place in two steps. The first step exports the data and stores it in intermediate files of the operating system. Note that the system stores the files in a special, database-independent format. After the export, the system performs the second step, the import into the target system. A correctly set-up system will execute the export automatically after release of the transport request.

Administrators must trigger the import themselves. They may, however, choose to automate the process with utilities provided by the operating system (e.g., cron under UNIX or at in Windows NT).

The transport control program tp plays a central role in this export/import mechanism. To ensure that this program functions correctly (see Section 7.9.7), the administrator must create a directory structure dependent upon the operating system.

Among other purposes, the directory tree serves as a storage medium for transport programs, parameter files, exported data and control files. When an R/3 system is installed with the installation program R3INST, the transport directories are created automatically. The difference in this regard between the operating systems supported by SAP is rather small: each system has its own naming convention. Accordingly, the general comments made below for UNIX also apply, with modification, to other operating systems.

The central transport directory serves as the starting point: in UNIX it is the directory /usr/sap/trans. Figure 7.22 shows the most important subdirectories under this central directory.

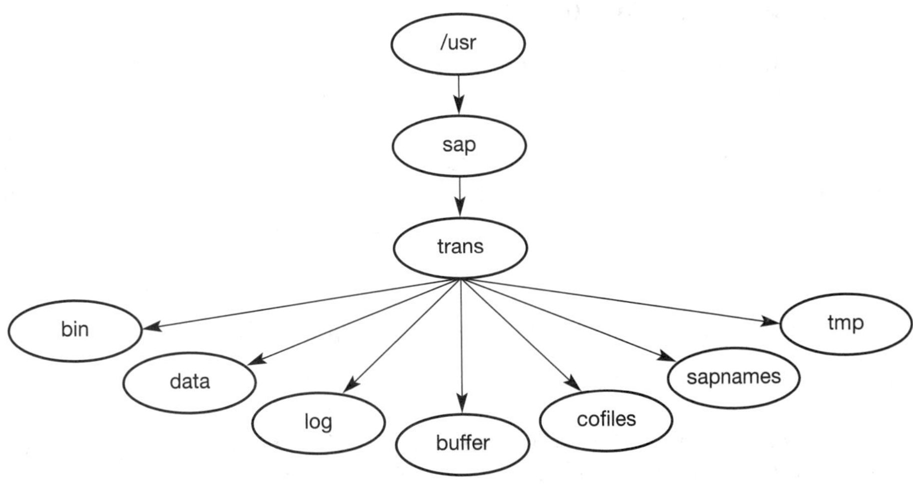

Figure 7.22 Transport directories of the CTS

The subdirectory `bin` contains the transport programs and the global transport parameter file `TPPARAM` (see Section 7.9.6).

A data file in the subdirectory `data` stores the exported objects of an R/3 system. The file name consists of a leading `R`, the sequential request number and the source system, as the following example shows. The data file of transport request SAPK900118 from system T01 is called R900118.T01.

The subdirectory `log` stores the transport logs. Several log files inform the user about the updates or results of executed transports. View the log with transaction `se09` (see Section 7.9.4); the transaction offers much more ease of use than the operating system editor.

The files stored in the subdirectories `buffer` and `cofiles` contain control information for the execution of transports. For each system within the system group, the subdirectory `buffer` contains a file named <SID>, the request buffer. The subdirectory `cofiles` stores information on transport requests. These files indicate which steps of the transport have already taken place and the return codes that ended each step.

When setting up a system hierarchy as required by the correction and transport systems, the administrator must decide which computer will house the central transport directory `/usr/sap/trans` (UNIX). This computer functions as the transport server. Other computers in the system group mount the central transport directory via NFS with the mount point `/usr/sap/trans`. All users of the various systems must have read and write access to the files of the central transport directory. For UNIX, set the right of the subdirectory to 777. This access ensures that each R/3 system can use the path `/usr/sap/trans` to access the files in the transport directories.

The central transport directory thus serves as the connecting point for all the R/3 systems counted in the configuration. Only this centralization permits the automation of transports.

7.9.6 Transport parameters

The system parameters relevant to transports are set in the parameter file `TPPARAM`, located in the subdirectory `bin` of the central transport directory.

The transport control program `tp` (see Section 7.9.7) uses the parameters as a profile for its work by evaluating the parameter lines. Users can define two types of parameters: those that apply to all SAP systems (global parameters) and those that apply only to a special system (local parameters). Define global parameters as follows:

```
<parameter>=<value>
```

Local parameters begin with the SAP system name, using the following notation:

```
<system_name>/<parameter>=<value>
```

Users can limit the validity of parameters to a specific operating system or database. Parameters specific to an operating system are written as follows:

```
<cpu>|<parameter> = <value>
```

Note the following options for cpu:

```
<cpu>:= aix | hp-ux | osf1 | sinix | sunos | wnt (Windows NT)
```

To define parameters relevant only to a specific database system, use the following syntax:

```
<db>:<parameter> = <value>
<db>:= ora (Oracle) | inf (Informix) | ada (ADABAS D)
```

When setting operating system-specific parameters, use the vertical bar (|) as a dividing character. Use a colon (:) as the dividing character when setting database-specific parameters.

The control program tp uses the settings in the file TPPARAM to determine the location of the central transport directory, the name of the database and which computer runs the database.

Configuration of the workbench organizer updates the parameter file TPPARAM. If the file does not yet exist, configuration creates it. After establishing the system group given in example B1, the parameter file appears as follows:

```
#@(#) TPPARAM.sap       20.6    SAP      95/03/28
#############################################################
#    Template of TPPARAM for UNIX                           #
#############################################################
# First we specify global values for some parameters        #
# then the system-specific incarnation of special parameters #
#############################################################

#############################################################
#                       Global Parameters                   #
#############################################################
transdir         = /usr/sap/trans/
dbname           = $(system)
alllog           = ALOG$(syear)$(yweek)
syslog           = SLOG$(syear)$(yweek).$(system)

##############################################################
#                       System-specific Parameters           #
##############################################################

##################################################
# E01 (Application development)                  #
##################################################
E01/dbhost       = ch
##################################################
# T01 (Test / Integration)                       #
##################################################
T01/dbhost       = liw
```

```
##################################################
# P01 (Production)                               #
##################################################
P01/dbhost        = rh
##################################################
# S01 (Training / Recovery-Tests)                #
##################################################
S01/dbhost        = fst
```

These specifications already allow for an exchange of objects within the system group.

The parameter `transdir` sets the central transport directory. The transport control program `tp` defines the files that store general log information by reading the parameters `allog` and `syslog`. The parameters also use built-in variables, explained in Table 7.11.

Table 7.11 Variables in TPPARAM

Variable names	*Meaning*
$(cpu)	CPU name (alphaosf | hp | rm600 | rs6000 | sun | wnt)
$(cpu2)	Operating system (aix | hp-ux | osf1 | sinix | sunos | wnt)
$(dname)	Weekday (SUN,MON,...)
$(mday)	Day of the month (1–31)
$(mname)	Name of the month (JAN,...)
$(mon)	Month (01–12)
$(system)	SAP system name
$(wday)	Weekday (00–06, Sunday=00)
$(yday)	Day of the year (001–366)
$(year)	Year (four places)
$(syear)	Year (two places)
$(yweek)	Calendar week (00–53)

Many different parameters can influence how the transport control program `tp` functions. Most have rather standard default values, so that users normally can work with a simple parameter file TPPARAM. Updating to a new version of R/3 software, however, is far more complicated. In this case, `tp` must be able to start and stop the system. The following additions to the file TPPARAM would accomplish such tasks for the system P01:

```
P01/startsap    =    /home/p01adm/startsap_rh_00 r3
P01/stopsap     =    /home/p01adm/stopsap_rh_00 r3
```

The settings given in the parameter file TPPARAM show very clearly that the name of a system within a system group must be unique.

7.9.7 The transport control program tp

The transport control program tp (transports and programs) controls transports between R/3 system and version updates of R/3 software. The transport program R3trans and various other tools execute transports. The wide range of functions provided by the transport program R3trans and its rather complicated use often make a direct call of this program superfluous. This book therefore does not present a detailed description of R3trans.

The advantages of tp over and against R3trans lie primarily in its ease of use and simplified parameter settings. In its very structure the program protects users from serious error conditions. No incorrect sequences when importing objects can occur, as tp automatically executes imports into the target system in the same order as the export from the source system.

Detailed transport logs allows the system administrator to trace and analyze transports (see Section 7.9.4).

Developers can begin an export of objects in R/3 with a mouse click by releasing a transportable change request or a transport request. Administrators, however, can first encounter the transport control program when importing objects. As true of many other programs, tp becomes much easier to use once users possess a basic knowledge of its implementation.

In addition to the preconditions described in Section 7.9.5, error-free use of tp in the target R/3 system requires configuration of at least two background processes (instance profile). These processes effect the transport steps implemented in ABAP/4. Call tp once all these preconditions have been met.

The following section explains the most important tp calls and options. Three essential types of tp calls exist:

- Commands to export objects,
- Commands to import objects,
- Utilities to control transports.

Exports, triggered from the R/3 system by release of a request, normally take place transparently to the user. The following comments shed some light on the automatic procedures involved in an export.

Objects are exported with tp at the operating system level as follows:

```
tp  export  <transport_request>
```

<Transport_request> stands for the document number assigned by the system, T01K90017, for example.

An export consists of a maximum of three partial export steps. The individual partial steps can be executed separately by the appropriate call options. The following overview describes the three phases and provides the corresponding tp call in brackets:

- R3trans export (tp r3e <transport_request>),
- Export of application-defined objects (tp sde <transport_request>),

- Test import (tp tst <transport_request> <SAP_system_name>).

Execution of the partial step R3trans export always takes place. This step exports the data and places a transport request (import claim) in the buffer of the target system.

Exportation of application-defined objects takes place only when such objects actually exist in the request.

The test import provides early recognition of conflicts or irregularities in the correction and transport system.

In actual practice, responsibility for exports lies with individual developers. Administrators, however, normally execute imports. To avoid blocking the operation of an up-and-running system, imports should take place during periods of lowered system activity. Start a complete import with the command:

```
tp  import  all  <SAP_system_name>
```

In this context, 'complete' means importation of all the transport requests stored in the buffer of the target system (buffer/<SID>).

The import process also consists of partial steps. These include:

- Repository import with R3trans,
- Activation of the repository,
- Calling the distributor,
- Structure conversion (tables),
- Moving the nametabs,
- Main import with R3trans (all data except table contents),
- Activation of enqueue modules,
- Structure conversion (matchcode objects),
- Import of application-defined objects,
- Execution of XPRA programs,
- Generation of programs and screen images.

The importation of objects is optimized so that the system runs only the import steps actually required for a given object. Imports can be restarted. After discovery and correction of an error, the same tp call continues the import. Normal operation will rarely require separate execution of individual steps.

During importation of client-dependent objects, note that the system imports objects into the same client as the source client. If the user desires an import into a different client, expand the import command with the parameter client=<target_client> as shown in the example:

```
tp import all client=007
```

The command tp import all automatically executes an importation into the target system in the same order as the export. In other words, users can introduce no errors regarding the sequence. A different circumstance prevails when importing individual requests. As long as users maintain the sequence of the export or make sure that no objects overlap or clash, no problems will appear. However, if users fail to heed these cautions, older versions may replace newer ones. If administrators cannot determine the correct sequence and still wish to execute the partial import ahead of time, they should use the following call:

```
tp import <transport_request> <SAP_system_name> U0
```

The option `U0` (see Table 7.12) ensures that the request remains in the request buffer of the target system and is reimported during the next `tp import all` (at the correct time according to the export sequence). This procedure presumes, of course, that the object involved has not changed in the meantime. Import individual requests only by way of exception to avoid redoubling efforts (reimportation). Table 7.12 lists additional unconditional modes. If using several options, link them together (e.g., U01).

Imports ready for execution are placed in the request buffer of the appropriate system. The transport control program `tp` uses this information to determine the imports it will perform. A file with the name of the SAP system represents a given system's buffer in a given system (e.g., SAP system P01 → buffer/P01).

Implementation of some transport steps, such as activation of repository objects, structural conversions or generation of programs and screen images, takes place in ABAP/4. Such implementation requires finely tuned communication between the transport control program `tp` and the ABAP/4 programs. An R/3 system containing transports from other systems must, therefore, be configured with two background processes. Make sure that the instance profile contains the appropriate entry for the parameter `rdisp/wp_no_btc`, which indicates the number of defined background processes.

Table 7.12 Unconditional modes for `tp`

Mode	*Transport step*	*Meaning*
0	Import	No deletion of the request in the request buffer of the target system after the import. Unconditional mode 1 is set in the request buffer for the request instead.
1	Export Import	Ignores incorrect request status. The request can be imported again (complete).
2	Import	Originals in the target system can be rewritten.
3	Import	System-dependent objects can be rewritten.
4	Import	Ignores that a change request was originally addressed to a different system.
5	Import	Although the target system is a consolidation system, objects can originate in any system.
6	Import	Objects in unconfirmed repair can be rewritten.
8	Import	Ignores limits to table classification.
9	Import	Ignores locks for transport type.

As of version 3.x, schedule the background job RDDIMPDP in all clients. Perform the scheduling as user DDIC in each client. Use program RDDNEWPP to schedule event-controlled execution of the background job. Use the older, time-controlled scheduling only in exceptional cases, when, for example, no communication is possible between tp and the message server. Program RDDPUTPP schedules time-controlled execution of RDDIMPDP (time interval: five minutes).

Transaction sm37 (*Tools → Administration → Jobs → Job overview*) displays the need for scheduling. We recommend that administrators choose * to display all scheduled jobs. If scheduling was successful, job RDDIMPDP or RDDIMPDP_CLIENT_xxx appears in the job overview, where xxx stands for the client number. In addition, tp offers this function. The following call returns information on whether or not RDDIMPDP is scheduled in system P01 (client 000):

```
tp checkimpdp P01
```

The system starts an event-controlled RDDIMPDP when the event SAP_TRIGGER_RDDIMPDP occurs.

The program RDDIMPDP actually functions as a dispatcher (task distributor). Tables TRBAT and TRJOB function as the communication link between tp and RDDIMPDP (ABAP/4 program).

After the actual import of the pure data (R3trans), tp triggers the event SAP_TRIGGER_RDDIMPDP. Using the entries in table TRBAT, RDDIMPDP determines which tasks require execution and starts the appropriate ABAP/4 programs (ABAPs) to implement the individual transport steps. Table 7.13 (see also the on-line documentation for RDDIMPDP) summarizes the ABAPs involved and the transport steps each implements.

RDDIMPDP can also recognize interrupted import steps by evaluating the entries in table TRJOB.

An example will demonstrate the communication between tp and RDDIMPDP:

The transport control program tp places the actions to be performed for transport request P01K900001 in table TRBAT. The following overview shows the contents of the table as it would appear after tp makes its entries and before the start of RDDIMPDP:

TRCORR	FUNCTION	RETCODE	TIMESTMP
P01K900001	J	9999	00000001
P01K900002	J	9999	00000002
HEADER	J	B	1996031815204456

The column TRCORR contains the transport request number. The column FUNCTION determines the action to be performed: possible entries include those given in Table 7.13. In this case, the function J signals that the transport request contains repository objects that require activation.

The column RETCODE provides information on the status of the work. The values mean:

- 9999 → Step waiting for execution,
- 8888 → Step is active,
- <=12 → Step has ended.

Table 7.13 ABAPs for implementation of partial transport steps

Function	Job name	Meaning
A		Mass activation of repository objects (old activator).
B		Mass activation of repository objects marked in table TACOB.
J	RDDMASGL	Mass activation of repository objects (except enqueue modules) (new activator).
M	RDDMASGL	Mass activation of matchcodes and lock objects (enqueue modules).
S	RDDDIS0L	Analysis of the database objects intended for conversion.
N | O	RDDGEN0L	Conversion of structural changes to database objects contained in table TBATG.
Y	RDDGEN0L	Conversion of structural changes to matchcode objects contained in table TBATG.
X	RDDDIC0L	Export of application-defined objects.
D	RDDDIC1L	Import of application-defined objects.
E	RDDVERSE	Version update during export.
V	RDDVERSL	Version update during import.
R	RDDEXECL	Execution of XPRAs.
G	RDDDIC3L	Generation of programs and screens.

RDDIMPDP reads the column TIMESTMP to determine the order of the actions that require execution. Completion of an action updates the TIMESTMP entry with the time that the action ended.

The HEADER entry in table TRBAT plays a special role. The transport control program tp uses it to inform the task distributor RDDIMPDP that it can start processing the individual requests. After it starts, RDDIMPDP sets the RETCODE value of the header to R (running) and starts the program appropriate to the value of FUNCTION. A running import might contain the following TRBAT entries:

TRCORR	FUNCTION	RETCODE	TIMESTMP
P01K900001	J	0	1996031816002034
P01K900002	J	8888	000002
HEADER	J	R	1996031815204456

This snapshot indicates the successful completion of the import step of transport request P01K900001 and that the mass activation of transport P01K900002 is currently running. After processing all requests, RDDIMPDP sets the header entry to F (finished).

While RDDIMPDP processes all requests in table TRBAT sequentially, tp also monitors the contents of table TRBAT. As soon as it encounters a completed action, it copies the log to the log directory and deletes the TRBAT entry. After extracting all logs, it also deletes the header.

RDDIMPDP uses table `TRJOB` to determine if a job required by a request is still active or if it terminated. To do so, it compares the `TRJOB` entry with the corresponding `TRBAT` entry.

Note some additional `tp` calls and their use.

If, after an export, a user determines that other systems also require deliveries, issue a import request manually with the following command:

```
tp addtobuffer <transport_request> <SAP_system_name>
```

Unconditional mode 4 (see Table 7.12) can trigger an import:

```
tp import <transport_request> <SAP_system_name> U4
```

To check if a connection to a special system is possible, use the following `tp` call:

```
tp connect <SID>
```

This call corresponds to a connect test. The following call provides global information on an SAP system:

```
tp getdbinfo <SID>
```

The output might appear as follows:

```
DBAHOME=/adabas/P01/db
DBACONN=P01
KERNVER=30D
SAPVERS=30D
DOKVERS=30D
```

Calling the transport control program `tp` with no parameters or invalid parameters provides an overview of all its functions. To receive more information on a special command, enter it without parameters.

A Authorization formulas

Hardware requirements. The data and formulas that follow were taken from Buck-Emden and Galimow (1996). Some suggestions and recommendations have been repeated verbatim.

Consider these remarks only as a first step in estimating the requirements of R/3 version 2.1, and only very carefully as an approach to R/3 version 2.2. Each case requires the services of a configuration specialist. Note the following abbreviations:

N	Total number of active users
Napp	Number of active users on the application server
PZ	Required CPU performance of the central system in SPECint92
PDB	Required CPU performance of the database server in SPECint92
Papp	Required CPU performance of the application server in SPECint92
MZ	Main memory requirements of the centralized system in MB
MDB	Main memory requirements of the database server in MB
Mapp	Main memory requirements of the application server in MB

We assume between 32 and 256 active users and that each user executes two to three screen changes. The RDBMS in use also influences the suggestions. These calculations depend on an Oracle RDBMS. If using a different RDBMS, expect differences in the final calculations. ADABAS D, for example, demands less disk space.

Calcualte the **CPU performance** as presented in Table A.1:

Table A.1 CPU performance requirements

Application	*Centralized system*	*Client/server system*
FI	PZ = 1.1 N	PDB = 0.3 N PApp = 0.8 NApp
MM	PZ = 2.5 N	PDB = 0.9 N PApp = 1.7 NApp
SD	PZ = 2.8 N	PDB = 1.3 N PApp = 1.6 NApp

For mixed operations involving different applications, add CPU performance depending on the actual users to calculate the total CPU performance required.

Calculate **main memory requirements** as presented in Table A.2:

Table A.2 Calculation of main memory requirements

Application	*Centralized system*	*Client/server system*
FI	MZ = 45 + 2 N	MDB = 50 + 0.5 N MApp = 35 + 1.7 NApp
MM	MZ = 65 + 2.2 N	MDB = 55 + 0.7 N MApp = 45 + 2.2 NApp
SD	MZ = 75 + 2.5 N	MDB = 60 + 0.7 N MApp = 50 + 2.2 NApp

For mixed operations involving different applications, take the highest constant value and add it to the variable main memory requirements for each application and number of users.

- *Disk space requirements*
  Depending on the RDBMS, between 4.5 and 6.5GB of disk space is required for a first installation without application data.
- *Performance capacity between the presentation server and the application server*
  Each screen change requires the transfer of approximately 1.5KB of data. Estimate by using the following formula: transfer rate = 2 N.
- *Performance capacity between the application server and the database server*
  Count on a transfer rate of about 2 megabits per second. For installations of a few hundred users, Ethernet or Token Ring networks are sufficient. For larger installations we recommend the use of high speed networks such as FDDI.

The calculation formulas have developed further since the introduction of R/3 version 3, primarily because of the new main memory management. Nonetheless, estimating the needs of an R/3 installation for a specific customer environment is no mean feat. System requirements depend on several factors: the performance of the hardware (computers, networks, etc.), the system software and the interplay between the two. Suggestions for configuration are therefore strongly influenced by test results at SAP and the experience of 'test customers' and SAP partners. The Early Watch Group and SAP's benchmark center collect information and prepare it for further use.

The following formulas and suggestions come from the groups noted above and indicate estimates for a specific situation. They are also property of SAP. We wish to name Dr Uwe Hommel, Bernd F. Lober, Dr Ulrich Marquard and Dr Wolfgang Müller as the authors and researchers of the formulas and specifications. As usual, neither SAP AG, the persons named above nor the authors of this book take any responsibility for any possible errors or as the result of using the formulas and specifications.

The following assumptions were employed:

- Ten users share a dialog work process.

- Three dialog work processes always have one batch work process and one update work process.
- The batch work process and the update work process run on the same application server.

N	Total number of active users (32 ⩽ N ⩽ 512)
Napp	Number of active users on the application server (32 ⩽ N ⩽ 512)
MZ	Main memory requirements of the centralized system in MB
MDB	Main memory requirements of the database server in MB
Mapp	Main memory requirements of the application server in MB

As displayed in Table A.3, the **main memory requirements** can be determined. The values calculated serve much more as a minimum threshold than as an average. The application FI can serve as a model for WM, SD for MM and CO, and SD for PS.

Table A.3 Calculating the main memory requirements in R/3 release 3

Application	*Centralized system*	*Client/server system*
FI	MZ = 90MB + 2.9MB * N	MDB = 100MB + 0.3MB * N MApp = 70MB + 2.5MB * NApp
PP	MZ = 180MB + 5.7MB * N	MDB = 150MB + 0.7MB * N MApp = 120MB + 5.3MB * NApp
SD	MZ = 150MB + 3.7MB * N	MDB = 130MB + 0.3MB * N MApp = 100MB + 3.3MB * NApp

Table A.4 assumes an Oracle system optimized for very high throughput. Values for other configurations are not yet available. In such cases, request help from both responsible groups at SAP.

Table A.4 Calculating the main memory requirements in R/3 release 3 for optimal throughput

Application	*Centralized system*	*Client/server system*
FI	MZ = 102MB + 3.9MB * N	MDB = 50MB + 0.54B * N MApp = 52MB + 3.5MB * NApp
FI. CO	MZ = 128MB + 4.8MB * N	MDB = 50MB + 0.4MB * N MApp= 78MB + 4.4MB * NApp
FI. CO. SD	MZ = 228MB + 4.8MB * N	MDB= 100MB + 0.4MB * N MApp= 128MB + 4.4MB * NApp
FI. CO. PP	MZ = 308MB + 4.8MB * N	MDB = 150MB + 0.4MB * N MApp = 158MB + 4.4MB * NApp
FI. CO. SD. PP	MZ = 358MB + 4.8MB * N	MDB = 180MB + 0.4MB * N MApp = 178MB + 4.4MB * NApp

The formulas and suggestions can be updated at any time. The broader the customer base of R/3 release 3 becomes, the more information available to determine criteria. Accordingly, always request the most recent figures from SAP.

B Profile entries

Many of the parameters described in the following can be assigned to a group of parameters that the R/3 administrator can manipulate. Only SAP employees or SAP consultants should change others. However, even when customers may adjust certain parameters, they should avail themselves of expert advice before making any changes. Unfortunately, no clear guidelines define the parameters belonging to either group. In any case, system installation provides some tools that help check parameter settings. Note the following tool:

sappfpar

To check the parameters, call:

sappfpar pf=<instance_profile> check

In many cases, using the values suggested during installation or the default parameters of the R/3 system is sufficient. The following parameter groups cannot be uniquely assigned to a particular profile. For example, the 'rdisp' entry exists in both the standard profile and the instance profile.

The following presents the most important parameters of R/3 version 3.0 and their meaning.

Configurations for the ABAP/4 environment

abap/atradir	This parameter sets up the ABAP/4 trace file. Do not change this parameter.
abap/atrapath	This parameter specifies the generic path names of ABAP/4 files in the host system. Change only in case of emergency.
abap/atrasizequota	Defines the total memory for the ABAP/4 trace file. The administrator can change the definition.
abap/buffersize	This parameter sets the size of ABAP/4 program buffers in SHM. The administrator can change the setting.
abap/dumponerror	This parameter triggers a system dump (core), if the R/3 system displays an ABAP/4 error message identical to the parameter value (name or error number). The administrator can change the entry.
abap/editor_file	The ABAP/4 editor uses these generic names for host system files. Only SAP can change this parameter.

abap/heaplimit	This parameter sets the amount of memory (in bytes) available for a work process. The work process restarts if the limit is exceeded. The administrator can change this parameter.
abap/heap_area_dia	This parameter limits the memory requirements for a user text to local working memory. The administrator can change this parameter.
abap/heap_area_tota	This parameter sets the memory requirements in the process-local working memory on an application server. The setting affects all user contexts. The administrator can change this parameter.
abap/ignore_icc	This parameter sets the check procedure for ABAP/4 consistency. Only SAP may change this parameter.
abap/locale_ctype	This parameter determines the character set used by the R/3 system. The administrator can change this parameter. Normal circumstances do not require changing the SAP default setting.
install/codepage/appl_server	This parameter sets the character set used by the SAP system to store data. It must be the same as abap/locale_ctype. The same rules apply as for abap/locale_ctype.
abap/swap_reserve	This parameter limits the process-local memory requirements for each user. The administrator can change this parameter.
abap/use_paging	This parameter shows whether to use old (value 1) or new (value 0) memory management. The administrator can change this parameter.
abap/warnings	This parameter sets the reactions of the R/3 system to warnings issued by the ABAP/4 runtime system. The administrator can change this parameter.

Alert parameters configure the CCMS 'Alert Monitor'

Do not change the alert parameters!

auth/check_value_write_on	This parameter determines whether to switch the recording of failed authorization checks (at system logon) on or off for each user. The administrator can change this parameter. A value of 0 switches the trace function off; the value of 1 switches it on.

Extended memory

em/blocksize_KB	This parameter specifies the size of segments allocated by the SAP memory pool if a user context exceeds the size of the default memory area (roll area). SAP can change the setting.

em/intial_size_MB	This parameter determines the size of the SHM area for the system's extended memory. Only SAP should change this setting.
em/stat_log_size_MB	Used for statistical purposes in new memory management (internal to SAP).
em/stat_log_timeout	Used for statistical purposes in new memory management (internal to SAP).
enque/table_size	This parameter specifies the size of the memory-resistant enqueue table in KB. Users can change this parameter.

Exe parameters: program names

These parameters provide SAP program names; only SAP should change them.

FN_parameters

The FN_parameter specifies file names used by the R/3 system and may be changed by SAP only.

FT_parameters

The FT_parameter contains file specifications used by the R/3 system. Only SAP may change the parameter.

gw parameters

This parameter group configures the SAP gateway server.

INSTANCE parameters

These parameters determine servers or instances; they are set automatically.

ipc parameters

This group of parameters configure inter-process communication and SHM.

ipc/sem_mon_level	This parameter activates semaphore statistics for the R/3 performance monitor. Only SAP may change this parameter.
ipc/sem_mon_rec	Sets the numbers of ring buffer records for statistical evaluation of semaphores. The administrator can change this parameter.
Ipc/shm_malloc_reserve	This parameter is required only for very rare operating system implementations. It is normally set to 0. It specifies the reserve area in bytes for later 'mallocs.'
ipc/shm_psize_xx	Specifies the size of logical SHM segments that administer the R/3 system. 'xx' is a two-character ID.

login parameters

This group of parameters configure the behavior of the R/3 system at login.

login/fails_to_session_end	This parameter specifies the repeat rate for login attempts. The administrator can change this setting.
login/fails_to_user_lock	This parameter specifies the number of login attempts permitted a given user before the system excludes him or her from additional attempts. The administrator determines the setting.
login/min_password_lng	This parameter configures the minimal length of the password. The administrator determines the setting.
login/password_expiration_time	This parameter sets the expiration date for a password. The administrator can change this setting.
login/system_client	This parameter specifies the default client at logon. The administrator can change the settings to this parameter.
login/no_automatic_user_sap	Setting this parameter to a value greater than 0 (zero) cancels the special status of the SAP user 'SAP*.' The setting should be contained in DEFAULT.PFL.

rdisp parameters

This parameter configures the dispatcher and its environment.

rdisp/TRACE	Setting the value range to 0–3 activates the developer trace (see Section 2.6). The administrator can change this parameter.
rdisp/appc_ca_blk_no	This parameter sets the number of SHM blocks for CPI-C communication. The administrator can change this parameter.
rdisp/autoabaptime	Process monitoring requires this parameter. SAP determines the setting.
rdisp/myname	This parameter assigns a user-defined, unique name to the application server. Background processing requires this parameter.
rdisp/btcname	This parameter specifies the name of the server established for background processing. The administrator can change this parameter.
rdisp/btctime	The administrator can use this parameter to determine the interval (in seconds) at which the background scheduler starts on a background processor.
rdisp/bufrefmode	This parameter specifies the possible settings for buffer synchronization of the R/3 system.

rdisp/bufreftime	This parameter specifies, in seconds, the interval at which to turn over the local buffer in a distributed application. The administrator can change this parameter.
rdisp/elem_per_queue	The administrator uses this parameter to determine the number of queries in a request queue in the dispatcher. The administrator can change this parameter.
rdisp/enqname	This parameter specifies the computer running the enqueue server.
rdisp/mshost	This parameter specifies the name of the computer running the message server.
rdisp/PG_LOCAL	This parameter dimensions the local paging buffer. The number specifies the size in 8KB blocks. The administrator can configure this parameter.
rdisp/PG_MAXFS	This parameter sets the maximum size of paging files in 8KB blocks. The administrator can change this parameter.
rdisp/PG_SHM	This parameter determines the size of the paging area in SHM. This size is counted in 8KB blocks. The administrator can change this parameter.
rdisp/ROLL_MAXFS	Here the administrator determines the maximum size of roll files in 8KB blocks.
rdisp/ROLL-SHM	Here the administrator specifies the size of SHM segments for the roll system in 8KB blocks.
rdisp/vbname	This parameter repeats the name of the computer running the update server.
rdisp/wp_ca_blk_no	This parameter determines the number of blocks for work process communication. The following parameters determine the size.
rdisp/wp_ca_btc_size	This default parameter should not be changed. It specifies the size of a block for work process communication (default value 12KB).
rdisp/wp_no_btc	The administrator configures the number of batch work processes with this parameter.
rdisp/wp_no_dia	This parameter allows the administrator to determine the number of dialog work processes.
rdisp/wp_no_enq	This parameter specifies the number of enqueue work processes that the administrator can set.
rdisp/wp_no_spo	The administrator can set the number of spool work processes with this parameter.
rdisp/wp_no_vb	The administrator determines the number of update work processes with this parameter.

rsdb parameters

This group of parameters configures the database interface.

rsdb/cua/buffersize	The administrator can set the size of the CUA buffer in KB with this parameter.
rsdb/dbconnects	The administrator configures the number of logons to the database during an R/3 system start with this parameter.
rsdb/dbhost	The administrator can set the name of the host system running the RDBMS with this parameter.
rsdb/dbid	This unchangeable parameter specifies the SID of the database server.
rsdb/ntab/ftabsize	The administrator can use configure this parameter to determine the size of the 'nametab buffer' in KB.
rsdb/oracle_home	This parameter should not be changed: it specifies the home directory of the Oracle RDBMS.
rsdb/oracle_host	This parameter specifies the name of the host system running the Oracle RDBMS. It may not be changed.
rsdb/oracle_sid	This parameter specifies the SID of the Oracle RDBMS. It may not be changed.

rslg parameters

These parameters configure the system log.

rslg/central/file	SAP specifies the name of the active central system log with this parameter.
rslg/central/old_file	This parameter specifies the name of the previous system log. Only SAP may change the parameter.
rslg/collect_daemon/exe_file	This parameter specifies the name of the collector process for the central log. Only SAP may modify this parameter.
rslg/collect_daemon/host	The administrator determines the host system running the central system log with this parameter.
rslg/collect_daemon/listen_port	Specification of sockets for network communication of the collector process. The administrator can change this parameter.
rslg/collect_daemon/talk_port	Specification of sockets for network communication of the collector process. The administrator can change this parameter.
rslg/local/file	SAP uses this parameter to determine the name of the local system log files.

rslg/max_diskspace/central	This parameter specifies the maximum size, in bytes, of the current and previous log files for the central case. The administrator can change this parameter.
rslg/send_daemon/exe_file	This parameter determines the name of the send process program. Only SAP may change this parameter.
rslg/send_daemon/listen_port	The administrator configures the send process socket with this parameter.
rslg/send_daemon/talk_port	The administrator configures the send process socket with this parameter.

rspo parameters

The SAP spool system parameters belong to this group.

rspo/host_spool/print	With this parameter the administrator specifies the output command for the host spool system.
rspo/archive_format	This parameter determines if the output format contains print control instructions (as of release 3.0) or not (for release 2.1).
rspo/default_archiver	This parameter specifies the default output device for print lists.
rspo/global_shm/printer_list	This parameter specifies the maximum number of output requests. It should not be changed.
rspo/host_spool/query	Use this parameter to specify a command to query the status of an output request from the host spool system. The parameter is valid only for UNIX systems and can be changed by the administrator.
rspo/lpq/temp_disable_slow	The administrator can use this parameter to configure an interval during which the host system output device must confirm a request made of it.
rspo/pq/temp_disable_time	This parameter specifies an interval during which the host system output device remains disabled. The administrator can change this parameter. The default interval is set to 300 seconds.
rspo/lpq/warn_time	This interval determines, in seconds, when the system should write a warning in the system log if the output device does not respond to a status query.
rspo/spool_id/chunk	This parameter determines the number of R/3 system spool IDs that can be reserved simultaneously.
rspo/store_location	This parameter defines where the TemSe system stores data.

rspo/tcp/retries	This parameter determines the number of attempts made to address a remote output device.
rspo/tcp/retrytime	This parameter sets the interval that can elapse between two logon attempts to a remote output device.
rspo/tcp/timeout/connect	This parameter limits the time during which a connection to a remote output device must be established. Requires connection types 'U' and 'S.'
rspo/tcp/timeout/read rspo/tcp/timeout/write	These parameters set the interval during which an individual data packet must be read by or sent to a remote output device.
rspo/to_host/datafile	This parameter specifies the name of a temporary file sent in formatted form to the host spool system.

rstr parameters

rstr parameters describe the possibilities for configuration of system traces.

rstr/file	This parameter specifies the absolute directory path of the trace file. Only SAP can change this setting.
rstr/max_diskspace	This parameter sets the maximum space limit for the trace file. The administrator can change this setting.

rsts parameters

Configure the TemSe database with these parameters.

rsts/ccc/cachesize	This parameter specifies the size, in bytes, available in SHM for the translation tables used for character sets. The administrator can configure this parameter.
rsts/maxsapcode	This parameter specifies the highest ID number of the SAP character set. The administrator should set it according to local circumstances.
rsts/files/root/G rsts/files/root/L rsts/files/root/T	These parameters can set a sample path specification for storing TemSe objects in the host system. The parameter is directly related to the parameter 'rspo/store_location.'

SAP parameters

Installation of the system automatically sets these parameters in the system profile. They may not be changed.

scsa parameters

The available SHM area is configured with this group of parameters.

scsa/shm/size	Only SAP should change this parameter. It sets, in bytes, the available SHM area used by the system log and trace options of the R/3 system.

stat parameter

This group of parameters set up the performance monitor of the R/3 system. As a rule, the defaults should not be changed.

stat/level	This parameter activates the response statistics of the R/3 system.
stat/btcrec	This parameter sets the maximum number of processing steps for a background request.
stat/bufsize	This parameter sets the default for the size of the statistics buffer required by each work process.
stat/rfcrec	This parameter specifies the number of log records for monitoring RFC communication.
stat/tabrec	Activates the default table statistics.
stat/version	This parameter varies the type and methodology of statistical output to equalize differences between versions of the SAP kernel.

zcsa parameters

These parameters configure the 'common system area' of the user's roll area (user context).

zcsa/calendar_area	Here the administrator sets the size, in bytes, of the calendar buffer (e.g., holidays, factory shut-downs).
zcsa/calendar_ids	With this parameter, the administrator sets the number of directory entries in the calendar buffer.
zcsa/db_max_buftab	The administrator should not set this parameter to too small a value. It specifies the number of entries in the resistant table buffer.
zcsa/presentation_buffer_area	The size of the buffer, in bytes, (> 1MB) for storing screens. Can be set by the administrator.
zcsa/table_buffer_area	This parameter allows the administrator to configure the size of the resistant table buffer. The size is given in bytes.

ztta parameters

These parameters configure the user's roll area (user context).

ztta/cua_area	SAP uses this parameter to configure the size, in bytes, of the CUA buffer.
ztta/dynpro_area	Here the administrator specifies the size, in bytes, of the SHM buffer for screens.
ztta/hold_data_area	Here the administrator can set the size, in bytes, of the SHM area for data transfer (user Set/Get data).
ztta/parameter_area	Here the administrator can specify the size, in bytes, of the buffer for the SPA/GPA parameters.
ztta/roll_area	Here the administrator can set the size, in bytes, of the roll area for storing ABAP/4 application program contexts. SAP must be informed of any changes.
ztta/roll_extension	The administrator uses this parameter to set the maximum size, in bytes, of the extended memory that a dialog process can claim.

DEFAULT.PFL

SAPSYSTEMNAME	=	FST
SAPDBHOST	=	axp
rdisp/mshost	=	axp
rdisp/sna_gateway	=	axp
rdisp/sna_gw_service	=	sapgw88
rdisp/vbname	=	axp_FST_88
rdisp/enqname	=	axp_FST_88
rdisp/btcname	=	axp_FST_88
rslg/send_daemon/listen_port	=	3701
rslg/collect_daemon/listen_port	=	3901
rslg/collect_daemon/talk_port	=	4001
rdisp/bufrefmode	=	sendoff,exeauto

Startprofil

```
#.*
#.*      generated by: R3INST
#.*
#.*-----------------------------------
SAPSYSTEMNAME        =FST
INSTANCE_NAME        =DVEBMGS88
```

```
#-------------------------------------------------------------------
# Start SCSA administration
#-------------------------------------------------------------------

Execute_00 =local $(DIR_EXECUTABLE)/sapmscsa -n
 pf=$(DIR_PROFILE)/FST_DVEBMGS88_axp

#-------------------------------------------------------------------
# start message server
#-------------------------------------------------------------------

_MS                     =ms.sapFST_DVEBMGS88
Execute_0               =local ln -s -f $(DIR_EXECUTABLE)/msg_server $(_MS)
Start_Program_0         =local $(_MS)
 pf=$(DIR_PROFILE)/FST_DVEBMGS88_axp

#-------------------------------------------------------------------
# start application server
#-------------------------------------------------------------------

_DW                     =dw.sapFST_DVEBMGS88
Execute_02              =local ln -s -f $(DIR_EXECUTABLE)/disp+work $(_DW)
Start_Program_02        =local $(_DW)
 pf=$(DIR_PROFILE)/FST_DVEBMGS88_axp

#-------------------------------------------------------------------
# start syslog collector daemon
#-------------------------------------------------------------------

_CO                     =co.sapFST_DVEBMGS88
Execute                 =local ln -s -f $(DIR_EXECUTABLE)/rslgcoll $(_CO)
Start_Program_03        =local $(_CO) -F
 pf=$(DIR_PROFILE)/FST_DVEBMGS88_axp

#-------------------------------------------------------------------
# start syslog send daemon
#-------------------------------------------------------------------

_SE                     =se.sapFST_DVEBMGS88
Execute_04              =local ln -s -f $(DIR_EXECUTABLE)/rslgsend $(_SE)
Start_Program_04        =local $(_SE) -F
 pf=$(DIR_PROFILE)/FST_DVEBMGS88_axp
```

Instance profile

```
SAPSYSTEMNAME       =FST
INSTANCE_NAME       =DVEBMGS88
SAPSYSTEM =88
rdisp/wp_no_dia=10
rdisp/wp_no_vb=5
rdisp/wp_no_vb2=2
rdisp/wp_no_enq=1
rdisp/wp_no_btc=6
rdisp/wp_no_spo=1
```

```
#.**********************************************
#.*                                            *
#.*       Instance Profile                     *
#.*                                            *
#.*       Version       = 00000                *
#.*       changed by    = R3INST               *
#.*       changed at    = Installation         *
#.*                                            *
#.*     Generated for usage of 2048 MB memory  *
#.*     and average number of 0100 active users *
#.**********************************************
em/initial_size_MB=500
ztta/roll_extension=210000000
rdisp/PG_SHM=6528
rdisp/ROLL_SHM=12928
rdisp/ROLL_MAXFS=32768
rdisp/PG_MAXFS=32768
abap/buffersize=200000

#---------- Shared Memory (Key=14) ----------
zcsa/presentation_buffer_area=8800000
sap/bufdir_entries=8800

#---------- Shared Memory (Key=19) ----------
zcsa/table_buffer_area=20000000
zcsa/db_max_buftab=3333

#---------- Shared Memory (Key=31) ----------
rdisp/elem_per_queue=2000
rdisp/wp_ca_blk_no=1000

#---------- Shared Memory (Key=33) ----------
rtbb/buffer_length=20000
rtbb/max_tables=400

#---------- Shared Memory (Key=34) ----------
enque/table_size=2000

#---------- Shared Memory (Key=41) ----------
rsdb/ntab/entrycount=8000

#---------- Shared Memory (Key=42) ----------
rsdb/ntab/ftabsize=4000

#---------- Shared Memory (Key=43) ----------
rsdb/ntab/irbdsize=2000

#---------- Shared Memory (Key=44) ----------
rsdb/ntab/sntabsize=1500

#---------- Shared Memory (Key=47) ----------
rsdb/cua/buffersize=8000
# @(#)ilprof.h    20.7.1.1    SAP    96/01/25
```

```
#-----------------------------------------------------------------
# Shared Memory Pool Sizes
#
# SAP uses shared memory segments for interprocess communication.
# Certain of these segments are grouped together in pools.
# The size of these pools is given in the parameters:
#
# ipc/shm_psize_10
# ipc/shm_psize_20
# ipc/shm_psize_40
#
# The pools must be defined large enough to contain the segments
# configured.
# The default contents of pools 10 and 40 are given below.
# To remove a logical segment out of a pool, use the entry:
#
# ipc/shm_psize_<key number> =0
#
# This causes the logical segment to be placed in its own physical
# segment.
# The actual SIZE of the various objects within the pool is determined
# by the parameter listed for each object below.
# (The ipc/shm_psize_<key number> parameter gives the size of the pools,
# whereas for other objects it simply controls the location of the
# object.)
#-----------------------------------------------------------------


#-----------------------------------------------------------------
# P O O L  1 0
#    contains
#          the calendar buffer (key 11)
#              zcsa/calendar_area
#          the TemSe cache (key 12)
#              rsts/ccc/cachesize
#          the presentation buffer (key 14)
#              zcsa/presentation_buffer_area
#          the semaphore administration area (key 16)
#              dependent on ipc/sem_mon_rec
#          the roll administration area (key 17)
#              dependent on rdisp/ROLL_MAXFS
#              (roughly rdisp/ROLL_MAXFS times 8 bytes)
#          the paging administration area (key 18)
#              dependent on rdisp/PG_MAXFS
#              (roughly rdisp/PG_MAXFS times 12 bytes)
#          the "100%" table buffer (key 19)
#              zcsa/table_buffer_area
#-----------------------------------------------------------------
```

```
#-----------------------------------------------------------------------
# P O O L  4 0
#    contains table dictionary descriptions (nametabs)
#         the DB statistics buffer (key 41)
#             size determined by number of tables in the database
#         the DB TTAB buffer (key 42)
#             roughly 100 times rsdb/entry_count
#         the DB FTAB buffer (key 43)
#             rsdb/ntab/ftabsize in kb plus management
#         the DB IREC buffer (key 44)
#             rsdb/ntab/irdbsize in kb plus management
#         the DB SNTAB buffer (key 45)
#             rsdb/ntab/sntabsize in kb plus management
#-----------------------------------------------------------------------

#-----------------------------------------------------------------------
# Length of time in seconds a work process may run before being
# stopped by the dispatcher.
#-----------------------------------------------------------------------
rdisp/max_wprun_time            =300

#-----------------------------------------------------------------------
# Update control
#      vbstart : attempt to update records which were not yet done
#                when the update server stopped.
#      vbdelete : period in days after which old update records are
#                 deleted.
#-----------------------------------------------------------------------
#rdisp/vbstart       =1
#rdisp/vbdelete      =50

#-----------------------------------------------------------------------
# Installed languages
#-----------------------------------------------------------------------
zcsa/installed_languages        =DE

#-----------------------------------------------------------------------
# Signon parameters
#-----------------------------------------------------------------------
# Default client on signon screen
#login/system_client             =001

#-----------------------------------------------------------------------
# System Language
#-----------------------------------------------------------------------
#zcsa/system_language =E

#-----------------------------------------------------------------------
# R/3 Extended Memory Management
#-----------------------------------------------------------------------
```

```
#-----------------------------------------------------------------------
# "Per-process" parameters
#-----------------------------------------------------------------------
# Short-term work area in bytes
#ztta/short_area            =550000
# Dynpro area in bytes
#ztta/dynpro_area           =64000

# Roll-able work area in bytes
ztta/roll_first             =1000000
ztta/roll_area              =6500000
# Heap Threshholds and Extended Memory Size

#-----------------------------------------------
# Shared Memory Pool Sizes
#-----------------------------------------------
ipc/shm_psize_10=36000000
ipc/shm_psize_40=28000000
```

Temu profile

```
SAPSYSTEMNAME       =FST
SAPSYSTEM           =88
DIR_EXECUTABLE      =/sapmnt/FST/exe
DIR_HOME            =/tmp
DIR_DATA            =/tmp
```

C Authorization profiles

This appendix contains the most important authorization profiles required for Basis administration. An 'X' in column *Comp* marks a composite profile. An 'X' in the column *Act* indicates an actively available profile.

Profile	*Comp*	*Act*	*Text*
S_A.ADMIN		X	Operator
S_A.CUSTOMIZ		X	Customizing (for all activities during system set-up)
S_A.DEVELOP		X	Developer
S_A.SYSTEM		X	System administrator (Superuser)
S_A.USER		X	Contact persons (Basis authorization)
S_ABAP_ALL		X	All authorizations in the ABAP area
S_ABAP_ANZ		X	BC ABAP – Processing authorization
S_ADMI_ALL		X	All administrative authorizations
S_BDC_ABTC		X	BC batch input – Batch processing of sessions
S_BDC_ALL		X	BC batch input – Authorization profile for all activities
S_BDC_ANAL		X	BC batch input – Session analysis
S_BDC_AONL		X	BC batch input – On-line processing of sessions
S_BDC_DELE		X	BC batch input – Delete sessions
S_BDC_FREE		X	BC batch input – Release sessions
S_BDC_LOCK		X	BC batch input – Locking and unlocking sessions
S_BTCH_ADM		X	BC batch – Processing authorization (Administrator)
S_BTCH_ALL		X	BC batch – All authorizations
S_CALENDAR_A		X	BC calendar – Maintenance authorization
S_CALENDAR_S		X	BC calendar – Display authorization
S_DDIC_ALL		X	BC DDIC – All authorizations
S_DDIC_SU		X	BC data dictionary – All authorizations
S_DOKU_AUTH		X	Documentation maintenance of all development classes

Profile	*Comp*	*Act*	*Text*
S_NUMBER		X	BC number range maintenance – All authorizations
S_RZL_ADMIN		X	RZ control station: Administration authorization
S_RZL_SHOW		X	RZ control station: Display authorization
S_SCRP_ALL		X	BC SAPscript texts, styles, forms – Maintenance authorizations
S_SPOOL_ALL		X	All spool authorizations
S_SYST_ALL	X	X	BC system authorizations (complete)
S_SYST_ANZ	X	X	BC for a department – Display (ABAP, tables)
S_SYST_FACH1	X	X	BC for a department – Maintenance (ABAP, Tab., Calendar, Co.Code.)
S_TABU_ALL		X	BC maintain all table with standard maintenance (SM31)
S_TABU_ANZ		X	Table display authorization
S_TABU_BSV		X	Authorization for status scheme maintenance
S_TABU_CLI		X	Maintain client-dependent tables
S_TAB_ANZEIG		X	Table display
S_TMS_NORM		X	Normal TemSe rights
S_TOOLS_EX		X	Call of external tools
S_TOOLS_EX_A		X	Performance monitor: Special monitor functions
S_TSKH_ALL		X	System administration authorizations
S_USER_ALL		X	BC user maintenance – All authorizations
S_USER_SAP		X	User and authorization maintenance SAP

D Editor commands

ABAP/4 editor line commands

Command	*Meaning*
*	Position cursor
<	Compress include
>	Expand include
A	Insert after line
B	Insert before line
B-	Cursor to last line
C	Copy line
CC	Copy block
CLEAR	Delete XYZ areas
D	Delete line
DD	Delete block
I	Insert after line
J	Join following line
M	Move line
MM	Move block
N	Insert comment block
O	Overlay line
OO	Overlay block
PP	Pretty print block
PR	Print block
R	Duplicate (repeat) line
RESET	Delete line command
RR	Duplicate (repeat) block
S	Split line
SH	Shift block

Command	*Meaning*
T+	Cursor to first line
U	Save (update) and compress include
W	Insert from clipboard
WW	Block after clipboard
XX	Block after X area
Y	Insert Y area
YY	Block after Y area
Z	Insert Z area
ZZ	Block after Z area

Editor commands

Command	*Meaning*
+	Next page
++	Last page
-	Previous page
–	First page
A..TTACH	Go to line...
B..OTTOM	Last page
BACK	Back
CH..ECK	Check
F..ETCH	Other program...
FI..ND	Find...
H..ELP	Help
I..NSERT	Insert line
IC	Statement pattern...
N..EXT	Find again
P..RINT	Print
PC	Download...
PC..DOWN	Download...
PCF..ETCH	Upload...
PP	Pretty printer
PRE..VIOUS	Search backwards

Command	*Meaning*
R..EPLACE	Replace...
RENU..MBER	Number
RES..TORE	Restore
S..AVE	Save
SAVEAS	Save as...
SET..PFAD	Set path
SHOW	Display structure
T..OP	First page
U..PDATE	Save without checking
VERS..ION	Display version

E System fields

Name	*Key*	*Type*	*Length/Dec*	*Meaning*
APPLI	INT2	X	2	SAP applications
COLNO	INT4	X	4	Current column during list creation
CPAGE	INT4	X	4	Current page number
CPROG	CHAR	C	8	Runtime: Main program
CUCOL	INT4	X	4	Cursor position (column)
CUROW	INT4	X	4	Cursor position (Line)
DATUM	DATE	D	8	SYSTEM: Date
DAYST	CHAR	C	1	Summertime active? ('daylight saving time')
DBCNT	INT4	X	4	Number of elements in edited dataset with DB operations
DBNAM	CHAR	C	2	Logical database for ABAP/4 programs
DBSYS	CHAR	C	10	SYSTEM: Database system
DCSYS	CHAR	C	4	SYSTEM: Dialog system
DYNGR	CHAR	C	4	Screen group of current session
DYNNR	CHAR	C	4	Number of current screen
FDPOS	INT4	X	4	Location of a string
FMKEY	CHAR	C	3	Current function code menu
HOST	CHAR	C	8	Host
INDEX	INT4	X	4	Number of loop passes
LANGU	CHAR	C	1	SAP logon language key
LILLI	INT4	X	4	Number of current list line
LINCT	INT4	X	4	Number of list lines
LINNO	INT4	X	4	Current line for list creation
LINSZ	INT4	X	4	Line size of list
LISEL	CHAR	C	255	INTERACTIVE: Selected line
LISTI	INT4	X	4	Number of current list line

Name	Key	Type	Length/Dec	Meaning
LOCDB	CHAR	C	1	Local database exists
LSIND	INT4	X	4	Number of secondary list
MACDB	CHAR	C	4	PROGRAM: Name of file for matchcode access
MACOL	INT4	X	4	No. of columns from SET MARGIN statement
MANDT	CHAR	C	3	Client number from SAP logon
MAROW	INT4	X	4	No. of lines from SET MARGIN statement
MSGID	CHAR	C	2	Message ID
MSGNO	NUMCN	3		Message number
MSGTY	CHAR	C	1	Message type (E, I, W, ...)
OPSYS	CHAR	C	10	SYSTEM: Operating system
PAGCT	INT4	X	4	Page size of list from REPORT statement
PAGNO	INT4	X	4	Runtime: Current page in list
PFKEY	CHAR	C	8	Runtime: Current F key status
PREFX	CHAR	C	3	ABAP/4 prefix for background jobs
REPID	CHAR	C	4	SYSTEM: SAP release
SCOLS	INT4	X	4	Columns on screen
SLSET	CHAR	C	14	Name of SELECTION-SETS
SROWS	INT4	X	4	Lines on screen
SUBRC	INT4	X	4	Return value after specific APAB/4 statement
SYSID	CHAR	C	8	SYSTEM: SAP system ID
TABIX	INT4	X	4	Runtime: Current line of an internal table
TCODE	CHAR	C	4	SESSION: Current transaction code
TFILL	INT4	X	4	Current number of entries in an internal table
TITLE	CHAR	C	70	Runtime: Title of ABAP/4 program
TLENG	INT4	X	4	Line width of an internal table
TMAXL	INT4	X	4	Maximum number of entries in an internal table
TNAME	CHAR	C	30	Name of internal table after an access
TOCCU	INT4	X	4	Occurs parameter with internal tables

Name	*Key*	*Type*	*Length/Dec*	*Meaning*
TPAGI	INT4	X	4	Flag indicating roll-out of internal table to paging area
TTABC	INT4	X	4	Number of last line read in an internal table
TTABI	INT4	X	4	Offset of internal table in roll area
TVAR0	CHAR	C	20	Runtime: Text variable for ABAP/4 text elements
TVAR1	CHAR	C	20	Runtime: Text variable for ABAP/4 text elements
TVAR2	CHAR	C	20	Runtime: Text variable for ABAP/4 text elements
TVAR3	CHAR	C	20	Runtime: Text variable for ABAP/4 text elements
TVAR4	CHAR	C	20	Runtime: Text variable for ABAP/4 text elements
TVAR5	CHAR	C	20	Runtime: Text variable for ABAP/4 text elements
TVAR6	CHAR	C	20	Runtime: Text variable for ABAP/4 text elements
TVAR7	CHAR	C	20	Runtime: Text variable for ABAP/4 text elements
TVAR9	CHAR	C	20	Runtime: Text variable for ABAP/4 text elements
TZONE	INT4	X	4	Time difference from Greenwich Mean Time (UTC) in seconds
UCOMM	CHAR	C	70	INTERACT.: Command filed function entry
ULINE	CHAR	C	255	Constant: Underline (______)
UNAME	CHAR	C	12	Session: SAP user from SAP logon
UZEIT	TIMS	T	6	SYSTEM: Time
VLINE	CHAR	C	1	Constant: Vertical bar
WILLI	INT4	X	4	Numner of current window line
WINCO	INT4	X	4	Cursor position in window (column)
WINDI	INT4	X	4	Index of current window line
WINRO	INT4	X	4	Cursor position in window (line)
WINSL	CHAR	C	79	INTERACTIVE: Selected window line
WINX1	INT4	X	4	Window coordinate (column left)

Name	Key	Type	Length/Dec	Meaning
WINX2	INT4	X	4	Window coordinate (colulmn right)
WINY1	INT4	X	4	Window coordinate (line left)
WINY2	INT4	X	4	Window coordinate (line right)
WTITL	CHAR	C	1	Standard page header indicator
XCODE	CHAR	C	70	Extended command field

F Transaction codes

Transaction codes can be entered with the following prefixes:

/n	Execute the following transaction in the same session
/o	Execute the transaction in a new session
/h	Execute the following transaction in debugging mode

0000	Popup for customizing
AL01	Global SAP alerts
AL02	Database alert monitor
AL03	Operating system alert monitor
AL04	Monitor call distribution
AL05	Monitor current workload
AL06	Performance report up- and download
AL07	Early Watch report
AL08	List of all logged on users
AL09	Data for database expertise
AL11	Display SAP directories
AL12	Display table buffer (expert mode)
AL13	Display shared memory (expert mode)
AL15	Customize SAPOSCOL destination
AL16	Local alert monitor for operating system
AL17	Remote alert monitor for operating system
AL18	Local file system monitor
AL19	Remote file system monitor
AL20	Early Watch: extended performance report
CREF	Cross reference
DB01	Analyze exclusive lockwaits
DB02	Analyze tables and indexes

DB03	Parameter changes in database
DB10	Monitoring security concept
DB11	Profile maintenance for Early Watch
DB12	Overview backup protocols
DB13	Database administration calendar
DBAk	Backup strategy calendar
DS01	Administration DN line for DS logon
DS02	Administration DN ACL for DS Add/Mod
F00	SAPoffice: short message
O032	Introductory guide from function choice
O052	Create client
O053	Customizing request administration
OCI1	Transaction for TCUSC maintenance
OS01	LAN check with ping
OS02	Operating system configuration
OS03	O/S parameter changes
OS04	Local system configuration
OS05	Remote system configuration
OS06	Local operating system activity
OS07	Remote operating system activity
OSS1	Logon to on-line service system
OY19	Table adjustment
RZ01	Job scheduling monitor
RZ02	Graphic of SAP instance network
RZ03	Presentation, control SAP instances
RZ04	Maintain SAP instances
RZ06	Alerts thresholds maintenance
RZ08	SAP-Alert monitor
S00	Short message
SCC3	Client copy log
SDC1	Dictionary nametab export (comparison)
SDC2	Dictionary nametab comparison
SE92	Maintain SysLog messages

SF07	Evaluate file names
SICK	Installation check
SKRT	SAPcomm: routing test
SLG1	Evaluate application log
SM0	User list
SM12	Display and delete locks
SM28	Installation check
SM49	Execute logical commands
SM50	Work process overview
SM51	List of SAP systems
SM58	Error log asynchr. RFC
SM59	RFC destinations (display and maintain)
SM69	Conceal/maintain logical commands
SMGW	Gateway monitor
SO20	SAPoffice: choose initial document
SO32	SAPoffice: create all users
SO36	Create automatic forwarding
SO51	Create addresses for SAPoffice
SO54	Download from Internet addresses
SO60	Call R/3 help library
SO61	R/3 library
SO75	Introduction to the R/3 system
SO99	Upgrade information system
SOLI	Load OLE TypeInfo
SOLO	OLE object browser
SP01	Spool control
SP03	Load spooler from formats
SP11	TemSe table of contents
SP12	TemSe administration
SPAD	Spool configuration
SPAU	Display modified DE objects
SPDD	Display modified DDIC objects
SPR1	Delta customizing for a project

SPR2	Delta customizing for an enterprise IMG
SPR3	Upgrade customizing for a project
SPR4	Upgrade customizing for an enterprise IMG
SRCN	Delete country-specific reports
SSC	SAP R/3 schedule (internal)
SSC0	SAP R/3 schedule (employees)
SSC1	SAP R/3 schedule (own)
ST01	System trace
ST02	Setup/tune buffers
ST04	Select activity of individual RDBMS
ST08	Network monitor
ST09	Network alert monitor
ST11	Display developer traces
STAT	Local transaction statistics
SUCH	CHECKs for translation
SVGM	SAP R/3 procedure model
SVGS	View of activity in the procedure model
SVMC	View maintenance with memory start
SWE3	Display instance connections
SWE4	Change event log status (on/off)
SWEL	Display event log
SWI2	Work item analysis (statistics)
SWI3	Workflow exit
SWI4	Task analysis
SWI5	Workload analysis
SWI6	Object links
SWPL	Step log for workflow
SWT0	Configure workflow trace
SWU0	Event simulation
SWU1	Users RFC monitor
SWU2	Event RFC monitor
SWU3	Consistency check: customizing
SWU4	Consistency check for standard task

SWU5	Consistency check for customer task
SWU6	Consistency check for workflow task
SWU7	Consistency check for workflow sample
SWU8	Switch technical traces on/off
SWU9	Display technical traces
SWUA	Start verification workflow
SWUD	Diagnosis of tools
TKPR	Display trace-file
TU01	Call statistics
TU02	Parameter changes of this instance
USMM	Entry: customer verification

G Morning Glory Gardening Center

Most of the development objects used in this book appear in the following example. The Morning Glory Gardening Center provides a model for the example. This application comprises the following tables:

All objects belong to development class 'ZZ01.' Report ZPFLLIST creates a list of all the plants sold by the garden shop, sorted according to color. Report ZPFLNEUE is a dialog-oriented ABAP, used to maintain the data in table ZPFLANZEN. The gardening center can add new plants to its inventory. Screen and statuses exist for the report. Transaction code 'z000' has been allocated to the transaction.

Transport request T01K900131 contains all the objects. The request can be imported into any R/3 system equal to or higher than 3.0A.

Note the following considerations:

- Correct installation of the CTS.
- If objects with identical names exist in the target system, the import will overwrite them.

Unfortunately, we cannot guarantee or take responsibility for accuracy and/or functionality in your system.

The enclosed diskette is in MS-DOS format.

Import the example as follows:

- Copy file R900131.T01 into the directory /usr/sap/trans/data
- Copy the file K900131.T01 into the directory /usr/sap/trans/cofiles
- Change to directory /sap/trans/bin
- Execute the following commands:
  tp addtobuffer T01K900131 <SAPSID>
  tp import T01K900131 <SAPSID> u4
- As described in Chapter 7, check the transport steps from within the R/3 system. If serious errors occurred (error code 8), correct the problems and try the import again.

The following DE objects are contained in transport request T01900131.

LIMU	COMM	ZZ01_2006
R3TR	DEVC	ZZ01
R3TR	DOMA	ZKENN_NR
R3TR	DOMA	ZNUM3

R3TR	DOMA	Z_CHAR10
R3TR	DOMA	Z_CHAR20
R3TR	DOMA	Z_CHAR30
R3TR	DOMA	Z_GELD
R3TR	DOMA	Z_HOCH
R3TR	DOMA	Z_LIEF
R3TR	DOMA	Z_NAME
R3TR	DOMA	Z_TIME
R3TR	DOMA	Z_TYP
R3TR	DTEL	ZANSCHRIFT
R3TR	DTEL	ZKENN_NR
R3TR	DTEL	ZLIEF
R3TR	DTEL	ZNAME
R3TR	DTEL	Z_FARBE
R3TR	DTEL	Z_FIRMA
R3TR	DTEL	Z_HOCH
R3TR	DTEL	Z_LIEF
R3TR	DTEL	Z_NAME
R3TR	DTEL	Z_NOTIZ
R3TR	DTEL	Z_ORT
R3TR	DTEL	Z_PFL_TYP
R3TR	DTEL	Z_PREIS
R3TR	DTEL	Z_STRASSE
R3TR	DTEL	Z_ZEIT
R3TR	PROG	ZPFLLIST
R3TR	PROG	ZPFLNEUE
R3TR	PROG	ZZREPO01
R3TR	TABL	ZANGEBOTE
R3TR	TABL	ZBESTELLD
R3TR	TABL	ZBESTELLU
R3TR	TABL	ZLIEFERANT
R3TR	TABL	ZPFLANZEN
R3TR	TRAN	Z000

R3TR	TABU	ZPFLANZEN
R3TR	TABU	ZANGEBOTE
R3TR	TABU	ZBESTELLD
R3TR	TABU	ZBESTELLU
R3TR	TABU	ZLIEFERANT

The example demonstrates the possibilities of the R/3 programming language in the simplest possible manner. Readers are invited and encouraged to expand and refine the example with their own developments. The example offers numerous possibilities.

ZPFLANZEN Items carried by the Gardening Center

Table class:	transparent	Delivery class:	A
Data type:	APPL0	Size category:	0

The table contains the items (plants) offered for sale to customers by the Gardening Center. The entry in the field 'IDENT' serves as the key.

Table structure

Table G.1 ZPFLANZEN

Field name	*Key*	*Data type*	*Length*	*Data element*	*Domain*	*Text*
IDENT	x	CHAR	5	ZKENN_NR	ZKENN_NR	Gardening Center ID
NAME		CHAR	20	Z_NAME	Z_CHAR20	Name
TYP		CHAR	10	Z_PFL_TYP	Z_TYP	Type of plant
COLOR		CHAR	10	Z_FARBE	Z_CHAR10	Characters 10
HIGH		NUMC	4	Z_HOCH	Z_HOCH	Expected height of growth
BEGINN		CHAR	2	Z_ZEIT	Z_TIME	Blossom time
ENDE		CHAR	2	Z_ZEIT	Z_TIME	Blossom time
PRICE		DEC	10	Z_PREIS	Z_GELD	Price
NOTICE		CHAR	30	Z_NOTIZ	Z_CHAR30	Comments

ZANGEBOTE List of items carried by plant suppliers

Table class:	transparent	Delivery class:	A
Data type:	APPL0	Size category:	0

This table contains items carried by companies that supply the Garden Center. The field SUPP_ID represents the internal key of the supplier. IDENT is the key to the plants offered by the supplier. DELIVPRICE contains the price at which the supplier delivers the plants.

Table structure

Table G.2 ZANGEBOTE Delivery data for the Gardening Center's orders

Field name	*Key*	*Data type*	*Length*	*Data element*	*Domain*	*Text*
SUPP_ID	x	CHAR	5	Z_LIEF	ZNUM3	Supplier's ID
IDENT	x	CHAR	5	ZKENN_NR	ZKENN_NR	Gardening Center ID
DELIVPRICE		DEC	10	Z_PREIS	Z_GELD	Delivery price

ZBESTELLU Delivery data for orders placed by the Gardening Center

Table class:	transparent	Delivery class:	A
Data type:	APPL0	Size category:	0

This table contains all the orders placed by the Morning Glory Gardening Center with its suppliers. ORDERNR is the order number assigned to a collective order by the Gardening Center. The key SUPPP_ID determines the supplier.

Table structure

Table G.3 ZBESTELLU

Field name	*Key*	*Data type*	*Length*	*Data element*	*Domain*	*Text*
ORDERNR	x	CHAR	4	CHAR4	CHAR4	
SUPP_ID	x	NUMC	3	ZLIEF	ZNUM3	3-digit supplier number
ORDER_DATE		CHAR	8	DATE	CHAR8	Date in CHAR format
DEVLIV_DATE		CHAR	8	DATE	CHAR8	Expected date of delivery
Z_SUM		DEC	10	Z_PREIS	Z_GELD	Price

ZBESTELLD Orders of the Busy Lizzie Gardening Center

Table class:	transparent	Delivery class:	A
Data type:	APPL0	Size category:	0

This table contains the Garden Center's orders for individual plants (ORDERNR). An order with supplier for a specific plant can be found with the order number. The table also contains the quantity ordered and the purchase price of each plant ordered.

Table structure

Table G.4 ZBESTELLD

Field name	*Key*	*Data type*	*Length*	*Data element*	*Domain*	*Text*
ORDERNR	x	CHAR	4	CHAR4	CHAR4	
IDENT	x	CHAR	5	ZKENN_NR	ZKENN_NR	Gardening Center ID
PIECES		NUMC	4	NUM4	NUMO4	4-digit number
ORDERPRICE		DEC	10	Z_PREIS	Z_GELD	Price

ZLIEFERANT Table of suppliers

Table class: transparent Delivery class: A
Data type: APPL0 Size category: 0

Finally, the Garden Center administers the addresses of its suppliers, sorted according to supplier number.

Table structure

Table G.5 ZLIEFERANT

Field name	*Key*	*Data type*	*Length*	*Data element*	*Domain*	*Text*
SUPP_ID	x	NUMC	3	ZLIEF	ZNUM3	3-digit supplier number
SUP_NAME	x	CHAR	35	ZNAME	NAME	Name
ADDRESS		CHAR	25	ZANSCHRIFT	CHAR25	Address
RESIDENCE		CHAR	30	ORT	TEXT30	Supplier's city

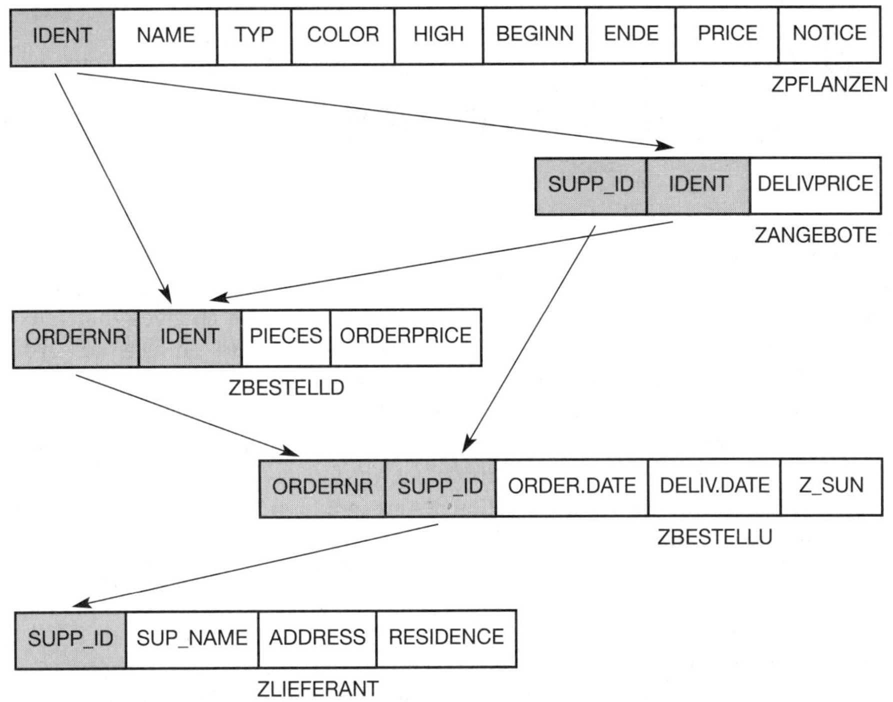

Figure G.1 Relations model for the Morning Glory Gardening Center

H Upgrade procedure

The SAP environment understands an upgrade as a change in the release level of the R/3 software and/or the RDBMS software. The explosive nature of an upgrade is caused not only by changing the level or the R/3 kernel, but also by the changes that affect the contents of the database. In the database sense, an upgrade affects all ABAP/4 applications as well as R/3 system metadata. A move from one R/3 version to the next requires structural changes to table structures, indexes of application and system tables and table contents. An upgrade therefore involves system down-time by definition. Most installations expect to provide round the clock system availability as the norm; an upgrade cuts deeply into in this expectation. SAP can aim only at reducing the required down-time to a minimum.

Release 3 of the R/3 software introduced a new technology to the upgrade procedure. Updates between 2.2 versions took place directly. At some point productive operation halted, new data was imported, specific objects exchanged and data converted. This method shut down the system from the beginning to the end of these phases.

A release change now uses the concept of a repository switch. The contents of an SAP database can be divided into two segments: customer data and basis data, the repository. The repository contains the data dictionary, screens, reports, documentation and generated objects such as matchcodes. An upgrade affects the repository first and foremost.

The first phase of the upgrade does not involve system down-time. This phase creates a shadow repository. In principle, this process creates a complete new repository of the new version parallel to the active repository of the start version. The new procedure offers a define advantage over the old: the R/3 system remains in operation during data import and the building phase.

The next phase compares the objects of the new and old repositories and determines the number of required conversions. The R/3 system continues to operate during this phase. The last phase of the upgrade executes the required conversions. It activates the new repository and deletes the old one (repository switch). Only the last phase requires stopping productive operation of the R/3 system.

As a logical consequence of doubling the repository, the database temporarily demands extra storage space. (For Informix and Oracle, the database can be reduced by an appropriate amount after completion of the upgrade.) The high level of modifications taking place in the database will add to the database logs written during normal operation. The input/output level will also increase during the data import.

Customers can choose between three basic options for executing an upgrade:

A_OFF

All modifications, including the rather involved data import, are executed without database logging. This strategy requires stopping the database at the beginning of the upgrade. Speed is a general advantage of this procedure. Since no database logging is performed, the I/O load is less than for other methods. Since the system is stopped, R/3 users cannot create any bottlenecks.

However, the lack of logging by the RDBMS means that the upgrade must begin from scratch if errors occur or the procedure terminates. In such a case, the data import must be completely restarted. Because no records exist, a rollback to a point before the termination is not possible.

A_ON

Unlike the above, this method places a priority on creating the shortest possible down-time. Logging remains active throughout the entire upgrade and records all modifications. To avoid make the total load too high, the administrator can choose a period of low usage and import the new repository in it.

This method allows a restart of the upgrade. Although slower than the method noted above, it reduces down-time to an absolute minimum. Productive operations must cease only at introduction of the repository switch.

A_SWITCH

This method combines the procedures A_ON and A_OFF. As is true of A_ON, users can define the period in which the data import occurs. In the process, the system remains active during creation of the new repository. The R/3 system must be stopped only when the equalization of the old and new repositories takes place. Up to that point, logging remains active in the database.

The following table summarizes the most important phases and their characteristics. The shaded table fields mark periods in which the R/3 system cannot be used productively.

Phase	*A_ON*	*A_SWITCH*	*A_OFF*
1. Preparation – Check disk requirements – Check software release for compatibility – Query and check passwords			
2. Import the new repository	at any time	at any time	additional DB backup: off or on line
3. Repository equalization Transfer modifications into the new repository and creation of a transport request to forward modifications into other systems			
4. Repository switch			
5. Backup DB contents			

Abbreviations

ABAP	Advanced Business Application Programming
CASE	Computer Aided Software Engineering
CCMS	Computing Center Management System
CPI-C	Common Programming Interface-Communication
CTS	Correction and Transport System
CUA	Common User Access
DB	Database
DBA	Database Administrator
DCE	Distributed Computing Environment
DCL	Data Control Language
DDL	Data Definition Language
DE	Development Environment
DML	Data Manipulation Language
DSA	Data Stripping Array (RAID 1)
DYNP	Screen Processor
Dynpro	Dynamic Program
EDM	Enterprise Data Model
EOD	End of Dynpro
GUI	Graphical User Interface
IDA	Independent Disk Array (RAID 5)
LAN	Local Area Network
LUW	Logical Unit of Work
MDA	Mirrored Disk Array (RAID 0)
NFS	Netware File System
ODBC	Open Database Connectivity
OLE 2	Object Linking and Embedding
OS	Operating System
OSS	Online Service System
PAI	Process After Input

PBO	Process Before Output
PC	Personal Computer
PDA	Parallel Disk Array (RAID 3)
Q-API	Queue-Application Programming Interface
R/3	Runtimesystem 3
RAID	Redundant Array of Independent Disks
RDBMS	Relational Database Management System
RFC	Remote Function Call
RMON-MIB	Remote Network Monitoring Management Information Base
RPC	Remote Procedure Call
SAA	Systems Application Architecture
SAP	Software and Application Programming
SNMP	Simple Network Management Protocol
SQL	Structured Query Language
TR	Transport Request
TCP/IP	Transmission Control Protocol/Internet Protocol
WAN	Wide Area Network
WOSA	Windows Open Services Architecture

Bibliography

Angeli, A., *et al. Relationale Datenbanksysteme für den Software-Entwickler*. Bonn: Addison-Wesley, 1989.

Bach, Maurice J. *The Design of the UNIX Operating System*. Englewood Cliffs, NJ: Prentice-Hall, 1986.

Buck-Emden, Rüdiger; Galimow, Jürgen. *Die Client/Server-Architektur des Systems R/3: Basis für betriebswirtschaftliche Standardanwendungen*. 3. Auflage zum Release 3.x. Bonn: Addison-Wesley, 1996.

CDI. SAP R/3: *Grundlagen, Architektur, Anwendung*. Haar bei München: Markt & Technik, 1994.

Codd, E.F. 'Is Your DBMS Really Relational?' *Computerworld* (14 October 1985).

Codd, E.F.: 'Does Your DBMS Run by the Rules?' *Computerworld* (21 October 1985).

Date, C.J.: *An Introduction to Database Systems*. 5th Ed. Vol. 1. Reading, MA: Addison-Wesley, 1990.

Hagen, Manfred; Will, Liane. *Relationale Datenbanken in der Praxis*. Berlin: Verlag Technik, 1993.

Hansen, Wolf-Rüdiger: *Client-Server-Architektur*. Bonn: Addison-Wesley, 1993.

Hein, M., *et al. Das Oracle-Handbuch*. Bonn: Addison-Wesley, 1990.

Keller, Gerhard; Meinhardt, Stefan. *DV-gestützte Beratung bei der SAP-Softwareeinführung*. Handbuch der modernen Datenverarbeitung: Theorie und Praxis in der Wirtschaftsinformatik, 31: 175. 1994.

Van der Lans, R.F. *SQL: Der ISO-Standard*. Munich: Hanser, 1990.

Lockemann, P.C., Schmidt, J.W., Eds. *Datenbankhandbuch*. Berlin: Springer, 1987.

Matzke, Bernd. *ABAP/4*. Bonn: Addison-Wesley, 1996.

McFadden, F.R.; Hoffer, J.A. *Database Management*. Redwood City, CA: Benjamin/Cummings, 1991.

Neumann, K. 'Kopplungsarten von Programmiersprachen und Datenbanksprachen.' *Informatik Spektrum* 15: (1992) 185–94.

Oracle. *Handbücher*. Munich: Oracle Deutschland GmbH, 1995.

Petkovié, Duöan. *Sybase- und Microsoft- SQL Server*. Bonn: Addison-Wesley, 1994.

Rahm, E.: *Hochleistungstransaktionssysteme*. Braunschweig: Vieweg, 1993.

SAP AG. *R/3-Systemverwaltung*. Walldorf, 1994.

Schlageter, G.; Stucky, W. *Datenbanksysteme: Konzepte und Modelle*. Stuttgart: Teubner, 1983.

Technical Committee ISO/IEC. *ISO/IEC 9075, 1992 Database Language SQL*. ISO, 1992.

Weikum, G. *Transaktionen in Datenbanksystemen*. Bonn: Addison-Wesley, 1988.

Wöhe, G. *Einführung in die allgemeine Betriebswirtschaftslehre*. 15th ed. Munich: Franz Vahlen GmbH, 1984.

Würth Akademie. *Tagungsunterlagen zum Würth R/3 Kongreß*. Künzelsau-Gaisbach, 1994.

Zehnder, C.A. *Informationssysteme und Datenbanken*. Stuttgart: Teubner, 1989.

Index